VANESSA JOY

The OFF-CAMERA FLASH Handbook

*32 Scenarios for Creating
Beautiful Light and
Stunning Photographs*

rockynook

The Off-Camera Flash Handbook
32 Scenarios for Creating Beautiful Light and Stunning Photographs
Vanessa Joy

Project editor: Maggie Yates
Project manager: Lisa Brazieal
Marketing manager: Mercedes Murray
Copyeditor: Maggie Yates
Design and type: Aren Straiger
Layout: Petra Strauch
Cover design: Aren Straiger
Indexer: Maggie Yates

ISBN: 978-1-68198-557-2
1st Edition (1st printing, February 2020)
© 2020 Vanessa Joy
All images © Vanessa Joy unless otherwise noted

Rocky Nook, Inc.
1010 B Street, Suite 350
San Rafael, CA 94901
U.S.A.

www.rockynook.com

Distributed in the UK and Europe by Publishers Group UK
Distributed in the U.S. and all other territories by Ingram Publisher Services

Library of Congress Control Number: 2019950811

Printed in Korea

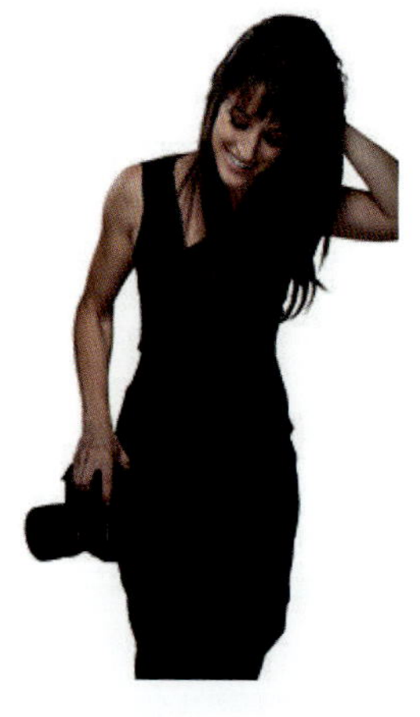

Vanessa Joy is a Canon Explorer of light and has been an influential speaker in the community for over a decade. Starting her photographic journey in 1998, she has since branched into public speaking, earned five college degrees, received a PPA Photographic Craftsman degree, been named a WeddingWire Education Expert, and been sponsored by Canon, Profoto, and Animoto to name a few. Vanessa has spoken at almost every major convention and platform in the event industry such as CreativeLIVE, The Wedding School, Clickin' Moms, WPPI, ShutterFest, Imaging USA, Wedding MBA, WeddingWire World, MobileBeat, in addition to hosting personal workshops and numerous small business and photography conventions around the globe. Recognized for her talent and business sense, her clients love working with her and industry peers love to learn from her tangible, informative and open-book style of teaching. Find her at www.VanessaJoy.com.

Instagram: @VanessaJoy
Twitter: @Vanessa_Joy
Facebook: www.facebook.com/vjoyphoto
YouTube: www.youtube.com/vanessajoy

Dedication

For my mom, who gave me an eye for photography,
for John Heyn, who showed me how to use it,
and for my dad, who taught me how to work for it.

Acknowledgements

As I started thinking about this section of the book and all of the people I knew I'd put in it, I realized I could and wanted to say the same thing about every single person. "I couldn't have done this without you."

It's true. Everyone in here, and probably some more, made it possible for this book to happen. And if any one of them wasn't a part of my life, I doubt this would've come to fruition.

First, thanks to George Varanakis and Profoto (Mark Rezzonico and Sara Strid). They had faith in me to work with off-camera flash while I was still boasting my "natural light photographer" status (because I didn't know how to properly use flash). Without George recommending me to Profoto and then Profoto's guidance through learning the B1s, I would still be cursing at my lights and missing all the beauty of creating my own light.

Thanks to my mom, Marjorie Scavone, who technically had me using off-camera flash in her studio set up when I was young. I remembering reading off light meter settings to her and assisting during her shoots like it was yesterday. Thanks for being patient with me all of the years and for cracking that smile on your face when I "broke the news" to you and dad that I didn't want to go to the dental school I had just been accepted to, and I wanted to go for photography instead.

Thanks to my dad for teaching me what running a business and providing for a family looks like, and for giving me my natural stage presence that makes teaching and speaking easy for me. Very few people have a dad that's a real-life rock star (he was the lead singer of Ram Jam, who had the hit song "Black Betty," and now tours with the Yardbirds), a wildly successful entrepreneur, and hands-down the best dad a girl could ask for. And to my brother Luke: Thanks for posing for me plenty of times for photo assignments, especially when I had no clue what I was doing and likely made you look like crap.

Rob, this book and my entire career aren't possible without you. You selflessly watch our kids while I chase my dreams, and tell me to get up when I'm whining in the fetal position on the floor and I feel like I can't do this anymore. You cheer me on when things are going great, and still manage to love me when I'm doing my best to remind you of how truly imperfect I am (even though I'm obviously a work of art under museum glass—Bill Burr joke guys, watch his 2019 Netflix special). And of course thanks for being my on-demand video production house, and for posing with a model for the chapter on couples portraits. I promise I'll (most likely) never tell you to smell another woman's hair again. Maybe.

Jaye, my life manager. I'm pretty sure that I couldn't survive without you. From reminding me I need to eat and scheduling days off for me, while dealing with all of my clients (some crazy ones too! They exist!) and managing your own photography business and life all while continually being upbeat—I literally do not know how you do it. You are the most hard-working, compassionate, supportive, and strong person I know. I'd say I'm lucky to have you but I know it's not luck that brought us together.

Seth, thanks for not letting me McFish this up. You have been so gracious in showing me where my knowledge gaps were and without you I'd still be thinking those retouched faces and over-edited scenes were straight-out-of-camera images. You have taken so many of my lighting-knowledge puzzle pieces and showed me how they fit together to open my eyes to light theory in a whole new way. You gave me the confidence to tackle this book.

Amie, thank you for all the behind-the-scenes photos throughout this entire book. All of the lighting setup photos are hers, unless taken by drone (those are Rob's), unless otherwise noted. Thanks so much for all you've done to boost my social media presence and get the word out about this book.

Thanks to my two main models for this book, Nikki and Claire. You guys are such a joy to photograph and always make me feel like I'm doing a good job. Thanks to all of my brides and grooms and their wedding guests that made an appearance here. You're all part of my journey in writing this book.

Thanks to everyone at Rocky Nook. Ted, thanks for entrusting me with this project and helping me define the vision of what it should be. Thanks so much to Maggie for turning my words into art!

And finally, to all of you that have been following me on YouTube and social media, your support (and heck even your hate) is what has pushed me along the entire time. I truly treasure the kind words that you send—even the not-so-nice-words, thanks for those too. Hey, sometimes you need a not-so-nice YouTuber troll to kick you where it hurts to make you better yourself. Whatever pushes us along is something to be thankful for, and that is all of you.

Table of Contents

PART 1

Getting Started with Off-Camera Flash (OCF)

CHAPTER 1

You Already Know This

This is for my fellow natural light photographers.

OFF-CAMERA FLASH SUCKS

I remember the first time I tried off-camera flash (OCF) on the job. I was posing a family group of about 30 people. I tested my light about 39,485,787 times before I started posing everyone; it worked fine all 39,485,787 times. I got all 30 people into position, made everyone look at me, and snapped the shot.

Nothing.

And everyone knew it. I heard a riveting chorus of "Your flash didn't fire!" from the perfectly posed peanut gallery judging me. Thank you Captain Obvious, I'm quite aware that it didn't #$*%&!@ fire!

That's the thing about OCF: It's one of the only ways your clients will think you have no idea what you're doing. They can see that things are going wrong and conclude, like mine did, that you're an idiot.

It could be because I threw it into the truck of my car and gave it the finger, but I never got my flash to work again that day. It wasn't until about 10 years later that I mustered up the courage to give off-camera-flash another shot.

When I did try to learn off-camera flash again, I quickly discovered that almost every tutorial and workshop I came across teaching about off-camera flash sucked. It really did. Flash was almost always taught in a way that was impossible for a beginner to learn. It was like listening to someone speak to me in some foreign language before they bothered to find out if I understood that language. And worse, if I admitted I didn't understand the language of flash—shame, shame, shame you fake photographer, who doesn't know flash like a "real" photographer should.

No more.

This book is going to give you exactly what you need to feel confident in your lighting abilities. By the end, I'll bet you'll find off-camera flash so easy and inspiring that it will become one of your favorite ways to take photographs.

Togs—I don't know if you know this, but OCF takes the imaging process away from molding the available lighting circumstances to your will, and puts full creative control back into your hands. You get to be a photographer that creates whatever you envision—not just alter what you see. Want it to be nighttime? Easy peasy. Need a golden hour glow? No problem. Craving light and airy when it's dark and gloomy? Sure thing. Want to make all of that look completely natural and in line with your brand? You've got it. You can make whatever you want to happen, happen in your photos.

REASONS TO START USING OCF

If I haven't convinced you yet, here are some things to consider.

Everyone else shoots natural light. So many photographers complain about the saturated industry. Guess what? They're right. There are a million (or more) of us. And they are *all* shooting in natural light, praying to God that it's a good quality that day. What if you could promise your clients the sun even when it isn't there? What if you didn't have to worry about an overcast day? Shooting with flash differentiates you from other shooters photographically, and your clients will be impressed that you can deliver the shots they want regardless of the weather.

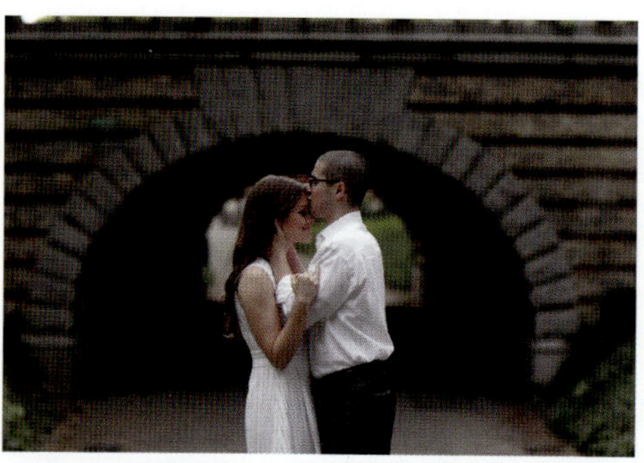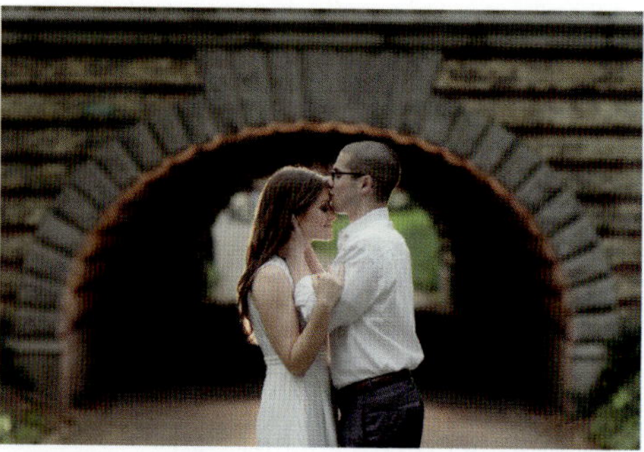

FIGURES 1.1 AND 1.2
CHECK OUT THIS CRAZY COMPARISON! LOOK HOW MUCH MORE THE OCF IMAGE (ON THE RIGHT) POPS!
BOTH IMAGES: CANON 1DX, CANON 85MM 1.2, ISO 200, F/2.2, 1/200
CANON 580EXII SPEEDLIGHT WITH CTO GEL

Annoy Uncle Bob. This is one of my favorite things to do. You know Uncle Bob? The one with the awesome, brand-new camera that he's testing out at his niece's wedding; the one with no regard to getting in your way or stealing your perfectly posed shots. Yeah, that guy. Well, shooting with flash lets you put your subject in heinous natural light. His photos will be crap, but your photos will be out of this world.

Be a better photographer. Learning to use a flash has been one of the best things I've done for my knowledge of natural-light photography. Learning about flash filled the gaps in my photographic knowledge like crazy. Do your craft a service and keep growing into it.

Make more money. There is a direct correlation to how many big, printed images I've sold and my use of OCF. If you're taking epic, gorgeous images, do you think your clients will be satisfied printing them as a 3x5 for an album? No way! These images will hang as 24x36 canvases on their walls!

It's not hard anymore. With the help of this book and the wonderful lighting and imaging technology that we have today, it's not nearly as difficult to master OCF as it used to be. So let's get going!

YOU ALREADY KNOW THIS

Attempting to learn off-camera flash was crazy difficult for me. When I looked at the flash, I felt like I was looking at a foreign object that defied all physical laws as I knew them. Not to mention that I'm seeing an almost-too-fast-to-see light flash, and somehow I'm supposed to know what it's going to do, or what it did after the fact.

Guess what? There's no crazy magic happening with a flash. The light that comes out of a flash follows the same rules as light from the sun. "Light is light" as they say. The only difference is that the flash light comes out in a quick burst versus sunlight, which lives in the sky all day. The light that comes out of any flash or piece of continuous-light-producing equipment follows the same rules that govern all light. Just think of it as your own portable mini-sun.

You're likely a natural-light photographer. Most of us started taking photos on our phones or point-and-shoot cameras before we ever thought of taking photography a step further. For many, it's more cost effective to buy just a camera, not a camera and a light.

As natural-light photographers, we're used to seeing light as it is and molding what is already there to work for our images. We see it, photograph it, and sometimes manipulate it with a window, reflector, or shade. Because of this, we often don't think about *why* and *how* the light from the sun is behaving and being altered.

To get started on the right foot, here are some things you already know, but haven't necessarily thought about before.

Light travels in straight lines. Every. Single. Time. No secret voodoo happening here.

Light reflects at equal angles. It's back to high school geometry class for this lesson! The angle of incidence of the light equals its angle of reflection. It's just like playing pool. When a ball hits the wall of the table at an angle, it bounces off at the same (but reverse) angle. Practically speaking, this means you can use a reflector with an off-camera flash just like you'd reflect the sun. Pretty cool.

The smaller the light is in relation to your subject, the harder the light will be. Think of the sun here. In relation to where we are in the universe, the sun is actually a super small light source (you can cover it by squinting one eye shut, or hiding it behind your pinky finger) in relation to us, even though it's a huge object. For an example of the quality of light this creates, think about the sun shining directly through slits in the blinds. You can see the lines of the blinds casting strong shadows into the room or onto your subject.

The larger the light is in relation to your subject, the softer the light will be. This soft light will create more gradual shadows. Using the sun example: If you were standing right next to our big, beautiful sun, it would be a large light source in relation to you. It would create a beautifully soft light wrapping around your gorgeous face. It'd burn you to a crisp, but you'd look great while screaming in terror. Totally IG worthy.

The closer the light is to your subject, the more contrast it will create between light to shadow. You see this all the time when you put something next to a window and take a picture of it. One side, the side shielded from the light, is super dark, and the other side, the one directly in the light, is super bright.

The farther the light is from your subject, the less contrast you'll see between the light and shadow. This is the opposite of the previous concept and there's a really great mathematical explanation for this if you're interested. Google "inverse square law" if you want extra credit.

You essentially have four elements (near, far, big, and small) at your disposal when molding and positioning your light.

1. You could have a big light source that's far away, such as a wall of windows, that's on the opposite side of the room. That would be a big, soft light that does not produce a lot of contrast between the light and dark of the shadows.

2. You could get closer to that big light source by walking over to the window side of the room. That light will be big and soft, but now it will have more contrast between the light and dark of the shadow.

3. You could have a small light source that's close to you. Say a cell phone flashlight an inch away from your face. That would be a hard light, with more defined lines. Also, it's close, so there will be a big contrast difference between the light and shadow side of the subject.

4. Move that same cell phone light four feet from your face. You still have a small light source creating hard lines, but you'll have a less drastic difference between the light and shadow sides of the subject.

MAKE IT HAPPEN

Look in your Y2K closet, go-bag, or under your bed, and grab your emergency flashlight. Take out your favorite Barbie doll or action figure (it'd easily be Wolverine for me), go to a dark room, and play with shadows. Move the flashlight closer and farther away from your subject and see how it affects the light and shadows.

Next, grab a piece of white paper and put it in front of the flashlight, close enough so that the light is only hitting the white paper. Your light source is now bigger. It's the size of the paper versus the size of the flashlight head. See what happens to the type of shadows that are on your subject's face when you put the piece of paper in front of the flashlight versus when there's nothing in front of it.

This type of exercise, without holding a camera at all, is a great way to start understanding (and then later predicting) how to mold light to create a certain effect. Later, when you start using a strobe as your off-camera flash, you can do the same type of exercise using the strobe's modeling light function. A modeling light is essentially the flashlight for the strobe you're using and you can use it to see what you're doing with the light before you start taking pictures. Very helpful.

ABOUT THIS TEACHING METHOD

I've created this book for the photographer that wants to learn flash but doesn't know where to start. Or maybe you tried to start, but got hit in the face with a firehose of information and got overwhelmed. Perhaps you grasped a little bit of information but still don't have the mastery you'd like. This book is for you.

This book is not for the photo guys with light meters around their necks and the inverse square law tattooed on their forearms. I love you guys, but you will absolutely 110% hate this book. I know, I know. Feel free to send nastygrams to @VanessaJoy on Instagram. I collect them so I have an excuse to eat Cold Stone Peanut Butter Cup Perfection ice cream, by the pint, by myself, with a glass of Napa red Zinfandel wine.

For everyone else who is ready to dive in, I solemnly swear that I am up to all good and hope to give you the easiest explanation of off-camera flash possible. I don't want to bore or intimidate you, and hinder you from picking up your flash. My goal is to get you using your off-camera flash as quickly as you can. If you listened to my "Make It Happen" instructions, then you've already used off-camera flashlight. Congrats!

You won't find complex narratives and diagrams about ratios and the inverse square law in here. They're great, and you should certainly learn them at some point. But I'm choosing to give you lighting basics that you can instantly use in your photography, without potentially overwhelming you with the technical jargon. I strongly believe that the best way to learn is by doing, and, if at the end of this book you've spent more time reading than doing, then I have failed you.

Hopefully I've inspired you to get moving. Go grab your camera and your flash(light) and a bottle of wine, and let's go. You've got this.

"If you don't make mistakes, you're not working on hard enough problems. And that's a big mistake." –Frank Wilczek

CHAPTER 2

Getting the Flash Off Your Camera

The basics of what you need and why you need it.

FIRST OF ALL…

Recently, a friend of mine commented that off-camera flash photography is sort of a recent thing.

Um, what?

Think about the history of photography. Flashes were essentially fireworks and flash powder ignited right as a photo was taken. Those flashes were all "off-camera." Even when flash bulbs were invented in 1927, they were one-time use and usually broke, and were still not actually attached to the camera.

Flashes were off of the camera until the hot shoe was invented, and a flash was able to sit in it on top of the camera body. So, flash was always just flash, not termed off-camera flash like we do today.

Mind. F@%#ing. Blown.

It's a little bit funny that we photographers (myself included) have feared something that's always been because we've grown accustomed to attached flashes around us.

This book is about off-camera flash, but please know that the concepts of flash are the same whether your light is connected to your hot shoe or connected to a trigger. It's simply the direction and position of the light that's changing.

WHAT YOU NEED

Our (the publishers and myself) goal with this book was to be brand agnostic. As they say, "light is light is light," and they're right. There are definitely differences between brands and models of flashes and everything else, but this book will talk about lighting scenarios in a generic way that can be applied to most types of flash equipment you are using.

That being said, I do want to list my gear so you understand what I'm working with. I also want to address the differences between certain types of gear so you can understand my priorities in shooting. This section will give you a solid basis of knowledge for when you next purchase or upgrade gear.

Lighting Gear

There are two major types of lights we'll talk about here: speedlights and strobes.

Speedlights:

- Hot-shoe mounted. Can be attached to a camera.
- Small, light, and portable.
- Less light/power output than strobes.
- Typically don't have a modeling light (except the Profoto A1).
- Don't work as well with larger modifiers.
- Can be triggered on and off the camera.

Strobes:

- Cannot be attached to a camera.
- Heavier than speedlights and less portable.
- Greater light/power output than speedlights.
- Typically feature a modeling light.
- Work well with almost any modifier.
- Can only be triggered off camera.

In my current arsenal I carry both speedlights and strobes on any given shoot. I find uses for both of them depending on my situation. Speedlights are great for when I'm on the go, especially if I'm shooting without an assistant. Strobes are necessary when I need more power, light spread, and a modeling light.

Modeling Light

Sounds glamorous, right? It may not be glamorous, but it is definitely useful on a shoot. A modeling light is a continuous light (think a light turned on like a lamp) that comes out of your strobe that *is not* the actual light that's going to flash when you take a picture. It seems trivial, but I assure you a modeling light is insanely useful.

Help with focus. Think about it. Typically when you need flash it's because you need more light. When it's dark, it's hard to focus. Pop on that modeling light to have a light on your subject that'll help you focus faster and more accurately.

Help the video guy. Or really, help yourself. If you're going outside, setting up a nighttime picture and the video guy follows you out and starts blasting really strong video lights, it'll mess you up. Instead, just pop on your modeling light and the video guy or gal has some light to work with.

Preview where your light is. It can be difficult setting up lights, especially from far away, and getting them to point exactly where you want the light to fall. With a modeling light, you're able to see exactly where the light is falling, which makes placing and directing the light a lot easier.

Video light. Modeling lights are usually super strong, but some, like the modeling light on the Profoto B10 series, are adjustable in intensity and color temperature. You can absolutely use them as a video light in some situations in case you want to shoot both photo and video.

Pupils. Ever photograph someone with brightly colored eyes, and then in the picture it looks like they're tripping on acid because their pupils are so enlarged? A modeling light will cause the pupils to shrink so you can see more of the color in the eyes in your photos.

Brand Differences

When you start shopping for lighting, you'll notice some pretty huge price differences between brands. There are a million YouTubers that'll fight for one brand or the other, so feel free to go listen to a few perspectives. In my experience, I have found that the more expensive brands, in general, offer better products based on color, power consistency, durability, usability, features, convenience, and customer services (especially if repairs are needed). It's a "you get what you pay for" situation. Do your research, of course, and choose what's best for you and your current needs. If you're just starting out you might not need the best of everything. But if you don't want to keep buying lights, then you might want to invest in the best right off the bat.

Here's my current gear list:

- Speedlight: Profoto A1
- Strobes: Profoto B1; Profoto B10
- Profoto Air Remote
- Camera Gear: Canon 1DXII; Canon Prime Lenses

Why No Light Meter?

I do not use a light meter. I used one back when I was shooting with film, but today I don't. I don't even own one.

Don't get me wrong, they're great and useful and more accurate than my method. But for me, the decision not to use one is about ease of use and speed during a shoot. My lights and camera essentially have light meters built into them so I find it more efficient to use them versus a light meter. I use TTL (essentially auto mode for your flash) frequently, if not always.

For me, I'm buying the technology, so I'm going to use it. It's certainly saved my butt when I only have nine seconds to take three photos (for at least one useable shot). Had I walked over to my subject for a light meter reading and walked back to my shooting spot, it would've taken up the entire nine seconds.

That being said, light meters are excellent tools that help figure out light ratios, assist with multiple-light setups, and help the photographer determine many factors when using flash. I am not discrediting light meters. I'm not even saying that I couldn't benefit from using one here and there. I'm simply not using them as the method to teach my scenario-based lighting in this book because most people find them to be a confusing hurdle. I'd like to eliminate as many roadblocks as I can between you and getting comfortable using flash.

Triggers

In order to get the flash to fire when it's not directly connected to your camera, you need a trigger (or Air Remote, as Profoto names it). A trigger mounts onto the hot shoe on your camera and tells the light when to fire so that it's in sync with your camera's shutter.

Not all triggers are made the same. Some are made to work only with certain camera brands. Some, like Pocket Wizards and Radio Poppers, are made to work across multiple platforms. Some have functionality in them that'll let you control every aspect of the light right from your camera (or an app on your phone). Others, like the Profoto Connect are super simple, with only an on and off button.

If you're first starting out in off-camera flash, this part can be extremely annoying, difficult, and potentially expensive. I can't tell you what to buy, but I can tell you this: It is exponentially harder and more frustrating to learn on equipment that is not reliable or consistent.

When you're ready to make your purchase, or upgrade, I highly suggest going into a camera store, like Adorama, to do it. Talk to an expert on the gear. Let them know your skill level and ask for recommendations. It'll help you navigate the plethora of options and give you somewhere to go when you have questions or problems after your purchase.

Light Stands

You cannot invest too much in your light stands. They are not only carrying very expensive pieces of equipment, but they are also protecting you from a liability. If you don't have an assistant, sturdy light stands and sand bags to weigh them down, are an absolute must.

I'm a fan of Manfrotto stackable stands because they're sturdy, take up less space in transportation, and extend as high as I need them to. If I need my stand to be even more portable, I enjoy my Matthew's 7.5′ Mini Extendable Reverse Stand. It's crazy compact, light, and can hold a speedlight or Profoto B10 easily.

Whatever you choose, make sure that you keep it grounded with either an assistant or counterweights. I've had light stands fall over, and I even had one fall off of a cliff. Miraculously, the built-tough Profoto B1 that fell over with it was completely fine.

OK, NOW GO SHOPPING

Actually, don't. Go renting instead. Or see if you can borrow another photographer's gear to try out some of the equipment in the scenarios I have listed. Experimenting with different lights and brands before making a significant purchase is a really good idea.

Gear, in a lot of ways, is a personal thing. Yes, you can compare specs and reviews until your eyes bleed. Ultimately, you're going to like what you like because you like it, because it feels good in your hands and makes your life easier. If you like it and it works for you, that's what you should use.

Happy shopping!

CHAPTER 3
Getting the Exposure

How to wrap your head around off-camera flash settings.

THE EXPOSURE ROOM

When you first learned photography, you may have had the exposure triangle explained to you. For me, the idea of an exposure triangle is by far one of the most irritating in photography. It does put the elements of exposure into a nice little box… err… pyramid; however, it doesn't help me visualize the elements of the light, nor does it help me balance it into one exposure. Plus, OCF would be the fourth point in the exposure triangle, and that doesn't really work.

I explain exposure to beginning photographers by having them picture a room with three windows: one for ISO, one for aperture, and one for shutter speed. You need a certain amount of light in the room to expose it correctly, so you open the shades. If you want to change one of your settings—say, lowering your ISO "shade"—you'll need to open one of you other shades to compensate in order to keep the amount of light in the room the same.

I suppose that's over simplifying it, and changing settings affects more than just the amount of light, but visually, the idea makes sense. Now, adding in off-camera flash is simply adding another window. Exposure-wise it behaves just like the rest of the windows. You open or shut your shade (i.e., raise or lower your light power) until you have the desired amount of light in the room (or your exposure). Then, if you want to change something in your exposure, you'll need to compensate by raising your light power (opening that blind a bit.)

There are definitely more elements that go into an exposure with off-camera flash and different ways it affects the image. However, if you're just starting out with all of this, it's very easy to overcomplicate it in your head. Do yourself a favor and keep it simple. You can always build upon your knowledge as you go. No need to try and drink from a fire hose right away; a water fountain will do just fine.

EXPOSURE SETTINGS

Whenever I'm setting up my exposure for an off-camera flash image, I first get the exposure I want for the background. My goal with OCF is typically to add just a kiss of light and make it look as natural and smooth as possible. Here are the steps I take to getting an exposure with OCF:

1. **Set your exposure for the background:** Basically this means that if you're taking a picture of someone outside, set your camera as if you were just photographing the landscape behind them.

   A. **Depth of Field:** Keep in mind how you'd like your images to look. If you usually have a shallow depth of field, keep that going here.

   B. **One Stop Under:** Some people like to set their background for a stop darker than for which it would normally be exposed. I don't do this typically, but you may want to try it if you want your background darker than your subject. It's your choice.

2. **Set your flash power:** There are two ways you can set your flash power on most lights. In my examples and setups, I'll tell you how I finagle through the lens (TTL) to work for me, but I also give suggestions for how to dial in settings manually, and I suggest a light meter when appropriate. The choice is ultimately yours for how you want to set your flash power. Refer back to this chapter throughout the book until you get used to setting your flash power how you see fit.

   A. **TTL:** This is basically auto mode for your flash. It stands for *through the lens* and it determines the amount of light power to pump out of the flash given your camera settings and environmental situation. I *highly* recommend setting your metering mode to spot metering when using TTL. Perhaps use the evaluative or matrix metering mode when exposing for your background, but switch to spot when exposing your light.

   B. **Manual:** This is where you decide and dial in how much power you want coming out of your light. You could use a light meter to determine the exact power it should be at based on your situation. Some photographers start by setting the light to a mid power range and then raise or lower their light power, checking their images as they go until they like the look of the image.

   C. **Both:** This is my method. Unfortunately, this method isn't available in all lights. It is available with any Profoto light, which is what I use (just one of the reasons I use their system!).

      I. I set my light(s) to TTL to let it determine about where the light power should be.

      II. I take a picture.

III. I switch my light to manual mode. The Profoto system will maintain whatever TTL-based light-power setting it had.

IV. I adjust my light to be brighter or darker as I see fit, looking at the back of my camera as a guide.

3. **Adjust the Image:** After you have a solid exposure, you may want to change things based on what you see. Maybe you'd like the whole picture to be brighter. Maybe you want just the background to be darker. Now is when you tweak the image, and more on how to do that later.

Adjusting Exposure with OCF

This may be the most confusing part of OCF, but feel free to refer back to this handbook at any time until you've got it down in your head.

When you're adjusting your exposure with OCF, there are a few things to keep in mind.

- The shutter speed *will not change* the flash power on your subject.
- The shutter speed *will change* the ambient (natural) light, which may change lighting on your subject, not because of the flash getting brighter or darker, but because of the ambient light getting brighter or darker on your subject.
- ISO and aperture *will change* the flash power and the ambient light on your subject all at once.

Go back and read that again.

One more time.

You still may not have the concepts down yet, and that's OK. As we go through the lighting scenarios, I'll remind you how it all applies to the specific situation we're in. All of those concepts have practical applications that you'll want to know.

- If you want your *overall picture* to be brighter or darker, raise or lower your ISO or aperture. This will also make the flash lighter or darker, so you may need to raise or lower your flash power if you don't like the change.
- If you want your *background* brighter or darker, raise or lower your shutter speed. This *will not* make the flash brighter in the scene, but your subject's exposure may change because of the increase in ambient light that you're letting into the camera.
- I recommend you only change one thing at a time. Don't change your ISO and flash power, and then take a picture. It's very easy to get thrown off course if you start changing multiple settings at once. Take it slow and only change one thing at a time. This way if you don't like it, you can easily change it back and try something else.
- When the ISO is lowered or the aperture is closed down (letting in less light), the flash needs to be at a higher power to affect the image. This means using more battery power. This is definitely something to consider if you shoot long event days like I do.

- High Speed Sync (HSS) sucks even more battery than a high flash power. We'll talk about HSS more later in the book, but for now just know that you will need HSS when you set your shutter speed above your camera's sync speed (different for each camera—mine is $\frac{1}{250}$ of a second. Most cameras are around $\frac{1}{200}$).

JUST LIGHT IT

All of this may seem daunting. I get it. I really do. But don't get frustrated and close the book now thinking you'll never get it. **You will get this**. But you have to do it to get better at it. It's not easy at first, and you will take a bad picture or two…hundred…thousand. Who cares?! You're likely shooting digital; it doesn't cost you money with each click. Just take another picture, learn something, and get better at it. Let's get out there and light something!

CHAPTER 4

Light Positions and Modifiers

How to pretty-up your light.

LIGHT POSITIONING

I'm pretty sure that light positioning is a topic that could be an entire book. In fact, I'm sure it must be out there somewhere. I'm going to go over some of basics here, but I highly recommend reading some books or taking classes all about how light positioning changes shadows and fall off, and how it shapes a person's face. It's an endless rabbit hole of information (but a fun one!). For our purposes, let's address the thought process behind where you place your lights. Think about what you're *not* lighting just as much as what you *are* lighting.

Two of the biggest mistakes I've made in lighting had to do with light positioning.

First, I thought that if I was lighting a person, I had to point the light directly at them. Not true at all. In fact, it's typically better to not point the light directly at your subject. It will lead to a harsher-looking image instead of one in which the light softly kisses your subject. There is a time and place for both, but normally I'm attempting to be subtle in my lighting.

Second, I wasn't paying attention to my light spill, and it was falling into parts of the picture that were not my subject. Light spill is basically the leftover light that you didn't want in your image. For example, in this image, while I love it, you can see a ton of light spill on the ground around them. It causes the viewer's eye to go down toward the ground instead of toward the bride and groom's faces. Not good.

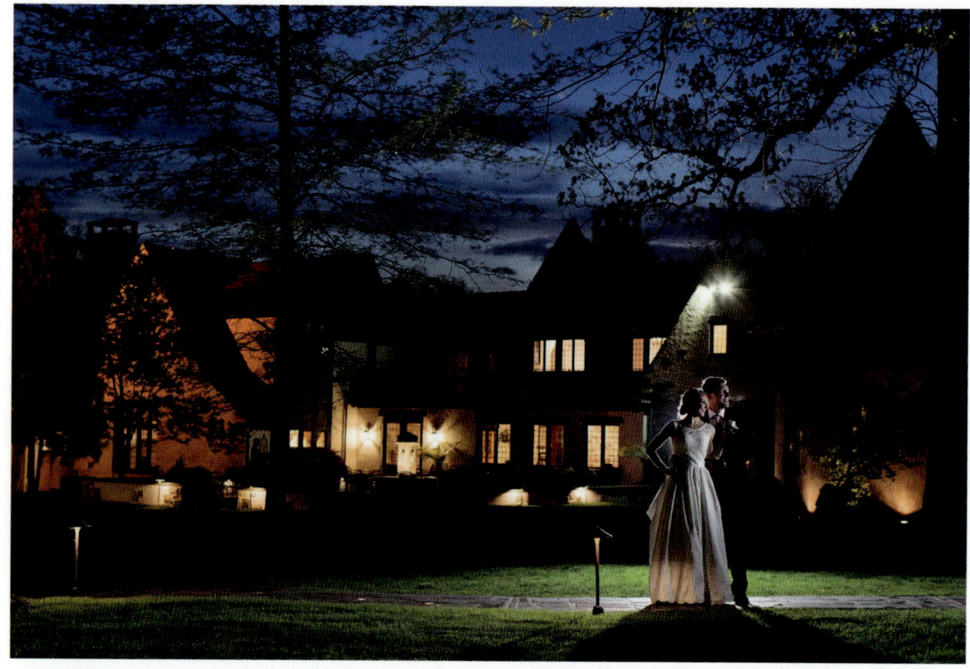

Feathering Light

Feathering light is a term used for tilting the light away from the subject so that it's not hitting them directly. If someone tells you "feather the light," they mean to direct the light away from the subject more. Mind you, that *doesn't* mean *move* the light farther away. Just point it, pan it, or tilt it in a direction that points it further away from the subject.

Here are some reasons to feather light:

- It softens the look of the light on the subject.

- It creates a softer look from light to shadow.

- It lowers the light intensity hitting the subject.

- It changes the shape of the light hitting the subject.

Light can be feathered in any direction. I like to feather the light in front of my subject so that it's really just the edge of the light that's grazing past my subject's nose. You could also feather the light up, down, and even behind the subject depending on the desired effect.

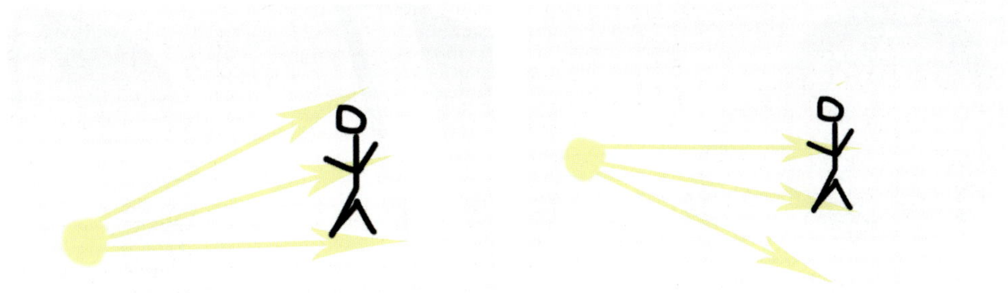

LIGHT MODIFIERS

Light modifiers (sometimes called light shapers) drove me up the wall for many, many years. These modifiers are the fluffy, boxy things that photographers stick onto their lights. I just didn't understand what they were or what they were doing. Not to mention that there are so many different types of modifiers with different names, brands, and sizes that it's hard to figure out what's good and what's not.

Forget the names of all of the modifiers. Here's what you're going to think about anytime you see a light modifier.

"It's just a window."

That's it.

I look at modifiers as pieces of equipment that go onto the strobe to mimic natural light scenarios. Think about the kind of light do you have with natural light coming through a really big window. It's a super soft, glorious light. What about a really tiny window? You'll have small, directional light. Whenever you see a light modifier, just think windows.

There is more that comes into play with different types of modifiers, but this is a good starting point. What follows are some of the basic light shapers and lingo that you might use.

Bare Bulb

A reference to shooting "bare bulb" means that there isn't any modifier on it at all. This term really refers to lights where you can actually see the strobe's light bulb and nothing is in front of it at all. Most old strobes were true bare bulb. Now a lot of strobes have some kind of glass covering them that helps protect the bulb as well as point the light more forward and diffuse it a bit.

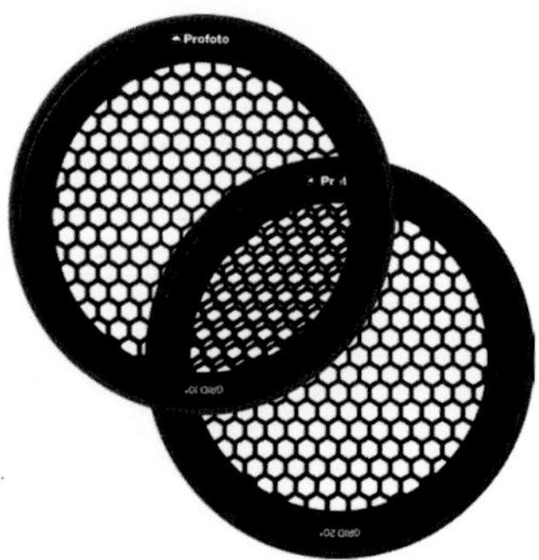

FIGURE 4.3
PROFOTO GRID KIT

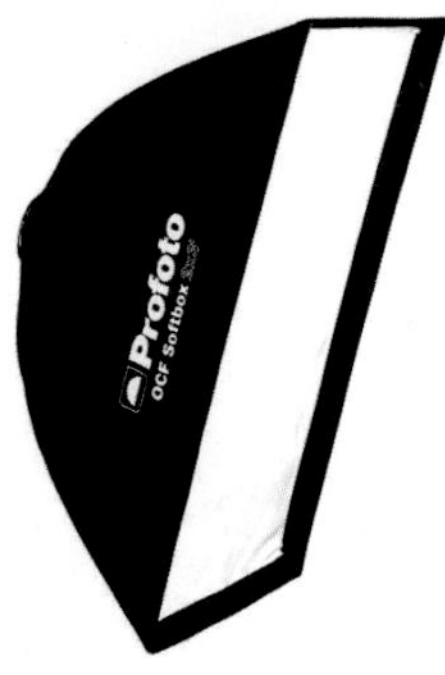

FIGURE 4.4
PROFOTO SOFTBOX

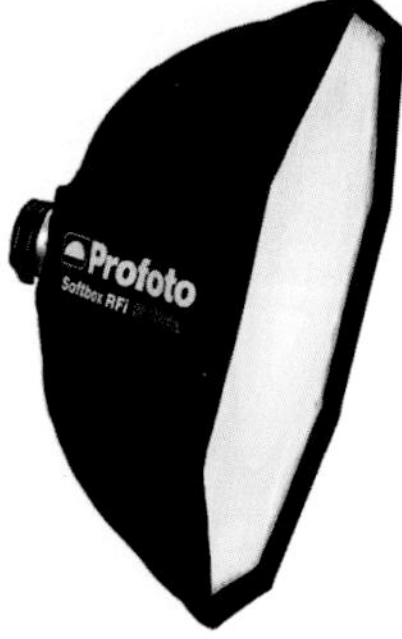

FIGURE 4.5
PROFOTO OCTA

Grids

Grids are honeycomb-shaped modifiers that you put in the front of your light to direct it with more intention. A grid is usually defined by the degree (20, 10, 5, etc.) to which the light is spreading. A smaller degree means more pointed light. A snoot (another type of modifier) would create a very pointed light, almost like shining a light through a door keyhole. You can put grids directly onto your light, or use them within other modifiers, like softboxes and beauty dishes to better direct the light so it won't spill out to other parts of your images.

Softboxes

These modifiers are the most accurate to my metaphor of windows because they are all rectangles. The can be very small like a 1' × 1', or very large like a 4' × 6'. They usually have diffusers on them (sometimes even two layers of diffusion) so that the light evenly spreads across then entire "window." Diffusers are also referred to as baffles or silks.

Octagon Softboxes

These softboxes are eight-sided and circular instead of four-sided and rectangular. Think of a circular window verses a rectangular one. Octas, as they're typically called, create a circular light that doesn't have the same straight edges that a regular softbox has.

Beauty Dish

A beauty dish has a unique light-bouncing setup inside of it. Instead of the light pointing directly through the diffusion layers like a softbox, there is a hard plate directly in front of the strobe. The light bounces off of the hard plate toward the back of the beauty dish, and then bounces back out toward your subject. This eliminates the hot spot in the middle of the light making the center of the light the least directly lit. You can use a diffuser or a grid with a beauty dish.

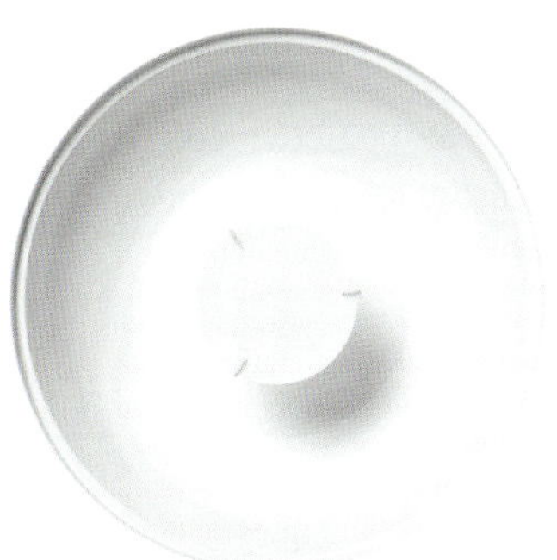

FIGURE 4.6
BEAUTY DISH

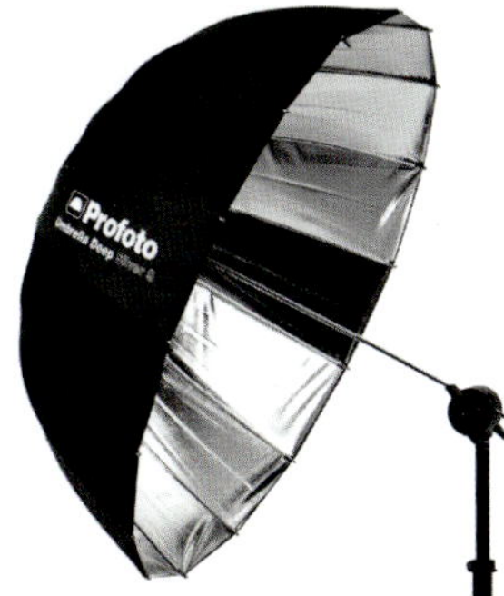

FIGURE 4.7
REFLECTIVE UMBRELLA

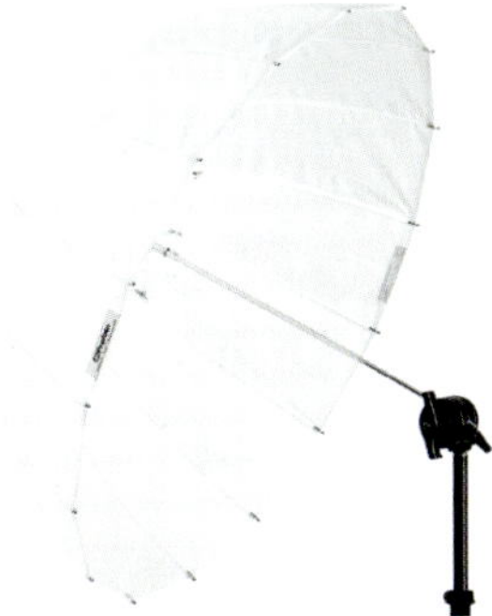

FIGURE 4.8
SHOOT-THROUGH UMBRELLA

Umbrellas

There are reflective umbrellas and shoot-through umbrellas. A reflective umbrella is opaque with a silver or white lining inside. You point the strobe at the back of the inside of the umbrella and bounce the light back at the subject. The shoot-through umbrella is translucent. Point the strobe at the back of the umbrella and through it to light the subject on the other side. Both are very portable and easy to set up. They create a widely spread light, which is why they're typically used for group photos.

Silver and White Reflectors

You'll notice that umbrellas, beauty dishes, and general reflectors will sometimes have a white or silver (in)side. The silver produces a brighter result, but also changes the quality of the light. A silver reflective surface will brighten the specular highlights, meaning the whites will become whiter, giving the image a more contrasty look. Do not use this on someone with oily skin. It will amplify the shine on their face.

Gels

Gels are translucent pieces of polyester (they used to be made of gelatin; hence the name) that come in many colors so you can change the color of your light. There are so many fun ways to use gels and we'll go over a lot of them!

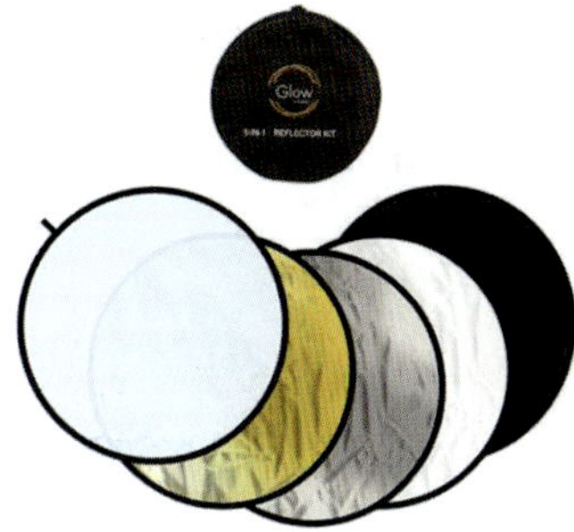

FIGURE 4.9
GLOW 5-IN-1 42" REFLECTOR FOUND AT ADORAMA.COM

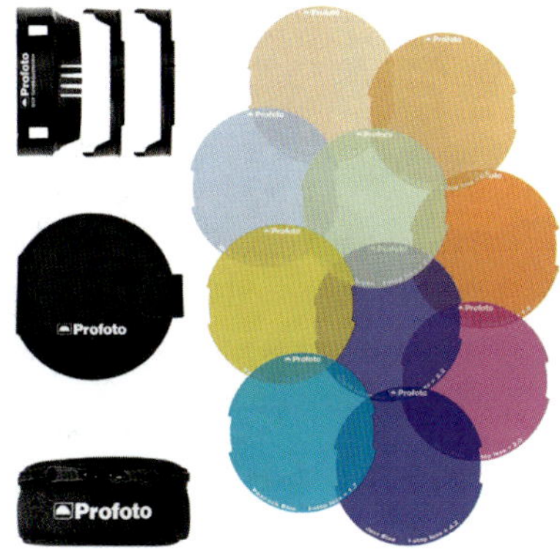

FIGURE 4.10
THESE ARE PROFOTO OCF GELS, BUT THERE ARE MANY, MANY TYPES OF GELS YOU CAN GET.

More on Diffusers and Grids

If you want, you can pull the diffusers off of your light modifier. You can also pull them off (*gasp!*) just a *part* of the light modifier. Maybe you only want the bottom of the light to have a grid on it while the top just has a diffusion layer. You can do that! Think outside the box.

WHAT I USE AND WHY

I want the decision of what you choose to use to come from you, but I do get this question a lot. I definitely have an arsenal of light modifiers, but I strategically use them depending on the shoot and what I'm looking to do.

Engagement and Portrait Sessions

- Profoto gels for sun flare.
- Profoto grids to direct light.
- Profoto OCF beauty dish because it's small and portable.

Headshot Sessions

- Profoto 2x3 softboxes, perfect for business headshots.
- Softbox grid to direct light, especially if I'm using a black background because I don't want any light to hit it.

Weddings

- Profoto Medium Umbrella because it's easy to set up. I use it for groups, mostly.
- Profoto gels for sun flare and other coloring tricks.
- Profoto grids to direct light.
- Profoto OCF beauty dish because it's small and portable.

SUMMARY

I've outlined modifiers in this chapter, but the truth is you need to start using them to really get the hang of how they work. If I were to recommend a "first modifier kit" purchase, I'd say an umbrella, grids, gels, and a portable beauty dish (in that order). They're what I use the most, and they will cover most basic lighting scenarios you come across.

There isn't a magic solution for every shot and you're going to like one type of modifier over another for a variety of reasons. A beauty dish not positioned correctly can end up not creating the look you want. Using a bare strobe bulb, if you know how to use it, you may be able to create exactly what you're looking for. Learning to use and position your light is more important than the modifier itself.

CHAPTER 5

How to Add More Lights

I promise, it's not that scary.

1 + 1 + 1 = 3

I dedicated an entire chapter to this because it was one of my hang-ups in learning the principles of off-camera flash. I remember looking at all of the lights that people were using and just thinking, "I can't even make one light look right; how on Earth do I do it with five lights?" I also thought there was a specific "positioning system" for three lights, and another specific system if you had four lights, five lights, and so on, which isn't necessarily correct. Adding more lights is just as simple as looking at your picture and thinking, "Hmmmm, I wish I had some light right there," and then placing a light in that spot.

Using multiple lights has value beyond photography. As my friend Daniel Norton says, "The more lights you use, the more you get paid." I agree with that since, even as a photographer, I would look at people using multiple lights and assume they knew more than me. Also not necessarily true but hey, if you can boost your perceived value, why not do so?

Adding more lights is not really an exact science as far as placement because you may want one thing over another in terms of style or look. What I want to concentrate on is the method for adding lights so that you don't get confused and end up with out-of-control lights all over the place. Here are the steps to get started:

- **The Fast-Start Method:** If you're using a system that has great TTL functionality, you can put your lights where you want them, put modifiers on them, turn them all on, and get your exposure automatically. Afterward you can adjust your lights to be brighter or darker.

- **The One-by-One Method:** This method is more ideal and lets you dial in settings for each light in a more fine-tuned fashion. I believe I actually learned this method from watching the aforementioned Daniel Norton on Adorama's Facebook page or YouTube.

  1. Get your background exposure first.

  2. Turn on your main light—I prefer to meter on TTL—and take a photo.

  3. Adjust your main light to be brighter or darker to your liking.

  4. Turn that main light head off. Note the power level before doing so if your light doesn't hold the power setting when you turn if off and on.

  5. Turn your second light on—I prefer on TTL—and take a photo.

  6. Adjust that light to be brighter or darker to your liking.

  7. Keep going with this system for as many lights as you're working with.

  8. Turn on all lights on manual. They should all be set to their previous setting, metered by TTL.

  9. Take a photo and adjust any of them to be brighter or darker as needed.

- **The Light Meter Method:** This way of setting your lights is similar to the previous method in that you measure and set the lights one at a time. However, instead of using TTL, you'll set your lights on manual and go through them one-by-one using the light meter to determine your power setting based on your desired exposure settings.

Important Things to Note

Some things to remember when you're using multiple lights:

- Keep them on separate groups so that you can adjust them all individually (until you run out of groups).

- Control your lights. There's not much of a point in using multiple lights if you're just light-bombing your entire photo without intention.

- Adjust one thing at a time. Going crazy thinking you can fix everything in one swoop will likely get you lost.

- Sometimes one light overpowers another. I just told you to set one light at a time and then add them all together. Occasionally a light will look great solo in your shot, but when you add another light you'll notice one of them isn't affecting the image in the same way it was before. This usually means that one or all of the other lights are overpowering it. Boost up the light that you're not seeing until you see it.

- Sometimes a photographer will use two lights in one position, pointed at the same subject from the same angle. This is usually because they need more power to affect the image so they use two, three, or four lights instead of one. You will likely see this with speedlights versus strobes, because they are less powerful, and during the daytime to overpower sunlight.

- Creating a multiple-light setup actually begs for the use of a light meter. While you can get away without one, utilizing one in this case is very useful and will probably get you to where you need to be faster and more accurately right off the bat. It'll also teach you to understand light power as you go, and before you know it, you'll know what power setting each light will be at based on the distance of them and your camera settings without needing to use TTL.

PART 2

Off-Camera Flash Techniques

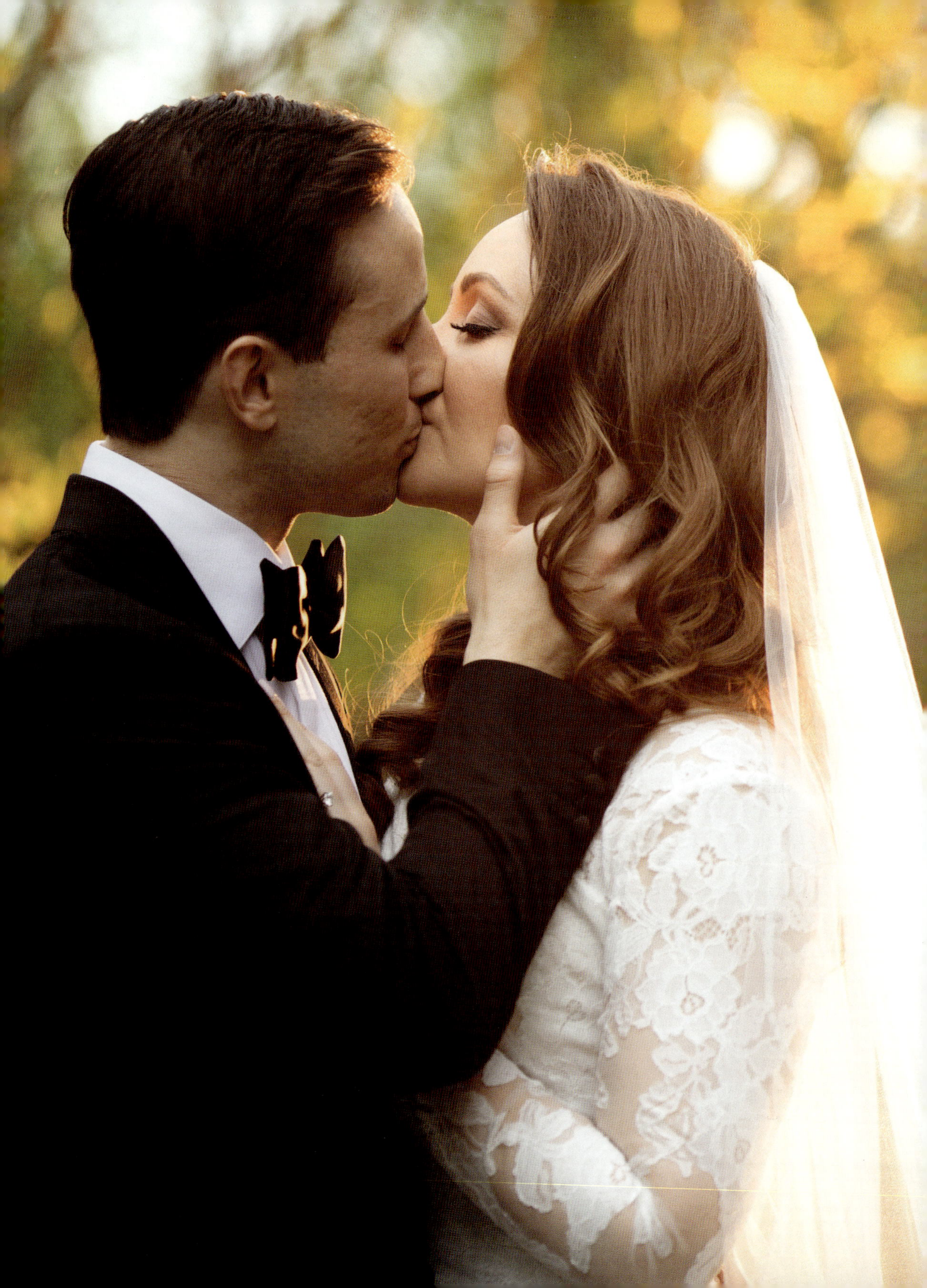

SCENARIO 1

Creating Gold Haze

For that warm glow whenever you want it.

GOAL IMAGE

With this trick you're looking to create that gorgeous just-before-sunset light. Think about using your off-camera flash to mimic the sun low in the sky. Shoot toward it to let the light directly hit your camera. All of the warmth of the "sun" beautifully spills over into your subject and you're left with an image that's soft and glowing. All images in this chapter are almost straight out of the camera, with only the areas of highlight (the white dress and shiny skin) taken down in Adobe Lightroom.

- Camera + Trigger
- Long focal length lens (100mm or higher recommended)
- Off-camera flash
- 2 Full CTO (color temperature orange) gels
- Light stand

In my experience, the easiest way to achieve this look is to use a longer lens and a lower aperture. They both contribute to any flare or bokeh in the image being smoothed out and softened as much as possible. You can create a haze with a wider lens, but it is more difficult to find the right angle that will produce a haze versus just a glowing light in the background of your image.

As always, your mindset should be to think about how you'd create this look with natural light, and then simply copy the light positions and colors. With natural light, you'd probably take this photo during golden hour. The light would be nice and low in the sky and behind your subject fairly far away. It would also be behind trees and bushes so place your light behind some foliage if possible.

The color of the sun at this time of day is warm. I recommend doubling up on your CTO (color temperature orange) gels so you have two full CTO gels in front of your flash. It'll suck up a little bit of light from your flash, but it will ensure that your light has the golden glow that you're looking for.

All of the images in this chapter are pretty much straight out of the camera with *zero* retouching involved. I want you to see what the light actually does, not what Adobe Photoshop does. If you wanted, you could cool the light down a little in post, or take some of the yellow tones out of the skin.

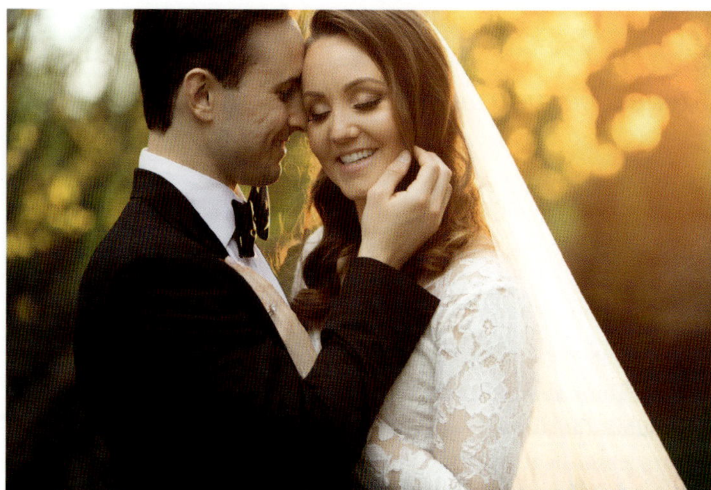

Step by Step

1. **Position your light:** Try to get the light at least 20 feet away from your subject, behind them and behind trees or bushes that'll break up the light and make it look more natural.

2. **Set the camera exposure:** Get an exposure for the natural light on your subject as if you weren't using off-camera flash. Try to keep your aperture as low as possible, about f/2.0. Take a test shot and check your histogram.

3. **Set the white balance:** Because the flash is gelled and you want it to look warm, you'll set your white balance for the light hitting your subject. If you're not into dialing in your white balance Kelvin setting manually, try using the cloudy day preset. Take a test shot and check the coloring of your photo.

4. **Set the flash:** I enjoy using TTL +2 in this scenario because it makes the backlight very prominent. If you're using a manual flash, start in the mid-high power range, or use a light meter and adjust up or down to your liking. Take a test shot and adjust your light based on the results.

5. **Change your angle:** This is where you get to play. Move your camera angle around to experiment with how the backlight is hitting your lens. The look of the haze will change a bit with each movement depending on the angle of the light to your lens.

6. **Make adjustments:** Once you have a solid image, feel free to change your exposure, white balance, or flash settings. Be sure to only change one thing at a time so you don't get so far away from what was working originally that you can't get back.

OPTIONAL: Use a white reflector in front of your subject to bounce some of the light from the sun or the off-camera flash back into their face and eyes.

Shot by Shot

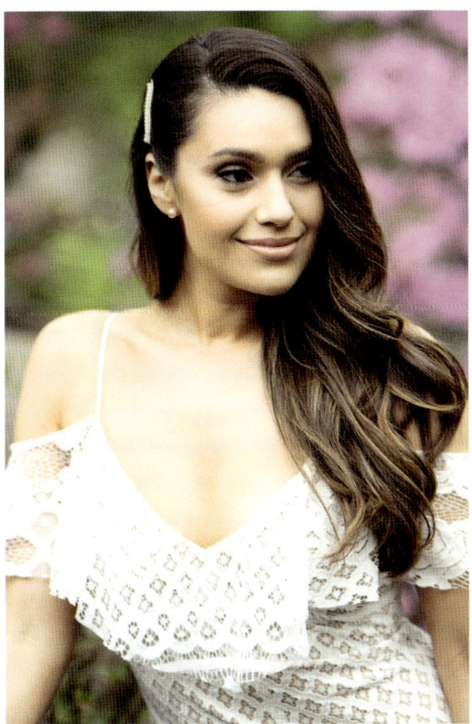

NATURAL LIGHT.
CANON EOS 5DS R, CANON 135MM 2.0, ISO 200, F/3.2, 1/200, WB 5700K

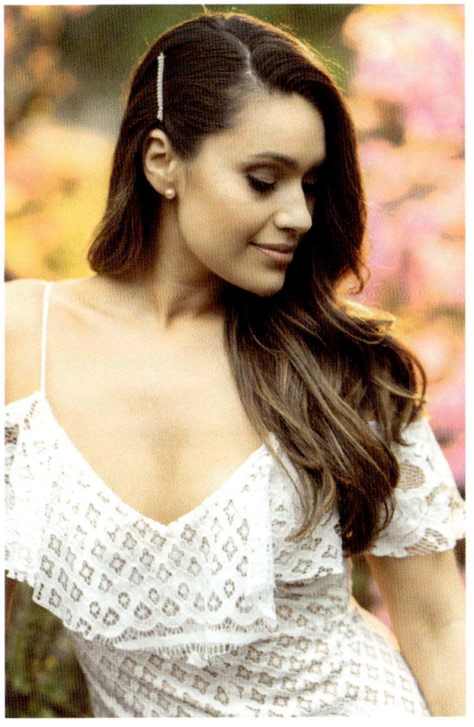

ADDING OCF IN BACK.
CANON EOS 5DS R, CANON 135MM 2.0, ISO 200, F/3.2, 1/200, WB 5700K

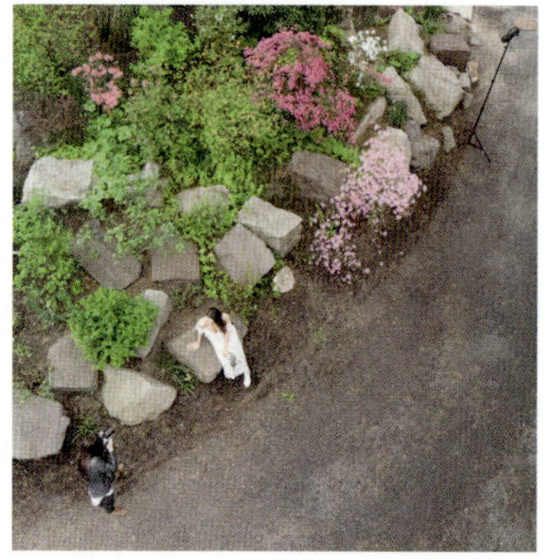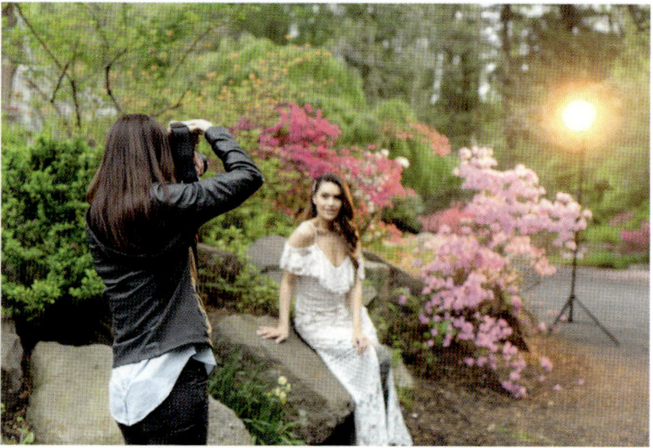

FIGURE 1.4

BEHIND THE SCENES.

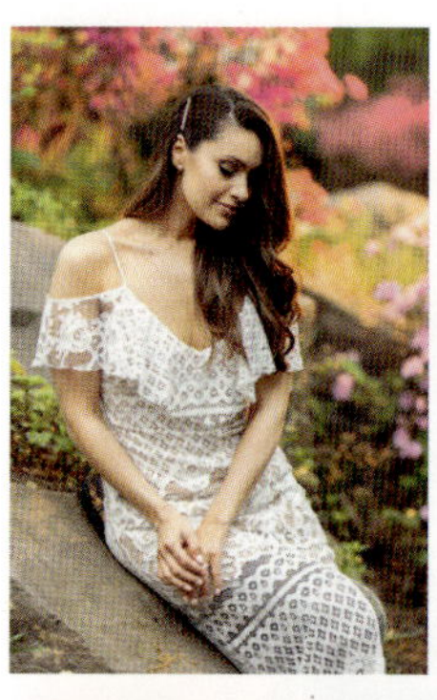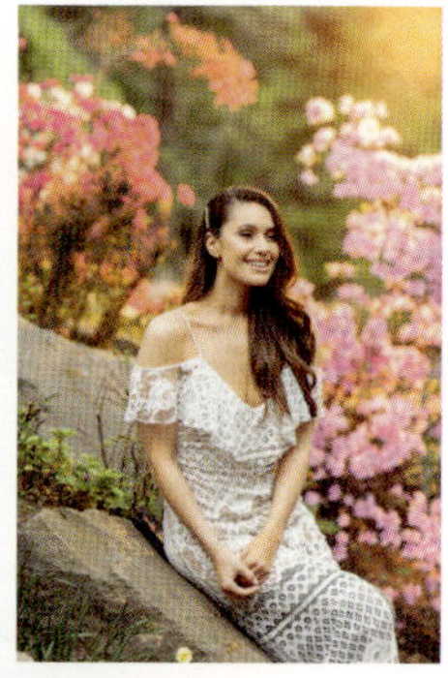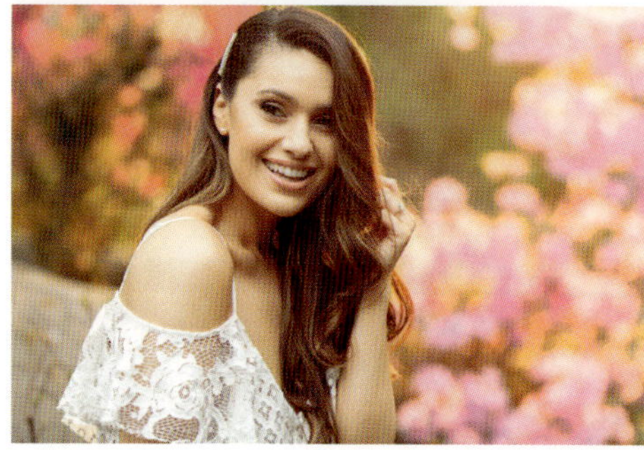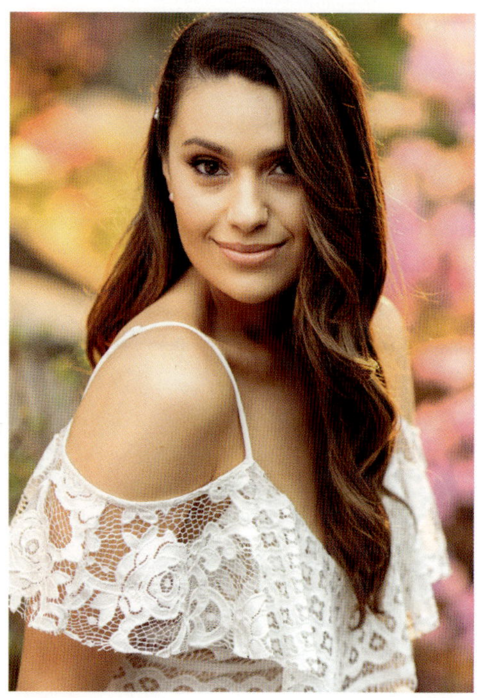

FIGURE 1.5

ALL SETTINGS: CANON EOS 5DS R, CANON 135MM 2.0.
ISO 200, F/3.2, 1/200, WB 5700K

FIGURE 1.6

ADDING OPTIONAL WHITE REFLECTOR.
CANON EOS 5DS R, CANON 135MM 2.0, ISO 200, F/3.2,
1/200, WB 5700K

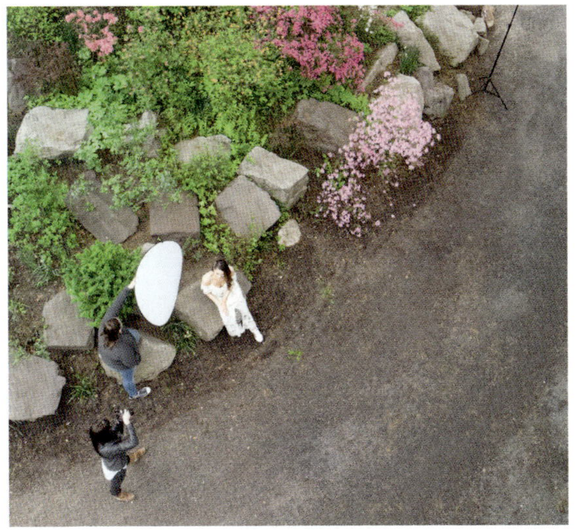
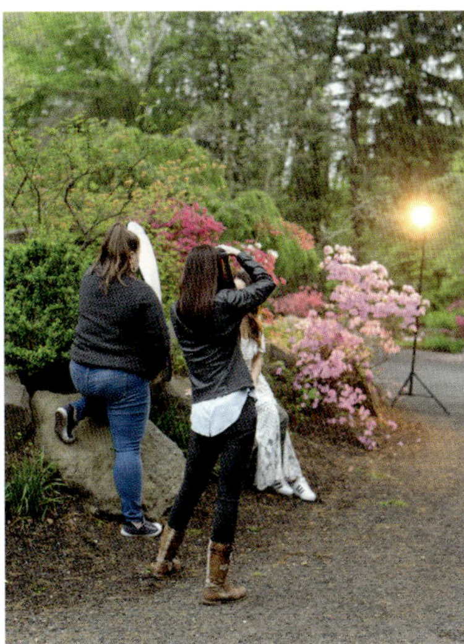

BEHIND-THE-SCENES AERIAL FOOTAGE USING AN OPTIONAL REFLECTOR.

Potential Problems

When you're creating backlight and letting it spill into the lens, it can be easy to overdo it. Keep in mind that the more haze you have, the less contrast you'll have in the image. This can make the image look a bit out of focus, or it can really distort the coloring of your subject's skin tone (it's already going to be a bit yellow because of the haze). The creativity is up to you though, so if you like that look then go for it.

Another possible problem is the placement of the light in relation to your subject. I don't recommend placing the light directly behind your subject because it will overexpose the image and create a distracting element right behind your subject. Do this: **Figure 1.8**; don't do this: **Figure 1.9**.

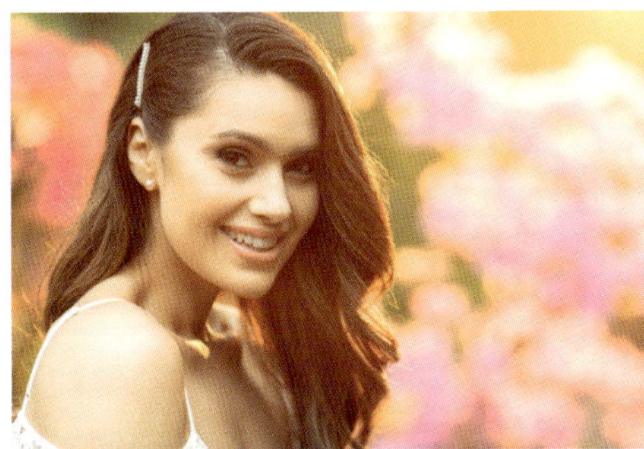

BEST PLACEMENT OF LIGHT.

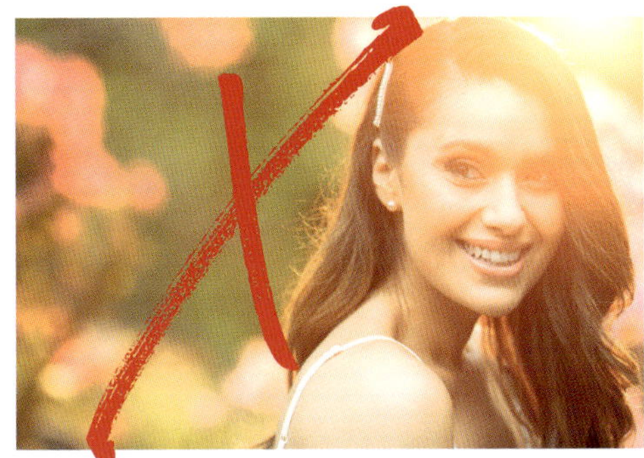

DISTRACTING PLACEMENT OF LIGHT.

Practical Uses

This is one of my favorite lighting setups on any given shoot. It's an easy, one-light setup that doesn't boggle the mind with all of the settings. It creates a soft dreamy look that wouldn't be possible without shooting during the golden hour.

Give this a try for individual and couple portraits, and for creating a magical, glowing scene in photos of children. If you advertise a warm photographic brand, you can use this technique consistently in your images.

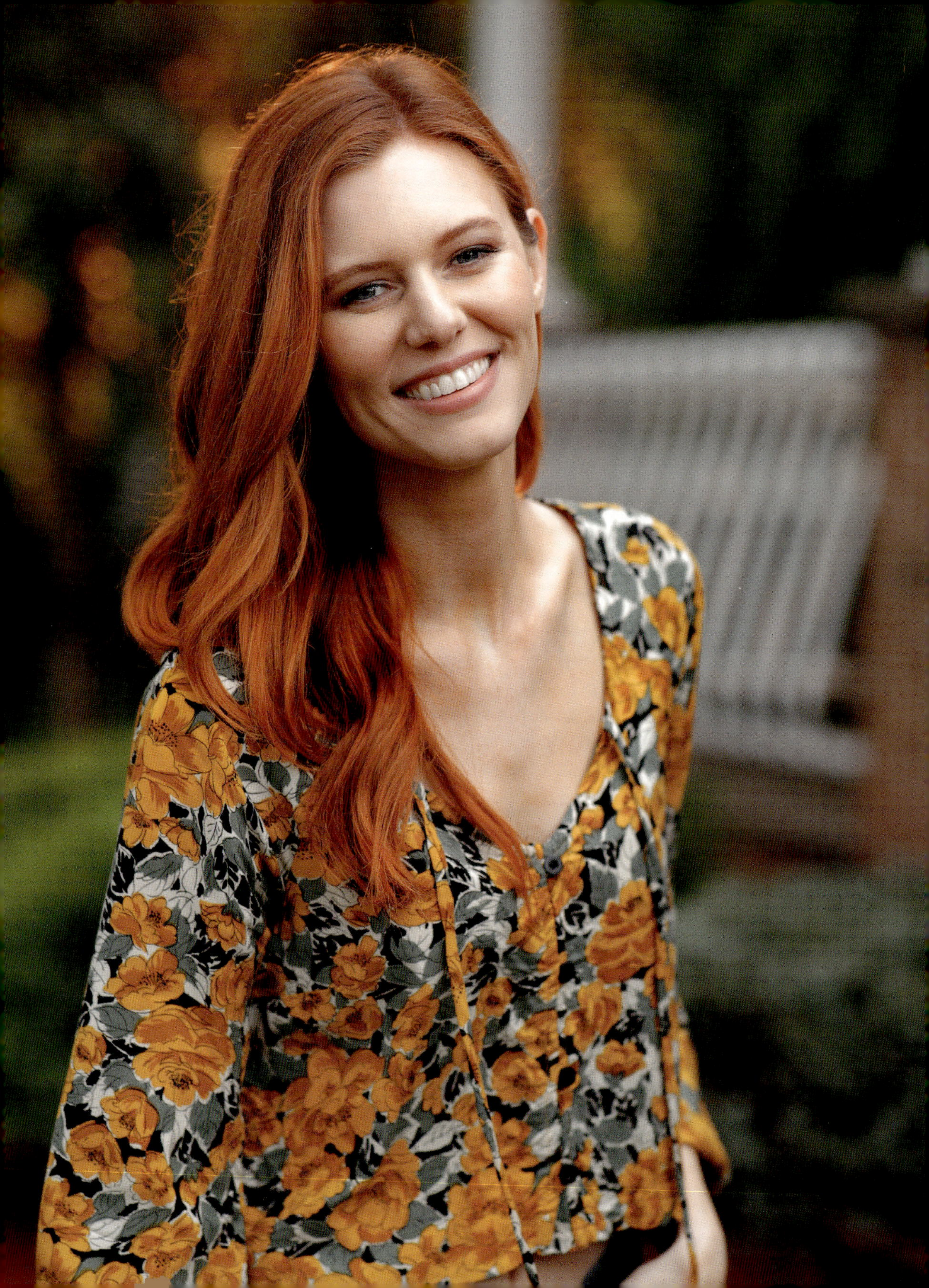

Creating Golden Hour

How to make it look like you're shooting at the best time of the day.

GOAL IMAGE

If you're looking for that perfect before-sunset time of day, this is how to create it no matter what time of day you're shooting. You can use your off-camera flash to copycat the sun low in the sky. Take advantage of it and make your whole frame glow. The best part is you can make the sun hit exactly where you want it to in your frame (**Figure 2.1**).

The secret to getting this right is finding some foliage. Having a flash appear out of nowhere isn't going to trick anyone. Placing that flash behind some greenery where the light gets broken up will make it seem more natural and far away, giving your image exactly what it needs to be believable.

GEAR NEEDED:

- Camera + Trigger
- Medium-to-long focal length lens (50mm or higher recommended)
- 2 Off-camera flashes
- 2 Full CTO (color temperature orange) gels
- 2 Light stands
- Soft modifier (umbrella, softbox, beauty dish, etc.)
- Large white reflector *(optional)*

Keep in mind how you would create this look with natural light, and then copy the light positions and colors. During the actual golden hour, the light would be nice and low in the sky and behind your subject fairly far away. It might also be behind trees and bushes, so place your light behind some plants if possible.

The color of the sun at this time of day is warm. I recommend doubling up on your CTO (color temperature orange) gels so you have two full CTO gels in front of your flash. It'll suck up a little bit of light from your flash, but it will ensure that your light has the golden glow that you're looking for.

Finally, if you were shooting during the golden hour with the light hitting the subject from behind, you'd likely need to fill in the face with a reflector or another flash. This will prevent your subject's eyes from looking like black holes.

Step by Step

1. **Position the "sun" backlight:** This is the light that will have the two CTO gels on it. Try to get the light at least 20 feet away from your subject and behind trees or bushes that'll break up the light and make it look more natural.

2. **Position your front light:** This light will have the soft modifier on it. You'll want it as close to your subject as possible, without being in the frame. I suggest placing it just to your right or left at about a 45-degree angle to your subject.

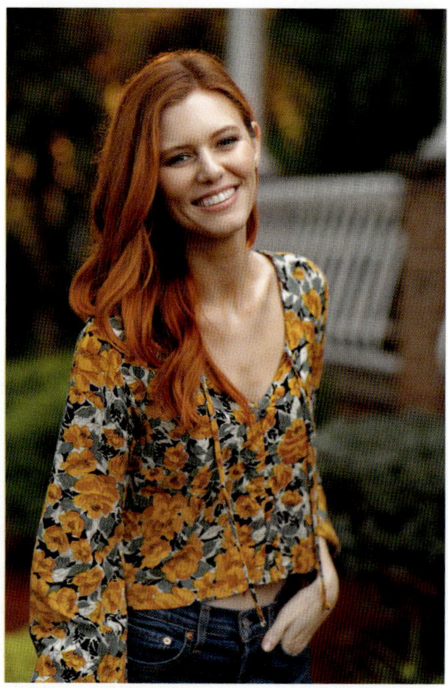

FIGURE 2.1
GOAL IMAGE.
CANON 1DX MARKII, CANON 85MM 1.4, ISO 50, APERTURE 2.5, SHUTTER 1/250, WB 5600

3. **Set the camera exposure:** Get an exposure for the natural light on your subject as if you weren't using off-camera flash. Take a test shot and check your histogram. You subject will likely be a little dark, especially in the eyes depending on the natural light in the scene.

4. **Set the white balance:** The flash that will hit the front of your subject won't have a gel on it so set your WB to the color temperature of the flash (usually 5600K). If you're not into dialing in your white balance Kelvin setting manually, try using the sunny day preset. Take a test shot and check the coloring of your photo.

5. **Set the back flash:** Turn on just your back flash and use TTL to get a power setting. Flip it to manual, keeping the same power setting, and adjust it until you like how powerful the "sun" looks.

6. **Set the front flash:** Turn on just your front flash, and use TTL to get a power setting. Flip it to manual, keeping the same power setting, and adjust brighter or darker for a proper exposure on your subject's face. Alternatively, for both flash settings you could use a light meter to set the power manually so that the light reads the same f-stop on the front and back of your subject. If you don't have a light meter or TTL available, start with a mid-range power setting on each flash, one by one, and adjust from there.

7. **Check both flashes:** Turn your back flash back on, still set with the power setting you got in step 5, and take a test shot with both flashes firing together. From here, adjust your flashes up or down until you get the look you're going for.

8. **Change your camera angle:** This is where you get to play. Move your camera angle around to experiment with how the backlight is hitting your lens. The look of the golden hour may change to a haze as you let the light spill into your lens. You can show the flash in the frame and let it flare into your lens as well.

9. **Make adjustments:** Once you have a solid image, feel free to change your exposure, white balance, or flash settings. Be sure to only change one thing at a time so you don't get too far away from what was working originally and can't get back.

OPTIONAL: Use a white reflector in front of your subject instead of the second flash. It will reflect back a warm color, but you may like the way it looks.

Shot by Shot

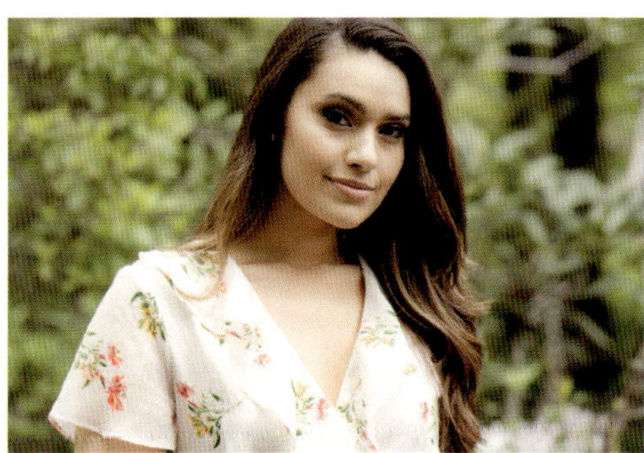

FIGURE 2.2
NATURAL LIGHT.
CANON 1D X MARK II, CANON 85MM 1.4, ISO 160,
APERTURE 3.5, SHUTTER 1/200, WB 5600

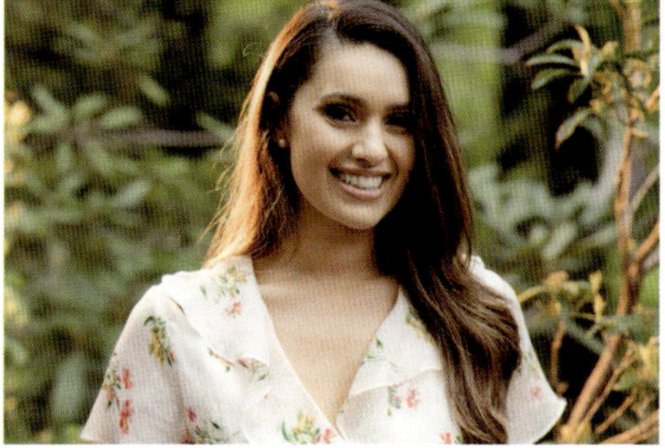

FIGURE 2.3
JUST THE BACK FLASH.
CANON 1D X MARK II, CANON 85MM 1.4, ISO 160,
APERTURE 3.5, SHUTTER 1/200, WB 5600

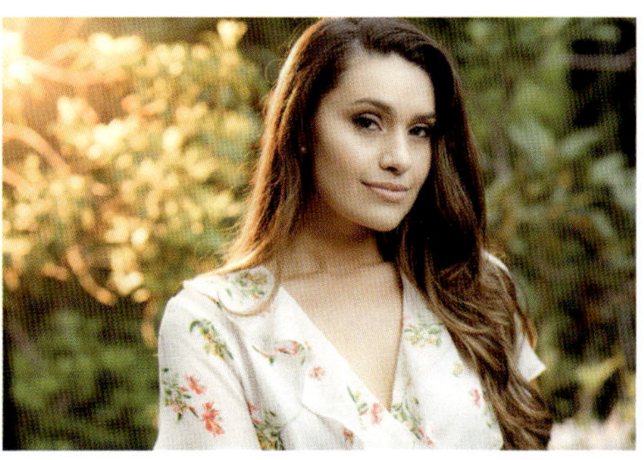

FIGURE 2.4
BOTH FLASHES FIRING.
CANON 1D X MARK II,
CANON 85MM 1.4, ISO 160,
APERTURE 3.5, SHUTTER
1/200, WB 5600

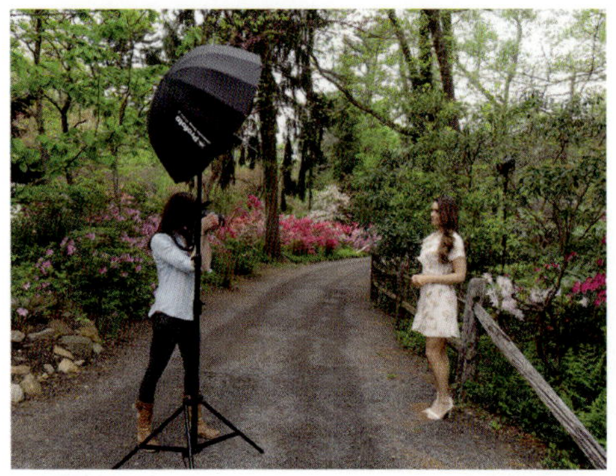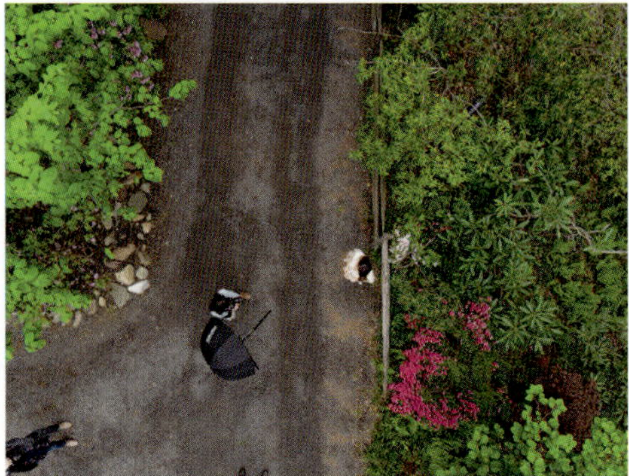

FIGURE 2.5
BEHIND-THE-SCENES SHOTS OF SETUP.

Potential Problems

Sometimes you'll take a look at your masterpiece and think the light in front looks "fake." This usually happens because it's too harsh or the wrong color. Feather your light so it's not directly smacking your subject in the face. You could also use a larger modifier or bring the light closer to your subject to soften it. If the color is the problem, warm up your white balance a little until you get a more balanced skin tone.

Occasionally, when you set this up and take your test shot using both flashes, you'll find the "sun" is not as bright as it looks when you're firing it alone. That typically happens when your front flash is too bright and is overpowering the back flash. Boost the power of the back flash, or change your overall exposure to let more light in and lessen the power of the front flash.

If you're attempting to do this in the middle of the day, rest assured it is possible, but it is much more difficult. The best natural-light scenario to do this in is a cloudy day or a sunny day in the shade. The lower the strength of the natural light in your scene, the easier it is for your flashes to match or overcome it. For more power, move the lights closer to your camera and subject.

If you're still having trouble, you may need to go into High Speed Sync (HSS) so you can lower the natural light using your shutter speed. Alternatively, you could use a neutral density filter so that you don't have to go into HSS. It's better to *not* go into HSS if you can avoid it because it will suck up your battery power *and* not produce as powerful of a flash.

Practical Uses

Don't just do this with close-ups. You can have bigger scenes that you've lit with the glowing "sun." Just keep in mind that in order for this to be believable, you need the "sun" to hit some other parts of the scene than just the subject. While the sun could be peeking in and streaming onto the back of your subject, it's pretty fun to let it explode around the rest of the photograph as well.

This *can* be done with just one light and no reflector at all. You just have to have a good natural light scenario, like you see in **Figure 2.7**, that won't give your subjects raccoon eyes. It's great fun being able to wow my clients with this technique and a huge confidence builder for me knowing that I can produce images that match my brand no matter what kind of day it is.

Examples with Just One Light

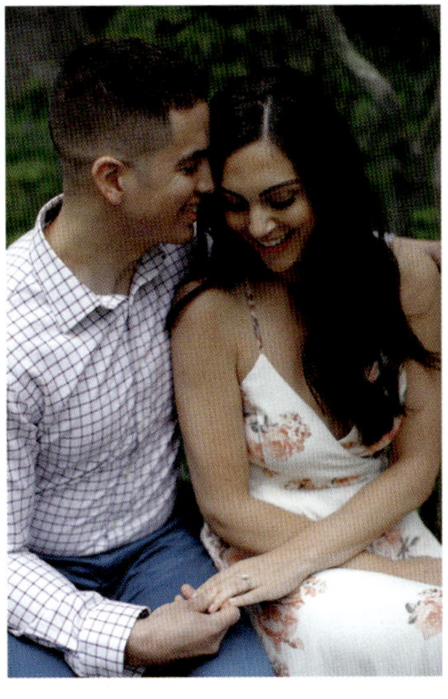
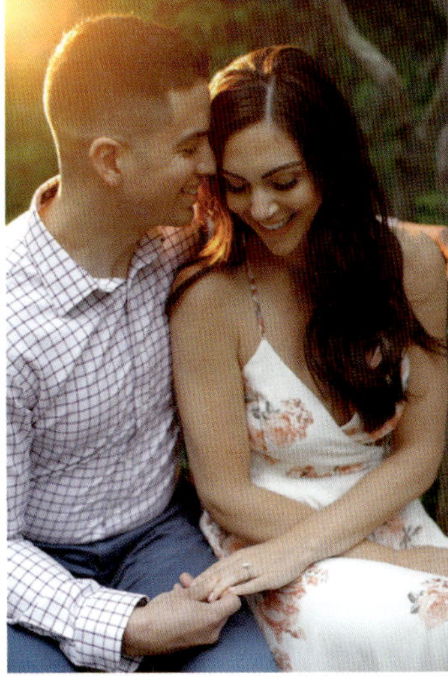

FIGURE 2.6
LEFT: NATURAL LIGHT.
RIGHT: FAKE GOLDEN HOUR.
CANON 1D X MARK II, CANON 50MM 1.2, ISO 640, APERTURE 2.2, SHUTTER 1/160

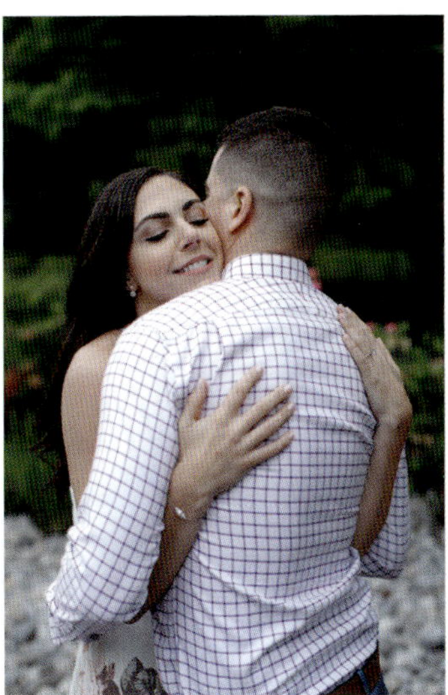
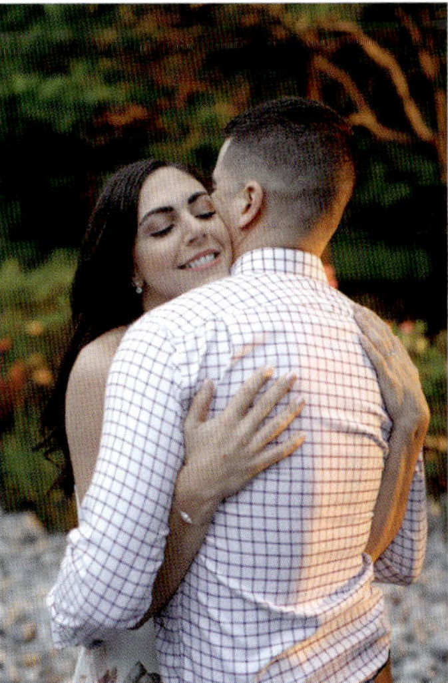

FIGURE 2.7
LEFT: NATURAL LIGHT.
CANON 1D X MARK II, CANON 50MM 1.2, ISO 500, APERTURE 2.5, SHUTTER 1/250
RIGHT: FAKE GOLDEN HOUR.
CANON 1D X MARK II, CANON 50MM 1.2, ISO 500, APERTURE 2.5, SHUTTER 1/250

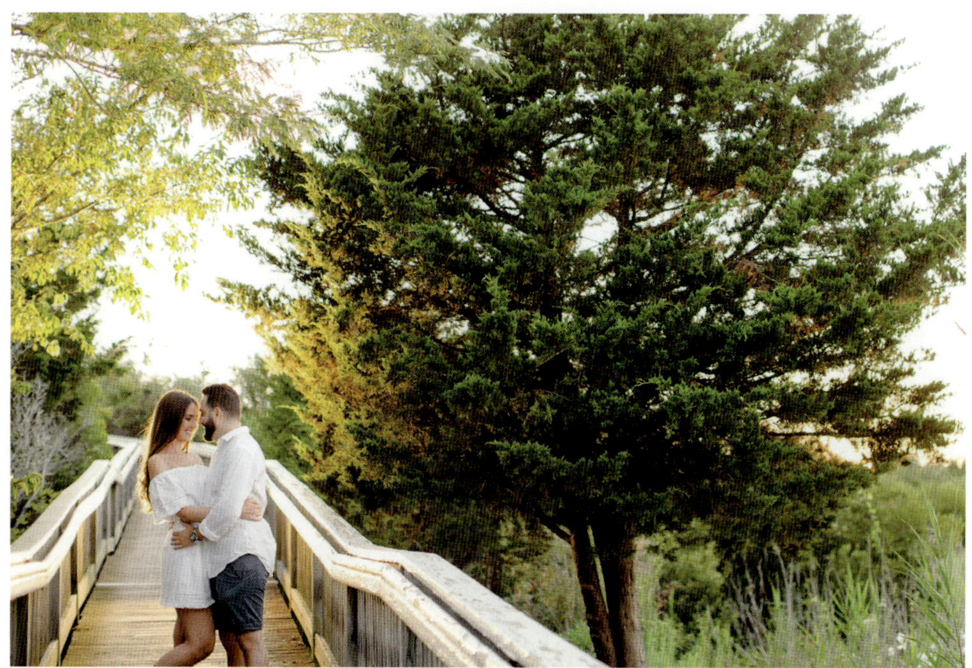

Give this a try for individual and couple portraits, and creating a magical, glowing scene in photos of children. If you advertise a warm photographic brand, you can use this technique consistently in your images.

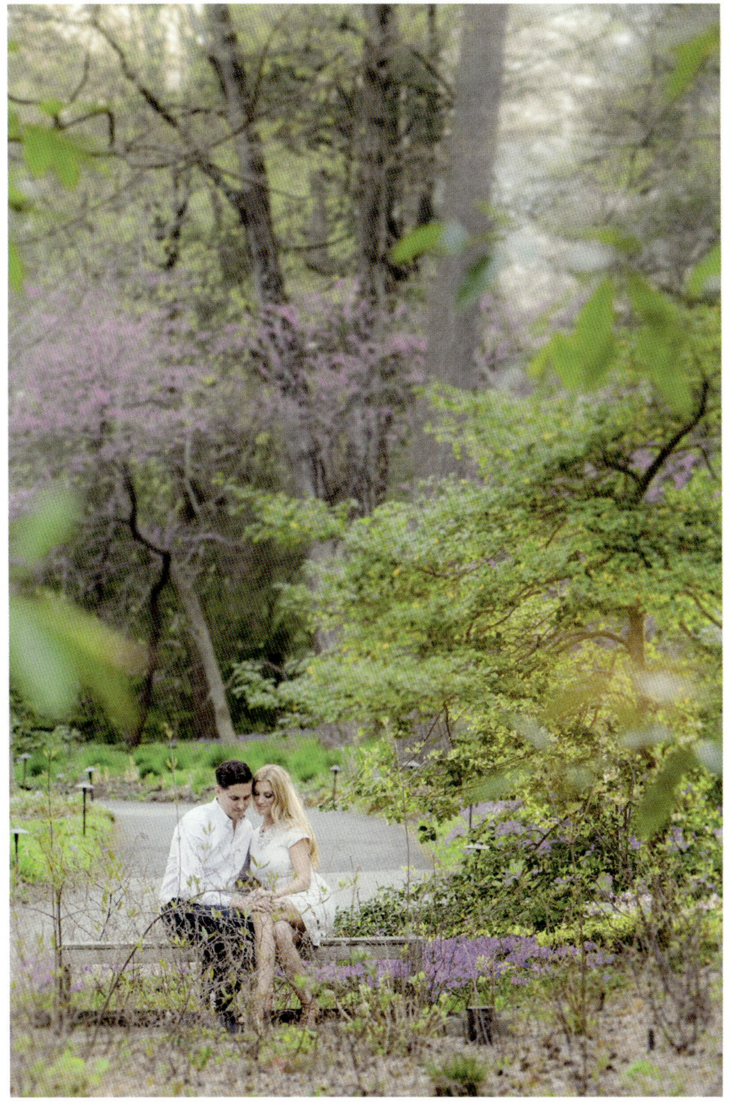

CANON 1D X, CANON 125MM 2.0, ISO 640, APERTURE 5.6, SHUTTER 1/250

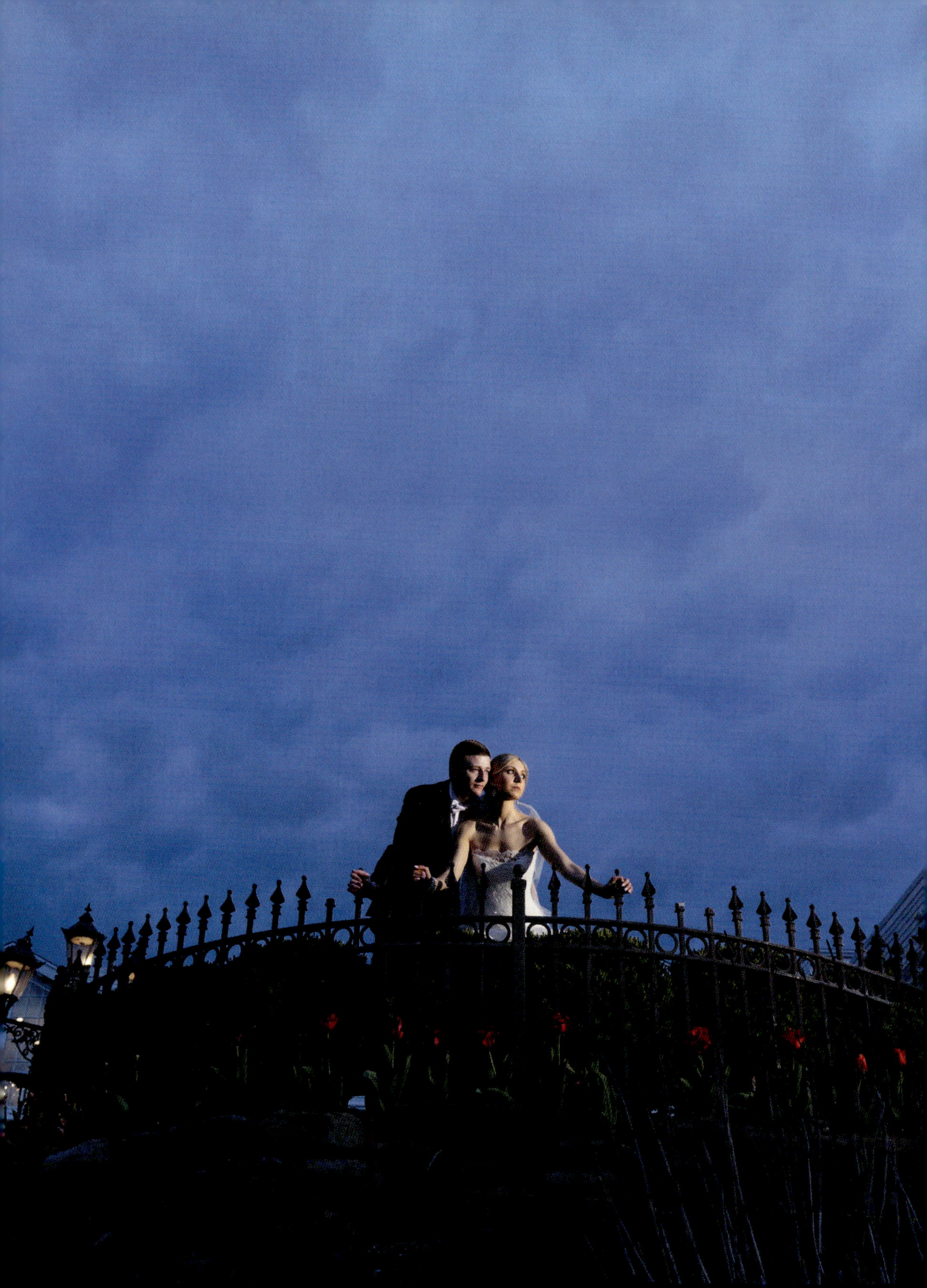

SCENARIO 3
Creating Twilight

Enhancing or creating that glowing, just-after-sunset blue sky.

GOAL IMAGE

I don't know about you, but more often than not I miss the sunset photo. Not because I'm not prepared, but because I'm listening to a (potentially long and embarrassing) best man's speech. There's only a small window to capture sunset, but I love twilight even more (**Figure 3.1**).

No, I'm not referring to the epic love story with a vampire-werewolf-human love triangle (team Jacob, over here). I'm talking about the way that the sky glows that magically saturated blue just after the sunset colors have passed. It's definitely my preferred "nighttime" shot (versus when the sky is pitch black).

I do advise that you take a look at Scenario 4, "Photographing a Sunset," before reading this one. It is not completely necessary, but the photography principles are pretty much the same except for one neat little trick that turns the sky blue. Actually, you might want to read Scenario 5, "Making a Magenta Sunset," as well. It all goes hand-in-hand.

Preferably, you'll be trying this shot during actual twilight when the sky is blue so you don't have to do too much to enhance it further. This will make it very easy to use a speedlight since you don't have the sun to compete with. However, you can make this happen after twilight and even in the middle of the day if you want to. In fact, there's a scenario on making it look like nighttime in the middle of the day in this book, so anything is possible.

To make this happen you have to play opposite day in the photo world. If you want a blue sky, then you actually need an orange gel to make it happen. It's much easier to light your subject instead of the entire sky.

If you wanted to "blue" a photograph, you would turn down your white balance to a temperature lower than what the actual light in the situation would generally need to make the colors seem realistic. That's all great until you put a person in the frame. They're instantly turned into a very blue Smurf or Smurfette (#80sreference), or a member of the Kree race living on Hala (if you're an *Avenger's* Universe fan like I am). Sounds fun, but not so cool to your clients, especially if one is wearing a white dress that is now blue.

To balance out the color on your subject, you need to add the opposite color light. Think of a color wheel. Colors on the opposite side of the wheel, when put together, cancel out each other's color and create a white light instead. The opposite of blue, for this purpose, is orange. Light your subjects with a Color Temperature Orange (CTO) gel to make them look like they have regular human skin tones.

The last thing you need to choose is the light modifier for your light. You absolutely can choose to not have one at all. Your light will be more direct and harsh looking. I prefer my twilight photos to have a more subtle light on my subject, so I use either a beauty dish or a softbox. However, I have used a grid if I need to position my light far away from my subject like I did in **Figure 3.1**. It's all relative to what you're trying to accomplish.

Step by Step

1. **Position your subjects:** Since we're using one light in this example, I suggest placing your subjects so that their faces are both turned towards the light. Turn their bodies away from the light so that the front of their torsos go into shadow. It creates a slimming effect and more dramatic lighting.

2. **Choose a lens:** Lens choice is up to you and your creativity. Choose a lens that will enable you to show the most sky you can in the frame. There's no point in turning the sky blue (or more blue) if it's only taking up a very small portion of your picture.

3. **Put modifiers on your light:** Put on the Full CTO gel. I usually won't go more orange than that because the light starts to look too unrealistic, but you are welcome use as much orange as you like. Also use the light modifier of your choice. This may suck up a lot of your light power, so keep that in mind.

4. **Position your light:** I typically shoot with my light to the right or left of my subjects at a 45-degree angle. Go even more to the side if you're looking for something more dramatic.

5. **Set your camera exposure:** Set your camera exposure as if you're taking a landscape photo of the nighttime sky. You may need to use a slow shutter speed. If that's the case, consider using a tripod, placing your camera on the ground, or holding your breath and stopping your heartbeat to avoid transferring any movement to the camera.

6. **Set the white balance:** Because the flash is your main source of light and you've covered it with a Full CTO gel, you'll set your WB to tungsten, or about 3200 Kelvin depending on the original color temperature of your light.

7. **Set your flash power:** I suggest setting your flash power to TTL +1 because of how many modifiers your light is passing through. With how TTL works, it theoretically shouldn't be a problem, but I find that the image can turn out too dark so I compensate for that upfront. If you're using a manual flash, start in the medium-high power range or use a light meter, and adjust up or down to your liking. Take a test shot and adjust your light to be more or less powerful according to your taste.

8. **Look at your colors and histogram:** Nighttime shots can be very deceiving when you're solely reviewing them on the back of the camera. I've fairly often loved a twilight shot on the back of my camera only to find that the backlight was making it look much brighter than it actually was. Take a look at your histogram to make sure that it's not too dark and that nothing is blown out. Adjust for more or less blue and light power as needed.

OPTIONAL: Add a rim light to the back of your subjects to further separate them from the background. I don't typically gel this light because I like the blue backlight it gives.

Shot by Shot

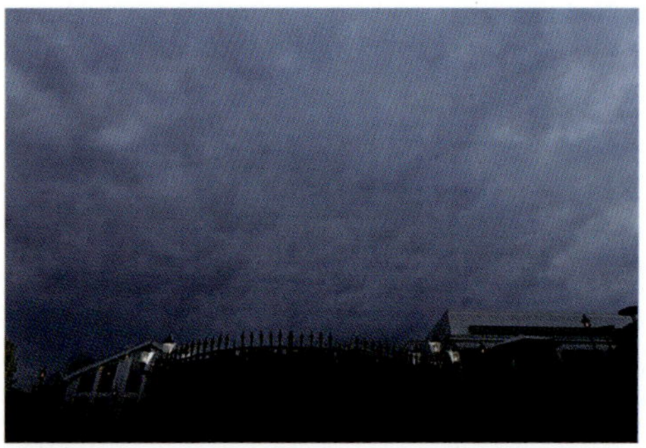

FIGURE 3.2
NATURAL LIGHT TWILIGHT SHOT.
CANON 1D X, CANON 24MM 1.4, ISO 500, APERTURE 7.1,
SHUTTER 1/250

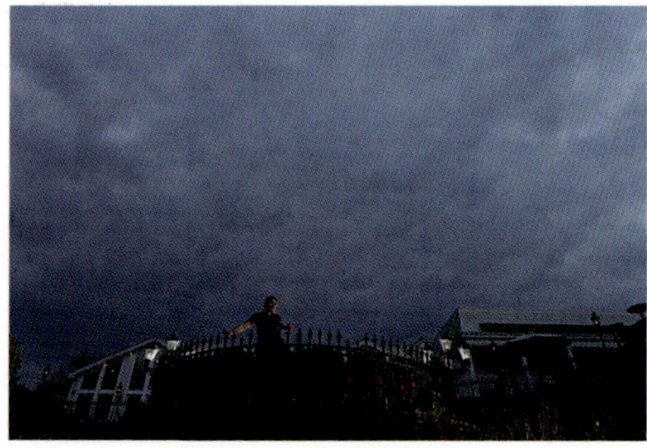

FIGURE 3.3
ADDING FRONT AND BACK FLASHES.
CANON 1D X, CANON 24MM 1.4, ISO 500, APERTURE 7.1,
SHUTTER 1/250

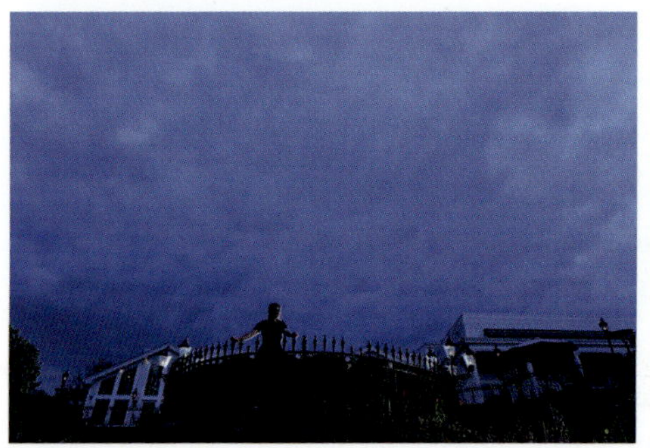

FIGURE 3.4
LOWERED WHITE BALANCE.
CANON 1D X, CANON 24MM 1.4, ISO 500, APERTURE 7.1,
SHUTTER 1/250

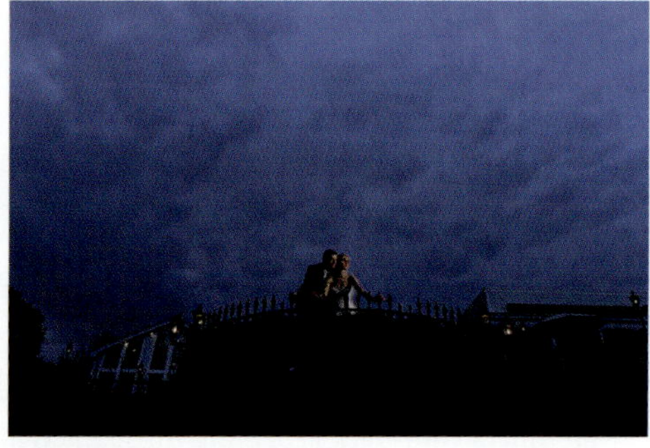

FIGURE 3.5
STRAIGHT OUT OF CAMERA IMAGE.
CANON 1D X, CANON 24MM 1.4, ISO 500, APERTURE 7.1,
SHUTTER 1/250

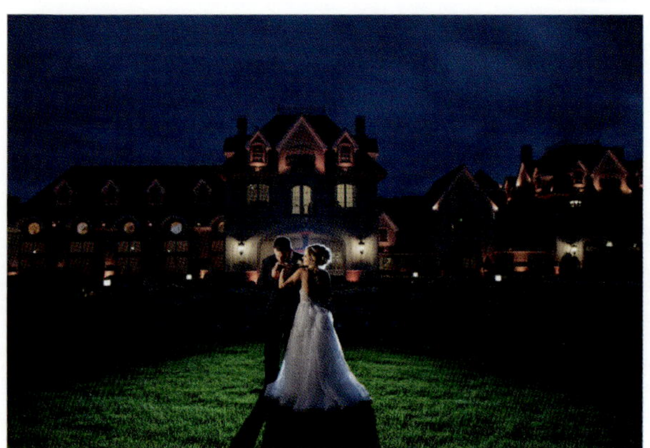

FIGURE 3.6
YOU CAN ADD AN OPTIONAL RIM LIGHT.
CANON 1D X II, CANON 24MM 1.4, ISO 1600,
APERTURE 3.5, SHUTTER 1/100

Potential Problems

There some potential issues that you can run into with twilight images. Here are the a few that I have come across:

- Anything else in the photo that's not lit by your CTO light will turn blue (note the blue building in the background of the first image in this chapter. That building is actually white). Avoid other objects in your shot by crouching low and shooting up toward the sky.

- You're lighting the subject, but some of the other landscape elements won't be lit and therefore will turn into silhouettes. Shoot at a lower angle to clean up your sky, or add CTO-gelled lights to your setup to light up other parts of the landscape.

- Check your histogram! I can't emphasize this enough. Do not trust the back of your camera!

- Watch for motion blur if you're using a slow shutter speed. Even if you're locked down on a tripod, your subjects can move to create a bit of a ghosting effect. Or, do that on purpose and have fun with it!

Practical Uses

This is a great technique for enhancing the blue night sky that's already there, or creating one if it's not there. Getting a handle on color shifting techniques like this will do wonders for your photographic knowledge to make you feel more in control of situations. Give it a try with one light first and build up from there. The two-light method (adding the optional rim light) is my go-to lighting setup for nighttime shots. It's a safety net that I have for any job that gives me confidence and creates an image that my clients look forward to having (and printing at a large size).

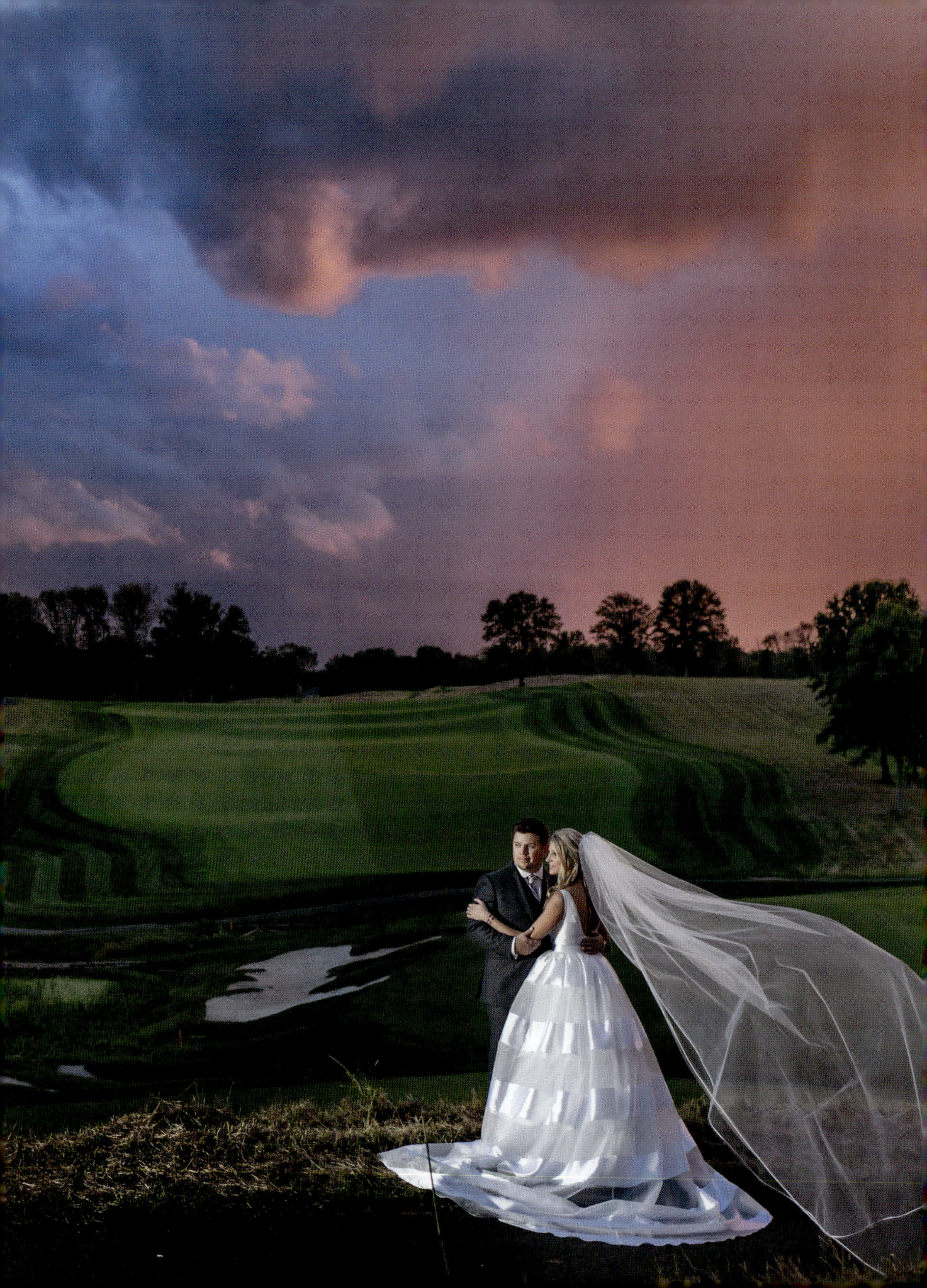

SCENARIO 4

Photographing a Sunset

How to take a portrait with a crazy awesome sky.

GOAL IMAGE

Ever have a couple that's drooling over the sunset on their wedding day but all you can produce is either a picture of them properly exposed or a photo of the sky with them silhouetted in it? Me too, my friend. Me too. That ends for you today. Taking sunset pictures is easier than you think (**Figure 4.1**)!

To start off, you'll want to think about the light modifier you choose to light your subject. You can choose to not have one at all, and your light will be more direct and harsh looking. I like my sunset shots to have a soft light on my subject without that light hitting the ground. I use either a beauty dish or a softbox, but typically not an umbrella. The first two options have stronger edges to them, which will let me point the light with more intention. An umbrella is more open, and won't be able to do this as easily. Light will almost certainly spill onto the ground, which can be distracting in a sunset picture.

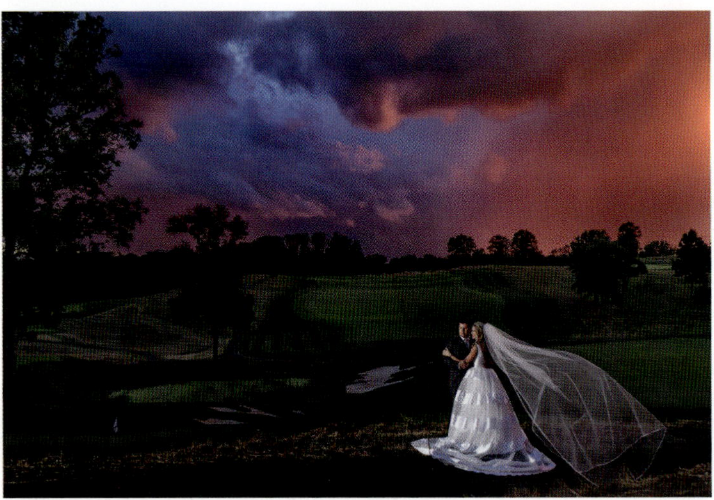

Step by Step

1. **Choose a lens:** Even for landscapes and sunsets, I like using longer lenses. If I have enough space to back up, I'll use a 50mm or 85mm lens for this shot. If you don't have that kind of space, go for a wider focal length so you can see the sky in the photo.

2. **Put a modifier on the light:** Use the light modifier of your choice on the light.

3. **Position the light:** Place the light as close as possible to your subject so that it's a bigger, and therefore softer, light source for your subject. I suggest feathering the light slightly in front of your subject so that the edges of the light just kiss them slightly. If you have a modeling light, turn it on so you can see exactly where the light is hitting your subject.

4. **Set the camera exposure:** Set your camera exposure as if you're taking a landscape photo of the sunset. Some photographers like to go a half or full stop darker, but that's up to you.

   In general, I set my shutter speed no higher than my max sync speed of $\frac{1}{250}$, and then I set my ISO as low as I can while maintaining a mid-range aperture like f/5.6. My goal is to keep my subjects nice and sharp, and having a slightly greater depth of field than I typically shoot with during the day helps with that. Plus, since it's darker when you're taking this photo, it helps to have a higher aperture in case you're not perfectly focused.

5. **Set your white balance:** Because the flash is the light source for your subject, set your WB to daylight, flash, or 5600 depending on the color temperature of your light.

6. **Set your flash power:** Find your power setting by setting your flash to TTL and adjusting from there. If you're using a manual flash, start in the medium power range and adjust up or

down to your liking, or use a light meter. Take a test shot and adjust your light to be more or less powerful according to your taste.

7. **Look at your histogram:** Sunset shots can be deceiving when you're reviewing them on the back of your camera because of the backlighting. Use your histogram to determine if you have a good exposure rather than going by the image on the back of the camera.

OPTIONAL: Add a rim light to the back of your subjects to further separate them from the background.

Shot by Shot

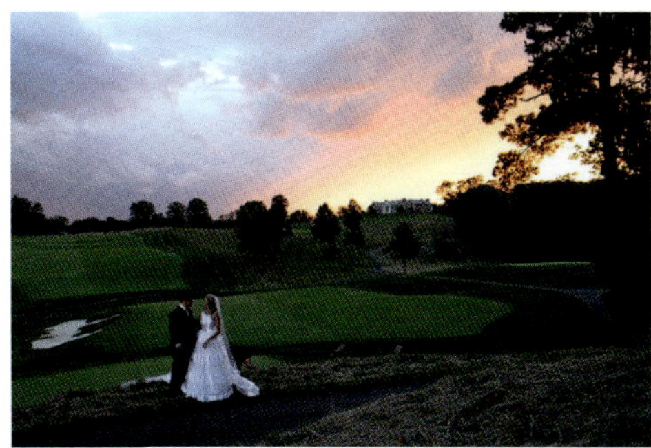

FIGURE 4.2
NATURAL LIGHT SUNSET.
CANON 1DX II, CANON 35MM 1.2, ISO 640, APERTURE 2.5, SHUTTER 1/400

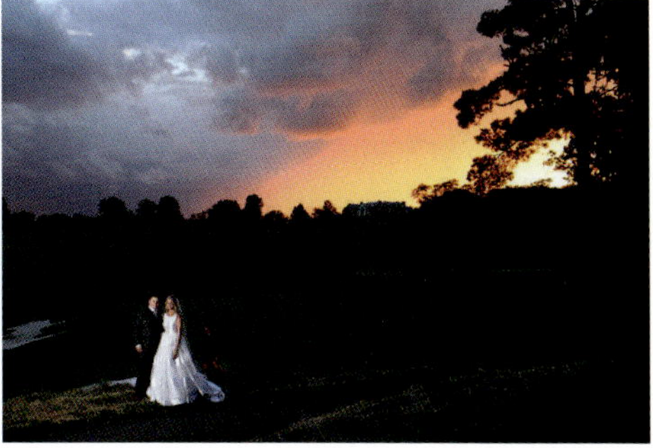

FIGURE 4.3
THIS PHOTO WAS TAKEN WITH AN ADDED PROFOTO B2, OCF BEAUTY DISH, AND OCF WITH TTL. I LOWERED THE ISO TO DARKEN THE SKY FOR A LESS GRAINY IMAGE.
CANON 1DX II, CANON 35MM 1.2, ISO 320, APERTURE 2.5, SHUTTER 1/400

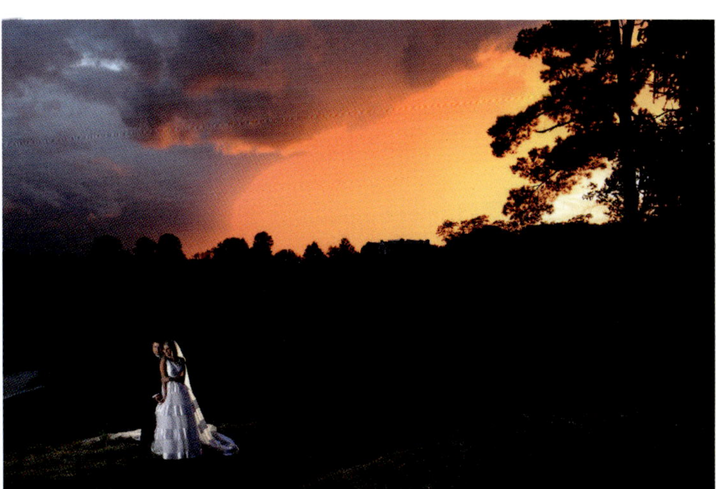

FIGURE 4.4
I LOWERED THE LIGHT POWER AND POSITIONED THE COUPLE. I RAISED MY APERTURE TO GET A GREATER DEPTH OF FIELD AND RAISED THE ISO TO COMPENSATE FOR THE EXPOSURE.
CANON 1DX II, CANON 35MM 1.2, ISO 500, APERTURE 3.5, SHUTTER 1/400

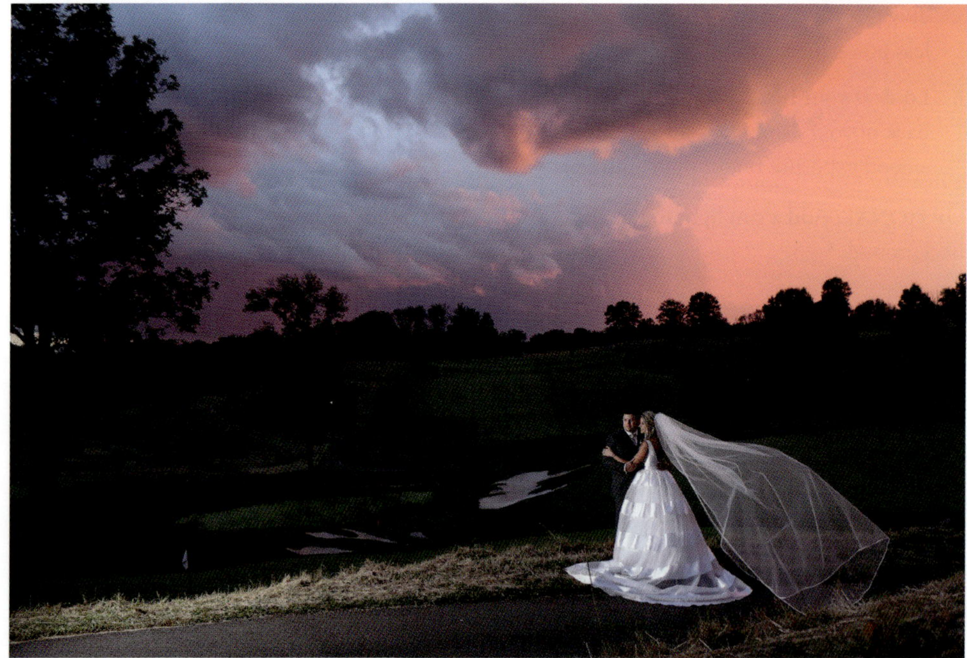

I DECIDED I LIKED THE SKY OVER TO THE LEFT SIDE OF THE IMAGE BEST, SO I NEEDED TO MOVE THE LIGHT FURTHER AWAY FROM THE COUPLE AND BOOST THE LIGHT POWER TO COMPENSATE FOR IT. I RAISED THE ISO AND LOWERED THE SHUTTER SPEED BECAUSE IT WAS GETTING DARKER.

IN HINDSIGHT, THERE WAS TOO MUCH LIGHT SPILL ON THE BOTTOM LEFT OF THE IMAGE; I SHOULD'VE TILTED THE LIGHT UP MORE, AND I HAD TO FIX THAT IN POST. IT ALSO WOULD HAVE BEEN BETTER TO GO SLIGHTLY LOWER ON THE SHUTTER SPEED TO GET OUT OF HIGH SPEED SYNC. THEN I COULD'VE LOWERED MY ISO FOR A CLEANER IMAGE. I BRIGHTENED THE SHADOW AREAS IN POST SINCE THERE WAS NOTHING I COULD DO ABOUT THAT IN-CAMERA WITH-OUT LOSING DETAIL IN THE SKY.

CANON 1DX II, CANON 35MM 1.2, ISO 800, APERTURE 3.5, SHUTTER 1/320

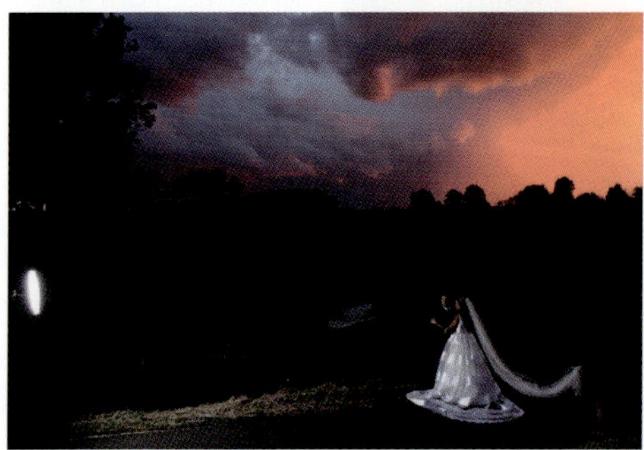

BEHIND-THE-SCENES SHOT.

Potential Problems

One of the biggest problems during sunset shots is focusing. It's darker, so most of the time it'll be harder to focus on your subject. For this scenario, and many others, I highly recommend using a flash that has a modeling light. You can turn it on and have a much easier job focusing on your subject without affecting your exposure.

When you first attempt an off-camera-flash-lit sunset shot, you'll likely be awed by the outcome—and you should be! One mistake I see a lot of photographers make is blowing out the light on the ground. The light from your off-camera flash shouldn't hit the ground too much, but you especially don't want it to make the ground so bright that it's brighter than your subject or the sunset (which sounds crazy, but it's really easy to do, especially if you're shooting on a light-colored ground like sand or a sidewalk). Our eyes go to the brightest part of the photograph first. To make sure that it's not the ground, tilt your flash upward until it's not hitting the ground so prominently, or use a grid as your light modifier.

Other Techniques

1. **Changing the color of the sunset:** I explain how to do this in Scenario 5, "Making a Magenta Sunset." Master this first, then head over there for more ideas on color.

2. **Use a slow shutter speed:** If you're photographing a sunset on a beach and you can see the water in the photograph, you can have a lot of fun experimenting with a slow shutter speed. You'll want a tripod for this, and a subject that can stand nice and still. Set your exposure with a shutter speed around $\frac{1}{10}$ of a second or lower. This will allow you to capture the motion of the waves, or maybe a bride's veil, with a dreamy, motion-blurred effect.

    I've actually never been in the position with a client to do this myself, but check out Los Angeles wedding photographer Michael Anthony, who has done some beautiful images with this added technique.

3. **Add a rim light:** Get your initial exposure first with the front flash balanced. Then, add a light, probably with a grid on it, behind your subject or behind them and off to one side. It separates them from the background quite nicely, like you see in **Figure 4.7**. It's optional to leave the starburst of light in the picture.

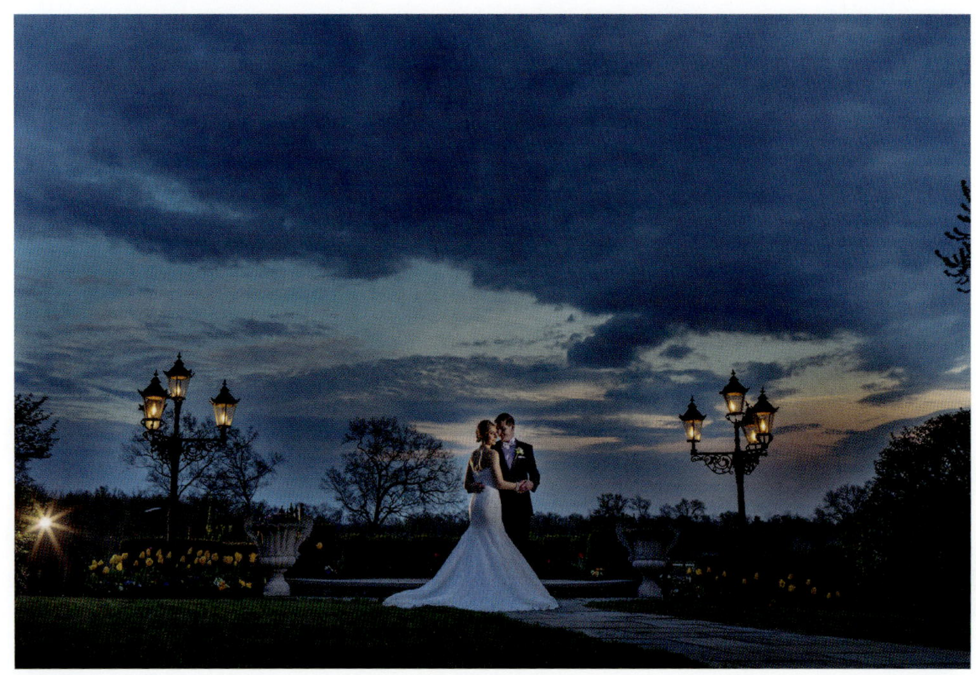

FIGURE 4.7

CANON 1DX, CANON 35MM 1.4, ISO 500, APERTURE 7.1, SHUTTER 1/200

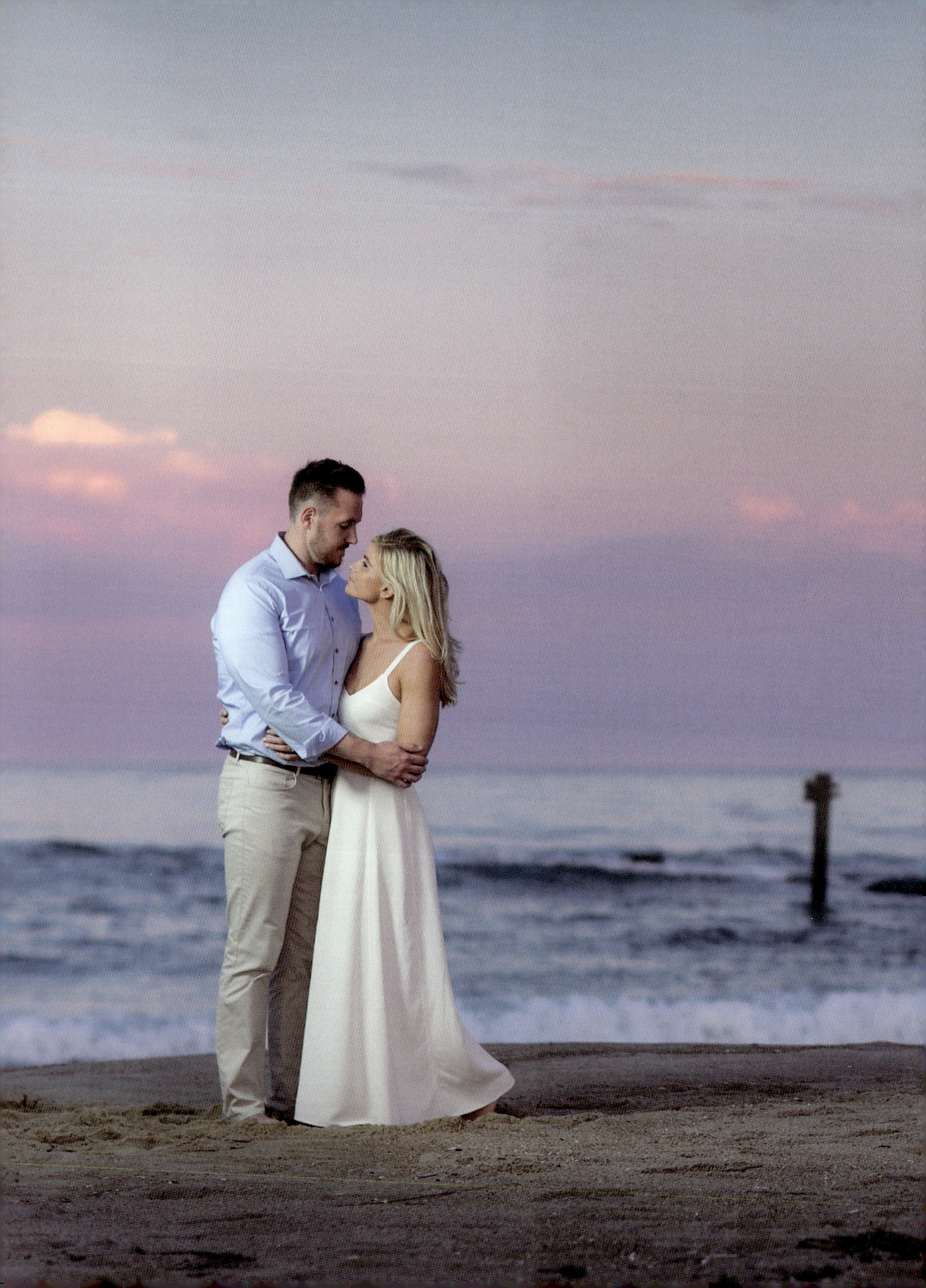

SCENARIO 5
Making a Magenta Sunset

Make magic light every night.

GOAL IMAGE

Everyone wants that magical sunset light and color. While I can't promise you the perfect clouds to go along with it, I can tell you how to make the sky appear to be that beautiful magenta color without swapping in Photoshop (**Figure 5.1**).

This concept is the same as creating a night-time look during the day, making a fiery sky, or enhancing twilight photos—but with different colors. Just like those examples, which you can read about in other chapters, you have to play the opposite color game here. If you want to blue your sky like twilight by using a light with a blue gel, you need to use the opposite color (yellow/orange) light on your subject so they don't look like Smurfs. If you light your killer sunset sky with a magenta light to add color, you need to put the opposite color light on your subjects so they don't look like they have really bad sunburns. What's the opposite color of magenta? Green. Green like the color your competition's skin will turn after they see this post on Instagram.

The other thing you need to think about is the light modifier you choose for your light. You absolutely can choose to not have one at all, and your light will be more direct and harsh looking. Personally, I like my sunset shots to have a more subtle light on my subject, so I use either a beauty dish or a softbox. They both create a diffused-light quality and the edges of those modifiers, as opposed to an umbrella, let me better control where the light is directed and where it falls.

GEAR NEEDED:

- Camera + Trigger
- Lens of any focal length
- Off-camera flash
- Light stand
- Light-softening modifier
- 1 or more green gels
- Second Off-camera flash *(optional)*

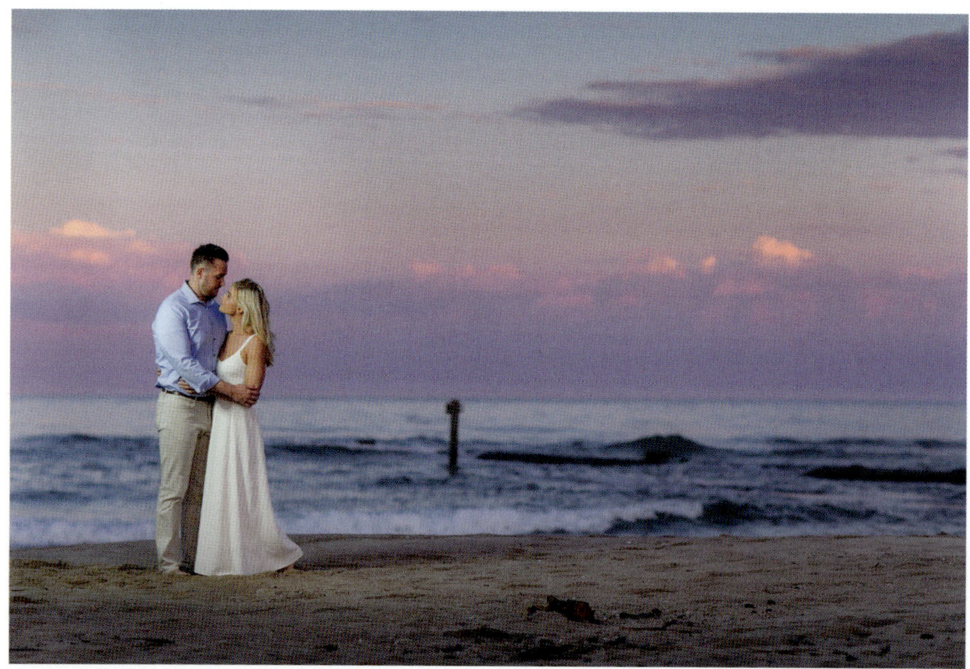

GOAL IMAGE. EDITED IN PHOTOSHOP TO BRIGHTEN SHADOWS AND INCREASE VIBRANCY. THE STRAIGHT-OUT-OF-CAMERA IMAGE APPEARS LATER IN THE SECTION.
CANON 1DX, CANON 85MM 1.2, ISO 200, APERTURE 2.5, SHUTTER: 1/800

Step by Step

1. **Position your subjects:** Since we're using one light in this example, I suggest placing your subjects so that their faces are turned towards the light.

2. **Choose a lens:** In the gear list I left this ambiguous because you need to choose a lens that will enable you to show the most sky you can in the frame. There's no point in turning the sky magenta if it's only in a small portion of the frame. Personally, I like using longer lenses. If I have enough space to back up, I'll use a 50mm or 85mm lens for this shot.

3. **Put modifiers on your light:** Put the green gel (or two if you want to go really magenta) and the light modifier of your choice on the light. This will suck up a lot of your light power. More on that later.

4. **Position your light:** This is a magical dance that you'll get used to, eventually. You want the light as close as possible to your subjects so that it's a bigger, and therefore softer, light hitting your subject. You also want it close because you're sucking up a lot of power with all the modifiers you have in front of your light. (However, you don't want the light in the shot.) Play with your light position and lens choice until you're happy with it.

5. **Set the camera exposure:** Set your camera exposure as if you're just taking a landscape photo of the sunset. Some people like to find that exposure and then go darker another half or full stop, but that's your call. I go for how I want the sky to look—that's my priority.

   In general, I set my shutter no higher than my max sync speed of ½₂₅₀, and then set my ISO as low as I can while maintaining a mid-range aperture like f/5.6. My goal is to keep my subjects nice and sharp; using a slightly greater depth of field than I typically shoot during the day helps with that.

6. **Set the white balance:** Because the flash is your main source of light, you'll set your WB to daylight, flash, or 5600 depending on the color temperature of your light.

7. **Set the color tone and white balance shift:** You need to get the sky magenta and take the green off of your subjects. You can't do this with white balance because the Kelvins will shift from blue to yellow. Instead, use color tone and white balance shift.

   Color tone specifically lets you adjust from green to magenta. Slide this setting all the way to the magenta side.

   White balance shift lets you adjust your colors anywhere you want. Adjust them towards magenta.

   What green gel(s) you put on your light will determine exactly how far magenta you're going to go. The more green on your light, the more magenta you need to have to balance the skin tones of your subjects back to normal. Consequently, the more magenta you use, the crazier pink your sky will get.

8. **Set your flash power:** I suggest setting your flash power to TTL +1 because of how many modifiers your light is passing through. With the way TTL works this theoretically shouldn't be a problem, but I find that it can turn out too dark, so I compensate for that upfront. If you're using a manual flash, start in the medium-high power range, or use a light meter and adjust up or down to your liking.

9. **Look at your colors and histogram:** Sunset shots can be deceiving when you're reviewing them on the back of the camera so take a look at your histogram to make sure that it's not too dark and that nothing is blown out. You'll get a good feel for how the colors look on the back of the camera. Adjust for more or less magenta and light power as needed.

OPTIONAL: Add a rim light to the back of your subjects to further separate them from the background.

Shot by Shot

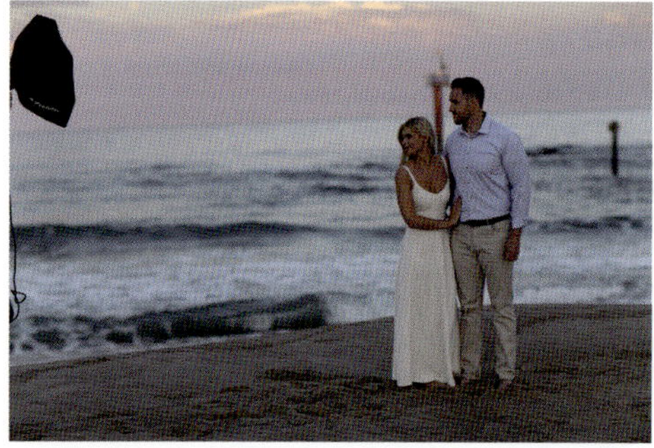

THIS IS A NATURAL LIGHT SUNSET SHOT (THE FLASH IS NOT ON).
CANON 1DX, CANON 85MM 1.2, ISO 160, APERTURE 2.2, SHUTTER: 1/500,

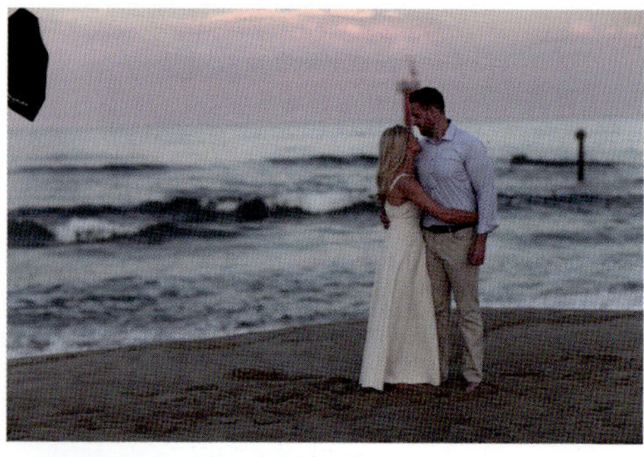

IN THIS ONE, THE COLOR TONE HAS BEEN CHANGED TO MAGENTA.
CANON 1DX, CANON 85MM 1.2, ISO 160, APERTURE 2.2, SHUTTER 1/500

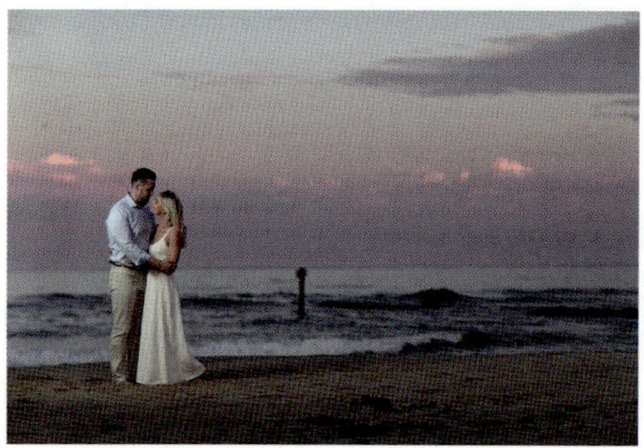

IN THIS STRAIGHT-OUT-OF-CAMERA SHOT, A PROFOTO B2, AN OCF BEAUTY DISH, AND GREEN GELS WERE USED, ALONG WITH A HIGHER SHUTTER SPEED, TO DARKEN THE SKY. I ALSO WANTED MORE DEPTH OF FIELD SO I WENT TO F/2.5 AND RAISED MY ISO TO COMPENSATE.
CANON 1DX, CANON 85MM 1.2, ISO 200, APERTURE 2.5, SHUTTER 1/800

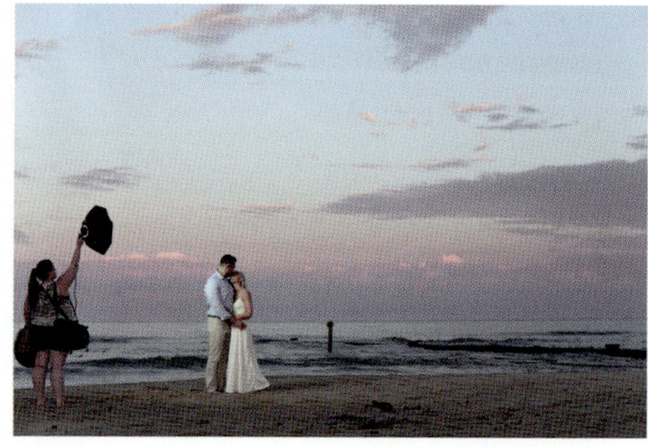

BEHIND-THE-SCENES SHOT.

Potential Problems

There are quite a few potential problems you can run into with sunset shots. Here are the ones that I come across most frequently.

- Anything else in the photo that's not lit by your green-gelled light will turn magenta, too. Avoid other objects in your shot by crouching low and shooting up towards the sky.

- You're lighting the subject, but some of the landscape around you isn't lit and will therefore turn to silhouette. Shoot at a lower angle to clean up your sky, or you can add green-gelled lights to light up other parts of the landscape.

- Maxing out your flash power can be an issue. Lower your aperture or raise your ISO to have more of the flash affect in your image.

Other Techniques

1. **Cloning out the light:** *A lot* of photographers choose to get the light super close to the subject and then remove it later with the clone stamp in Photoshop. This is advantageous because you'll get a beautifully soft light on your subject. It can be annoying removing it in post, so if you choose to do this, try to have the background behind your light fairly clean.

   Alternatively, you can take a second picture of just the sky, without the light in it, so it's easy to paste that sky onto the lit image. You'll need a tripod for both shots to make sure your frame doesn't move and it's easy to copy and paste that portion of the sky from one photo to the other.

2. **Adding magenta in post:** Instead of futzing around with your color tone and white balance shift in-camera, you could take the picture with your subjects lit like little green Martians and then just change the color tone in post.

3. **Fixing lighting in post:** You can decide to not worry about the light spill or even the light exposure and fix that all in post, too. The light spill onto the ground is a result of not directing your light onto your subjects accurately. It can be fixed by taking two pictures just like I mentioned and cloning out the light, except you'll be cloning out parts of the photo that were lit that you didn't want to be.

I don't like any of this. These are all perfectly acceptable solutions, but they all take time in front of the computer and I prefer to make my money holding a camera and not a mouse (credit to my friend Moshe Zusman for that saying). In addition, the more altering and correcting you do in post, the more it deteriorates your image. There's also the risk of your perception warping to the image until you've accidentally Photoshopped it to death. Do yourself a favor: Get it as right in-camera as possible and spend time with your friends and family instead of with your computer.

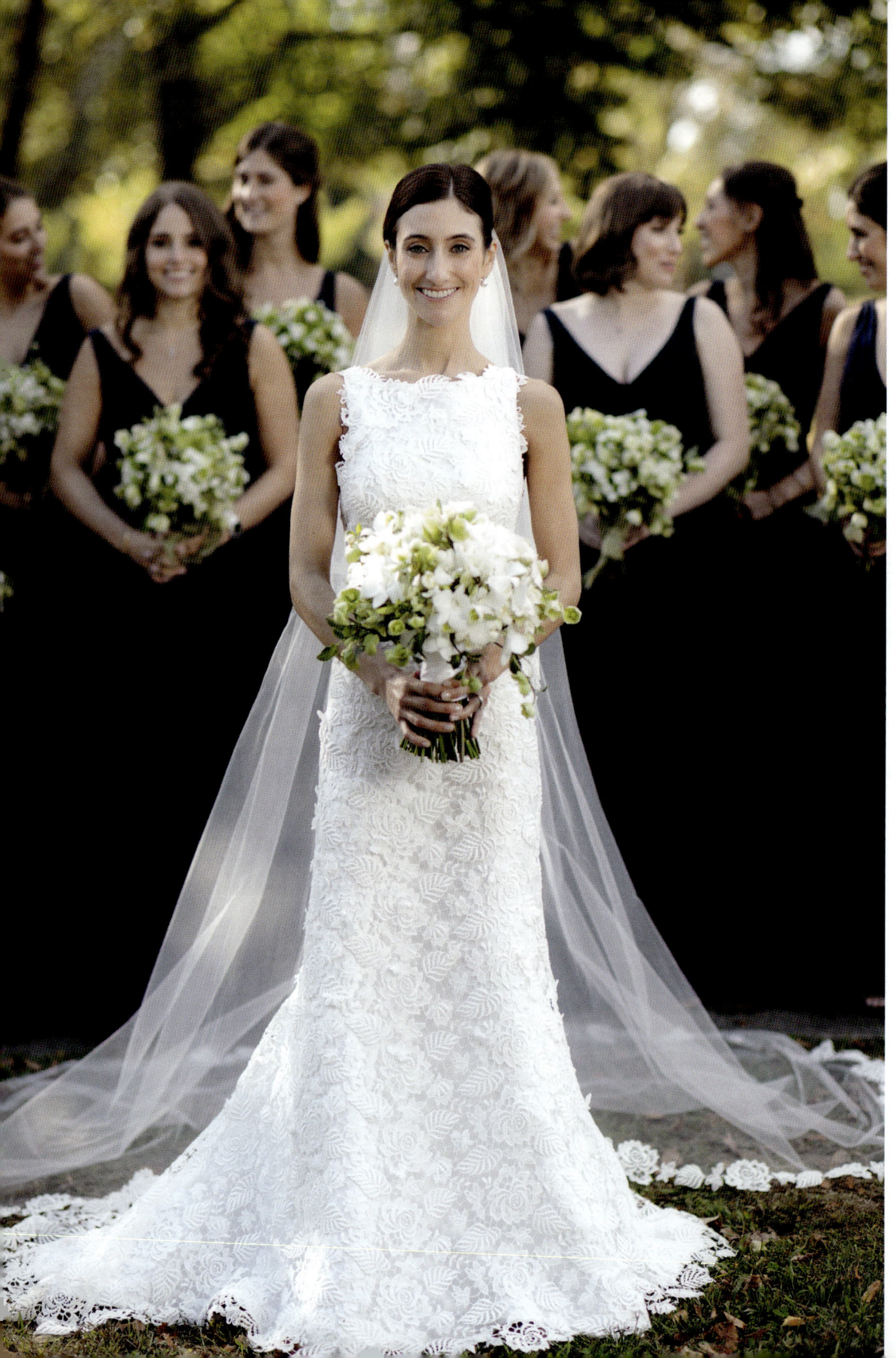

SCENARIO 6

Group Shots with One Light

Set it and forget it for large groups of people.

GOAL IMAGE

Most of us didn't get into photography because we like photographing large groups of rowdy people. But no matter what genre of photography you've gotten yourself into, you've likely spent a good amount of time taking pictures of those crazy groups anyway. The last thing you want to think about is your light when you're managing a family list the size of Manhattan. Here's how I do it (**Figure 6.1**).

To start off, you'll want to find a location that has even lighting. Inside or open shade with the sun behind my subjects is usually what I go for. Having chairs and stairs nearby is another good idea depending on how large your group is. If you are inside and have the luxury of finding a room with white walls, definitely use that space.

GEAR NEEDED:

- Camera + Trigger
- Lens of any focal length
- Off-camera flash
- Light stand
- Umbrella modifier *(optional but not needed if you have a large white wall)*

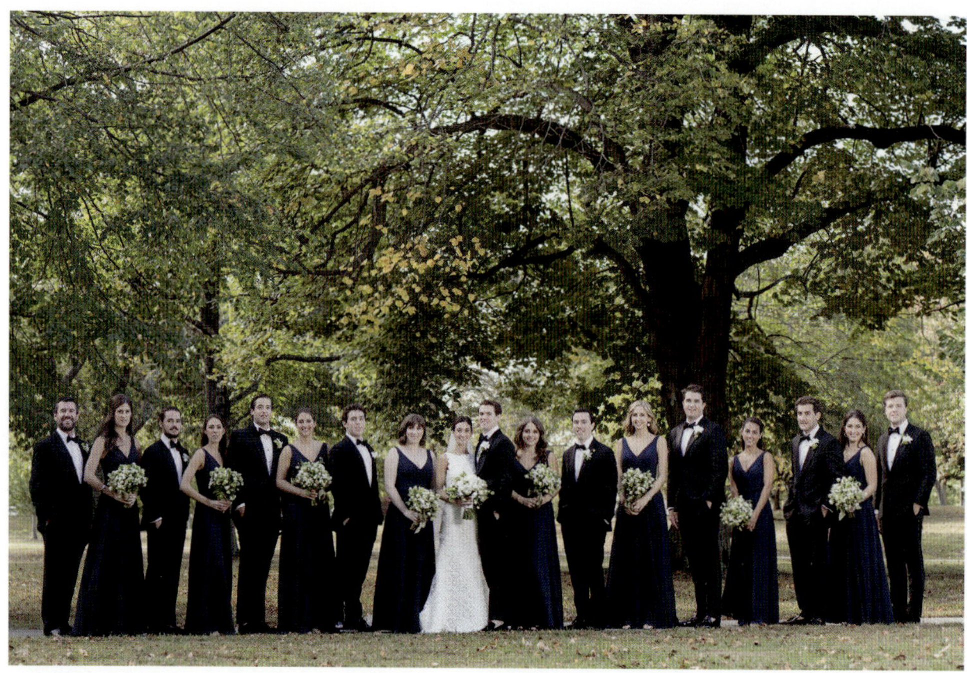

There's a whole method to posing big groups like families and a bridal party at a wedding. It's an art and a skill. If you don't know how to do that effectively, check out www.SpeedPosing.com. It'll change your life.

A lot of people think that because it's a big group of people, you must need multiple lights. This is not necessarily true. As long as you are shooting indoors or in open shade and have a light powerful enough to balance the existing light in the area, you'll be fine with just one.

If you're shooting in a room with white walls, then you won't need a modifier. You'll just point the light towards the white wall behind you. That huge white wall is your super-soft light source. It's as if you just turned the wall into floor-to-ceiling window. If you don't have a white wall, use an umbrella. A shoot-through umbrella will give you nice, evenly spread light, but some of it will be wasted because it will spread everywhere.

I shoot my groups with a deep, medium-sized white umbrella with a diffuser over it. This gives my light more direction. The light is still even, but because of the modifier's definitive edges and the fact that it's only pushing light forward, it's not wasting light that's spilling onto the floor or behind you and all around like the shoot-through umbrella would.

Step by Step

1. **Position your subjects:** Find your open shade or indoor location (with chairs and stairs if possible). I recommend putting a test subject there first while you set everything up, rather than positioning a large group of people and making them wait while you set your camera and lights.

2. **Choose a lens:** Choose your lens based on how large your groups are and how much space you have to back up. I highly recommend shooting with the longest focal length lens that you can. The longer the focal length, the more the people will be compressed together, making them appear closer and more cohesive. It will prevent the people in the front from looking huge while those in the back look tiny.

3. **Position the light:** It is easiest to place the light between 8–10' high, pointed towards the group, and as close to the camera as you can get (versus over to the right or left). This will cause the shadows to fall low and behind people, rather than on the faces of those next to them. It should be a good distance away from the group to prevent the people closest to the light being too bright while the people farthest from it are not lit well enough (inverse square law at work). If you choose to put the light to one side of the camera, point the light to the opposite side of the frame/group of people so the light spills evenly over the group (**Figure 6.2**).

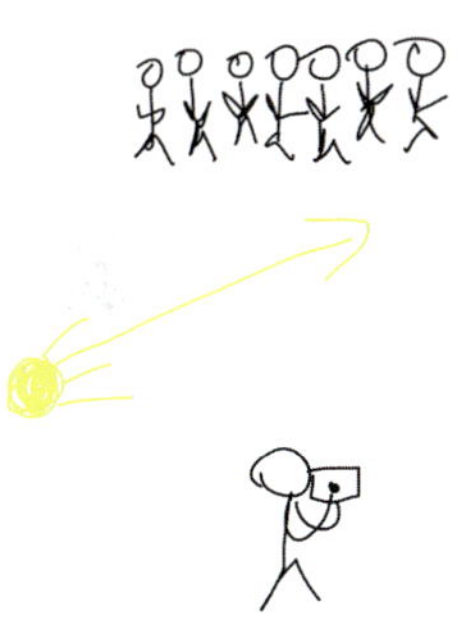

FIGURE 6.2

LIGHTING DIAGRAM.

4. **Set the camera exposure:** Set your camera exposure as if you're taking a picture of the background. Make your aperture your priority since you'll need a greater depth of field shooting groups of people. I suggest f/5.6 or higher.

5. **Set the white balance:** Because the flash is your main source of light, set your white balance to flash or 5600 Kelvin depending on the original color temperature of your light.

6. **Set the flash power:** Set your flash power to TTL and take a test shot. Flip to manual, holding that power setting, and adjust if necessary. If you're using a manual flash, start in the medium-high power range, or use a light meter and adjust up or down to your liking. Take a test shot and adjust your light to be more or less powerful according to your taste.

7. **End in manual mode:** In my opinion, if you start by getting your flash power setting in TTL, it's important that you switch to manual to hold that correct power setting static. If you don't, the light power will change up and down depending on the colors that people are wearing in the photograph. It will be a nightmare to edit later!

OPTIONAL: Use a light meter to measure the light on the left, middle, and right side of the image to see if your light is spreading evenly.

Shot by Shot

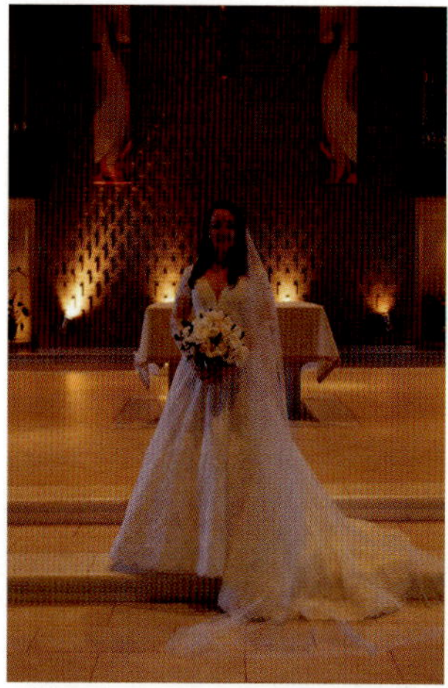

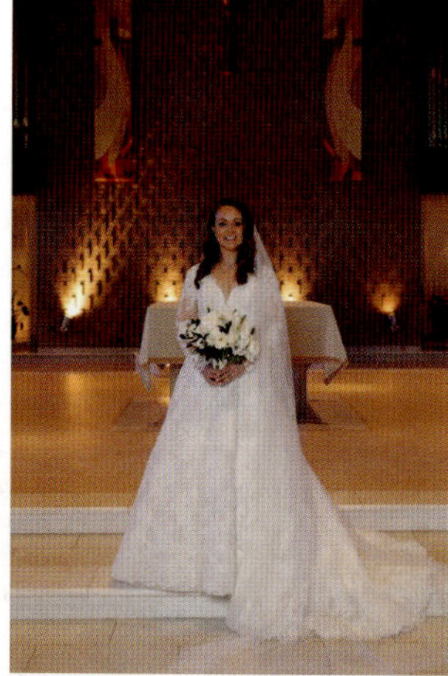

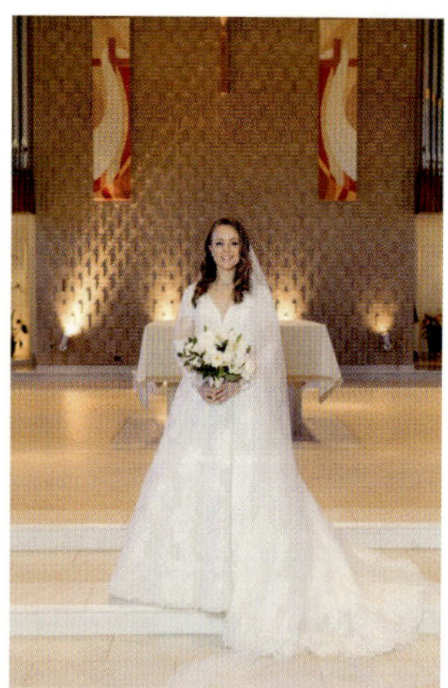

FIGURE 6.3

A NATURAL LIGHT SHOT TO GET
THE BACKGROUND EXPOSURE.
CANON 1DXII, CANON 50MM 1.2,
ISO 1000, APERTURE 5, SHUTTER
1/100

FIGURE 6.4

FOR THIS IMAGE I ADDED A PROFOTO B1 ON TTL WITH A MEDIUM UMBRELLA
AND DIFFUSER. ADMITTEDLY, IT WAS A STOP DARK, BUT I DIDN'T WANT TO
SACRIFICE A LOWER APERTURE BECAUSE I NEEDED DEPTH OF FIELD; OR A
HIGHER ISO FOR FEAR OF GRAIN; OR A LOWER SHUTTER SPEED FOR FEAR OF
CAMERA SHAKE. IN THE SECOND PHOTO, THE EXPOSURE HAS BEEN BROUGHT
UP IN LIGHTROOM.
CANON 1DXII, CANON 50MM 1.2, ISO 1000, APERTURE 5, SHUTTER 1/100

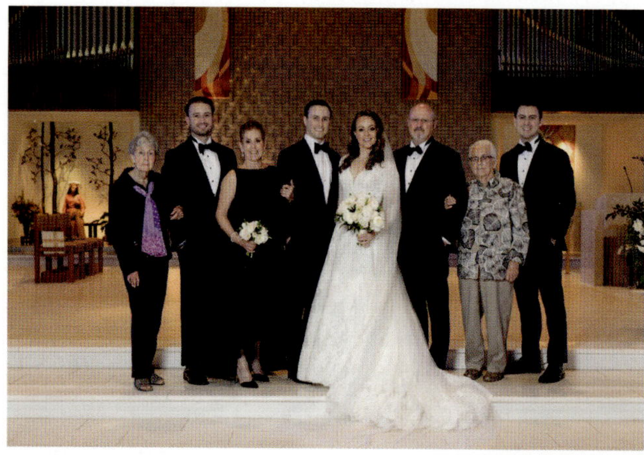

FIGURE 6.5

I SWITCHED TO MANUAL AND STARTED GOING THROUGH THE FAMILY LIST.
CANON 1DXII, CANON 50MM 1.2, ISO 1000, APERTURE 5, SHUTTER 1/100

Potential Problems

- **Super-bright and super-dark subjects:** The farther away your light is from the group, the more evenly lit the group will be. This is because of the inverse square law. If one side of the photograph is too light and the other side is too dark, back your light up a bit more. However, the farther away your light is, the harder it will be, so you have to find a happy medium.

- **The flash isn't bright enough:** If the natural/ambient light in the area is too bright then this may happen. Try maxing out your shutter speed to the highest sync speed to cut down on the ambient light. You could also go into High Speed Sync to do this more effectively, but you may have trouble with battery life and power.

- **Color changing:** Even with your power setting and white balance on manual, it's possible that your flash is experiencing a color shift from shot to shot as the flash warms up. This is one of the defining characteristics between less expensive and more expensive flashes and strobes. The more expensive ones are known to hold their color output consistently. It'll save you hours upon days of editing over the life of your lights.

- **Fighting the sun:** You can use this technique outdoors in midday like you see in **Figure 6.6**. The difference is that you'll definitely need to use a powerful strobe and will likely need a darker initial exposure. You want to position the sun at your subjects' backs, but you still might get highlights. At very least this will balance out the exposure so the background isn't completely blown out and there is light on their faces.

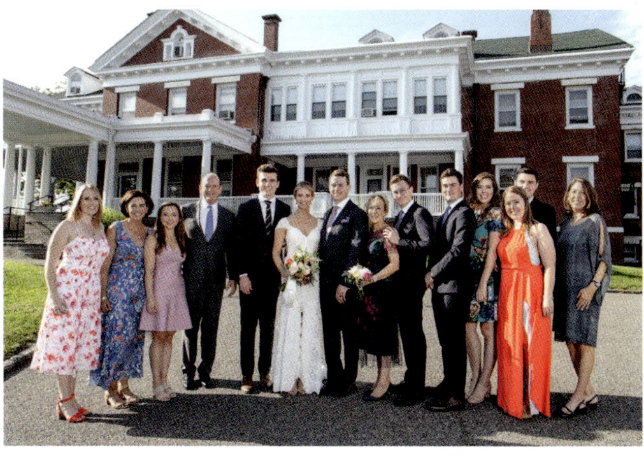

I USED A PROFOTO B1 AND AN OCF BEAUTY DISH ON CAMERA RIGHT
POINTED TOWARD THE LEFT SIDE OF THE FRAME.
CANON 1DXII, CANON 24MM 1.4, ISO 400, APERTURE 10, SHUTTER 1/250

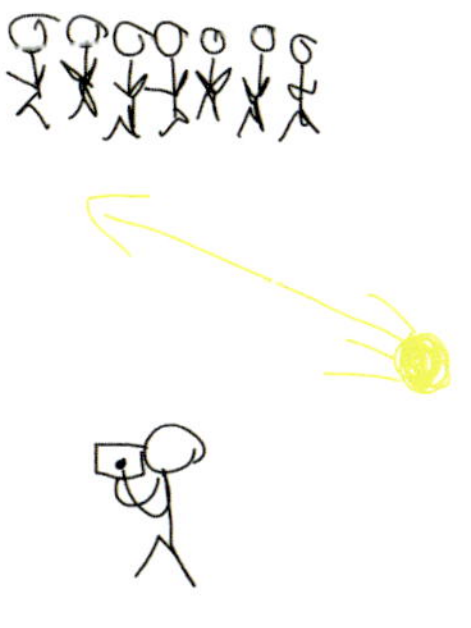

FIGURE 6.7
LIGHTING DIAGRAM.

Other Techniques

The most important thing to remember with this one-light group photo is that the inverse square law seriously comes into play here. It's probably one of the most practical applications of it that I experience routinely. I highly suggest reading not only what I've written to summarize it in this book, but what other sources have to say about it as well. It can be a fairly complicated concept, but once you understand it you'll have exponential growth in your photography skills.

Using two lights is another popular technique for lighting groups, and it solves the problem of your flash not being bright enough if you're running into that dilemma. The process is the same as above, expect for the light positioning.

I position the lights about 5 feet away from me directly to my right and left. They're both pointed at the *opposite* end of the group; the light on your right is pointing across the group to the person on the far left, and the light on your left is pointing across the group to the person on the far right. This helps light the group evenly without one side being brighter than the other. This works as long as you're using two of the same lights at the same power setting, with the same modifiers on them.

However: if you're the luckiest person in the world, and you're lighting a big group with one light, and you happen to have lightly colored walls around you, you have another option. As I mentioned briefly in the beginning of the section, you don't need a modifier. Just turn your strobe around and bounce the light off of the wall directly behind you, or slightly to the left or right behind you. This will produce beautifully even light for the largest of groups because the light source is farther away (inverse square law in play here). If it's a large wall, the light will be soft. The bigger the light source, the softer the light will be. Depending on how big the room is and your camera settings, you may need to use a strobe versus a speedlight to have enough power to light the whole group.

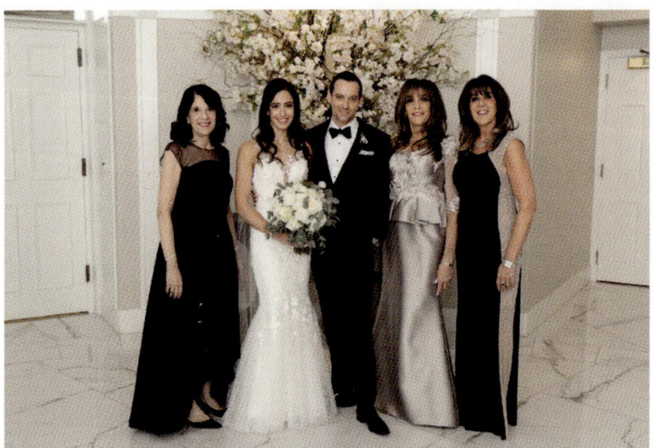

FIGURE 6.8

AN EXAMPLE OF THIS TECHNIQUE IN ACTION.
PROFOTO B10 BARE BULB, CANON 1DXII, CANON 85MM 1.4, ISO 500,
APERTURE 4, SHUTTER 1/200 WB 5600

FIGURE 6.9

LIGHTING DIAGRAM.

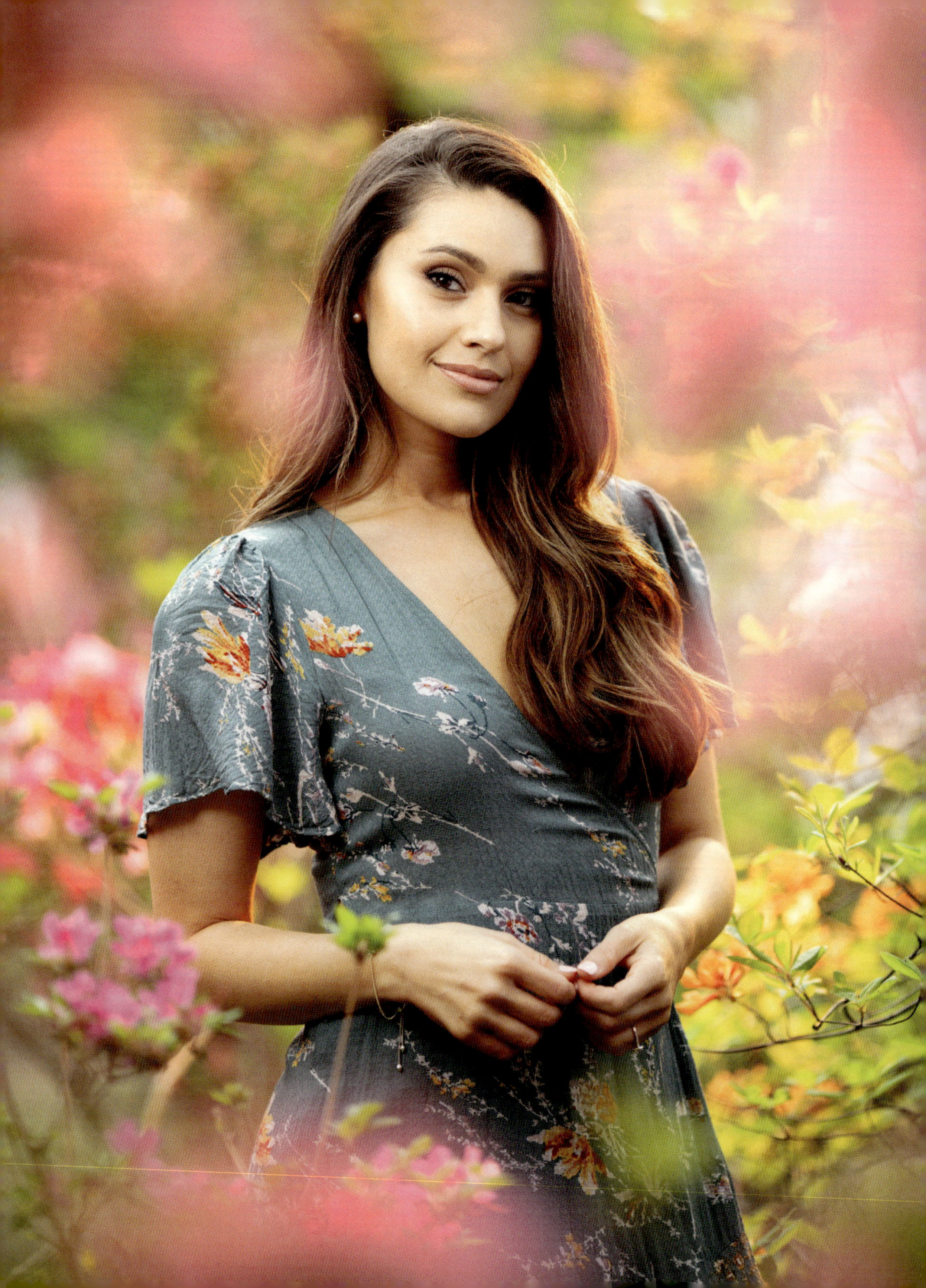

SCENARIO 7
Individual Portraits

Re-create my absolute favorite, natural,
to-die-for golden-glow lighting for portraits.

GOAL IMAGE

Hooray! This is the "how I got the cover shot" section! This technique is by far my favorite way to light someone. It gives a beautifully soft natural-looking light that almost no one would think looks like flash. It's an ideal lighting setup for a cloudy day, but you can use it at anytime of the day or night. All of the images in this chapter are straight out of the camera (**Figure 7.1**).

You'll find this setup very similar to the Golden Hour setup, but with a few caveats. My goal in an image like this is to not just think about lighting the subject, but the environment around them as well. I want everything to be evenly lit.

GEAR NEEDED:

- Camera + Trigger
- Medium to long focal length lens (50mm or higher recommended)
- 2 Off-camera flashes
- 2 Full CTO (color temperature orange) gels
- 2 Light stands
- Umbrella
- Reflector *(optional)*

I want to be able to shoot close-ups as well as ¾-length and full-length shots. A longer lens is preferable not just because it's considered a portrait lens, but also because it's easier to get my lights closer to my subject without them showing up in the frame. I don't want to do any Photoshop work afterwards.

If you're photographing this during a cloudy day you'll have no problem using a speedlight for it. If you're in bright sun, you may want the power of a strobe. It'll make things easier for you, and you won't have to worry as much about battery power or if you light will be powerful enough.

I highly recommend that you use a medium or large umbrella with a diffuser on it. You could use a shoot-through umbrella, but given that this is being shot in an open space, it's wasting light bouncing back off of the umbrella. A 5′ octa would also do the trick. Anything that'll create a large, diffused light will work well.

Step by Step

1. **Position the back light:** This is the light that will have the two CTO gels on it. Try to get at least 20 feet away from your subject, slightly to the right or left of them, and behind trees or bushes that'll break up the light to make it look more natural. Don't point the light directly at your subject's head! Aim to point it a little bit behind and past their head so that the light spreads softly across them and all of their surroundings.

2. **Position the front light:** This light will have the umbrella or large modifier on it. You'll want it to be as close to your subject as possible without being in frame. I suggest placing it just to your right or left at about a 45-degree angle to your subject, and about 8 feet high. Feather the light a bit in front of and across your subject so everything is lit evenly.

3. **Set the camera exposure:** Get an exposure for the natural light on your subject as if you weren't using off-camera flash. Take a test shot and check your histogram. You subject will likely be a little dark, especially in the eyes, depending on the natural light in the scene. I prefer a shallow depth of field with this setup, so I usually aim for around f/2.2–3.2.

4. **Set the white balance:** The flash that will hit the front of your subject won't have a gel on it, so set your WB to the color temperature of that flash (usually ~5600K). If you're not into dialing in your white balance Kelvin manually, try using the sunny day preset. Take a test shot and check the coloring of your photo. Feel free to warm or cool it slightly depending on your taste.

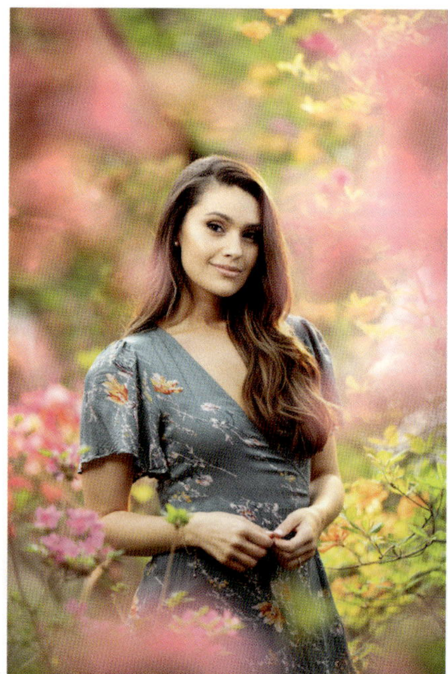

FIGURE 7.1
GOAL IMAGE.
CANON 5DS R, CANON 135MM 2.0, ISO 320,
APERTURE 2.2, SHUTTER 1/250

5. **Set the back flash:** Turn on just your back flash and use TTL to get a power setting. Flip it to manual keeping the same power setting and adjust it until you like how powerful the "sun" looks. Turn this flash head off.

6. **Set the front flash:** Turn on just your front flash and use TTL to get a power setting. Flip it to manual, keeping the same power setting, and adjust it brighter or darker for a proper exposure on your subject's face. Alternatively, for both lights you could set your camera to manual and set the flash power to mid-range, and adjust up or down to your liking. You can also use a light meter to measure and set both lights to have the same exposure on the front and back of your subject.

7. **Check both flashes:** Turn your back flash back on, still set with the power setting you got in step 5. Take a test shot with both flashes firing together. Adjust your flashes up or down until you get the look you're going for.

8. **Change your camera angle:** Although the goal of this setup isn't to get "sun flare," you definitely can grab that if you'd like. Try backing up, moving closer, and changing lenses. You're set to manual so you won't see much of a difference in the light between lenses and can keep shooting without worrying about resetting your exposure.

9. **Make adjustments:** Once you have a solid image, feel free to change your exposure, white balance, or flash settings. Be sure to only change one thing at a time so you don't get too far away from what was working originally and can't get back.

OPTIONAL: Use a reflector to bounce light back on the shadow area of your subject. This will soften the look of the flash and create less contrast in the image.

Shot by Shot

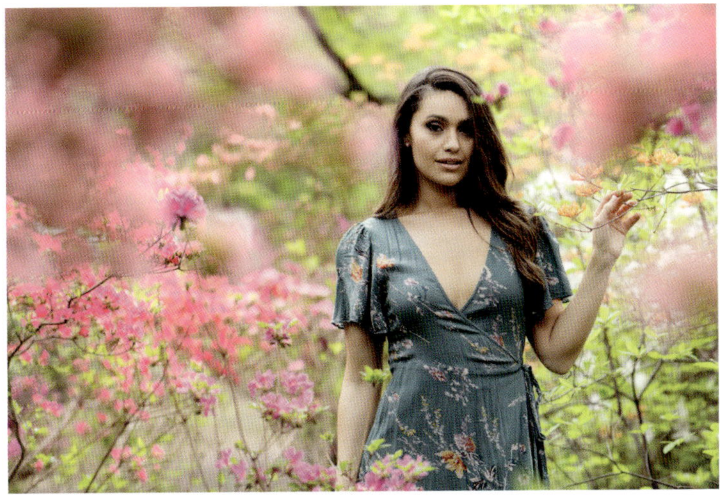

FIGURE 7.2
NATURAL LIGHT.
CANON 5DS R, CANON 85MM 1.4, ISO 250, APERTURE 2.5, SHUTTER 1/200

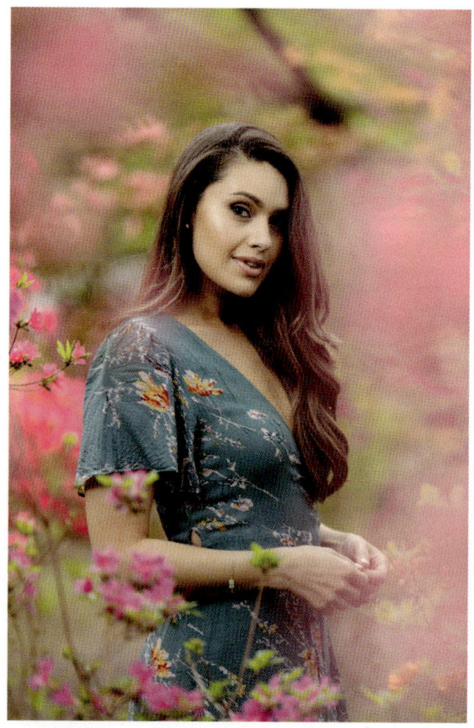

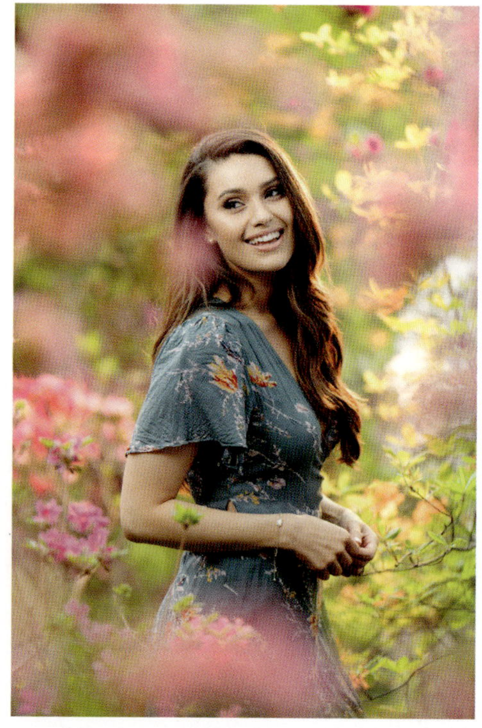

FIGURE 7.3
JUST THE FRONT FLASH.
CANON 5DS R, CANON 135MM 2.0, ISO 320, APERTURE 2.2,
SHUTTER 1/250

FIGURE 7.4
BACK FLASH AND REFLECTOR ADDED.
CANON 5DS R, CANON 135MM 2.0, ISO 320, APERTURE 2.2,
SHUTTER 1/250

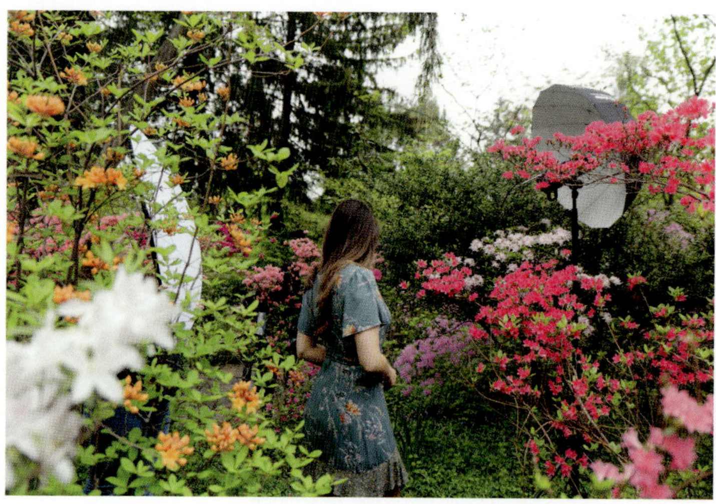

7.5
BEHIND THE SCENES.

Potential Problems

Sometimes you'll take a look at your masterpiece and think the light in front looks "fake." This usually happens because it's too harsh or it's the wrong color. Feather your light so it's not directly smacking your subject in the face, but it's also hitting their surroundings. Light hitting everything evenly in the photo makes it look more natural. If the color is the problem, warm up your white balance a little until you get a more balanced skin tone.

Setup during bright sunlight is going to be difficult because you have to overcome the light of the sun in order to make your own light. Try to find a shady spot with a shady background as well.

If you're still having trouble, you may need to go into High Speed Sync (HSS) so you can lower the natural light using your shutter speed. Going into HSS will lower the effectiveness of your flash power, so depending on your circumstances that may not help you. Alternatively, you could use a neutral density filter so you can use the full power of your flash and not need HSS.

Practical Uses

This lighting is gorgeous for a bride, senior portrait, children's portraits, couples, and families— pretty much anything! If you want your subjects to have the freedom to move a bit more, bring your front light a little closer to you so it's not at such a strong angle. This will cause the light to be more flat and even across the photo, and you won't have to worry about one person's face being in shadow while another's is properly lit (e.g., if you have them looking at each other).

Give this a try for individual and couples portraits, and for creating a magical, glowing scene in photos of children. If you advertise a warm photographic brand, you can use this technique consistently in your images.

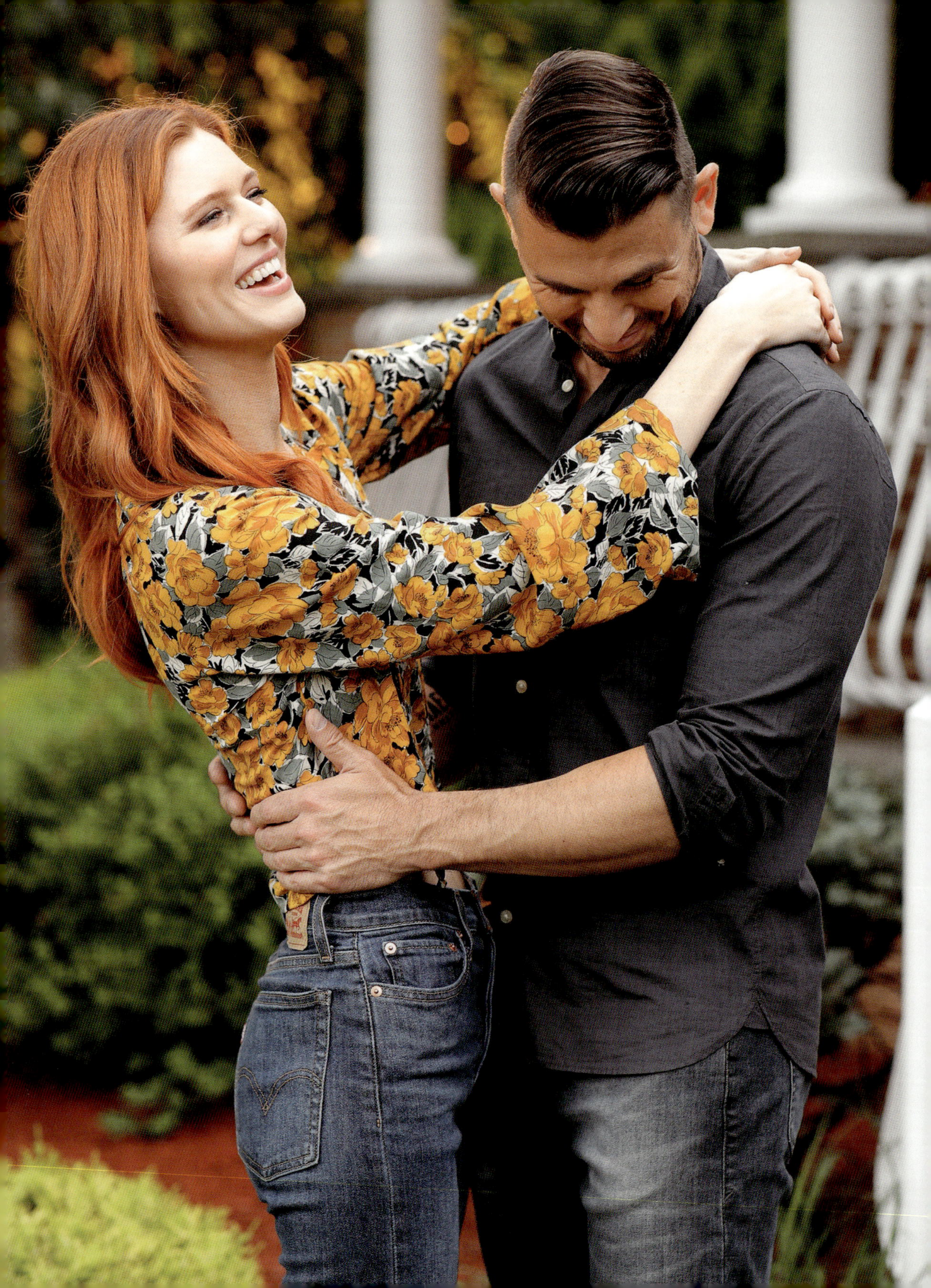

Portraits of Couples

How to get two people to look amazing together.

GOAL IMAGE

Let's start this chapter off with me admitting that I do not do this during all of my couple's shoots. Do I want to? Heck yes. However, if natural light is looking good and I can get a quality image with just a reflector, that's what I'm going to do. Why? Because it's easier and, more importantly, it makes it easier for me to connect with my clients. They can move around more freely and respond to my prompts without anyone worrying about light direction (**Figure 8.1**).

However, if I don't have great natural light, or I want to control it a bit more, this is my go to setup. It's the same as my favorite individual portrait light setup, with a few changes that help with photographing couples. As for the previous scenario, my goal in an image like this is to light not only the subject, but also the environment around them so that everything looks evenly lit.

If you're photographing this during a cloudy day you'll have no problem using speedlights for this setup. If the sun is bright, you may want the power of a 250-watt (or higher) second strobe. It'll

GEAR NEEDED:

- Camera + Trigger
- Medium to long focal length lens (50mm or higher recommended)
- 2 Off-camera flashes
- 2 Full CTO (color temperature orange) gels
- 2 Light stands
- Umbrella

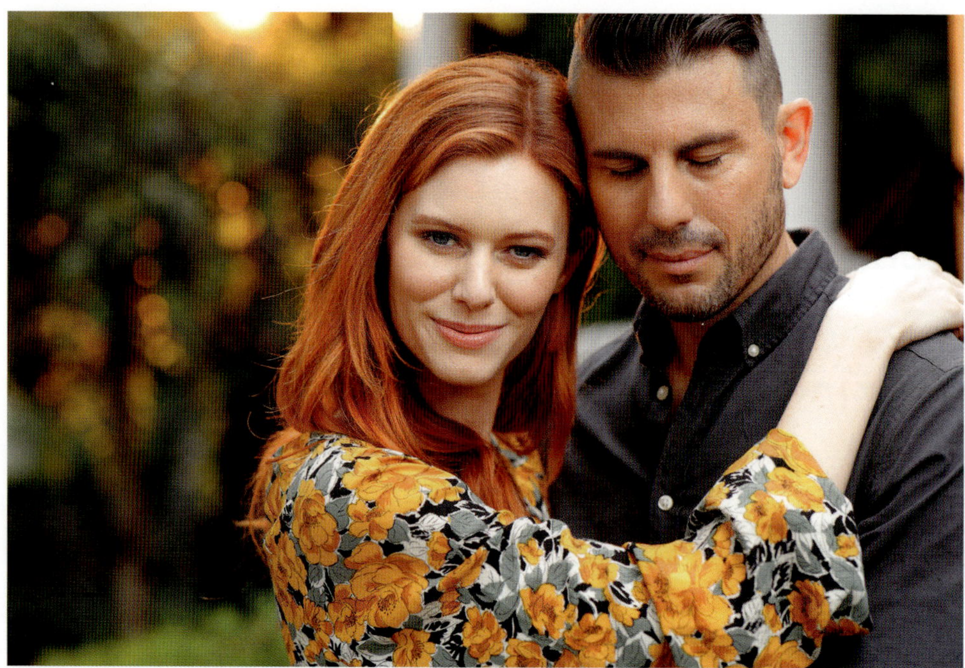

just make things easier for you so you don't have to worry as much about battery power and whether or not your light will be powerful enough for the scene.

I highly recommend that you use a medium or large umbrella with a diffuser on it for this scenario. You could use a shoot-through umbrella, but because this is being shot in an open space, some light would be wasted. A five-foot octa would also do the trick. Any light that is large and diffused will work. All images in this chapter are straight out of the camera.

Step by Step

1. **Position the back light:** This is the light that will have the two CTO gels on it. Try to be at least 20 feet away from your subjects, slightly to the right or left of them, and behind trees or bushes that'll break up the light and make it look more natural. Don't point the light directly at their heads! Aim it behind and past their heads so that the light spreads softly across them and their surroundings.

2. **Position the front light:** This light will have the umbrella or large modifier on it. You'll want it as close to your subject as possible without being in frame. I suggest placing it just to your right or left at less than a 45-degree angle to your subjects and about 8 feet high. Feather the

light a bit in front of and across your subjects so it lights them and their surroundings. The closer your light gets to your camera, the less chance you'll have at throwing unwanted shadows around and the easier it will be to pose the couple freely.

3. **Set the camera exposure:** Get an exposure for the natural light on your subjects as if you weren't using off-camera flash. Take a test shot and check your histogram. Your subjects will likely be a little dark, especially in the eyes depending on the natural light in the scene. I prefer a shallow depth of field with this setup, so I usually aim for around f/2.2–3.2.

4. **Set the white balance:** The flash that will hit the front of your subjects won't have a gel on it so set your WB to the color temperature of the front flash (usually ~5600K). If you're not into dialing in your white balance Kelvin manually, try using the sunny day preset. Take a test shot and check the coloring of your photo. Feel free to warm or cool it slightly depending on your taste.

5. **Set the back flash:** Turn on just your back flash and use TTL to get a power setting. Flip it to manual keeping the same power setting and adjust the light until you like how powerful the "sun" looks. Turn this flash head off.

6. **Set your front flash:** Turn on your front flash and use TTL to get a power setting. Flip it to manual, keeping the same power setting, and adjust the light brighter or darker to get a proper exposure on your subjects' faces. Alternatively for both lights you could set your camera to manual and set the flash power to a mid-range. Adjust up or down to your liking, or use a light meter to measure and set both lights to have the same exposure on the front and back of your subjects.

7. **Check both flashes:** Turn your back flash back on, still set with the power setting you got in step 5, and take a test shot with both flashes firing together. Adjust your flashes up or down until you get the look you're going for.

8. **Change your camera angle:** While the goal of this setup isn't to get "sun flare," you definitely can grab that if you'd like. Try backing up, moving closer, and changing lenses. You're set to manual so you won't see much of a difference in the light between lenses so you can keep shooting without worrying about the exposure.

9. **Make adjustments:** Once you have a solid image, feel free to change your exposure, white balance, or flash settings. Be sure to only change one thing at a time so you don't get too far away from what was working originally and you can't get back.

OPTIONAL: Only use one of the lights instead of both. You might like the outcome better!

Shot by Shot

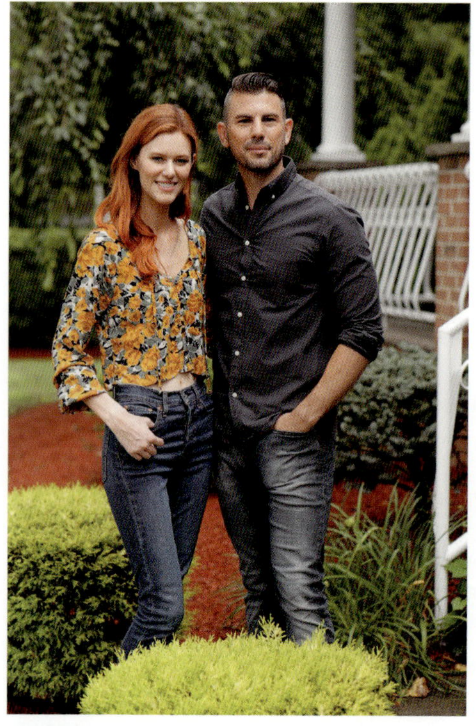

FIGURE 8.2
NATURAL LIGHT.
CANON 1DXII, CANON 85MM 1.4, ISO 125, APERTURE 3.2,
SHUTTER 1/250, WB 5700K

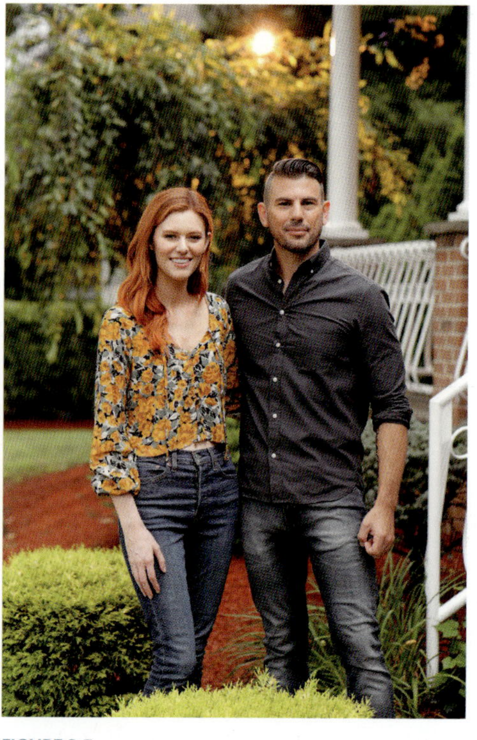

FIGURE 8.3
TURN ON THE BACK PROFOTO B1 (WITH TWO FULL
CTO GELS) ON TTL.
CANON 1DXII, CANON 85MM 1.4, ISO 125, APERTURE 3.2,
SHUTTER 1/250, WB 5700K

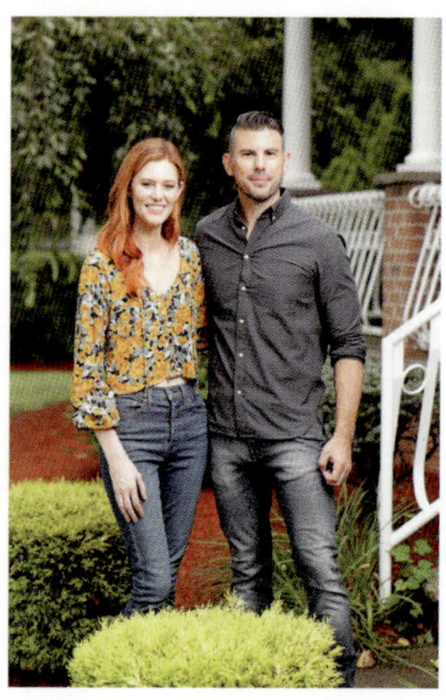

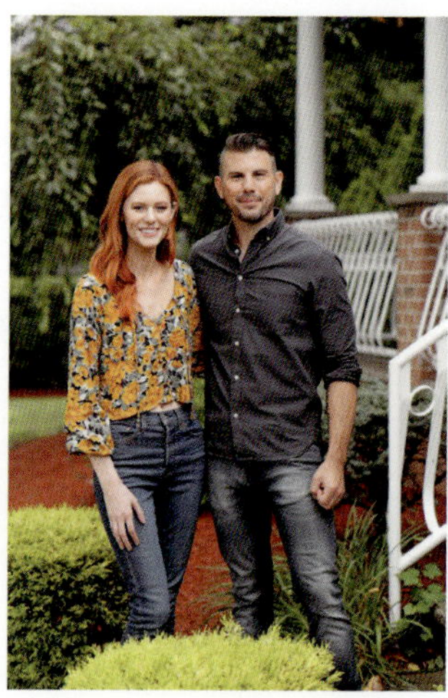

FIGURE 8.4
I TURNED ON THE FRONT FLASH,
BUT IT WAS TOO BRIGHT. I SWITCHED
TO MANUAL AND LOWERED THE
POWER IN THE SECOND PICTURE.
SETTINGS FOR BOTH: PROFOTO B1
WITH MEDIUM UMBRELLA AND
DIFFUSER.
CANON 1DXII, CANON 85MM 1.4,
ISO 125, APERTURE 3.2,
SHUTTER 1/250, WB 5700K

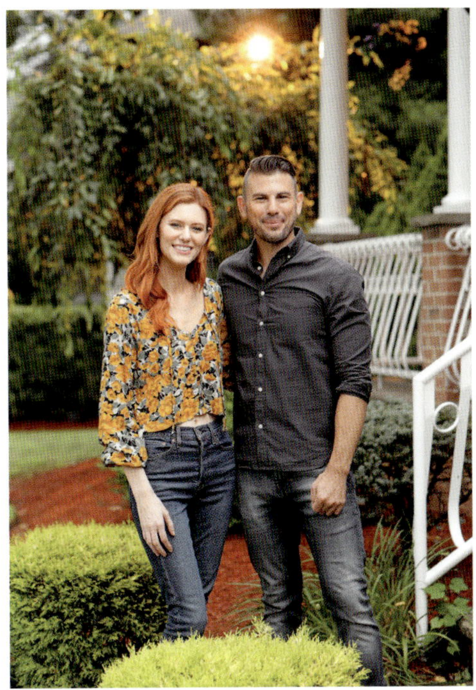

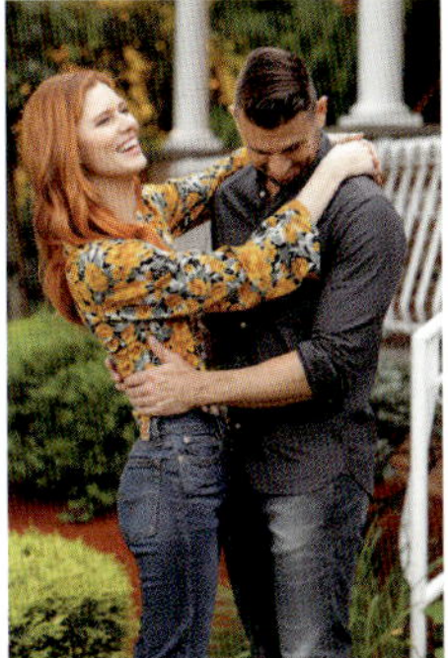

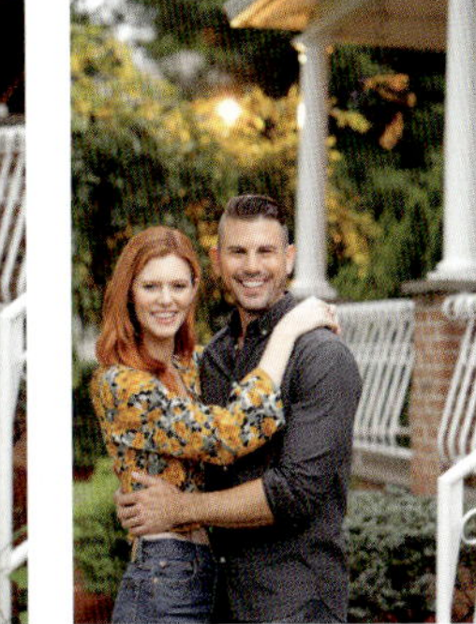

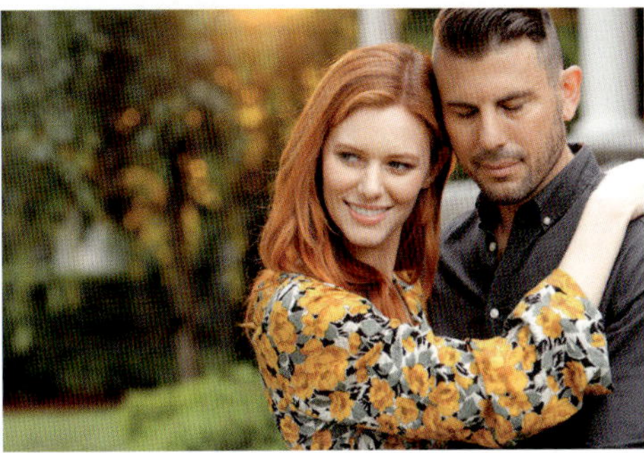

FIGURE 8.5

I TURNED ON THE FLASHES, BOTH OF WHICH WERE STILL SET TO WHERE I LEFT THEM.

CANON 1DXII, CANON 85MM 1.4, ISO 125, APERTURE 3.2, SHUTTER 1/250, WB 5700K

FIGURE 8.6

WE SWITCHED UP THE POSE AND DID A FEW CROPPED VARIATIONS AND EXPRESSIONS.

SETTINGS ARE THE SAME FOR ALL. CANON 1DXII, CANON 85MM 1.4, ISO 125, APERTURE 3.2, SHUTTER 1/250, WB 5700K

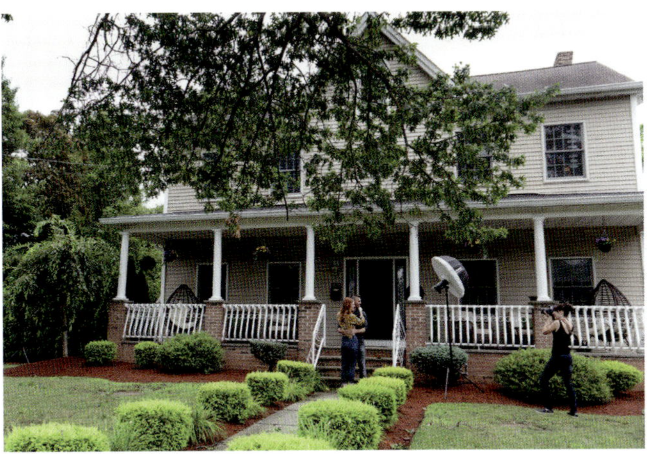

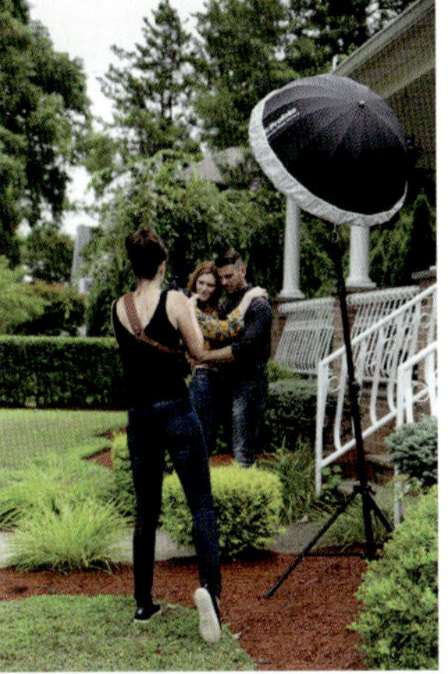

FIGURE 8.7

BEHIND THE SCENES.

Potential Problems

The biggest hurdle to overcome in this scenario is favoring the light to one side or the other. Ideally, I like to have directional light on my subjects' faces, but that becomes an obstacle with a couple. I need to have them both facing the same direction or one subject's face will be lit, while the other's is in shadow and the back of their head is lit.

In this case, I use the main light more directionally, and intentionally pose the couple so both of their faces are turned towards the light. Then I position the main light to be a bit more flat so they can turn and move any way they'd like without the casting shadows on each other or one of them turning away from the light.

Also, I have to give a huge thank you to my hubby for posing as the male model in this chapter with our model, Claire. He wasn't particular thrilled about it as he's not a huge fan of having his picture taken, but did it anyway.

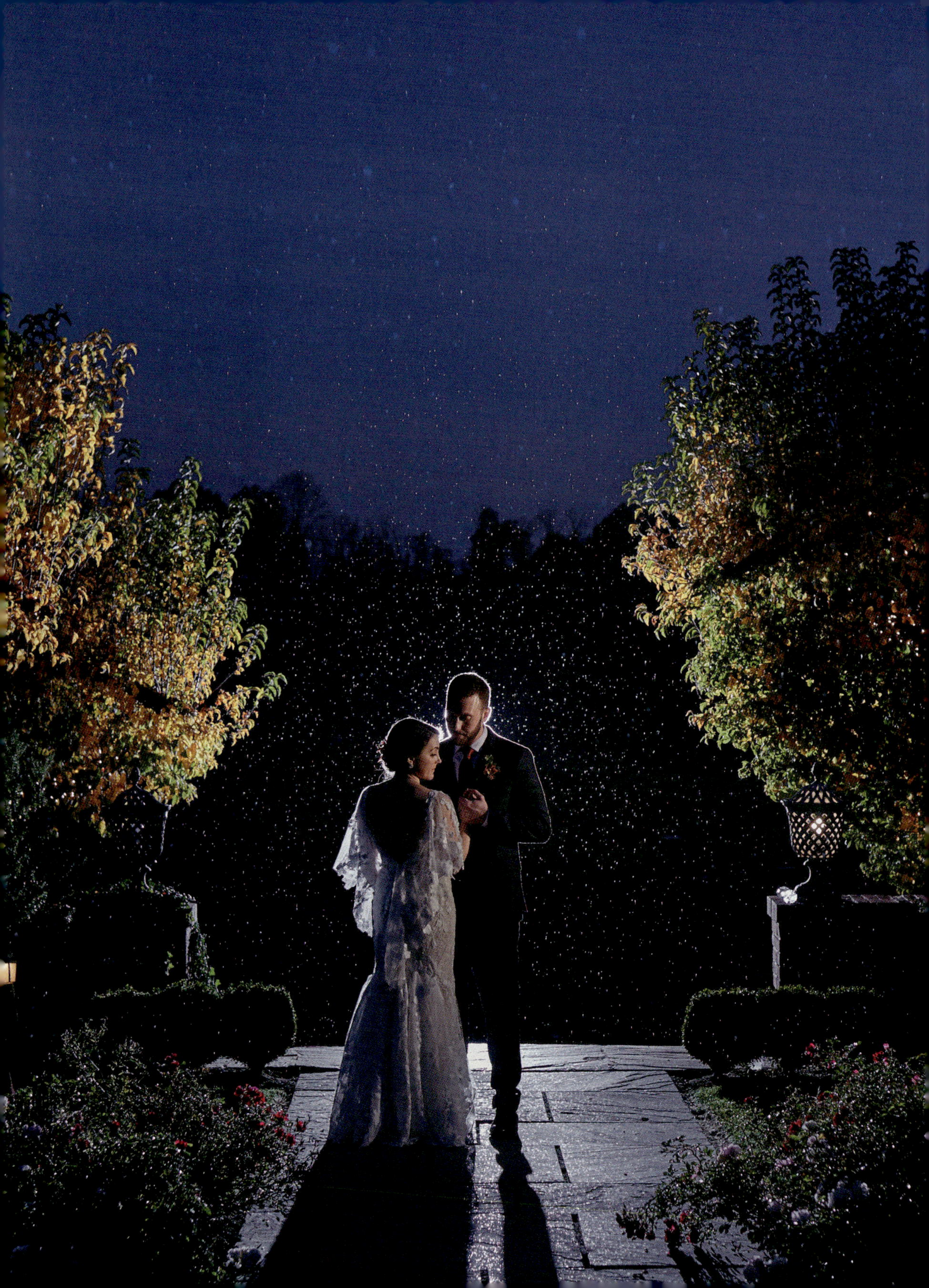

Epic Rain or Snow

You'll start praying for rain so you can get this shot!

GOAL IMAGE

Get ready to wow your clients with this epic image. You won't dread rain or snow on your shoots quite as much. It's simple and fast, and your subjects don't need to get wet at all (**Figure 9.1**).

The first thing to note is that most off-camera flashes are *not* waterproof or even water resistant. Take care of your equipment and protect it from the weather when executing this shot. You can have an assistant hold an umbrella over your flash, or cover it with something to protect it from the rain or snow. I've used things like reflector bags to cover my lights in the past. Don't use something like a plastic bag because you risk your light heating up and melting the plastic, which may damage your light.

GEAR NEEDED:

- Camera + Trigger
- Medium focal length lens (50mm)
- Off-camera flash
- Light stand
- Shoot-through umbrella *(optional)*
- Second off-camera flash *(optional)*
- Large silver reflector *(optional)*

The key to this shot is to backlight the rain or snow while rim lighting your subject. It can take some time getting used to placing the light so that it's evenly hitting your subject all around, so don't get frustrated if it's not the way you like it the first time around. It's also light years easier to do at night versus during the day. My example here was shot during the day since that's the more difficult image to make. At night, you'll easily be able to get this shot with a shutter speed below your camera's sync speed so you get more power from your light by not needing to use HSS.

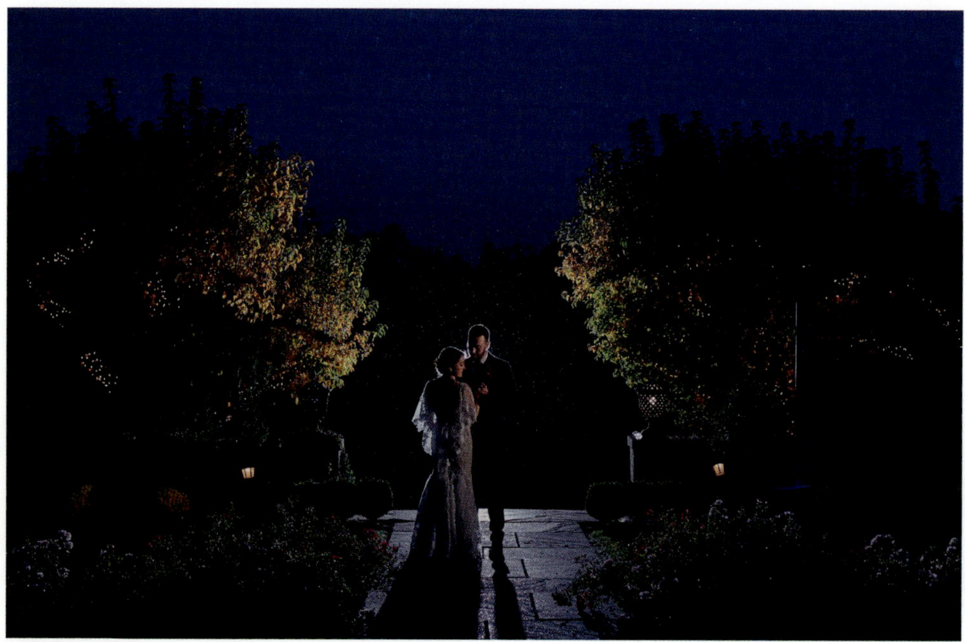

Step by Step

1. **Position the subjects:** Aim for a dark background in your frame. This will help the raindrops pop and make it easier for you to set your camera exposure later.

2. **Position the light:** Try to get the light at least 10 feet away from your subject, and point it toward your subject's head or a little higher to avoid a ton of light spill on the ground. You'll want the light far enough away from your subject to be able to hide it behind them and ensure enough light spread to hit all the rain or snow around them.

3. **Set the camera exposure:** Set the natural light exposure so that you get a black frame. The only light you want affecting the image is your off-camera flash. I prefer setting my exposure with a higher f-stop in this scenario. It'll keep all of the precipitation nice and crisp, as well as your subjects.

4. **Set the white balance:** Because the flash is your main source of light, set your WB to daylight, flash, or 5600 depending on the color temperature of your flash.

5. **Set the flash:** I usually enjoy using TTL +2 in this scenario because I want the backlight to blast light throughout the whole frame. If you're using a manual flash, start in the medium-high power range, or use a light meter and adjust up or down to your liking. Take a test shot and adjust your light to be more or less powerful according to your taste.

6. **Light the subject** *(optional):* This is if you want to move past a rain silhouette and show more of your subject's face. The more power you give your light, the better chance there is of it reflecting off a nearby surface and throwing light onto the front of your subject.

    You could also use a silver reflector, or add an additional flash (on- or off-camera) to light them in the front. If your subject is holding a white umbrella, point the flash slightly upward toward it and some light will fall back down on your subject with the overhead reflection from the umbrella.

OPTIONAL: Put a modifier on your light, such as a shoot-through umbrella (which would double as a protector for your light in poor weather conditions). This would help spread the light all around to hit every possible raindrop in the sky while keeping the light softly distributed around your subject.

Shot by Shot

FIGURE 9.2
NATURAL LIGHT BLACK FRAME.
CANON 1D X II, CANON 50MM 1.2, ISO 100, APERTURE 4.5,
SHUTTER 1/8000

FIGURE 9.3
ADDING OFF-CAMERA FLASH.
CANON 1D X II, CANON 50MM 1.2, ISO 100, APERTURE 4.5,
SHUTTER 1/8000

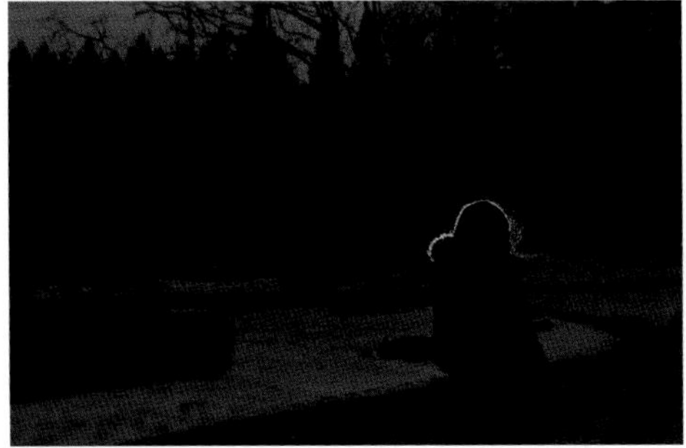

FIGURE 9.4
RAISE THE ISO TO LET MORE OF THE STROBE LIGHT IN.
CANON 1D X II, CANON 50MM 1.2, ISO 640, APERTURE 5,
SHUTTER 1/8000

FIGURE 9.5
POSITION THE COUPLE.
CANON 1D X II, CANON 135MM 2.0, ISO 640, APERTURE 5,
SHUTTER 1/8000

FIGURE 9.6

BRING UP THE HIGHLIGHTS AND SHADOWS IN LIGHTROOM.
CANON 1D X II, CANON 135MM 2.0, ISO 640, APERTURE 5,
SHUTTER 1/8000

FIGURE 9.7

BRING UP THE ENTIRE EXPOSURE IN LIGHTROOM.
CANON 1D X II, CANON 135MM 2.0, ISO 640, APERTURE 5,
SHUTTER 1/8000

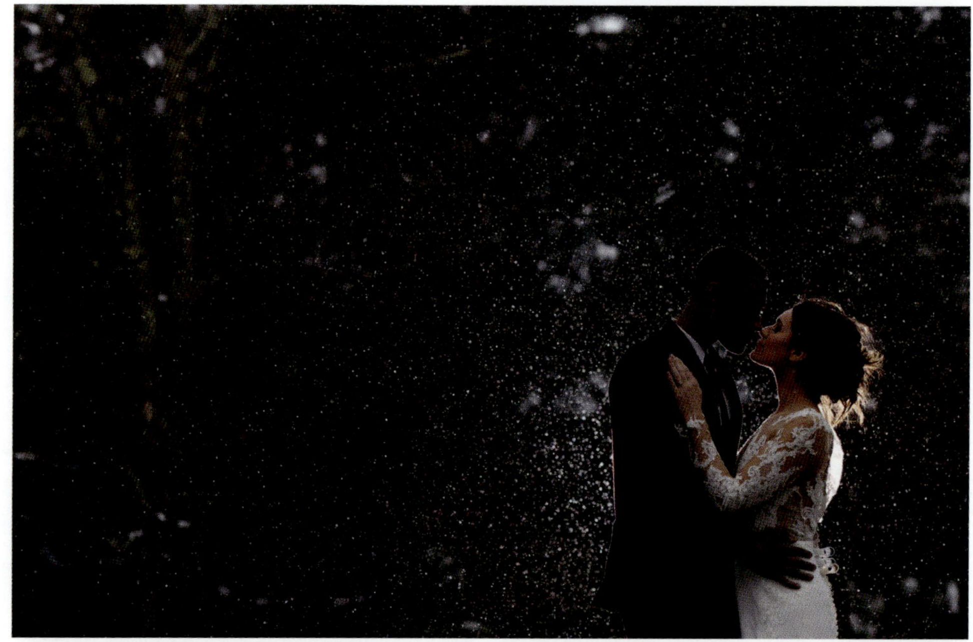

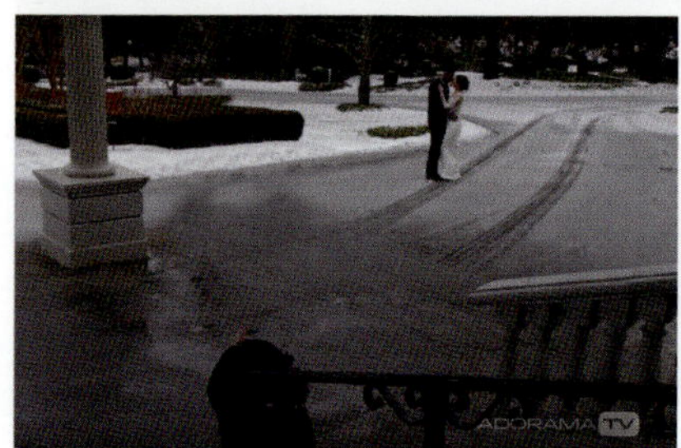

FIGURE 9.8

BEHIND THE SCENES: THE LIGHT IS DIRECTLY
BEHIND THE COUPLE.

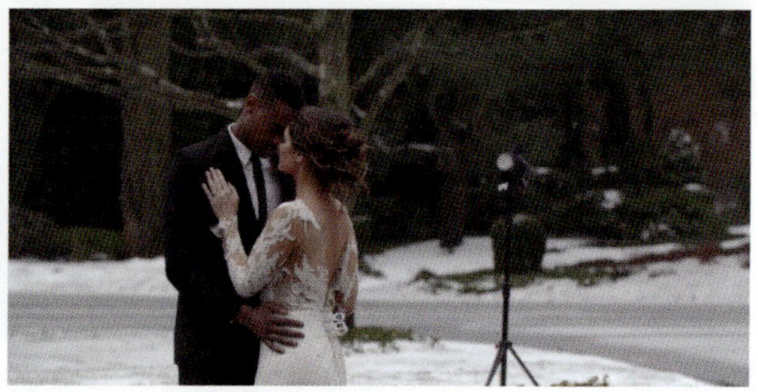

FIGURE 9.9

BEHIND THE SCENES: THIS SIDE ANGLE ALLOWS YOU
TO SEE THE LIGHT.

Potential Problems

If you're photographing this shot at night, which is the easiest time to do it, it can be hard to focus on your subject. Use some kind of continuous light to get focus, and then turn it off when you're ready to take a picture. Be careful not to overexpose the edges of your subject, which can be easy to do if you're photographing a bride. The veil or edges of the dress are easily blown out and can become a distracting element in the image.

If you're photographing during the day, like I did in the example, you'll likely need to use High Speed Sync (HSS) to darken the natural light exposure as much as possible so the rain will show up. This will kill battery power so choose your shots and don't go crazy snapping into oblivion.

Going into HSS will also lower the intensity of the light, which was my ultimate problem here. I could've used another example that was more "successful," but it's more beneficial for you to see a shot that isn't perfect and how to deal with it.

In HSS my light was at max power and it wasn't enough. I couldn't move the light any closer because I needed the light spread to show off the rain. Pulling out another flash or putting on an neutral density (ND) filter so I could get out of HSS would've caused my couple to get more aggravated in the sleet and freezing conditions. I chose to raise the ISO to let in a bit more of the strobe light (I didn't want to lower the aperture because I was having trouble with focus as it was) to give me something to work with in post and let my couple go inside.

This is not ideal, and I certainly don't recommend the "holy-crap-fix-it-in-post" technique. However, I would be amiss if I didn't admit that sometimes there are very tough situations where you're maxed out on light power and you need to apply what you know to get something salvageable. This was one of those times. You can view an entire behind-the-scenes video of this shoot on Adorama's YouTube channel. Just search "Vanessa Joy How to Shoot in the Rain."

Brush up on your silhouette posing before attempting this lighting technique. Posing your subject(s) in a flattering way will make or break this image. Think of creating long lines and separating body parts (such as separating the arms from the waist) and people (such as separating shoulders and faces so there are two distinct figures).

Other Techniques

Feel free to play around with showing the off-camera flash behind your subject. While showing the flash may be considered "incorrect" photographically, if you do it right, your clients will love it. Boosting your f-stop will cause the flash to starburst if it shows up in your image. Lowering it will give the light a softer, more circular look. Try letting it appear around the waistline of your subject so it doesn't behead them.

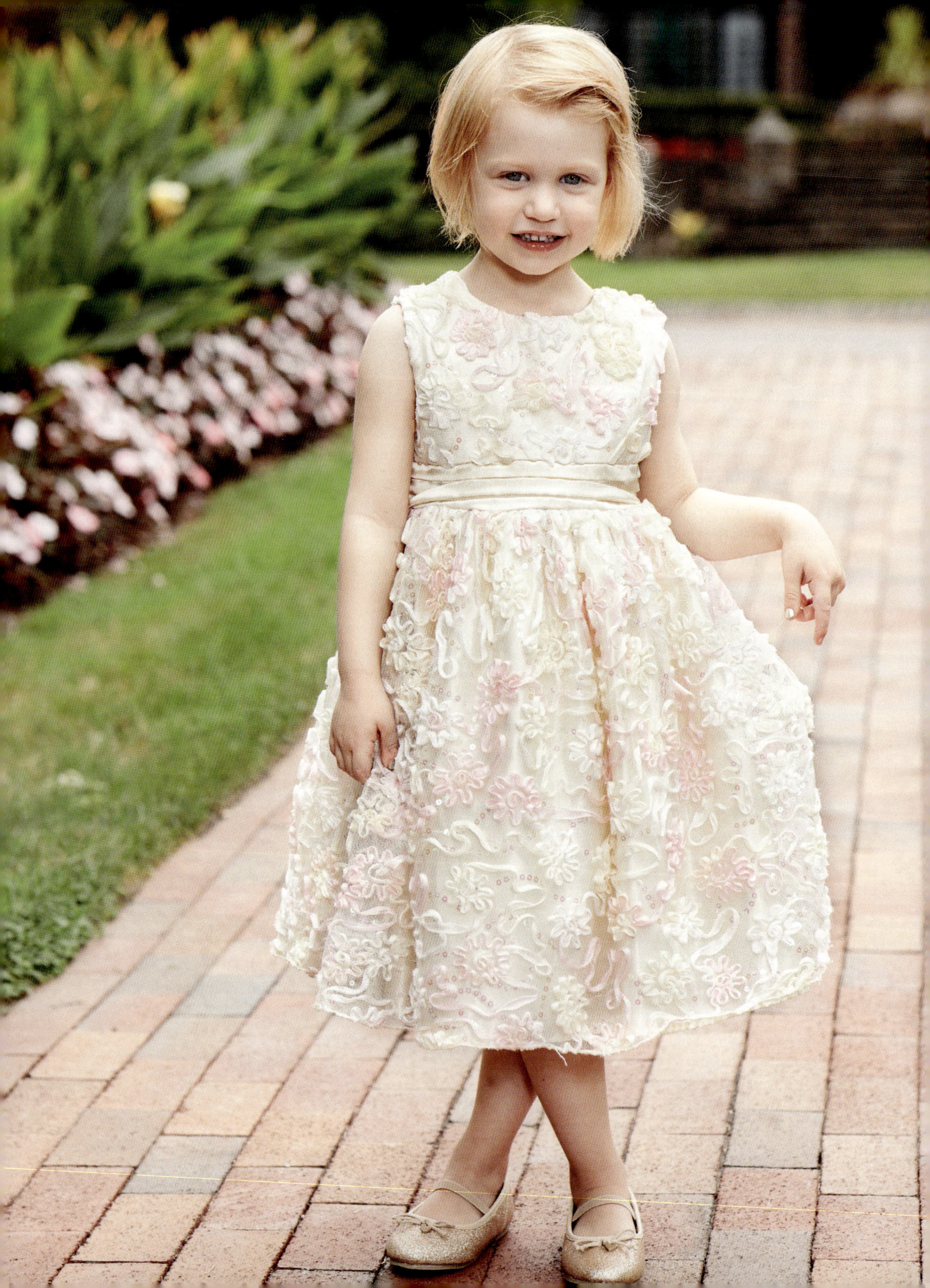

Enhancing Natural Light

What to do when you've got a day with gorgeous natural light that you want to step up even further.

GOAL IMAGE

Let's get one thing straight: I know I'm writing a book about off-camera flash, but if the natural light is gorgeous, use the natural light! Flash is not *mandatory* by any means. If the pictures look great with natural light, use it! I certainly do. Flash is a tool just like any other piece of equipment we have, and we can choose if, when, and how to use it.

All images in the step-by-step walkthrough are straight-out-of-camera.

GEAR NEEDED:

- Camera + Trigger
- Medium to long focal length lens (50mm or higher recommended)
- Off-camera flash
- Light stand
- Umbrella / softbox / octa

The first way I really learned to use off-camera flash was with this technique. My photo friend Rich Schaub helped my friend Ahmet Ze and I learn off-camera flash this way because this method is great for a sunny day, a cloudy day, or even if the sun keeps moving in and out from behind the clouds. The sun will mostly affect the background exposure, and not the flash power on the your subject's skin, which is the most important part of the photo.

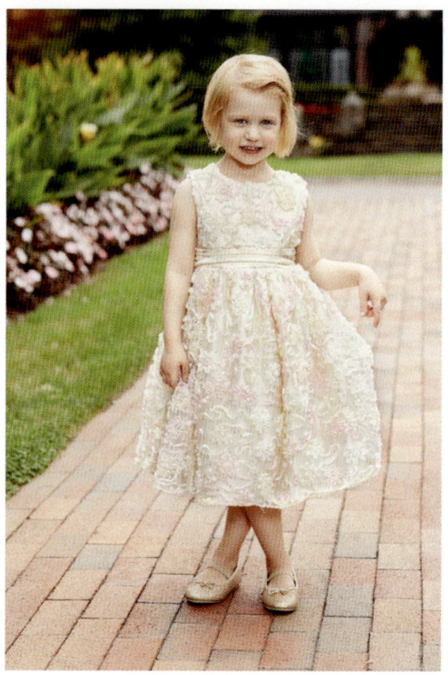

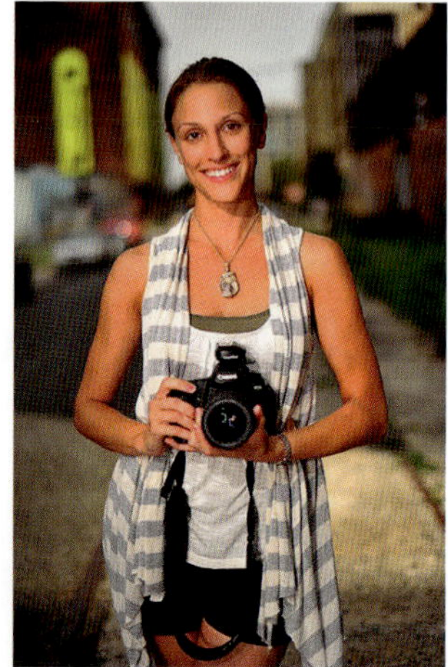

FIGURE 10.2
PHOTO BY RICH SCHAUB

Just like that horrible old photo I can't believe I let you see, we'll be using the sun as a backlight in this scenario and a flash to light the front of the subject. You might think, "why not just use a reflector?" You certainly could, but here are some reasons why that might not be the best solution:

- Reflectors usually require an assistant to hold them.

- Reflectors move a lot.

- OCF will allow you to change the color of the photo.

- OCF gives you more control over how bright or dark your background will be.

- Reflectors require the sun to be out and not dipping behind clouds, or else your exposure changes. Using a flash works well even if the sun keeps moving in and out of the clouds.

Step by Step

1. **Position the subject:** Place your subject so that the sunlight is hitting the back of their head. The sun may be going in and out of clouds, but that won't change your flash exposure.

2. **Position the light:** This light will have an umbrella/softbox/octa modifier on it. You'll want it to be as close to your subject as possible without being in frame, so it's nice and soft. I suggest placing it just to your right or left at about a 45-degree angle to your subject, about 8 feet high. You're welcome to experiment with placement, especially if your subject's head will be turning to the side.

3. **Set the camera exposure:** Get an exposure for the natural light on your subject as if you weren't using off-camera flash. Take a test shot and check your histogram. You want the subject to be a little dark so that your flash is what is primarily lighting the face.

4. **Set the white balance:** The flash that will hit the front of your subject won't have a gel on it so set your WB to the color temperature of the flash (usually ~5600K). You could also use the sunny day preset. Take a test shot and check the coloring of your photo. Feel free to warm or cool it slightly depending on your taste.

5. **Set the flash power:** Turn on just your front flash and use TTL to get a power setting. Alternatively, you could set your camera to manual and set the flash power to a mid-range value and adjust up or down to your liking, or use a light meter. Flip it to manual, keeping the same power setting, and adjust brighter or darker for a proper exposure on your subject's face.

    If you don't like how your background looks, change the shutter speed *after* you've figured out the correct flash power for the subject's face.

6. **Make adjustments:** Once you have a solid image, feel free to change your exposure, white balance, or flash settings. Be sure to only change one thing at a time so you don't get too far away from what was working originally and you can't get back.

Shot by Shot

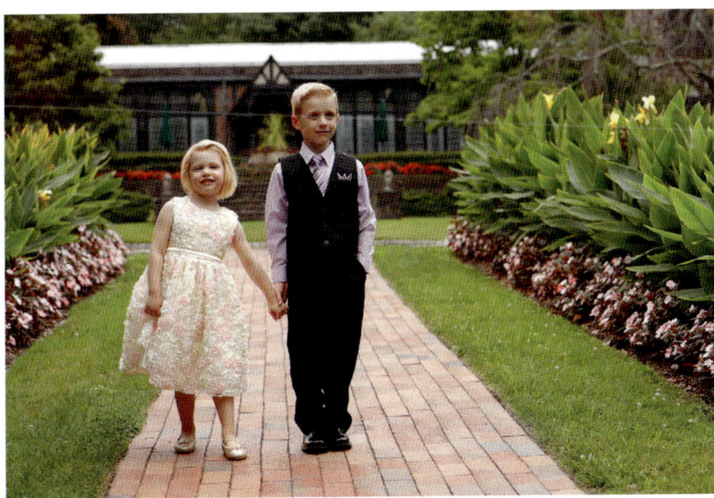

FIGURE 10.3
NATURAL LIGHT.
CANON 1DXII, CANON 85MM 1.4, ISO 200, APERTURE 5, SHUTTER 1/250, WB 5900

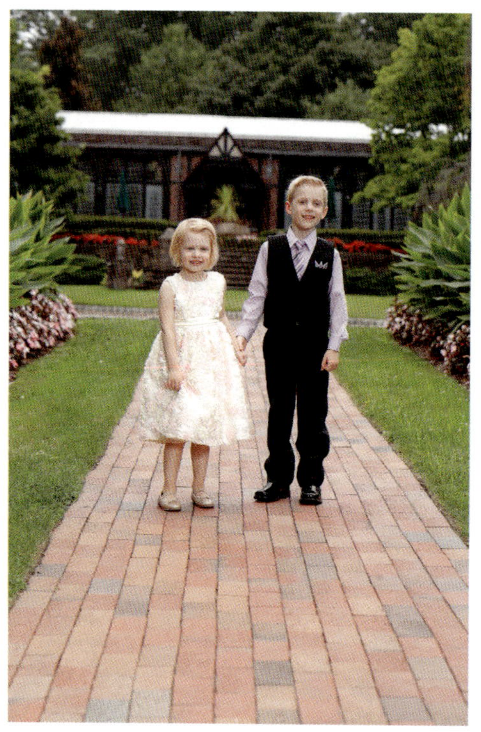

FIGURE 10.4

THIS IMAGE HAS THE ADDITION OF A PROFOTO B10 WITH A SMALL WHITE UMBRELLA AND DIFFUSER TO CAMERA RIGHT.

CANON 1DXII, CANON 85MM 1.4, ISO 200, APERTURE 5, SHUTTER 1/250, WB 5900

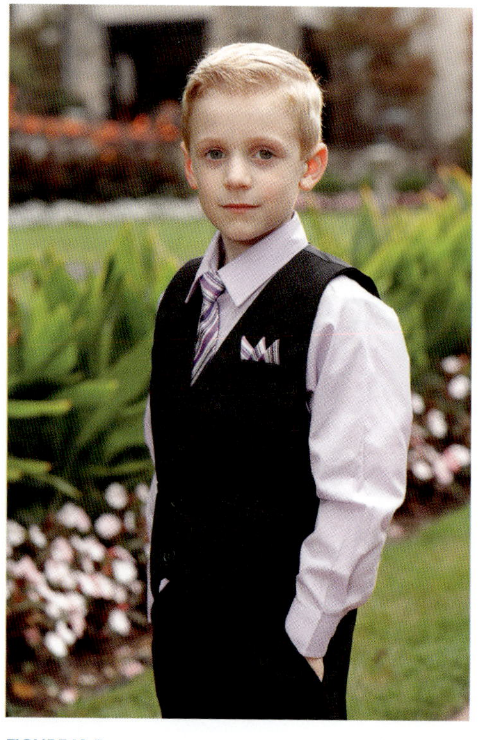

FIGURE 10.5

I LOWERED THE APERTURE TO BRIGHTEN THE FLASH SINCE THE SUBJECT MOVED FARTHER AWAY FROM IT. THERE IS A PROFOTO B10 WITH A SMALL WHITE UMBRELLA AND DIFFUSER TO CAMERA RIGHT.

CANON 1DXII, CANON 85MM 1.4, ISO 200, APERTURE 4.5, SHUTTER 1/250, WB 5900

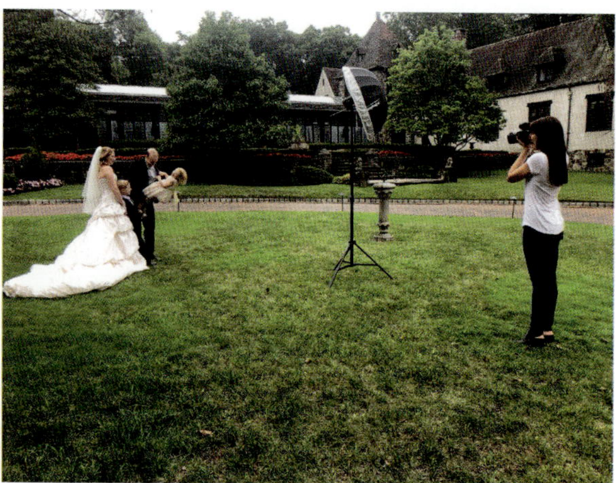

FIGURE 10.6

BEHIND-THE-SCENES SHOT.
PHOTO BY JUAN ACEA

Potential Problems

If you have a partly cloudy day on your hands, you may get frustrated with the sun going in and out of the clouds, changing the way your background looks from shot to shot. It's helpful to put your subject in a spot where their back is lit by the sun but their face is in the shade (and lit by your flash). The more your frame (both the subject and the background) is in the shade, the less your shot will be affected by the sun.

Either way, try to set your shutter speed around $\frac{1}{125}$ of a second. This will give you the freedom to move your shutter speed up or down a couple of stops to compensate for your background going brighter or darker. This won't affect the flash exposure on your subject, and you won't need to go into HSS. If the changes are super extreme, you may need to go into HSS to give yourself more leeway.

Special thanks to photographer Vail Fucci, who not only trusted me to photograph her and her family, but also allowed me to use their images in my book! Thanks girl!

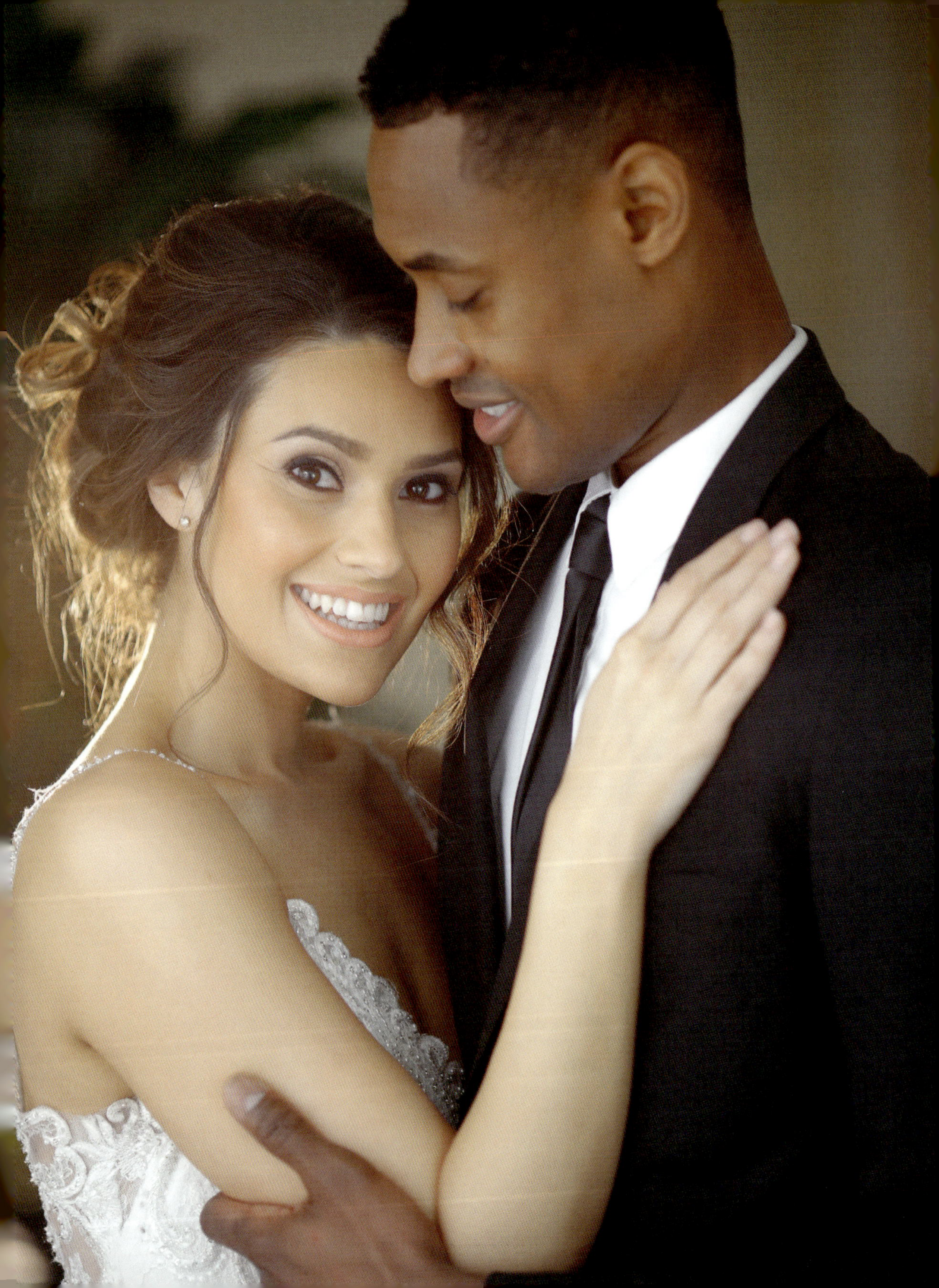

Making Indoors Look Like Outdoors

Make beautiful images even if there's a hurricane outside.

GOAL IMAGE

I'm from the Northeast, which means I've had jobs in hurricanes (multiple times) and have definitely had to hide inside due to frigid or wet weather. Needless to say, it kills my client's day (their wedding day especially) when their vision of glowing outdoor images is quashed by sleet or rain. But no fear! I can make them happy anyway and so will you after this section! All images in this section are straight-out-of-camera, so you can see what it looks like without me enhancing it in Photoshop.

The concept here is almost exactly like Scenario 2, "Creating Golden Hour." The difference is that because we're inside, we don't need to compete with the power of the sun. We can more easily use speedlights in this case, which makes for a less expensive and less cumbersome setup.

GEAR NEEDED:

- Camera + Trigger
- Long focal length lens (100mm or higher recommended)
- 2 Off-camera flashes
- 2 Full CTO (color temperature orange) gels
- 2 Light stands
- Soft modifier (umbrella, softbox, beauty dish, or a big white wall to bounce light off of)
- Reflector *(optional)*

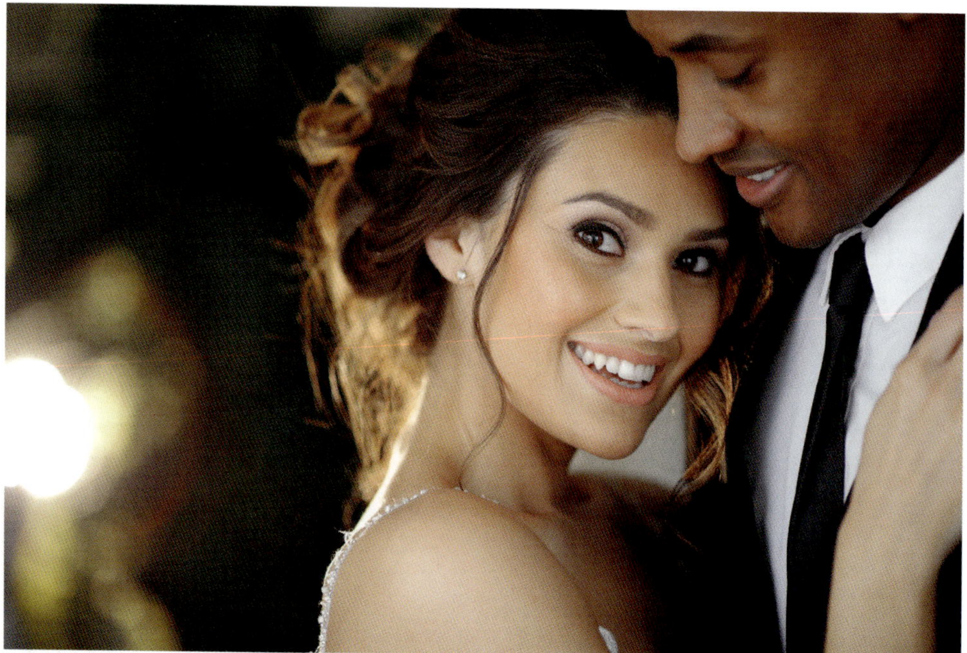

The secret to getting this right is finding some foliage, except this time you're probably going to move it. I've been know to "borrow" plants that I find around the venue and set them up where I want to photograph this pseudo-outdoor setup. You'll place one flash behind the plant to make it look like real greenery outside with the sun behind it.

Sometimes "borrowing" plants from the venue simply means moving them away from the wall. To get this shot effectively, you'll want to shoot in a room where you have about 5 feet of space behind the plants and a white wall in front of or to the side of the plants. You'll be using a longer lens for this shot so you need to be in a room where you have plenty of room to back up. All of that considered, I usually have to move plants around to make the shot work.

Step by Step

1. **Turn all other ambient lights off:** You need to control not just the amount of light in the room, but the color of it as well. If you have ugly tungsten lights throwing gross colors on your subjects, it's not going to be pretty. Do yourself a favor and turn them off!

2. **Position the plants:** It sounds ridiculous, but it works. Place the plants in position behind your subjects so the greenery fills the background of the image almost completely. You also need to have about 5 feet of space behind the plants to place your flash far enough away from them that the light will hit all of them.

3. **Position the "sun" backlight:** This light will have two CTO gels on it. Try to place it at least 5 feet away from your plants and point it through the greenery toward your subjects. This will rim light your subjects nicely in addition to making your greenery glow.

4. **Position the front light:** This light will have the soft modifier on it or (and I prefer this) be pointed toward a large white (or lightly colored) wall. If you're lucky enough to have white ceilings as well, point the light toward a corner of the room. It'll act like a huge umbrella by bouncing the light back and lighting your subject. The light should be hitting the front of the subject, maybe off to the right or left a little to give everything a little dimension.

5. **Set the camera exposure:** Get an exposure for the natural light on your subject as if you weren't using off-camera flash. Because you're inside, this might not be much. But if you're in a room with windows, let a bit of that light affect your image if possible. Personally, I like to use a very low aperture so that the background blurs as much as possible, hiding any elements that would give away that this was shot indoors.

6. **Set the white balance:** The flash that will hit the front of your subject won't have a gel on it so set your WB to the color temperature of the flash (usually ~5600K). If you're not into dialing in your white balance Kelvin manually, try using the sunny day preset. Take a test shot and check the coloring of your photo.

7. **Adjust positioning:** For this to be believable, the greenery needs to fill the background. It's not going to look like it's outside if you only see a little bit of greenery on one side of the frame, and wallpaper and a chandelier on the other. Using a longer lens helps compress the image and makes it easier to fill the background with the greenery. It may take some adjusting; move your subject closer or farther away from the greenery until it looks right.

8. **Set the back flash:** Turn on just your back flash and use TTL to get a power setting. Flip it to manual, keeping the same power setting, and adjust the light until you like how powerful the "sun" looks. Turn this flash head off.

9. **Set the front flash:** Turn on just your front flash and use TTL to get a power setting. Flip it to manual, keeping the same power setting, and adjust the light brighter or darker for a proper exposure on your subject's face. If you're bouncing this flash, you may be at a fairly high power setting. Alternatively for both flash settings you could use a light meter to set the power manually so that the light reads the same f-stop on the front and back of your subject.

10. **Check both flashes:** Turn your back flash back on. It'll still have the power setting you got in step 5. Take a test shot with both flashes firing together. Adjust your flashes up or down until you get the look you're going for.

11. **Make adjustments:** Once you have a solid image, feel free to change your exposure, white balance, or flash settings. Be sure to only change one thing at a time so you don't get too far away from what was working originally and you can't get back.

OPTIONAL: Add a reflector on the opposite side of the front flash to fill in any shadows.

Shot by Shot

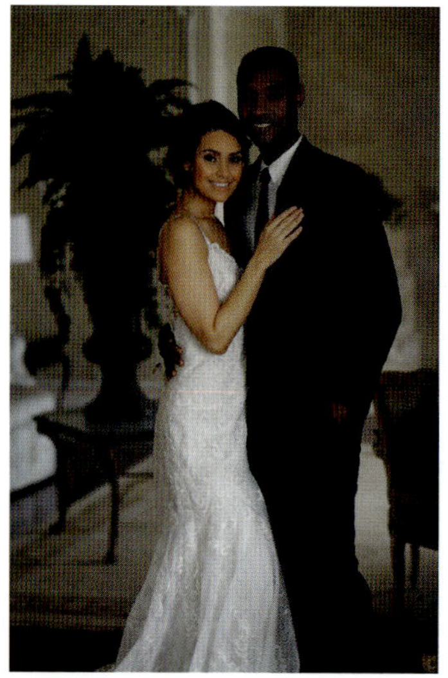

FIGURE 11.2

NATURAL LIGHT.

CANON 1DX II, CANON 85MM 1.4, ISO 1600, APERTURE 2, SHUTTER 1/160

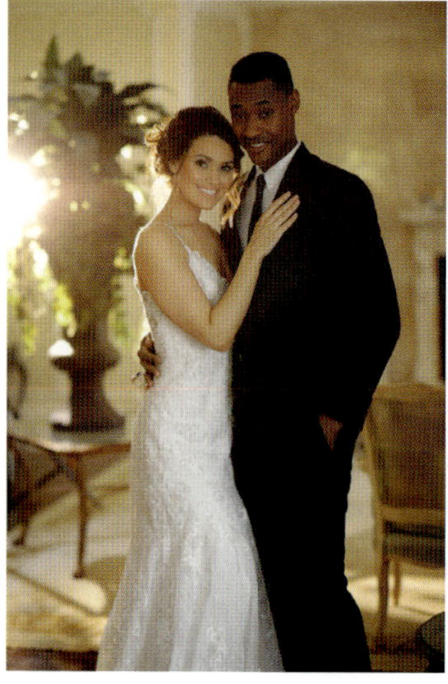

FIGURE 11.3

SHOT WITH JUST THE BACK FLASH.

CANON 1DX II, CANON 85MM 1.4, ISO 1600, APERTURE 2, SHUTTER 1/160

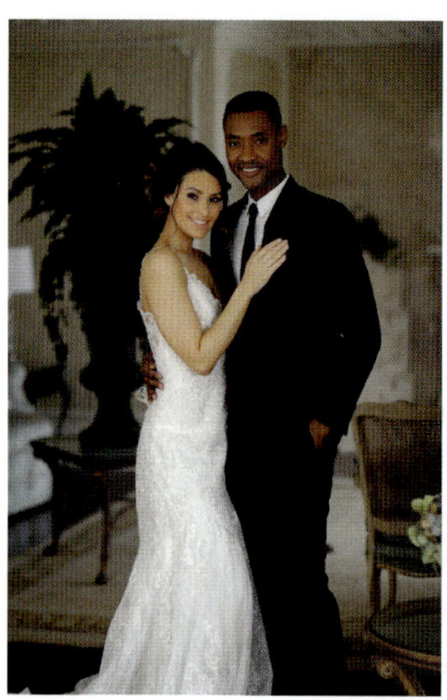

FIGURE 11.4

SHOT WITH JUST THE FRONT FLASH.

CANON 1DX II, CANON 85MM 1.4, ISO 1600, APERTURE 2, SHUTTER 1/160

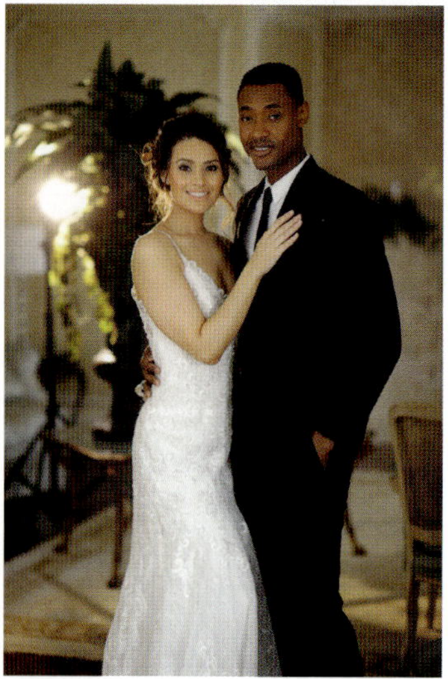

FIGURE 11.5

SHOT WITH BOTH FLASHES.

CANON 1DX II, CANON 85MM 1.4, ISO 1600, APERTURE 2, SHUTTER 1/160

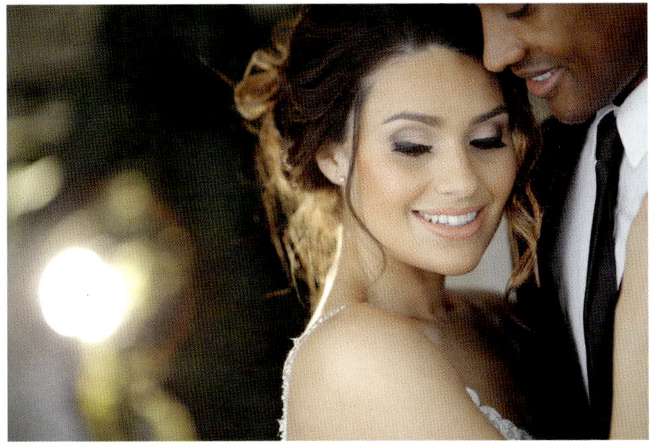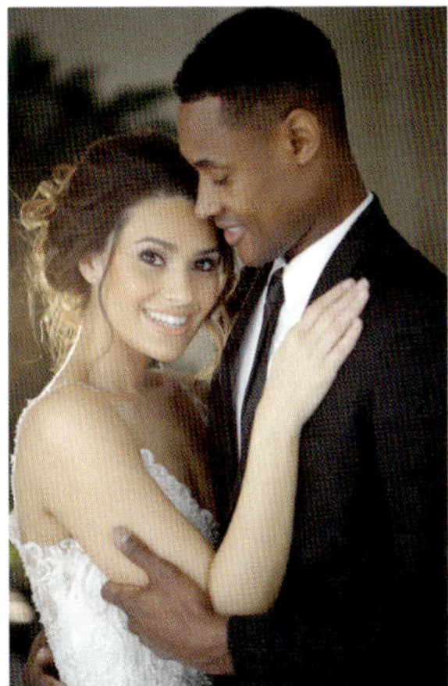

FINAL PHOTOS, CROPPED TO HIDE THE INDOOR ELEMENTS.
ALL SETTINGS ARE THE SAME: CANON 135MM 2.0, ISO 1600, APERTURE 2, SHUTTER 1/160

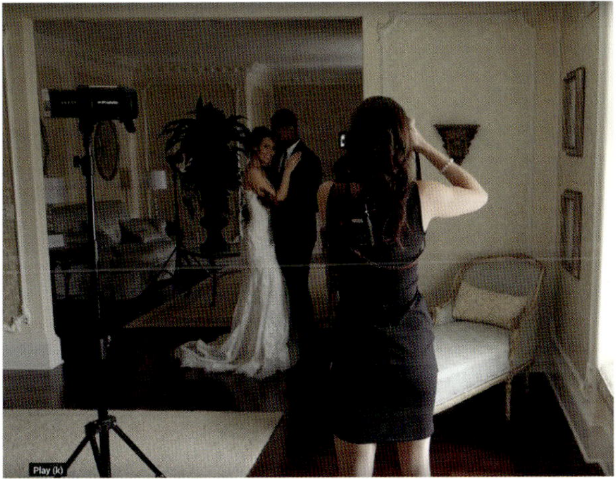

SETUP, BEHIND THE SCENES.

Potential Problems

This image can look "flashy" if it's not done correctly. This usually happens because the flash is too harsh or the wrong color. If you're not bouncing your light, feather it so it's not directly pointing at your subject. You could also use a larger modifier or bring the light closer to your subject to soften it. If the color is the problem, warm up your white balance a little until you get a more balanced skin tone.

Occasionally, when you set this up and take your test shot using both flashes, you'll find the "sun" not being as bright as it looks when you're firing it alone. That typically happens when your front flash is too bright and overpowering the back flash. Boost the power of the back flash, or change your overall exposure to let more light in and lessen the power of the front flash.

Finally, if you don't think the image looks natural enough, let more natural light of the space in. The easiest way to do this without ruining your flash settings is to lower your shutter speed. This won't change the way the flash looks in the image, but it lets more of the natural light show up. It may make the image look more believable for this setup.

Practical Uses

I love being able to cheer up clients that are bummed about not being able to shoot outdoors. It can instantly brighten their day when you show them the back of your camera. To them, it's magic. You're giving them something they thought was taken away from their day. Even if you can only pull off a few close up pictures like this, it can alter the mood of the entire shoot.

Give this a try for individual and couples portraits. It will definitely cheer up your clients! Also, if you advertise a warm photographic brand, you can use this technique consistently in your images.

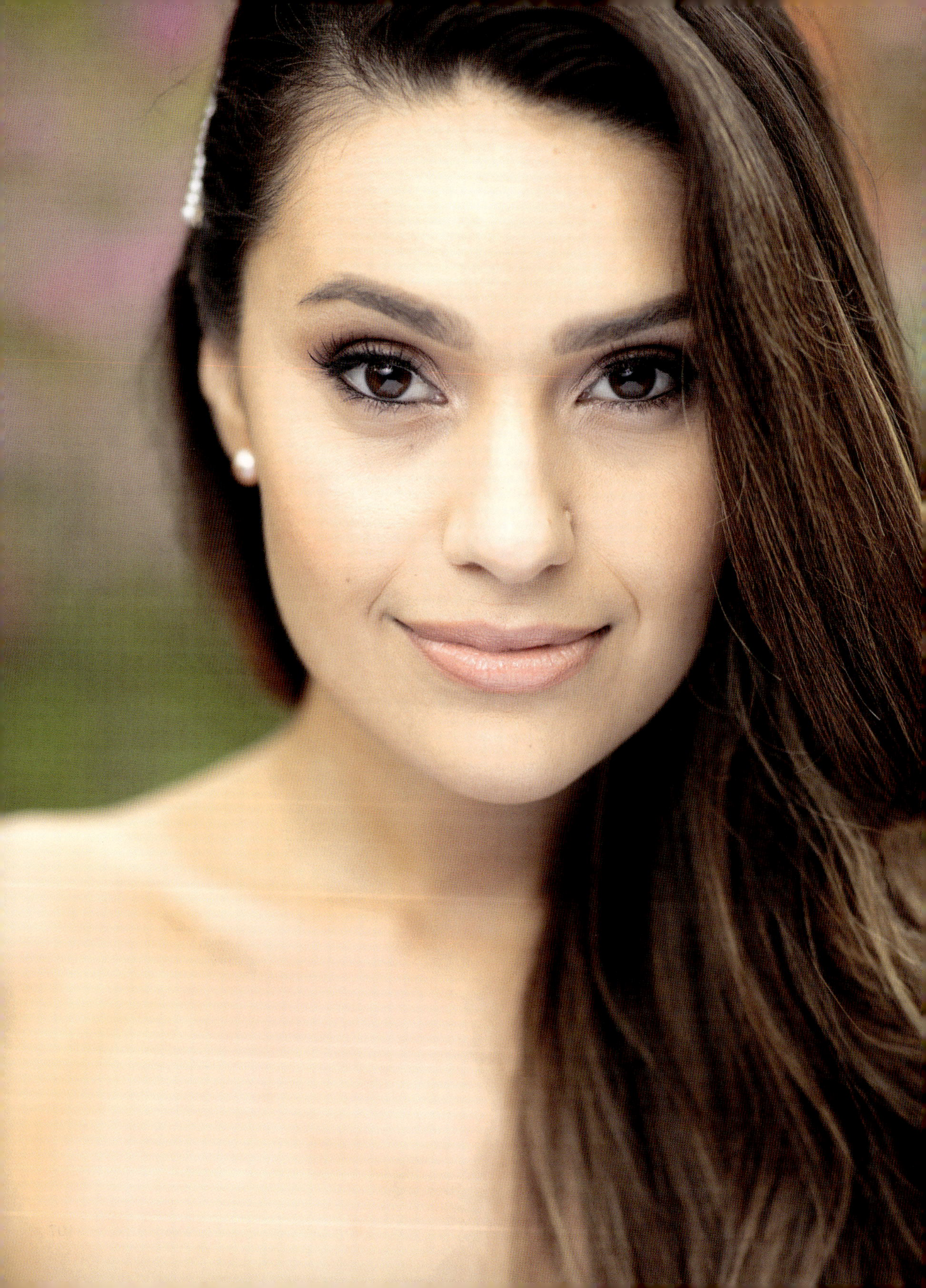

SCENARIO 12

Super Soft Portrait Light

*Create a natural-light look with studio-quality light
in this simple setup.*

GOAL IMAGE

Sometimes when you're photographing in natural light, even though it may be soft and overcast, it's just not attractive on a face. Regardless of cloud coverage, the angle of light is what can make or break a portrait. Having control over your light in order to flatter your subject's face is paramount. All images in this chapter are straight out of the camera.

This is one of my favorite setups because it can be done very inexpensively and with a strobe or a speedlight in pretty much any lighting condition you find yourself in. It will help you create a beautiful look that'll flatter almost any face, and give you control over what the rest of your background looks like.

I've done this on quite a few shoots, demos, and weddings, and not only does it yield a gorgeous look, but it also draws a bit of attention as well. It's not a typical thing you'd see a photographer doing during a shoot so on-lookers get curious, and that is always a great marketing tool.

- Camera + Trigger
- Portrait focal length lens (85mm or higher recommended)
- Off-camera flash
- 5-in-1 Reflector
- Light stand *(optional)*
- Reflector holder *(optional)*

Step by Step

1. **Position your light:** You can put your speedlight or strobe on a light stand or have your
   assistant hold it. I do recommend a light stand
   here because if you do have an assistant, it's
   better that the extra pair of hands holds the
   reflector instead. The light will be about a foot
   or so higher than your subject and pointed
   down at him or her.

2. **Take apart the reflector:** I use the Glow 5-in-1
   42" reflector for this (found at Adorama),
   because it has a diffuser in addition to the
   white, silver, gold/silver, and black sides. We'll
   be using the diffuser *and* the white side.

3. **Position the diffuser:** The diffuser needs to be
   above your subject, angled slightly down so
   that the light pours onto your subject from in
   front of their face instead of directly over it.
   The diffuser needs to be far enough away from
   your light so that the light, when fired, hits
   the diffuser all the way around the edges.

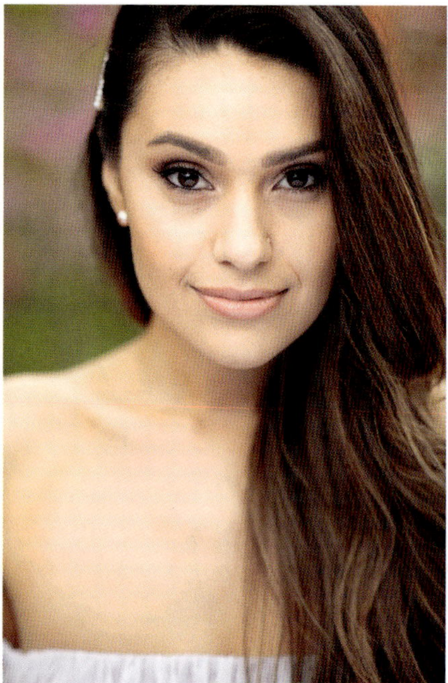

4. **Position the reflector:** What's left from the
   5-in-1 reflector, after you take out the diffuser, is the white covering. You can still use this!
   Position it as a reflector below your subjects face. You may need to have your subject hold one
   side while you hold the other, or have the assistant hold your side, or have another arm
   coming off the light stand to hold a side. However you manage it, have the white part spread
   out as much as possible.

5. **Set your camera exposure:** Get an exposure for the natural light in the *background* of your
   image. Depending on your lighting scenario, you may need to go darker in order to take some
   of the natural light off of your subjects, face so that the flash does most of the lighting.

6. **Set your white balance:** Your flash will be hitting your subject, so set your white balance to
   flash or 5600 Kelvin (depending on your flash).

7. **Set your flash:** I start with TTL here and then flip to manual and go brighter or darker
   depending on what I'd like my images to look like. You could also set your camera to manual
   and start at the mid-power level range, or use a light meter.

8. **Change the exposure:** Mess around with brightening or darkening your background using
   shutter speed. If you're not getting the look you'd like, change your other exposure settings
   and adjust the flash brighter or darker accordingly.

Shot by Shot

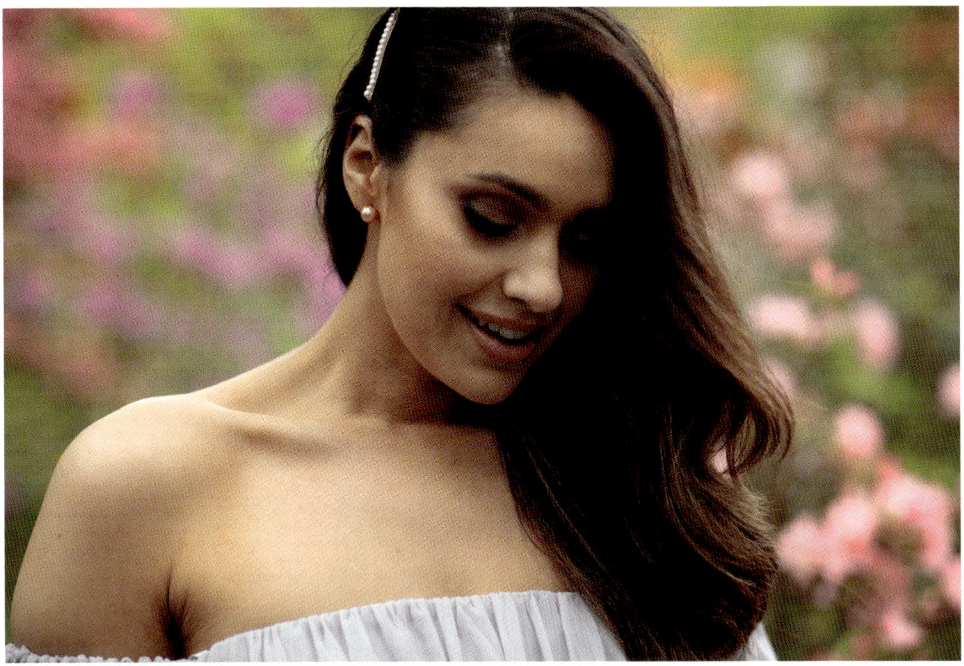

NATURAL LIGHT AND MISSED FOCUS, BUT THE POINT OF THIS PICTURE IS TO GET THE EXPOSURE I WANT ON THE BACK-GROUND SO, GOAL ACCOMPLISHED.
CANON 5DS R, CANON 85MM 1.4 IS, ISO 160, APERTURE 2.2, SHUTTER 1/200

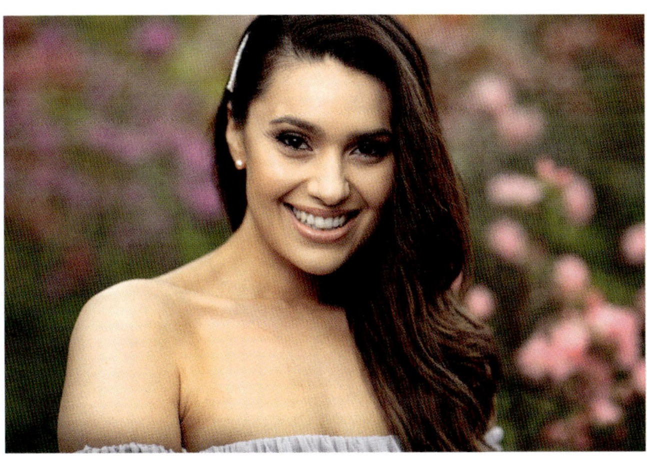
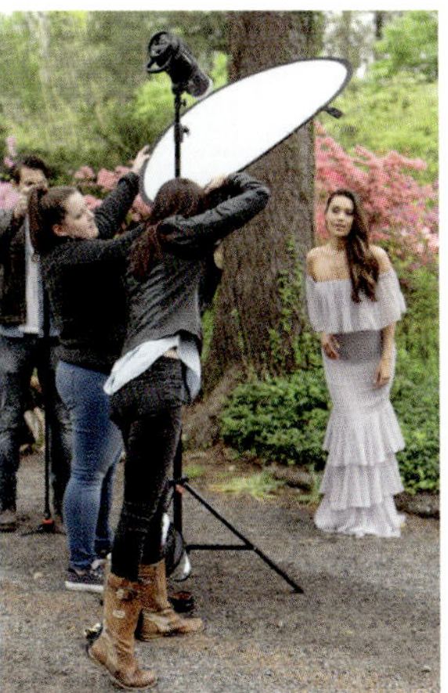

ADDING A PROFOTO B1 OCF SHOOTING THROUGH THE 42" WHITE DIFFUSER. I RAISED MY SHUTTER SPEED BECAUSE THE TOPS OF THE FLOWERS WERE BLOWING OUT IN THE BACKGROUND. YOU CAN SEE THE BEHIND-THE-SCENES SHOT IN THE IMAGE ON THE RIGHT.
CANON 5DS R, CANON 85MM 1.4 IS, ISO 160, APERTURE 2.2, SHUTTER 1/250.

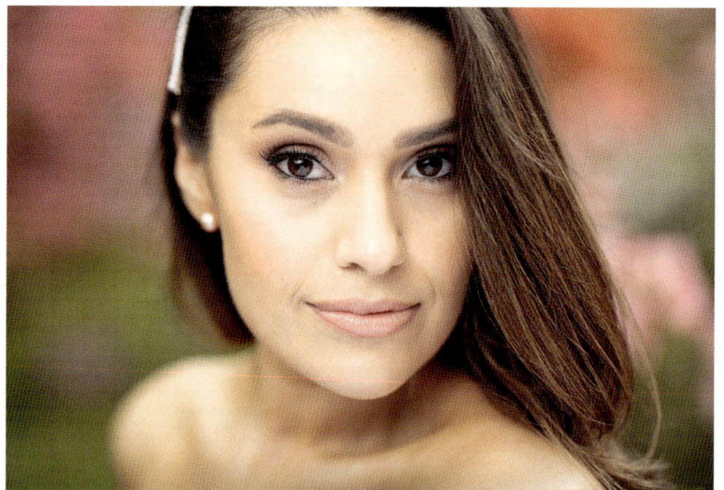

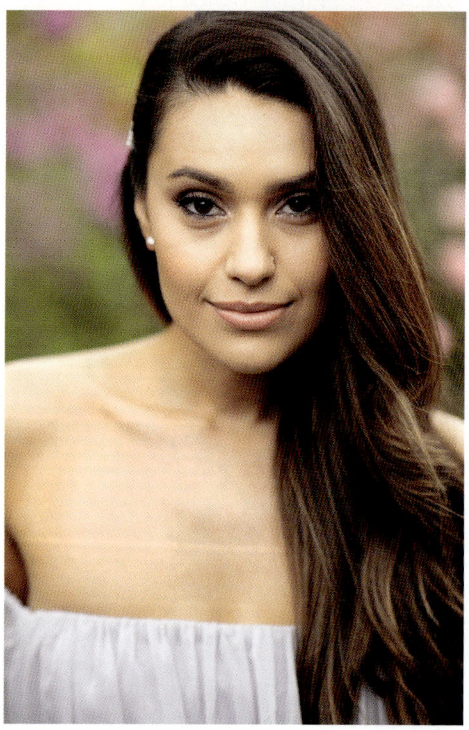

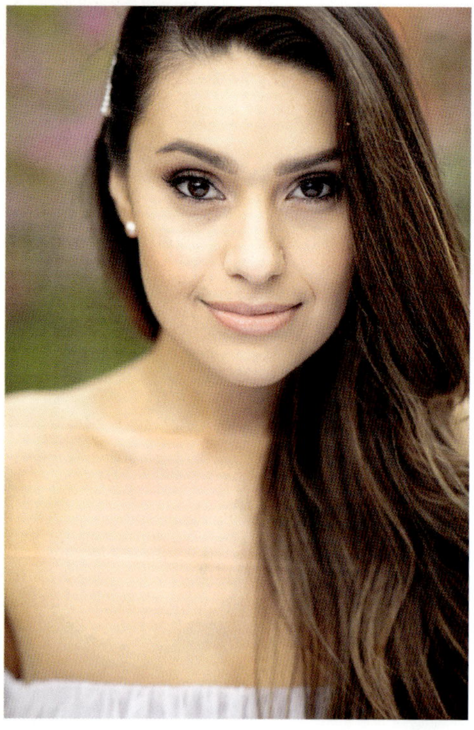

FIGURE 12.5

SIDE-BY-SIDE DIFFERENCE WITH AND WITHOUT HAVING THE REFLECTOR ON THE BOTTOM. IT MAKES A **HUGE** DIFFER-
ENCE IN FILLING IN UNDER-EYE SHADOWS!
SETTINGS THE SAME FOR BOTH IMAGES: CANON 5DS R, CANON 85MM 1.4 IS, ISO 250, APERTURE 2.2, SHUTTER 1/250

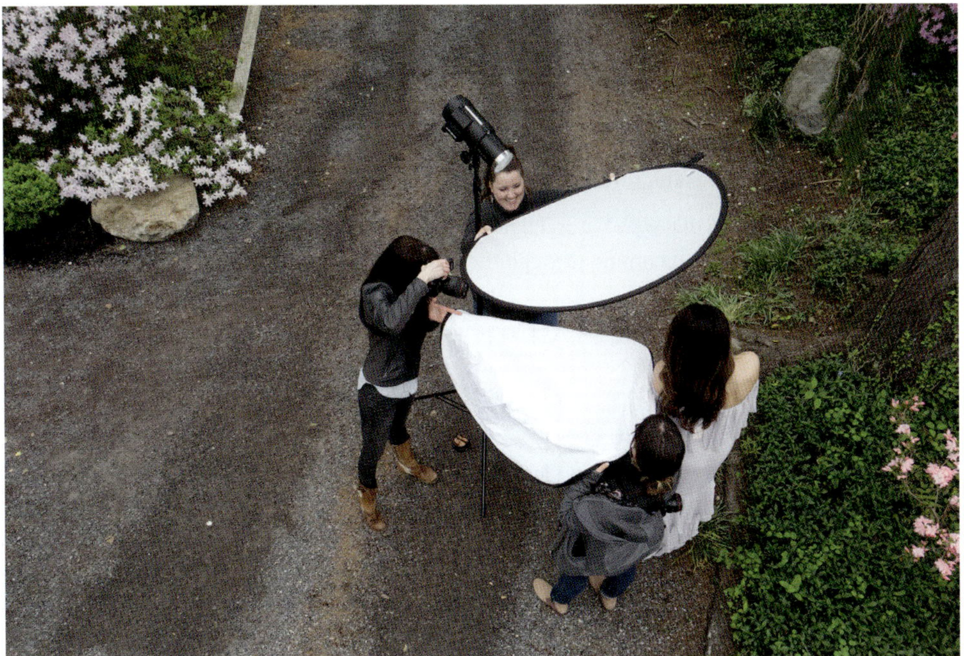

Potential Problems

The key to getting a nice soft light in this method is getting your light source to be as big as possible. To do that you need your flash hitting the entire diffuser that you're using. If you think that the light looks too harsh, fire a test shot while looking at the flash hitting the diffuser. If it's not hitting the entire diffuser, and instead maybe just hitting the middle, back your flash up off of the diffuser. If you're using a speedlight, adjust your zoom to be as wide as possible.

Balancing the look of the light can be tricky as well. If you find yourself looking at the image and thinking it looks too "flashy," try changing your exposure so that the flash power goes down and a bit more of the natural light peeks into the image. You are, in a way, using this technique to intentionally fill flash the image, so you may need to play around with it a bit in order to get the look that you're going for.

Practical Uses

This is a great trick to use when you're photographing headshots or portraits outside. It's essentially a clamshell setup, but with a lot less equipment and an inexpensive light modifier that's serving two purposes instead of one. You could do this with a couple as well, just adjust your positioning so that they are a bit further away from the lights so that they fit in your frame.

As a side note, you can do this with natural light as well. See the shots below I did with the exact same setup, just using the sun coming through the diffuser instead of the flash.

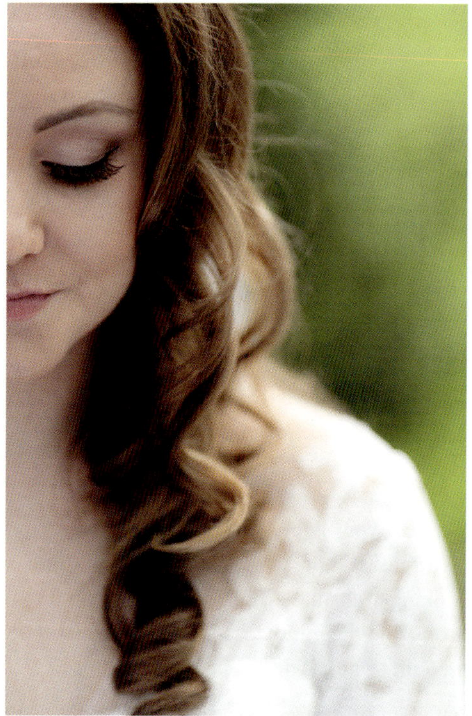
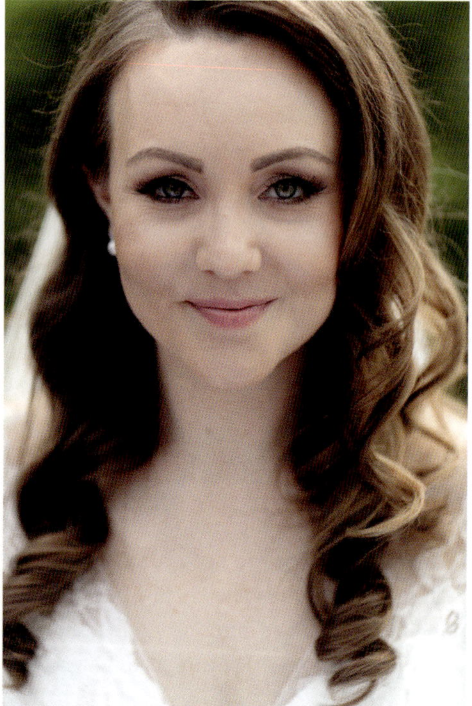

NATURAL LIGHT—NO FLASH USED, JUST THE SAME REFLECTOR SETUP.
SETTINGS THE SAME FOR BOTH: CANON 1DX II, CANON 135MM 2.0, ISO 250, APERTURE 2, SHUTTER 1/400

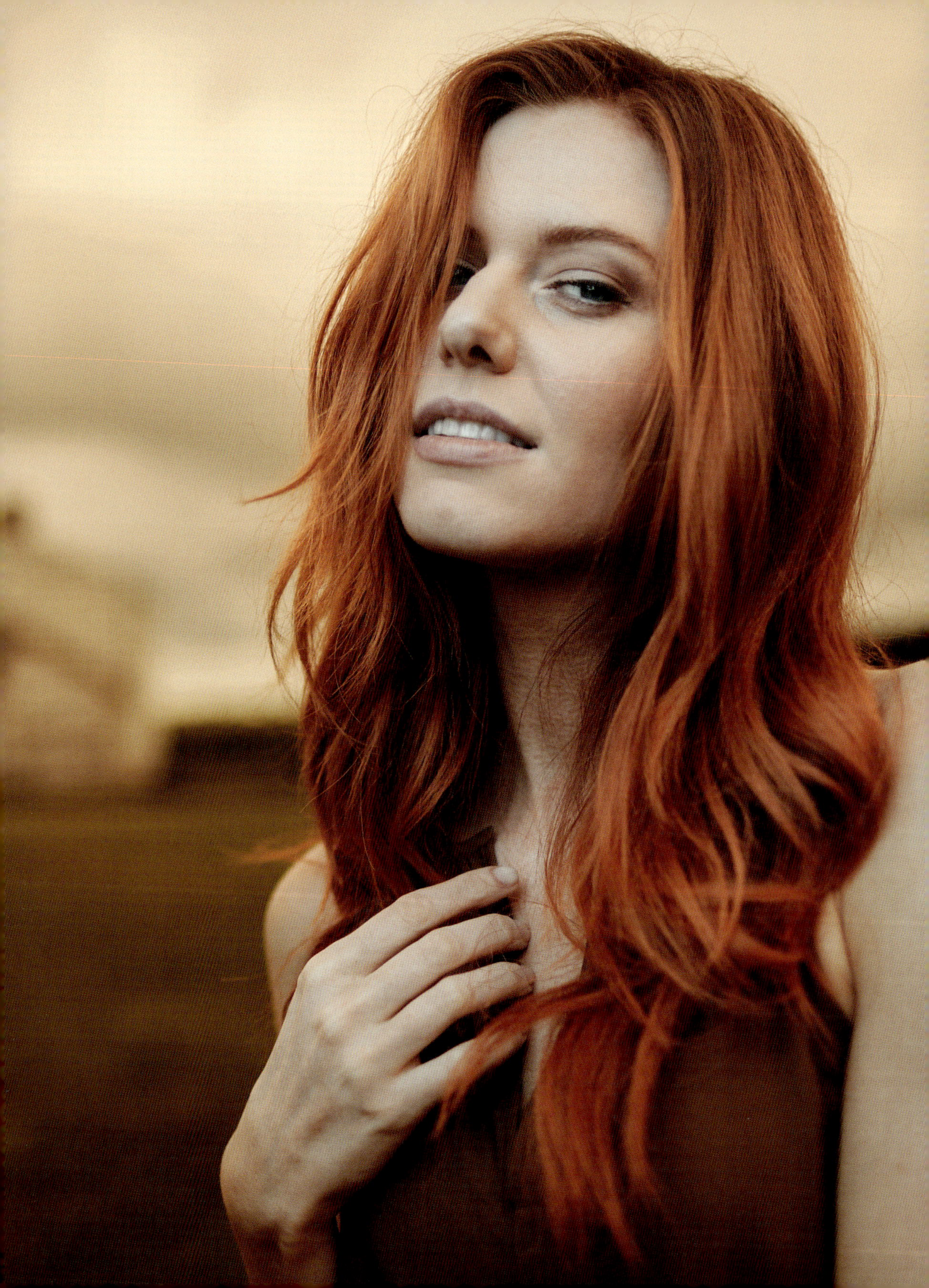

SCENARIO 13

Warming Up the Sky

Create a gorgeous, warm sky completely in-camera.

GOAL IMAGE

One of the current photography (or should I say editing) trends is to have a crazy warm image, void of blues and greens. It creates a dreamy feel, but when you look closely, or in comparison to true color, this technique makes the subject very orange. It's a bit unnatural and reminds me of my fellow New Jersians' extreme fake tanning habits. I'm going to show you how to create a similar warm-world feel without affecting skin tones.

This lighting technique is the exact opposite of Scenario 3, "Creating Twilight." The color theory is similar, but it's used in the opposite way. In creating twilight, you use an orange gel on skin tones so that you could lower your white balance to make the sky blue. With the method in this scenario, you'll use a blue gel to balance skin tones as you raise your white balance to make the sky orange/yellow.

GEAR NEEDED:

- Camera + Trigger
- Lens of any focal length
- Off-camera flash
- Full CTB gel
- Light stand
- Light-softening modifier *(optional)*
- Reflector *(optional)*

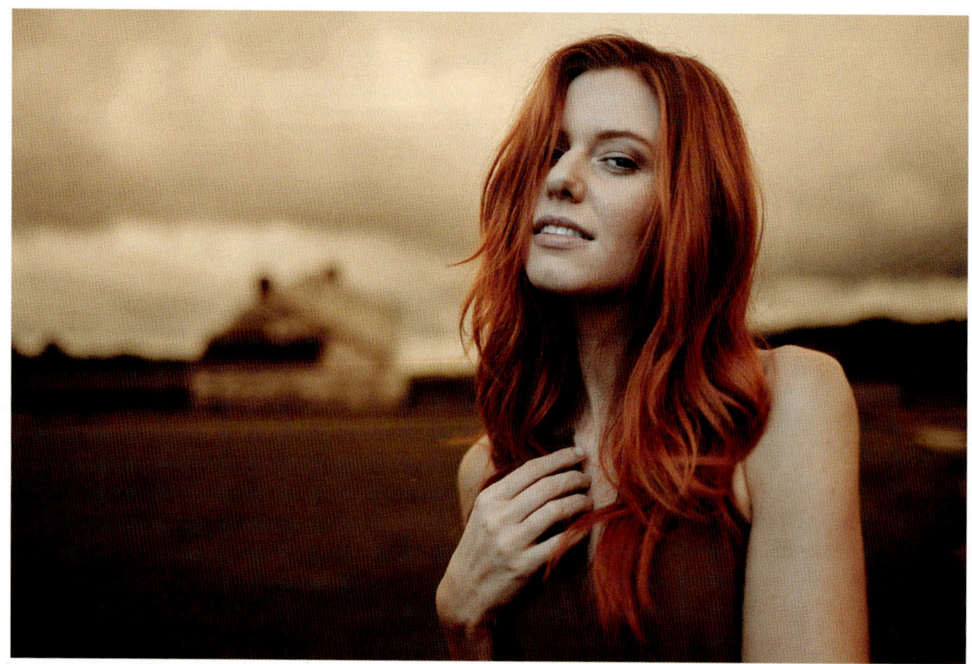

GOAL IMAGE. THIS IMAGE WAS EDITED IN CAPTURE ONE TO ADD MORE WARMTH SINCE I WAS MAXED OUT AT 10,000 KELVIN ON MY CAMERA. THE STRAIGHT-OUT-OF-CAMERA IMAGE IS **FIGURE 13.7**.
CANON 1DX II, CANON 35MM 1.4, ISO 200, APERTURE 1.8, SHUTTER 1/8000

If you execute this shot when the sun is lower in the sky, it'll be easier on you and your light. It will be very easy to use a speedlight since you won't have bright sun to compete with. You can make this concept work in the middle of the day if you want to, but these images really come to life with a slightly darker sky or, if you're fortunate enough, a cloudy sky.

This is another case of opposite day in the photo world. If you want a warm sky, then you actually need a Color Temperature Blue (CTB) gel to make it work. Why? Because it's easier to light the subject than the entire sky.

If you wanted to "warm up" a photograph, you would turn up your white balance to a higher temperature. Once you do that, however, the way your subjects look will also warm up. They'll become what I lovingly call "Jersey Orange," a magical mix of spray-tan and fake-baking that you can only find in the Garden State. If you actually photograph Jersey people, the last thing you need is to make them more orange! Typically I'm trying to find a way to desaturate and brighten orange and red skin tones. I even have a Photoshop action I created called "De-Jersey Skin." (I'm NJ born and raised, and totally guilty of fake-baking in the past, so I can poke a little fun here.)

To balance out the color on your subject, you need to add the opposite color light. The opposite of yellow is blue, so use a Color Temperature Blue gel (CTB). Light your subject with that, and voila! They're back to regular non-Jersey skin tones.

The last thing you need to choose is the light modifier (or choosing not to have one so your light will appear more direct and harsh). I prefer my photos to have a more subtle light on my subject so I use either a beauty dish or a softbox. However, I have used a grid if I need to position my light far away from my subject like I did in the first photo of this chapter. It's all relative to what you're trying to accomplish.

Step by Step

1. **Position your subjects:** Attempt to place your subjects against the darker side of the sky. It will have more saturation in it, and the effect will appear more successful because you'll be able to see the color shift more distinctly.

2. **Choose a lens:** Lens choice is up to you and your photographic preferences. Choose a lens that will enable you to show some background so that you can see what it is that you're essentially changing. Keep in mind this doesn't have to be the sky. You can warm up trees, buildings, or anything else.

3. **Put modifiers on the light:** Put on a full CTB gel. I usually won't go more blue than that because the image starts looking too unrealistic, but you are welcome to stack a second gel if you'd like. Add the light modifier of your choice and you're set. Keep in mind that the more modifiers you use, the more power you'll need coming out of your light to affect the image.

4. **Position the light:** Let's try something different than the rest of the scenarios for this one. Place your light about 9 feet above your subject, just to the right or left of you. It'll mimic more of a "sun overhead" look.

5. **Set the camera exposure:** Set your camera exposure as though you're taking a landscape photo of the background. Keep your depth of field preferences in mind and try to get your ISO as low as possible for a clean image.

6. **Set your white balance:** Because the flash is your main source of light, and you've covered it with a full CTB gel, set your WB to about 8000 Kelvin depending on the original color temperature of your light.

7. **Set the flash power:** I suggest starting off with your flash power set TTL, then switching to manual and adjusting if you need more or less power. If you're using a manual flash, start in the medium-low power range, or use a light meter and adjust up or down to your liking. Take a test shot and adjust your light to be more or less powerful according to your taste.

8. **Look at your colors and histogram:** This is where you'll play with just how orange you want your sky to be. If you want it to be warmer, then raise your Kelvin temperature and you may need to add more blue gels onto your light. If you want to cool it down, then lower your Kelvin temperature and you may need to go down to a half CTB gel.

OPTIONAL: Add a reflector to fill in shadows.

Shot by Shot

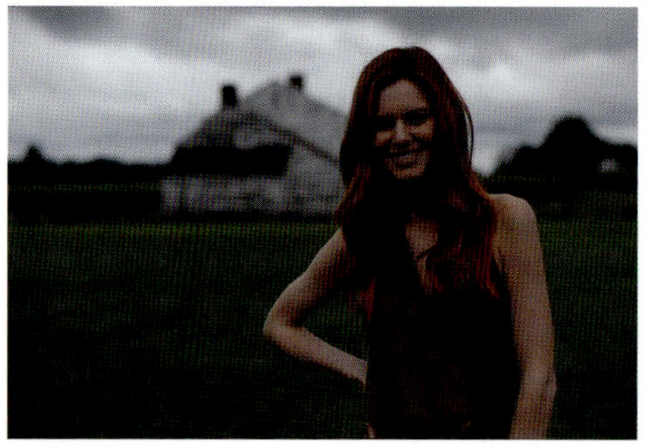

FIGURE 13.2

NATURAL LIGHT SHOT TO GET THE BACKGROUND BASE EXPOSURE.

CANON 1DX II, CANON 50MM 1.2, ISO 100, APERTURE 2.2, SHUTTER 1/3200

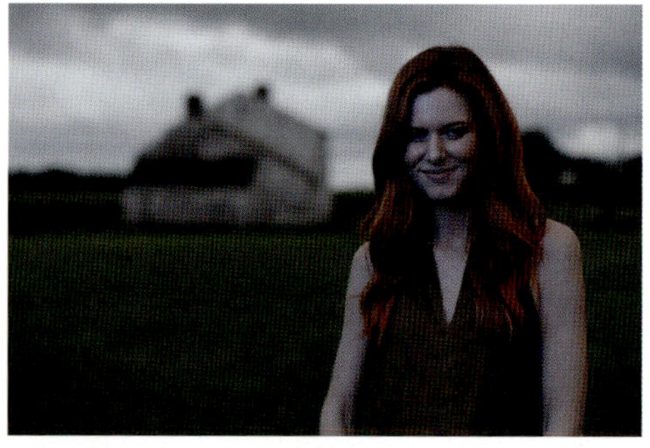

FIGURE 13.3

SHOT WITH A PROFOTO B1 OCF WITH BLUE GEL AND PRO-FOTO MEDIUM UMBRELLA.

CANON 1DX II, CANON 50MM 1.2, ISO 100, APERTURE 2.2, SHUTTER 1/3200

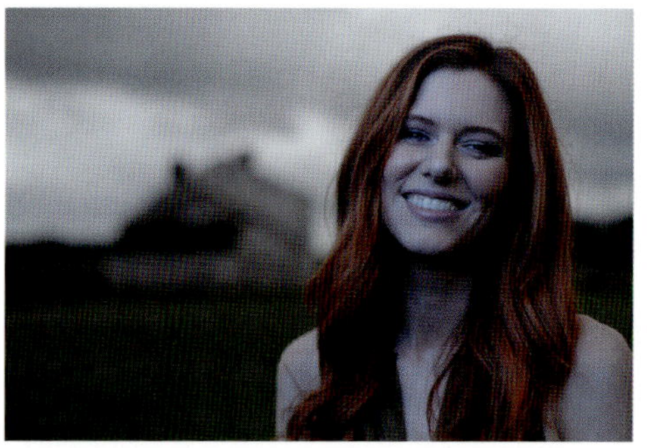

FIGURE 13.4

MY LIGHT WAS AT MAX POWER, SO I RAISED MY ISO TO MAKE THE ENTIRE IMAGE BRIGHT AND THEN RAISED MY SHUTTER SPEED TO MAKE THE BACKGROUND DARKER.

CANON 1DX II, CANON 50MM 1.2, ISO 250, APERTURE 2.2, SHUTTER 1/8000

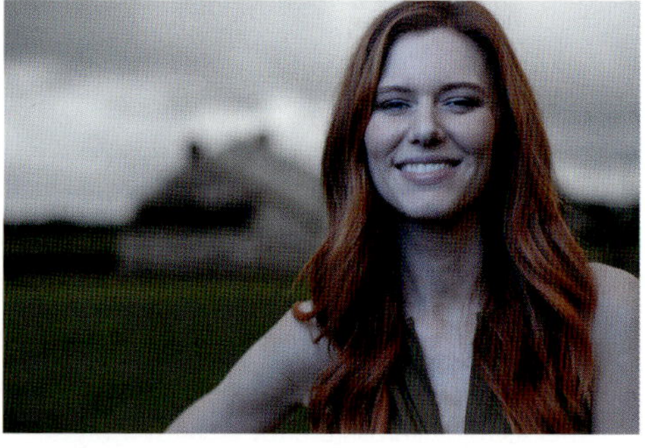

FIGURE 13.5

I NEEDED A LITTLE MORE LIGHT SO I RAISED MY ISO AGAIN.

CANON 1DX II, CANON 50MM 1.2, ISO 320, APERTURE 2.2, SHUTTER 1/8000

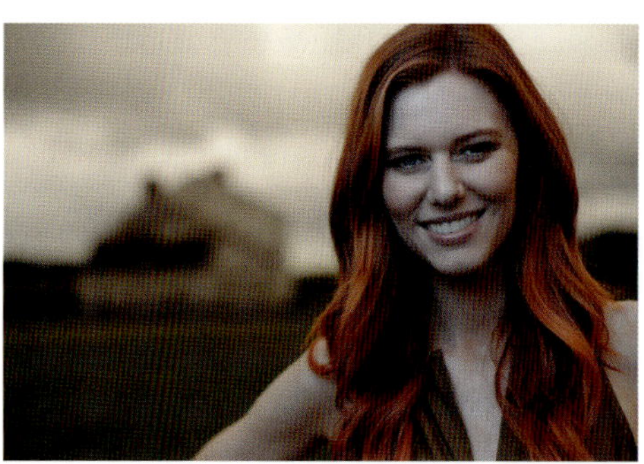

FIGURE 13.6

I WARMED UP MY WHITE BALANCE ALL THE WAY TO 10000K.

CANON 1DX II, CANON 50MM 1.2, ISO 320, APERTURE 2.2, SHUTTER 1/8000

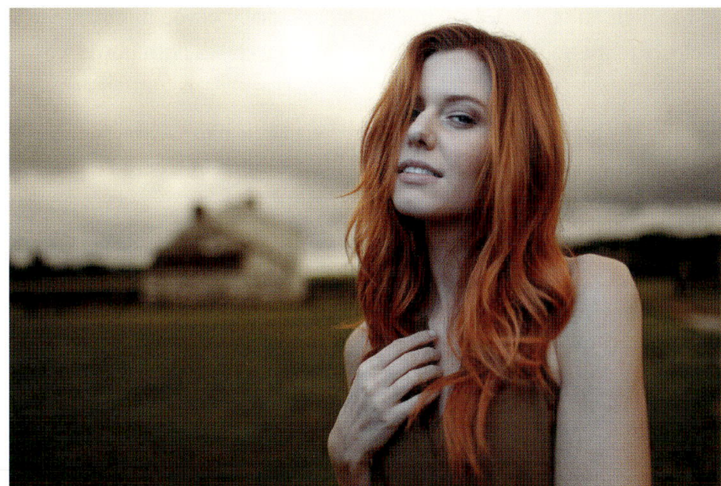

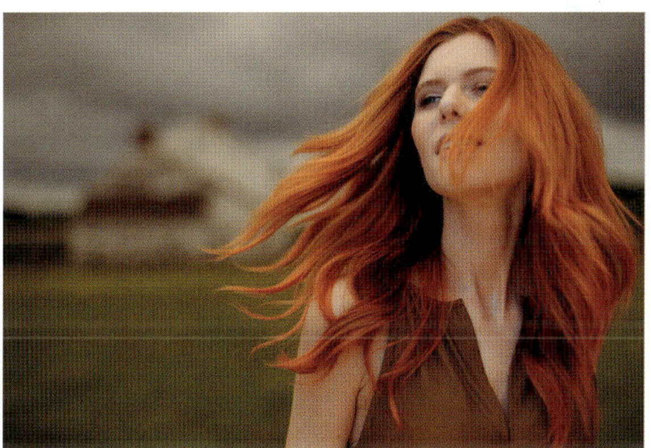

FIGURE 13.8
SHOT WITH AN ADDED REFLECTOR TO FILL IN SHADOWS.
I LOWERED THE ISO TO DARKEN THE ENTIRE PHOTO.
CANON 1DX II, CANON 50MM 1.2, ISO 125, APERTURE 1.8,
SHUTTER 1/8000

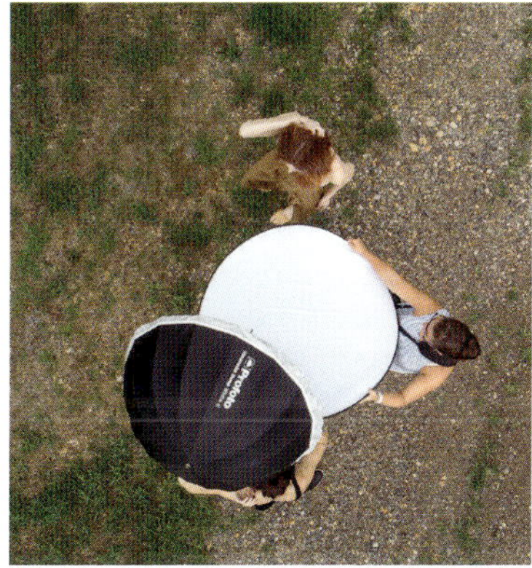

FIGURE 13.9
BEHIND THE SCENES.

Potential Problems

Anything in the photo that's not lit by your CTB light will turn orange. You might like this, but you might not, so keep your background in mind, especially if it includes any dead giveaways that the shot isn't "real" (e.g., a red stop sign that now looks orange).

Check your histogram for lighting! I can't emphasize this enough. Do not trust the back of your camera for an accurate reading of your exposure!

If the power of your flash is too high, the CTB gel will not saturate as nicely as you might like or need. Try moving the light closer to the subject so that you don't need as much flash power to affect the image.

Sometimes you'll want a warmer sky but can't go any higher on your white balance. In this case you'll have to do it in post-processing, so plan for that when you're shooting. You could try putting a warming filter over your lens as another alternative.

Finally, remember to check your histogram for lighting! I can't emphasize this enough. Do not trust the back of your camera!

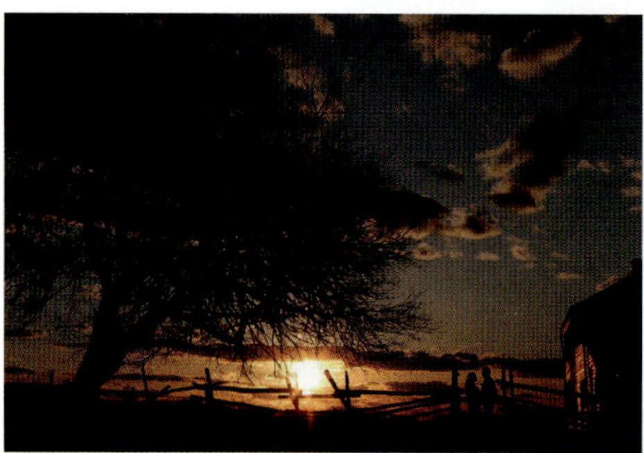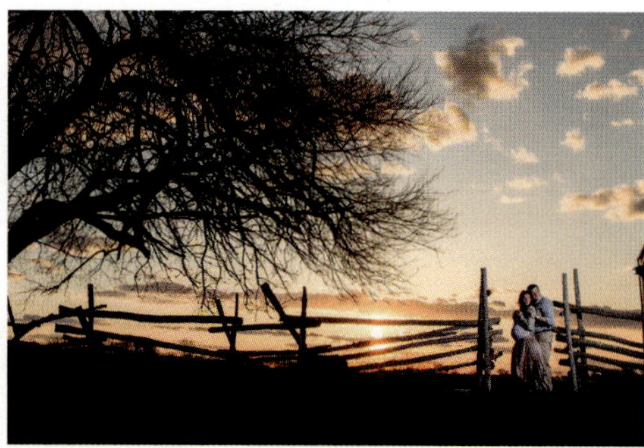

FIGURE 13.10
THIS IS ANOTHER EXAMPLE OF NATURAL LIGHT (LEFT) WITH NORMAL WHITE BALANCE VERSUS THE SAME SCENE LIT WITH A BLUE GEL AND WARMED UP (RIGHT).
NATURAL LIGHT SHOT: CANON 1DX, CANON 50MM 1.2, ISO 100, APERTURE 16, SHUTTER 1/250
SHOT WITH FLASH: PROFOTO B2 WITH GRID AND A CTB GEL AND A WARMED-UP WHITE BALANCE. CANON 1DX, CANON 50MM 1.2, ISO 100, APERTURE 14, SHUTTER 1/250.

Practical Uses

This is a fun lighting method for creating something otherworldly. You can also use it to maintain consistency with your warmly colored images, even when your background is anything but. I like using this technique for hero images (my main images that I use in my portfolio) that I know will be jaw-dropping for the client to see and print. It's always a goal of mine to have a few "wow" images that are outside of the imagination of my clients—pictures that don't look like the natural light we were shooting in. It amazes my clients and gives them something they wouldn't be able to mimic on their own. It validates why they hired me and leaves them excited about the photos. It also keeps me inspired to create something different. With the shoot for this book I got super creative and went outside my brand, and I loved it! Sometimes shooting is just for you.

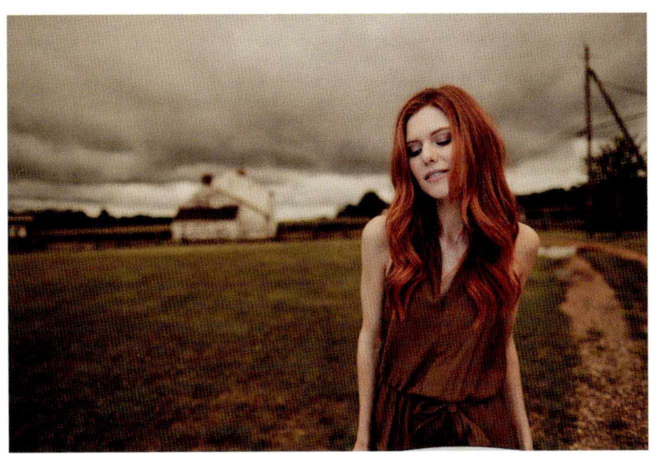

FIGURE 13.11

CANON 1DX II, CANON 24MM 1.4, ISO 125, APERTURE 1.8, SHUTTER 1/8000

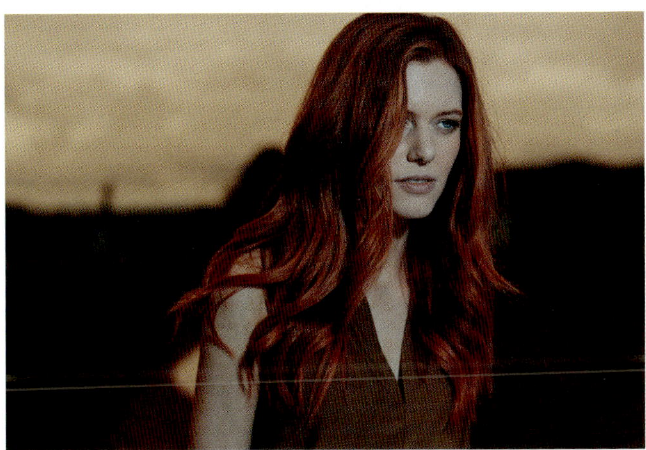

FIGURE 13.12

CANON 1DX II, CANON 50MM 1.2, ISO 125, APERTURE 2.5, SHUTTER 1/8000

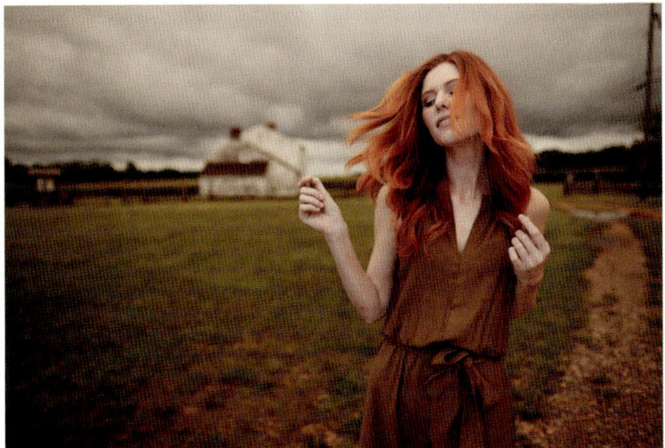

FIGURE 13.13

CANON 1DX II, CANON 24MM 1.4, ISO 125, APERTURE 1.8, SHUTTER 1/8000

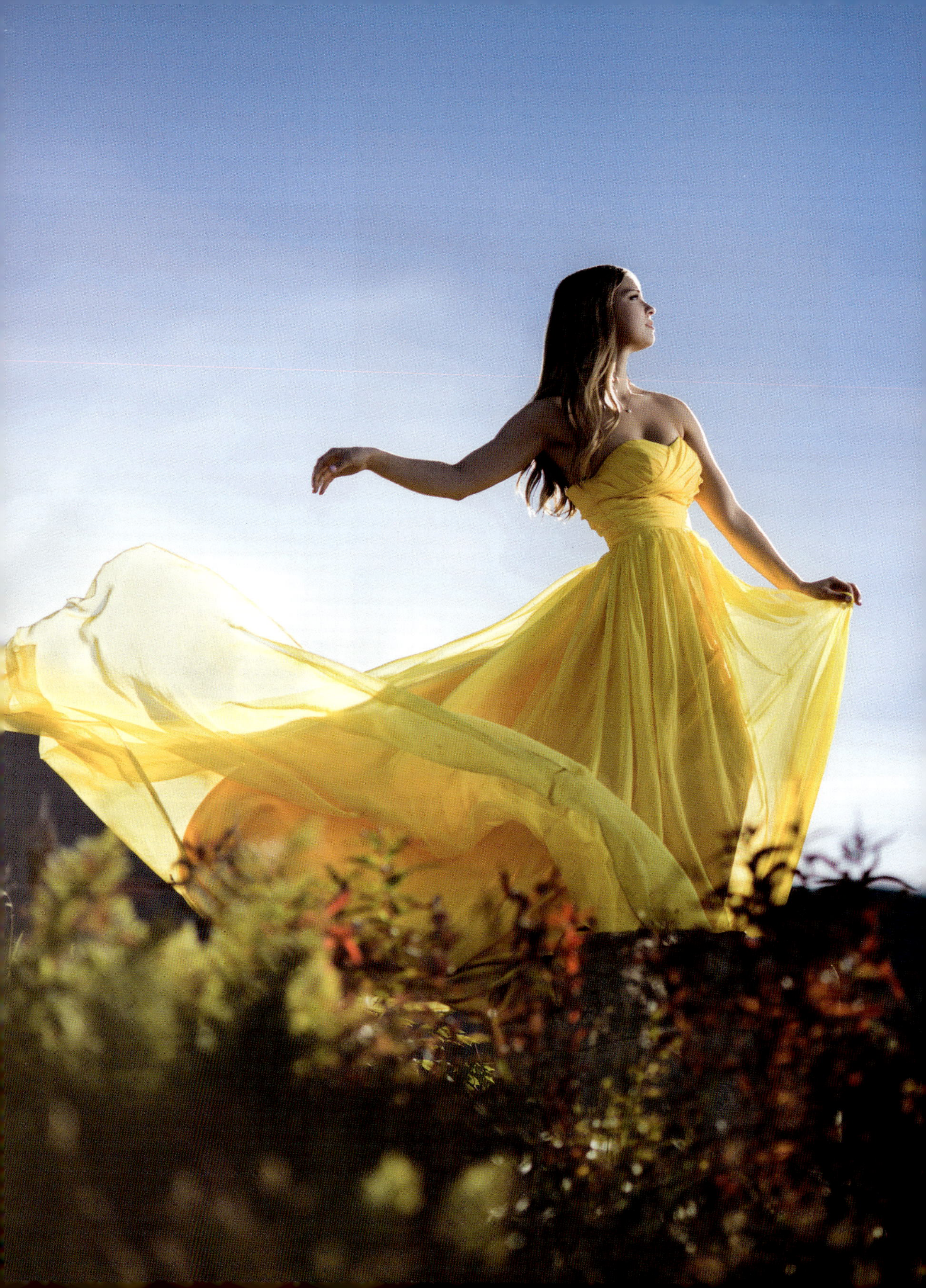

SCENARIO 14

Keeping a Blue Sky

How to show off a beautiful blue sky when you have it.

GOAL IMAGE

While natural light produces some beautiful imagery, it can often result in a blown-out white sky on a beautifully blue-sky kind of day. Depending on your style, you might like one over the other. Personally, I'm a big fan of complimentary colors, so when I saw this beautiful yellow dress in the example image, I just had to put it up against the bright blue sky we were under (**Figure 14.1**).

To avoid making an image like this look "flashy," you need to position your light to be facing the same direction as the sun. Think of molding the existing light with your off-camera flash rather than trying to fight it. Think about how you'd create this look with natural light, and copy the light position. With natural light, the easiest option for taking this photo is with the sun at your back. The light would ideally be low in the sky and perhaps lighting your subject slightly from the side.

GEAR NEEDED:

- Camera + Trigger
- Lens of any focal length that'll let you see the sky in your shot
- Off-camera flash
- Light modifier (such as a 2x3 softbox)
- Light stand
- ND filter *(optional)*
- Half CTO gel *(optional)*

Step by Step

1. **Position your subject:** Find the bluest part of the sky to position your subject against. The sun won't be in the picture, because you're pretending your flash is the sun. I like finding a spot for my subject to be higher up so I can shoot up toward the person to show more of the sky.

2. **Position the light:** You'll have to get your light pretty close to your subject here. You're essentially fighting the power of the sun, so the closer your light is to your subject the better. Place the light to be shining in the same direction as the sun, opposite of wherever you see the shadows falling on the ground.

3. **Set the camera exposure:** Set your camera as though you were just taking a photo of the background and that beautiful blue sky. If you like a lot of depth of field in your image and don't mind using a higher f-stop, keep your shutter speed below your camera's sync speed (1/250 or so) so you don't have to put your flash into High Speed Sync. HSS will use up a lot of extra battery power and won't be as bright. Personally I like a more shallow depth of field in my images, so I tend to go into HSS and keep my battery usage in mind.

   Alternatively, you can use a neutral density (ND) filter to darken the image, making it possible to use a lower f-stop for a shallower depth-of-field look. These filters darken the entire image so you don't have to darken the image using your exposure.

4. **Set the white balance:** The flash is the main source of light hitting your subject, so set your WB to flash or 5600 Kelvin depending on the color temperature of your light.

5. **Set the flash:** I typically find TTL works really well in this scenario because it's fairly straightforward. If you're using a manual flash, start at the highest power setting or use a light meter and adjust down to your liking. Either way, take a test shot and adjust your light to be more or less powerful to correctly expose your subject.

6. **Make adjustments:** Once you have a solid image, feel free to change your exposure, white balance, or flash settings. If you want the entire image to be dark, adjust your ISO or aperture. If you just want to darken or lighten the background/sky, adjust your shutter speed. Be sure

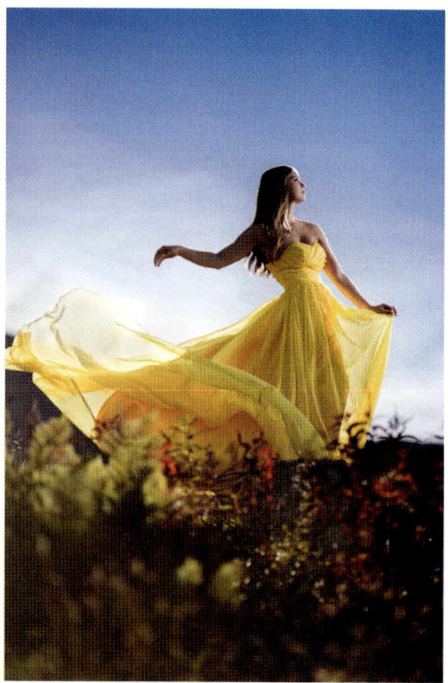

FIGURE 14.1

GOAL IMAGE. SHOT WITH A PROFOTO CANON AIR REMOTE, PROFOTO B10, AND A PROFOTO 2X3 OCF SOFTBOX. SEE FIGURE 14.5 FOR THE STRAIGHT-OUT-OF-CAMERA IMAGE.
CANON 1DX MARKII, CANON 135MM 2.0, ISO: 125, APERTURE: 2, SHUTTER: 1/4000, WB: 5600K

to only change one thing at a time so you don't get too far from what was working originally and can't get back.

OPTIONAL: Put a half CTO gel on your light and change your white balance to roughly 4000K. This will let you blue the sky and background even more to show it off while keeping a normal color on your subject. Be careful not to make it look unnatural if that's not what you're going for.

Shot by Shot

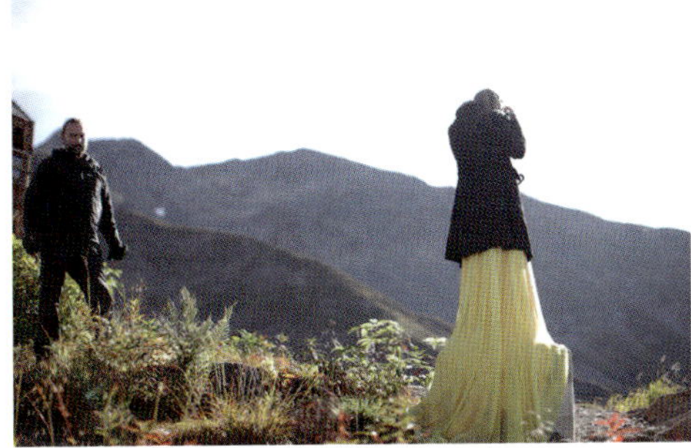

FIGURE 14.2
NATURAL LIGHT SHOT TO EXPOSE FOR THE SUBJECT.
CANON 1DX MARK II, CANON 50MM 1.2, ISO 50,
APERTURE 1.8, SHUTTER 1/1000

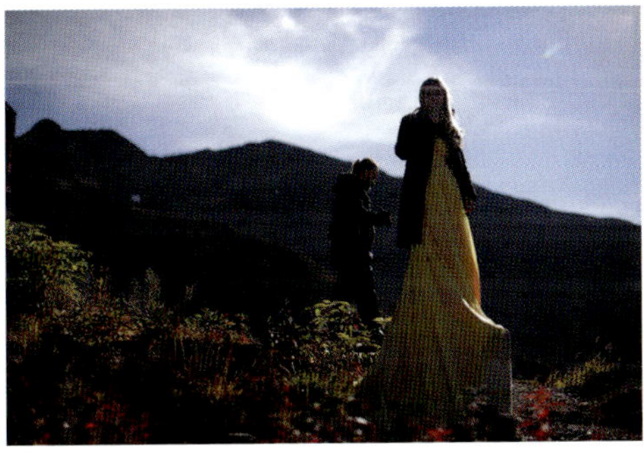

FIGURE 14.3
NATURAL LIGHT SHOT EXPOSING FOR THE SKY.
CANON 1DX MARK II, CANON 50MM 1.2, ISO 50,
APERTURE 1.8, SHUTTER 1/4000

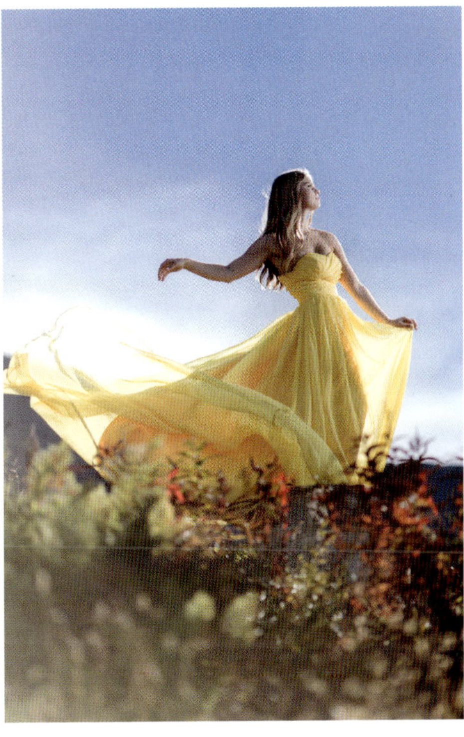

FIGURE 14.4
I CHANGED LENSES AND RAISED THE ISO TO ADJUST
FOR THE APERTURE DIFFERENCE BETWEEN THE LENSES.
SHOT WITH A PROFOTO CANON AIR REMOTE, PROFOTO
B10, AND A PROFOTO 2X3 OCF SOFTBOX
CANON 1DX MARK II, CANON 135MM 2.0, ISO 125,
APERTURE 2, SHUTTER 1/4000, WB 5600K

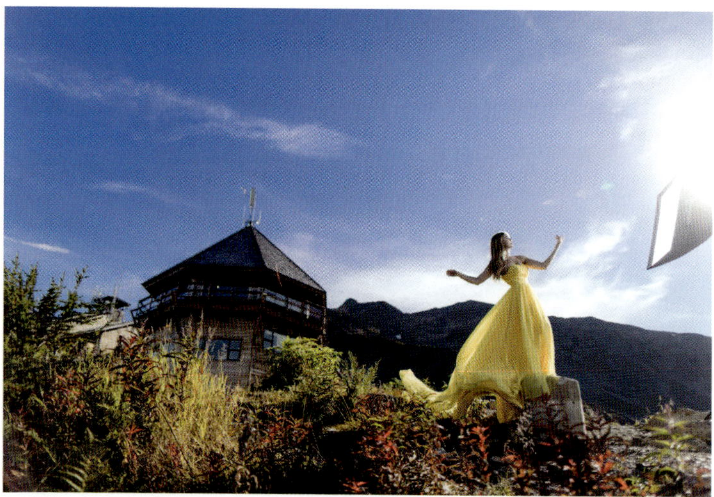

FIGURE 14.5

LIGHTING SETUP: BEHIND THE SCENES WITH OCF. USING A PROFOTO CANON AIR REMOTE, PROFOTO B10, AND A PROFOTO 2X3 OCF SOFTBOX.
CANON 1DX MARK II, CANON 50MM 1.2, ISO 50, APERTURE 1.8, SHUTTER 1/4000

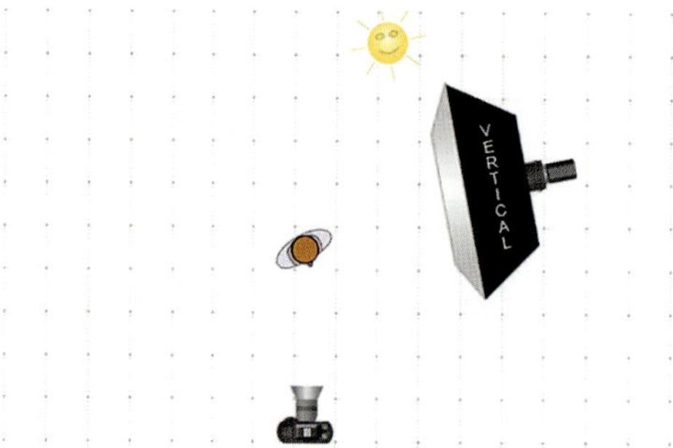

FIGURE 14.6

LIGHTING DIAGRAM.

Potential Problems

A shot like this is going to use all the power in your flash. I recommend using a more powerful strobe with 250 watt seconds or higher, or you'll have a hard time getting the light to affect your exposure. If you only have speedlights at your disposal, use two, three, or even four of them all coming from the same direction to essentially create one more powerful light.

Practical Uses

This is a great technique to use on a shoot when you'd like to give your client multiple looks, or if you have an epic sky you're trying to show off. I've used this method on more than one occasion when a storm was coming or had just passed and there was a crazy, cloudy sky. Without off-camera flash there would be no way to properly expose both my subject and the sky in these scenarios.

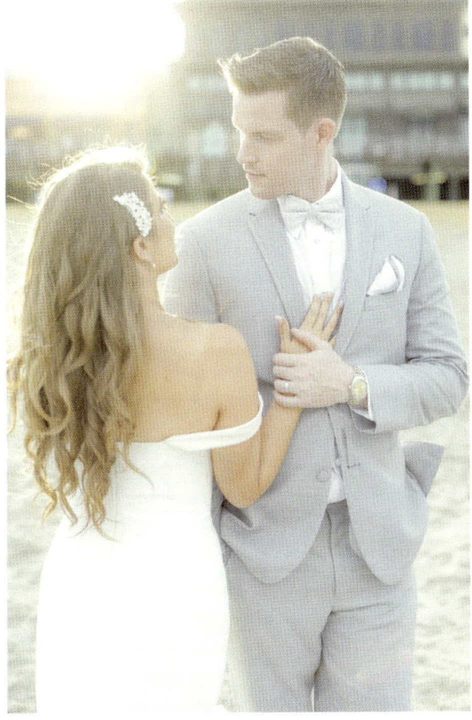

FIGURE 14.7
NATURAL LIGHT.
CANON 1DX MARK, CANON 50MM 1.2, ISO 320,
APERTURE 2.5, SHUTTER 1/400

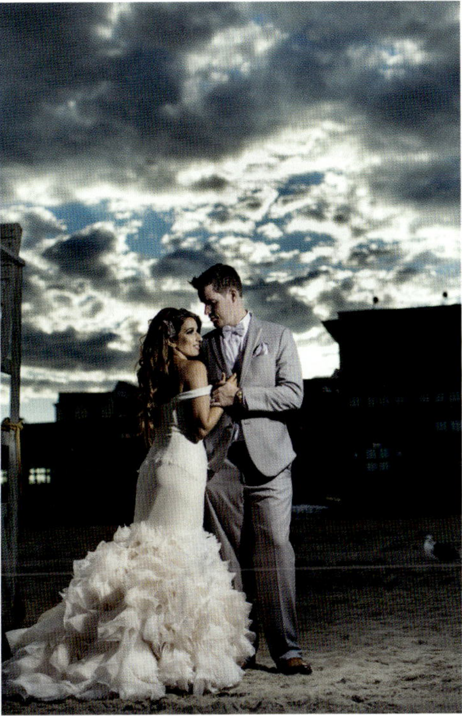

FIGURE 14.8
WITH FLASH SECONDS LATER.
CANON 1DX, CANON 50MM 1.2, ISO 320, APERTURE 2.8,
SHUTTER 1/6400

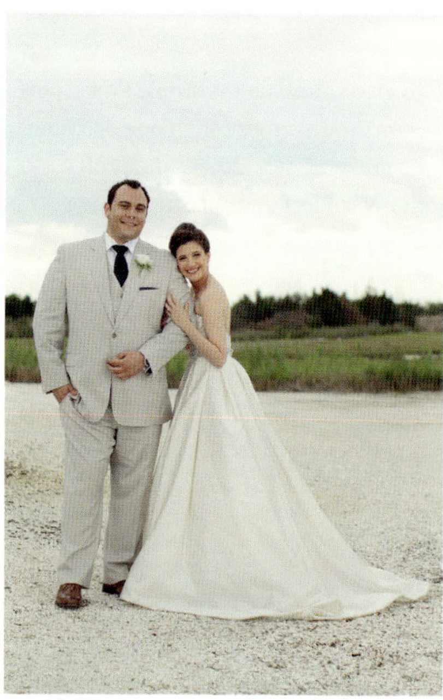

NATURAL LIGHT.
CANON 1D MARK IV, CANON
50MM 1.2, ISO 200, APER-
TURE 2.5, SHUTTER 1/200

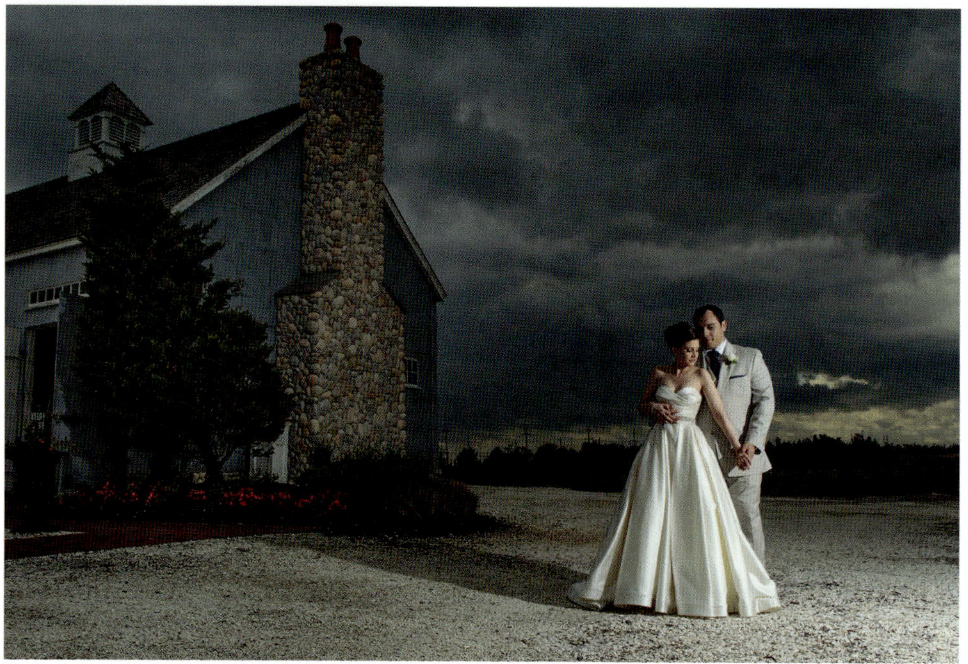

FIGURE 14.10

WITH FLASH SECONDS LATER.
CANON 1D MARK IV, CANON 24MM 1.4, ISO 200, APERTURE 10, SHUTTER 1/250

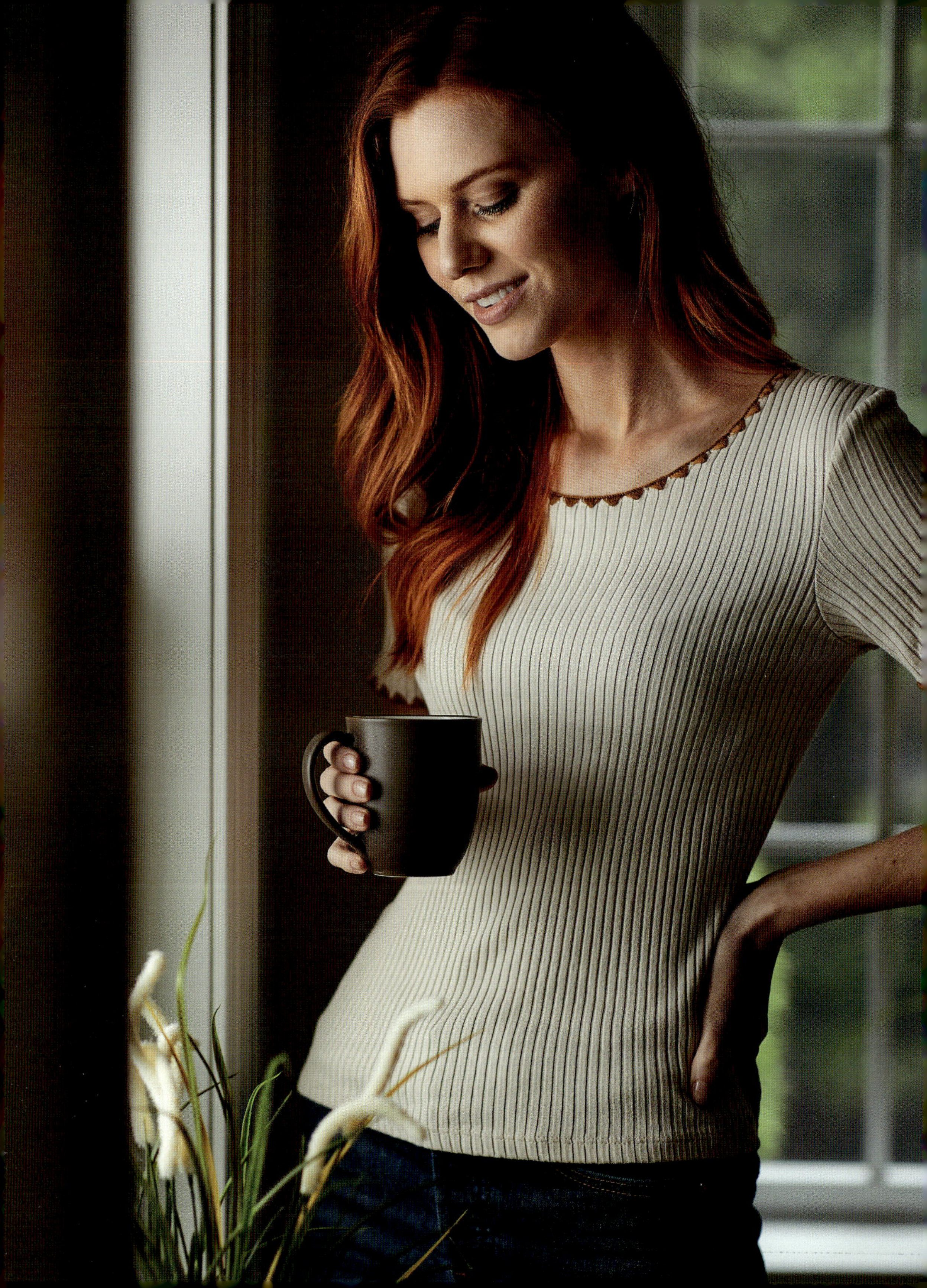

Light Like It's Coming Through a Window

In this shot, you can see how light seems to be pouring through the window.

GOAL IMAGE

This can be a pretty cool shot to get. It can be a dramatic, moody image, but it's very fun to do and it definitely wows your clients. One of my absolute favorite shots I've seen with this technique is by Susan Stripling from a wedding in the spring of 2019. It was every bit of grand and magical storytelling that any wedding photographer (and couple) would want in their images. It's posted on her Facebook page (www.facebook.com/SusanStripling Photography) on April 9, 2019, if you'd like to take a look.

GEAR NEEDED:

- Camera + Trigger
- Mid to wide focal length lens
- Off-camera flash
- Light stand *(optional)*
- Reflector *(optional)*
- Large modifier *(optional)*

For this technique, ideally you have a large window to work with; however, any size of window will do. The larger the window, the wider your OCF light spread has to be to cover the entire window from outside to mimic natural light. That means you may need to set your light up fairly far away from the window, resulting in a need for more power output. I recommend using a strobe over a speedlight for this technique; however, if you're shooting this in a low-light situation, a speedlight (or two) might have enough power to pull it off.

Step by Step

1. **Position your subject:** Place your subject in the path of where the light will fall through the window. I suggest directing their face toward the window so the light illuminates their face and eyes.

2. **Position the light:** Place the light outside the window as high as the middle of the window or above. Place it too low, and the effect won't look real since the sun doesn't light windows from the bottom up.

3. **Set the camera exposure:** Set your camera exposure as though you're taking a picture of the background. You have a choice to make: If you want the image to be more dramatic and the window light to contrast with the rest of the image, darken your exposure so the room gets darker. If you want soft window light, brighten your exposure so the flash will become more of an accent light rather than the only thing lighting the photo. Set your shutter speed to around $\frac{1}{160}$ of a second so you have room to raise or lower your shutter shutter speed to darken or lighten the natural light in the room without affecting your flash.

4. **Set the white balance:** Because the flash is your main source of light, set your white balance to flash or 5600 Kelvin depending on the original color temperature of your light.

5. **Set the flash power:** Set your flash power to TTL and take a test shot. Flip it to manual, holding that power setting, and adjust if necessary. If you're using a manual flash, start in the medium-high power range or use a light meter and adjust up or down to your liking. Take a test shot and adjust your light to be more or less powerful according to your taste.

OPTIONAL: Use a reflector close to your subject to fill in shadows and make the image less contrasty.

OPTIONAL: Put a large modifier on your light so that you add a layer of diffusion. Then you can move the light closer to the window. This will result in a softer light.

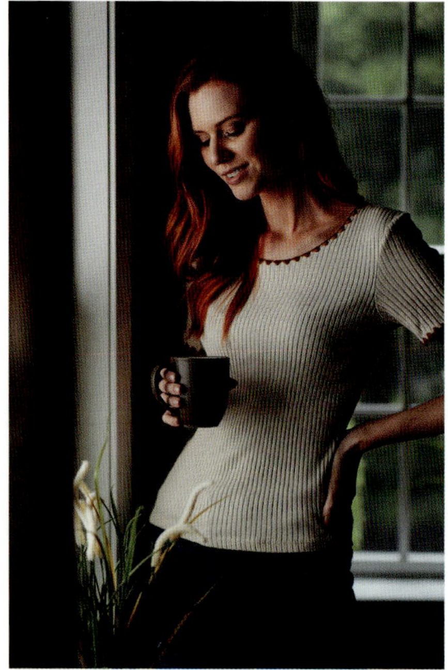

FIGURE 15.1
GOAL IMAGE.
CANON 1DXII, CANON 85MM 1.4 IS, ISO 160, APERTURE 2.2, SHUTTER 1/200

Shot by Shot

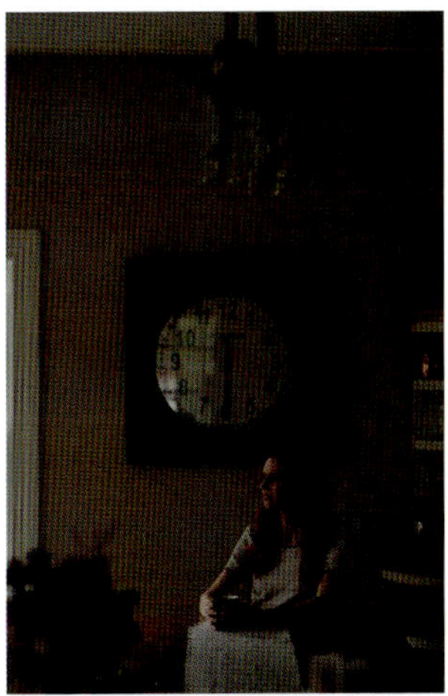

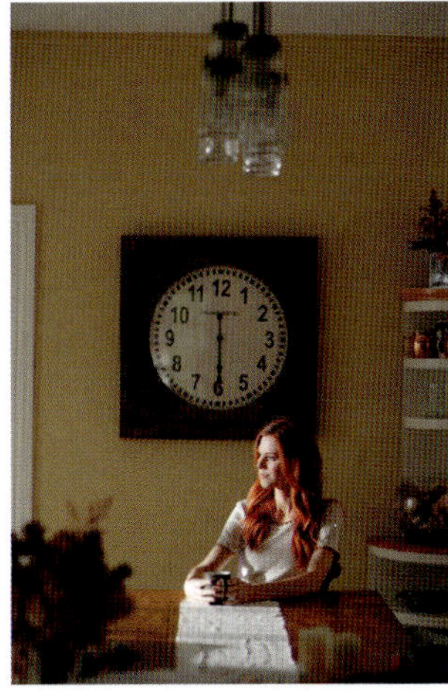

FIGURE 15.2 (LEFT)
NATURAL LIGHT INDOOR SHOT.
CANON 1DXII, CANON 85MM 1.4 IS,
ISO 500, APERTURE 2.2, SHUTTER 1/250

FIGURE 15.3 (RIGHT)
SHOT WITH ADDED OCF ON TTL:
PROFOTO B1 WITH NO MODIFIER BUT
THE LIGHT WAS TOO BRIGHT.
CANON 1DXII, CANON 85MM 1.4 IS,
ISO 500, APERTURE 2.2, SHUTTER 1/250

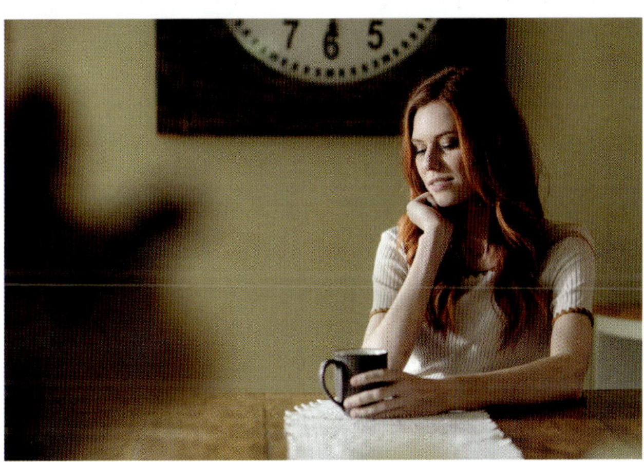

FIGURE 15.4
HERE I SWITCHED TO MANUAL,
LOWERED THE LIGHT POWER, AND
SHOT WITH A PROFOTO B1 WITH
NO MODIFIER.
CANON 1DXII, CANON 85MM 1.4 IS,
ISO 500, APERTURE 2.2, SHUTTER
1/250

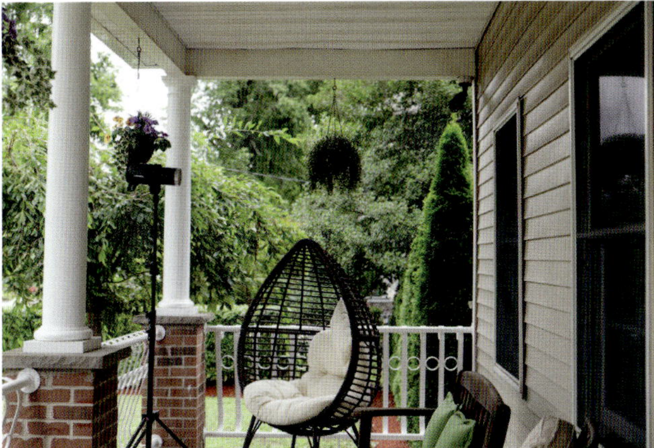

FIGURE 15.5
BEHIND THE SCENES: PLACEMENT OF
THE LIGHT OUTSIDE THE WINDOW.

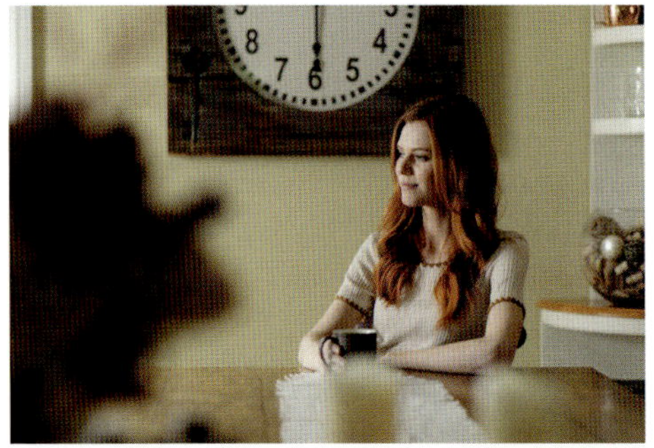

FIGURE 15.6

SHOT WITH A 2X3' SOFTBOX TO PROFOTO B1.
CANON 1DXII, CANON 85MM 1.4 IS, ISO 500, APERTURE 2.2,
SHUTTER 1/250

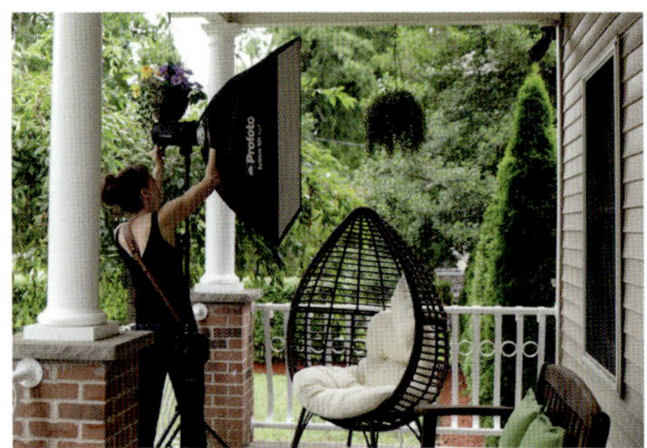

FIGURE 15.7

BEHIND THE SCENES: LIGHT WITH MODIFIER.

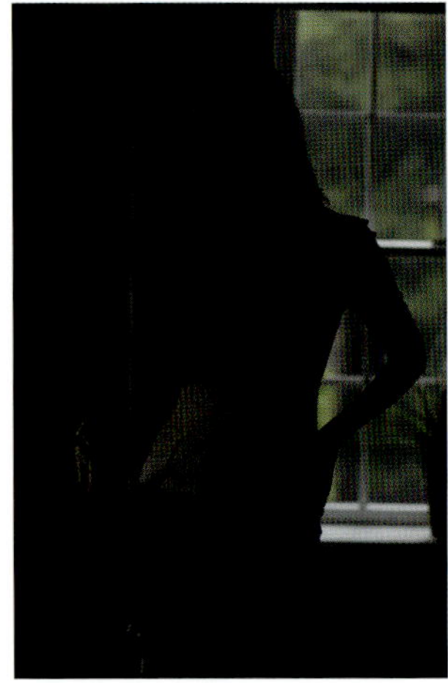

FIGURE 15.8

I MOVED THE MODEL RIGHT NEXT TO
THE WINDOW. NATURAL LIGHT SHOT.
CANON 1DXII, CANON 85MM 1.4 IS,
ISO 160, APERTURE 2.2, SHUTTER
1/200

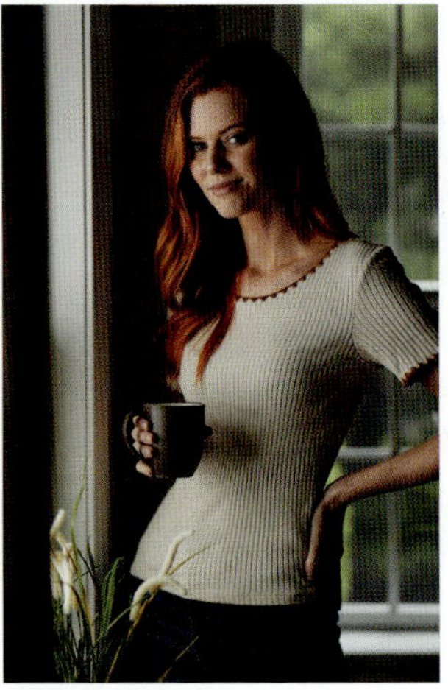

FIGURE 15.9

SHOT WITH AN ADDED PROFOTO B1 WITH 2X3 SOFTBOX RIGHT OUTSIDE
THE WINDOW.
CANON 1DXII, CANON 85MM 1.4 IS, ISO 160, APERTURE 2.2, SHUTTER 1/200

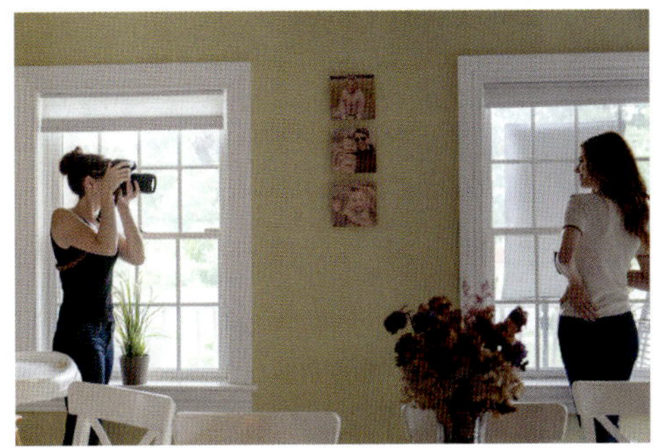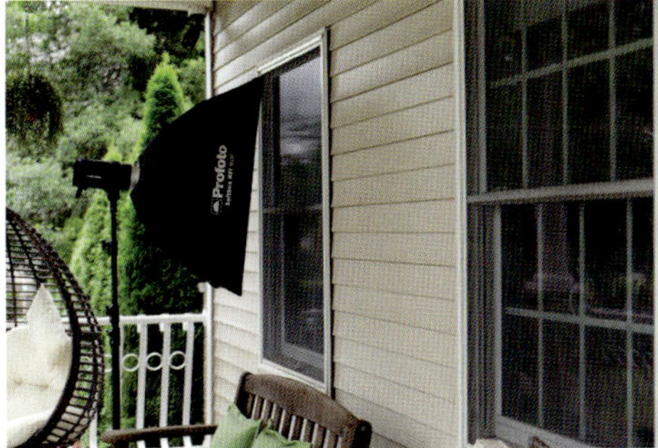

FIGURE 15.10

BEHIND THE SCENES: FAKING WINDOW LIGHT.

Potential Problems

The light inside the room that you're shooting into may have different colored lights than your window light. To remedy this, you can choose to gel your flash to color correct (see Scenario 25, "Using Gels to Color Correct"). You also have the option of turning the lights off manually, or by getting a black exposure before starting.

Practical Uses

This technique is great for rainy days when you can't bring your subjects outside, or in a room with windows on a cloudy day that doesn't provide enough natural light.

Faking window light is great for overpowering ugly ambient light when you can't darken the room enough to "turn it off." This method creates "wow" images that completely change the look and feel of the room from what the eye sees.

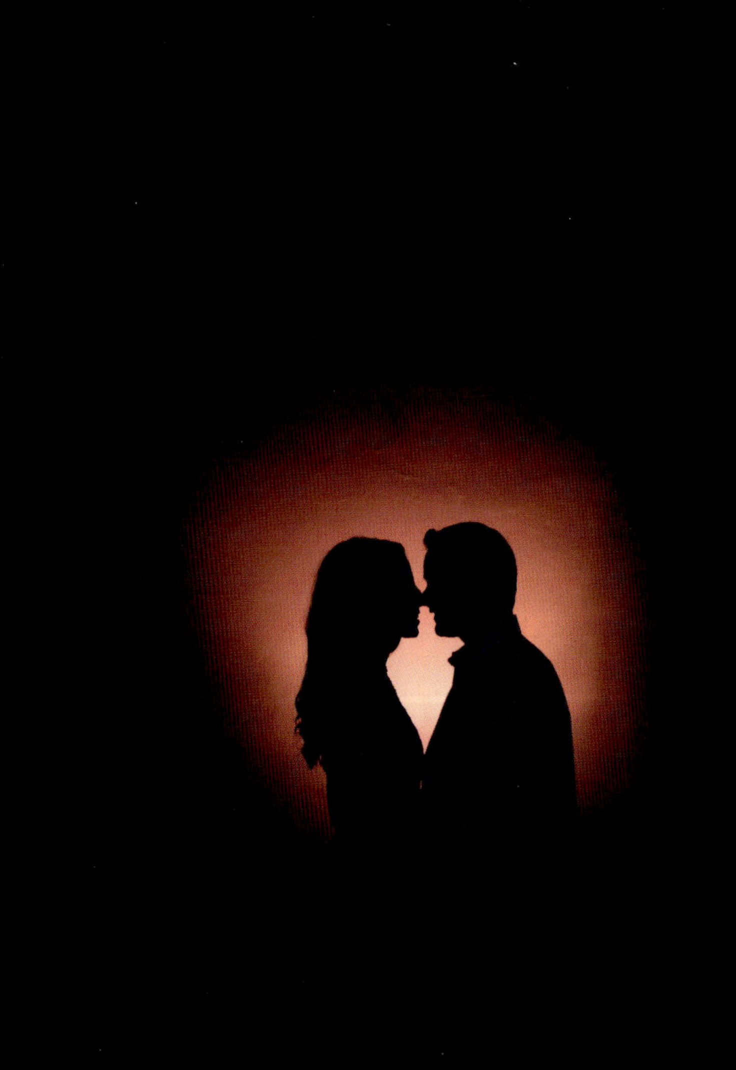

SCENARIO 16
Creating a Silhouette

Quick drama anytime day or night.

GOAL IMAGE

This is a fun technique with a myriad of applications. I've seen some incredible photographers using this technique to silhouette a subject while another part of the frame is properly exposed. I often use this when I have a not-so-sexy room to photograph in and I want to give my client something more dramatic (**Figure 16.1**).

The idea behind this technique is that you're blacking out your subject by creating a brighter light behind them that you can expose for. Depending on your lighting conditions, you may need to use High Speed Sync to cut out the natural light enough that there isn't any hitting your subject.

GEAR NEEDED:

- Camera + Trigger
- Lens of any focal length (though I prefer wider)
- Off-camera flash
- Colored gels *(optional, but recommended)*
- Light stand *(optional)*
- Second off-camera flash *(optional)*

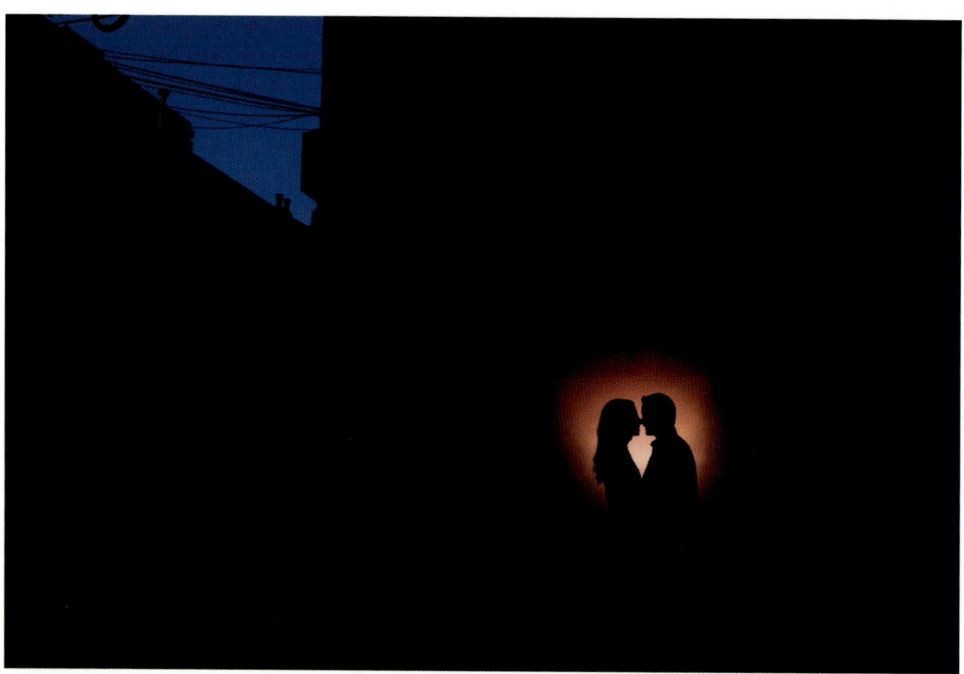

Step by Step

1. **Position your subject:** This technique is easiest with your subject about 5–10 feet from a blank wall. Choose a pose that will be flattering in a silhouette.

2. **Put a colored gel on your light:** This is optional, but I have a lot of fun playing with different colors lighting the background behind the subject.

3. **Position the light:** I like to have my light position close to the couple and pointed at the wall. A modeling light is very helpful here, but if you're using a speedlight that doesn't have one, just test fire the flash to see where your light is falling. I go for a nice even circle around the subject.

4. **Set the camera exposure:** Find an exposure that makes your subjects go completely black. This may mean that the rest of the photograph goes completely dark as well.

5. **Set the white balance:** Because the flash won't affect the light on your subject, auto WB or flash would be fine here.

6. **Set the flash:** If you needed to set your shutter speed over your camera's sync speed, be sure to turn on High Speed Sync on your flash. Try TTL first to see how bright the flash is in the

image. You could set your flash to manual at the mid power range, or use a light meter on the wall to determine flash power. If you're using a colored gel, you may want to lower the flash power so that you get a more saturated color on the wall. The higher the flash power, the less saturated the color will be.

OPTIONAL: Place an additional light with a different-colored gel, like a speedlight, pointed directly at your lens and "flash yourself." See Scenario 29, "Making Front Bokeh," for more information on doing this effectively.

Shot by Shot

FIGURE 16.2

NATURAL LIGHT (BLACK IMAGE).

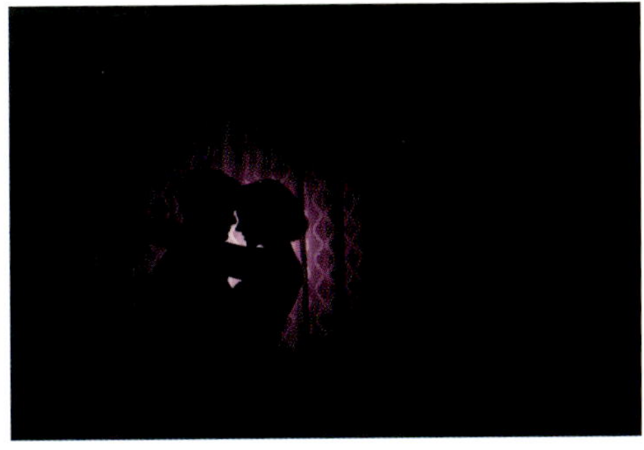

FIGURE 16.3

SHOT WITH A PROFOTO B10 WITH PINK GEL TO CREATE A SILHOUETTE.
CANON 35MM 1.4, ISO 1000, APERTURE 18, SHUTTER 1/250

FIGURE 16.4

"OPTIONAL FLASHING YOURSELF TECHNIQUE" WITH A PROFOTO B10 WITH A TEAL GEL POINTED AT AND RIGHT NEXT TO MY LENS. IT WAS TOO BRIGHT.
CANON 35MM 1.4, ISO 1000, APERTURE 18, SHUTTER 1/250

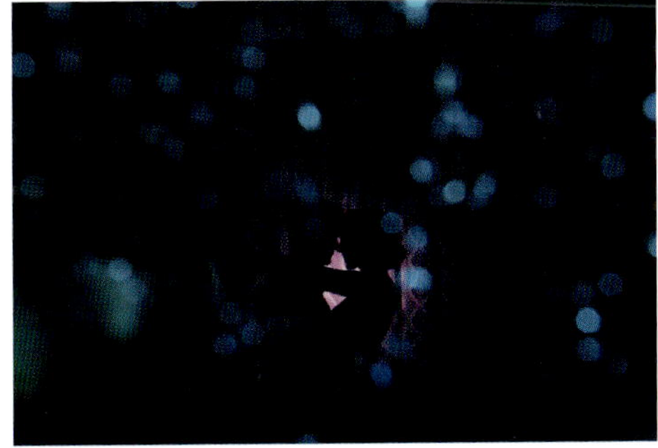

FIGURE 16.5

I RAISED THE APERTURE TO 22 TO GET THE BEST "BOKEH BALLS" AND LOWERED THE INTENSITY OF THE FRONT LIGHT. I RAISED THE BACKLIGHT TO KEEP THE SCENE AS BRIGHT AS IT WAS IN THE PREVIOUS PICTURES.
CANON 35MM 1.4, ISO 1000, APERTURE 22, SHUTTER 1/250

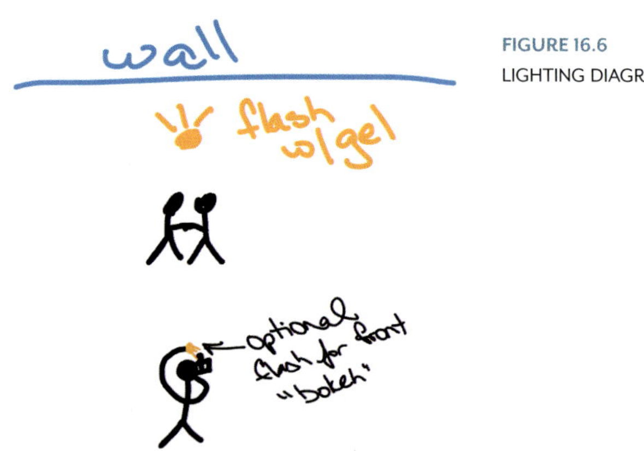

Potential Problems

Because you may be attempting this shot during the day, there's a chance you will need to use High Speed Sync in order to get a blacked-out exposure on your subject. When you enter HSS, the flash isn't as powerful and will suck up more battery power. If you can, find a location that is dark, inside, or in shadow, and you'll have an easier time with the flash. Another option is to use an ND filter to darken your image, making it easier to stay below your camera's sync speed.

Sometimes when I use a gel during this shot, the color isn't quite what I want it to be. Since you don't have any light on the subject, change your white balance, color tint, or white balance shift to get the color you want. It won't affect how your subject looks because they're in silhouette.

Practical Uses

This technique easily produces a "hero" image. If you're in a creative slump or not thrilled with your shooting location, this is a perfect way to get a wide, epic image. It's always a goal of mine to capture a hero image like this one because it will look great spread across an album or printed as wall art.

Give this a try for individual and couples portraits, getting a "nighttime" shot in the middle of the day, hiding an unattractive location and getting an epic image, and creating a base layer for a multiple-exposure photograph.

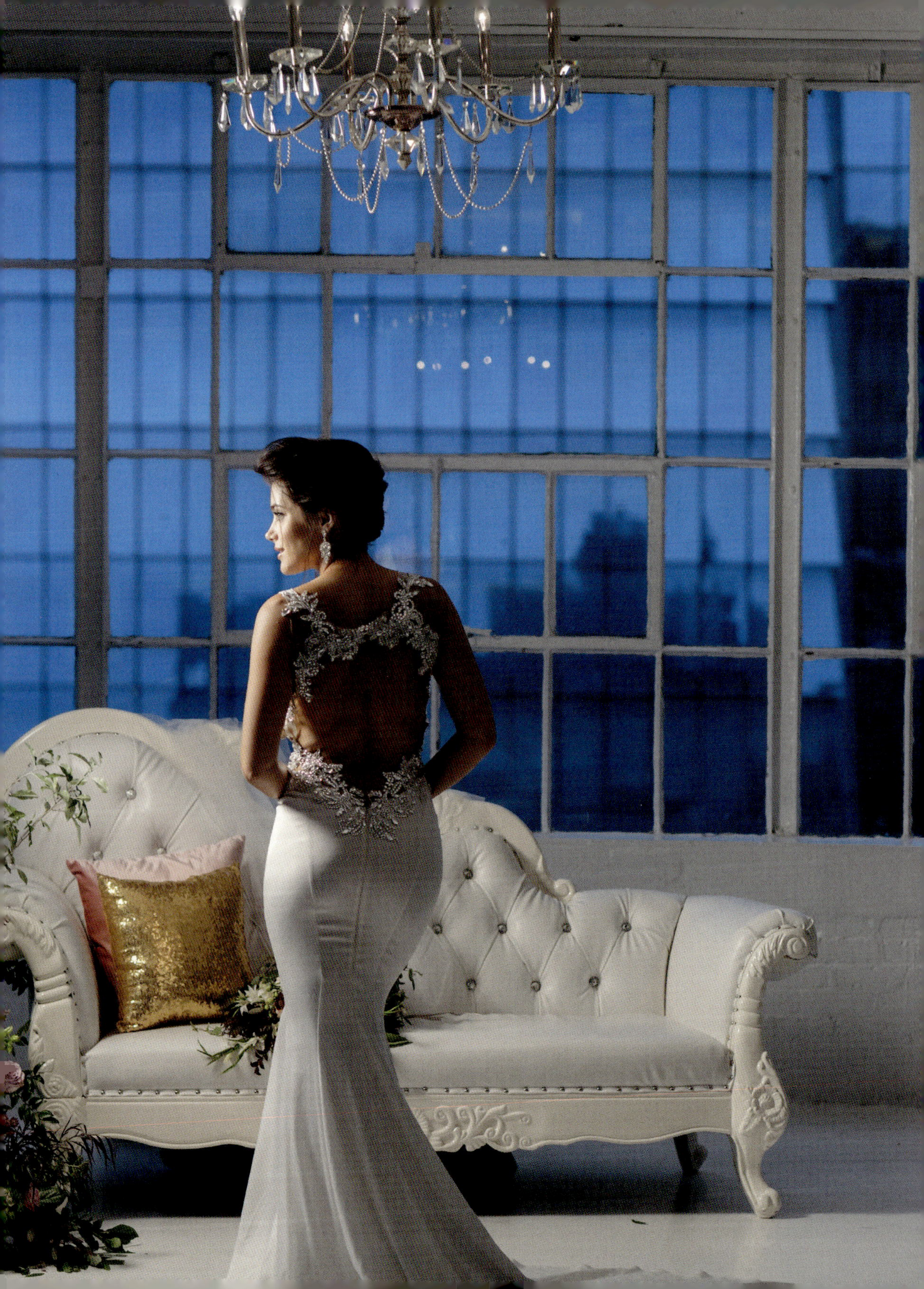

SCENARIO 17

Turn Day into Night

Control the way the Earth turns—sort of.

GOAL IMAGE

This is a favorite trick of mine for any photo shoot, but especially when I am photographing a wedding and there won't be time for a true "night" shot. Having the ability to create night is not only fun, but it wows your clients and gives them a unique image that they won't be able to pass up (**Figure 17.1**).

This technique is actually much more simple than you'd think. It's exactly like the concept in Scenario 3, "Creating Twilight," in which you use a gel to balance the skin tone of your subject while altering the look of the background with your white balance.

Since the example I gave in that chapter is an outdoor one, I'll show you an indoor day-to-night shoot this time. (*Psst:* Indoors is easier in my opinion!) Check out Scenario 3 for an in-depth explanation of how and why this works. This chapter is going straight to the step-by-step instructions. All the images in the shot-by-shot examples are straight-out-of-camera.

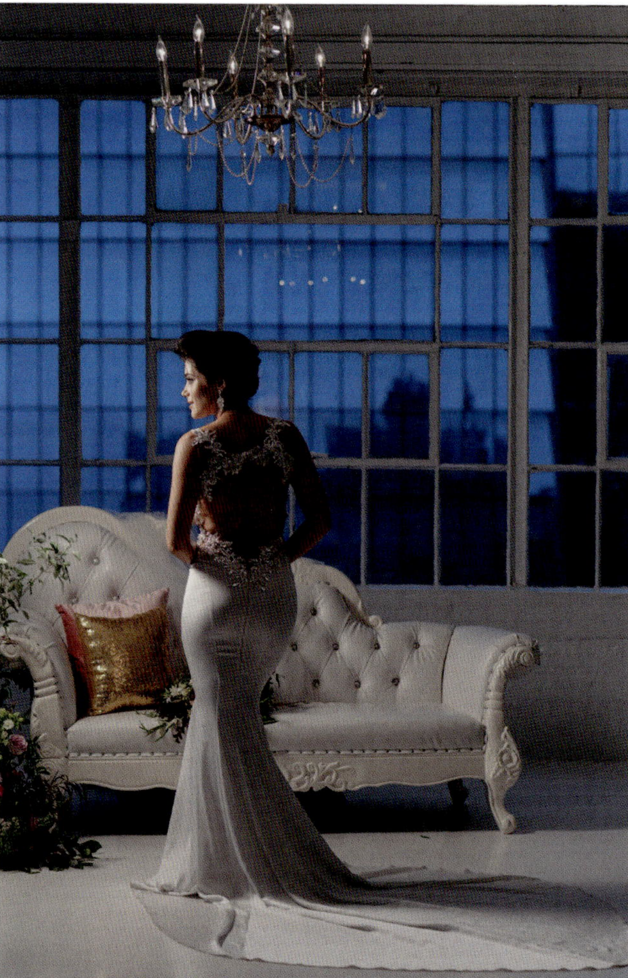

GOAL IMAGE. I WISH I COULD GIVE YOU THE SETTINGS FOR THIS, BUT MY METADATA GOT ERASED!

Step by Step

1. **Find a spot:** When I'm looking for a location to turn day into night, I'm usually looking for a window. Showing a window will help create a contrast between indoors and outdoors. Without showing the outside, there's no indicator to the viewer that the image was taken at night (even though it wasn't).

2. **Position your subject:** Just because we're showing a window doesn't mean that the subject has to be right up against it. In fact, it's better to create some space. It'll be easier to work with the light reflection that way. I suggest placing the subject at least 10 feet away from the window.

3. **Choose a lens:** Lens choice is up to you and your creativity. I love using long lenses, especially for situations like this where I want to bring the window "closer" to my subject.

4. **Put modifiers on the light:** Put on the full CTO gel. I usually won't go more orange than that because it gets too unrealistic looking, but you are welcome to. Also put the modifier of your choice on the light. You're inside and you aren't fighting the sun, so you don't have to worry too much about sucking up batter power.

5. **Position the light:** I typically shoot with my light to the right or left of my subjects at a 45-degree angle. Go even more to the side if you're looking for something more dramatic. For this example I wanted a little more drama since it was a night shot, so I put the light at a 90-degree angle, to the side of my subject.

6. **Set the camera exposure:** Set your camera exposure as if you're taking a photo that will expose outside of the window—maybe a stop or two darker. You don't want it to look bright outside, so manipulate your settings to make it look dark.

7. **Set the white balance:** This is where you make it look like night. Set your white balance to about 3200 Kelvin. You may change this depending on how the flash looks, but go for what makes the background look right first.

8. **Set the flash power:** I suggest setting your flash power to TTL +1 because of how many modifiers your light is passing through. If you're using a manual flash, start in the medium-low power range or use a light meter and adjust up or down to your liking. Take a test shot and adjust your light to be more or less powerful according to your taste.

9. **Look at your colors and histogram:** Take a look at your histogram to make sure that you're not too dark or too light. Adjust for "blue" and light power as needed.

Shot by Shot

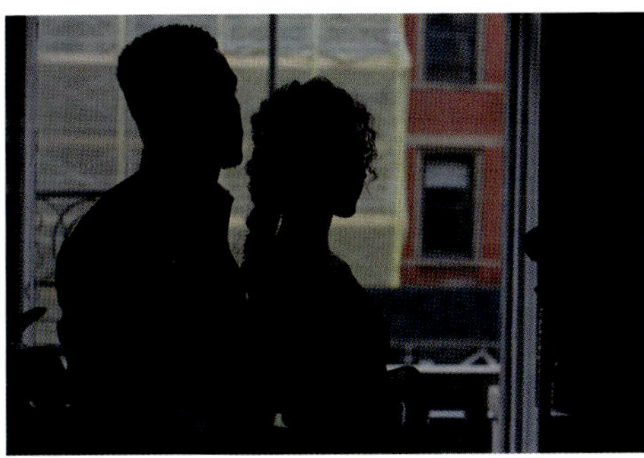

FIGURE 17.2
EXPOSING FOR THE BACKGROUND.
CANON 1DX II, CANON 50MM 1.2, ISO 100, APERTURE 3.2,
SHUTTER 1/250

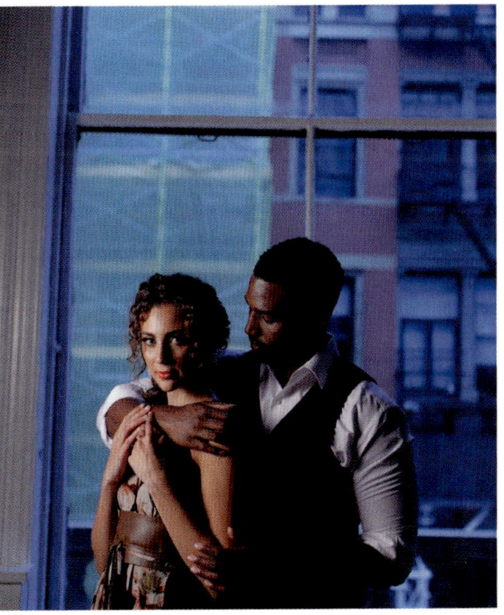

FIGURE 17.3
ADDED A PROFOTO B2 WITH 2X3 SOFTBOX AND CTO GEL.
CANON 1DX II, CANON 50MM 1.2, ISO 100,
APERTURE 3.2, SHUTTER 1/250

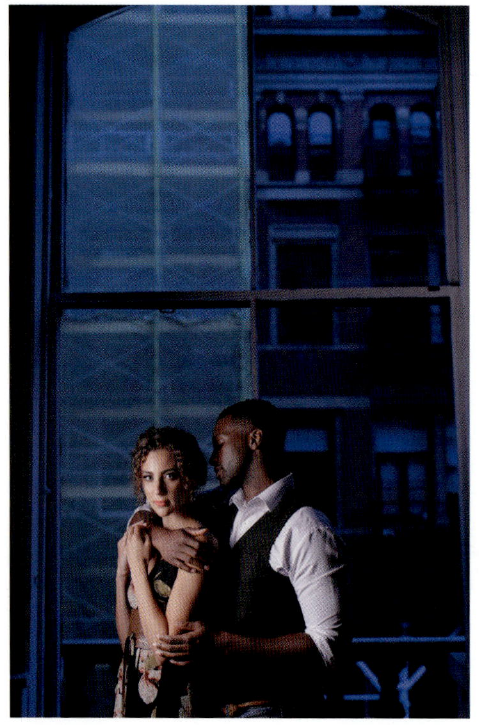

FIGURE 17.4

LOWERED WHITE BALANCE.

CANON 1DX II, CANON 50MM 1.2, ISO 100, APERTURE 3.2, SHUTTER 1/250

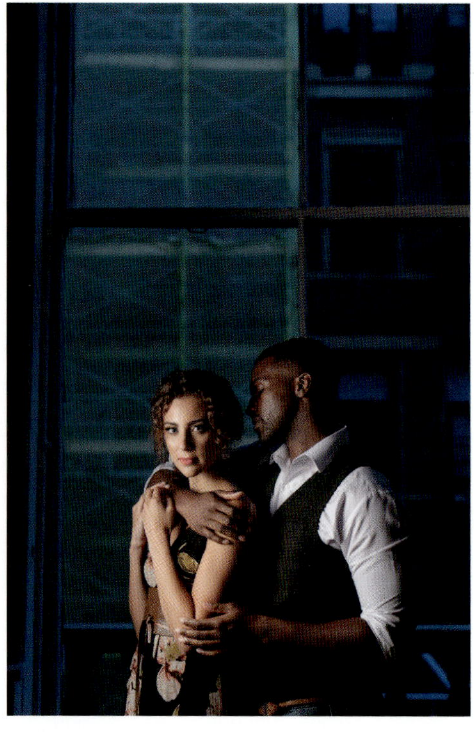

FIGURE 17.5

THE FINAL IMAGE, EDITED IN LIGHTROOM.

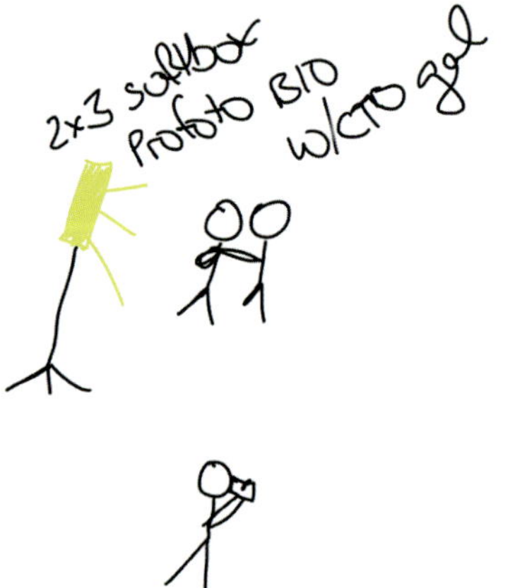

FIGURE 17.6

LIGHTING DIAGRAM.

Potential Problems

Turning day into night can be tricky. If you think that your subject's skin tone looks too blue, warm up the image by raising the Kelvin. However, this may make the background not look like night anymore. If you find that happening, set your Kelvins to what you want the background to look like, and then add more CTO gel to counter the blue. They make quarter, half, and full CTO gels so you can back off by going to a half CTO, or add more by stacking quarter, half, or full CTOs on top of each other.

Depending on your photographic brand, you may want to add a fill light that will spread light everywhere. To do this, set up a second light with the same CTO gel on it and a light modifier that will spread it everywhere (like an umbrella or a shoot-through umbrella). Position that light right behind and above you, pointing toward the middle of your frame. It'll fill in the shadows with a warm color that'll create even more of a contrast between the outdoor blue look and the inside warm look. It'll also make the lighting look a bit softer.

Other Techniques

Once you've mastered this technique, build on it. You can add a rim light or light flare or anything else you want to shape your light. If you have buildings or streetlights in your image, you might want to add some "illumination" in post-processing. I don't necessarily recommend it, but if you're shooting into a window at "nighttime" and there are buildings outside, it stands to reason that people in those buildings would have their lights on. It'll make the image more believable, and it's not something that you can do in camera, so it has to be done in post.

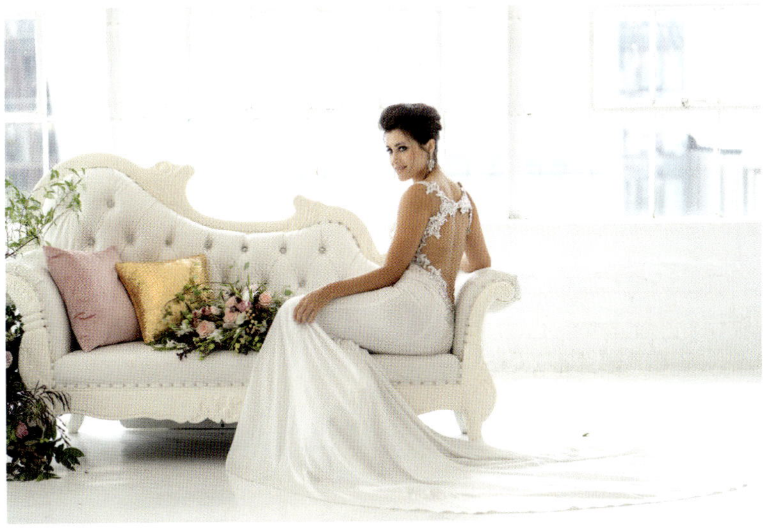

FIGURE 17.7

NATURAL LIGHT IN THE ROOM.

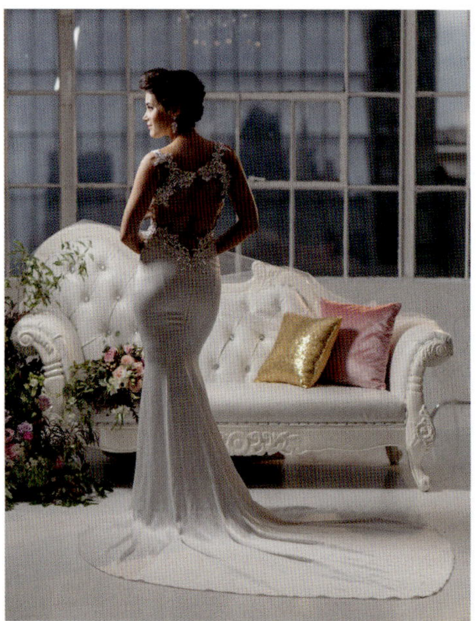

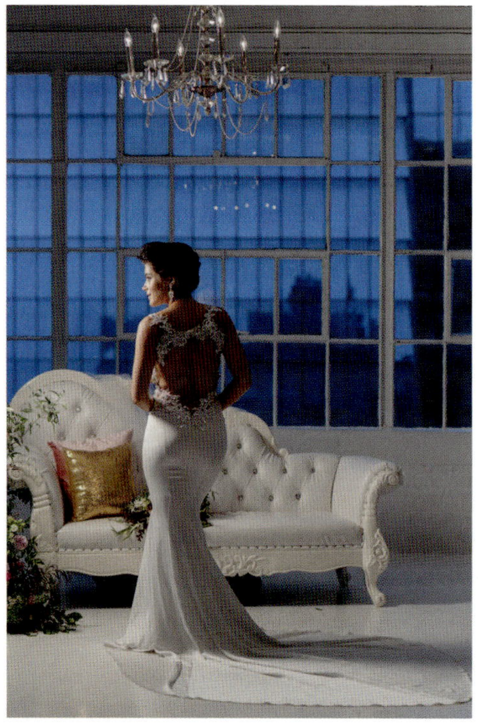

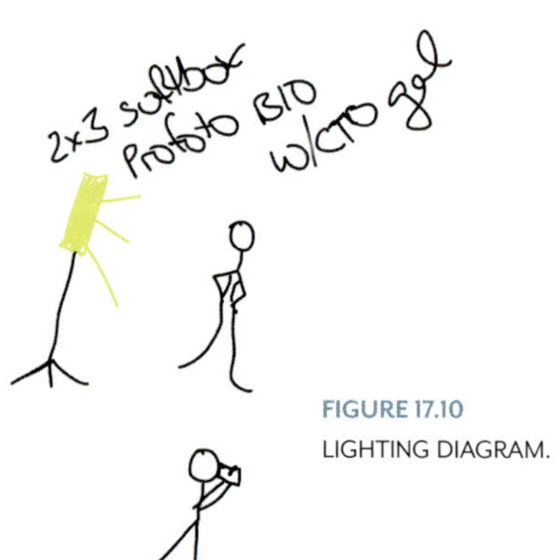

FIGURE 17.10
LIGHTING DIAGRAM.

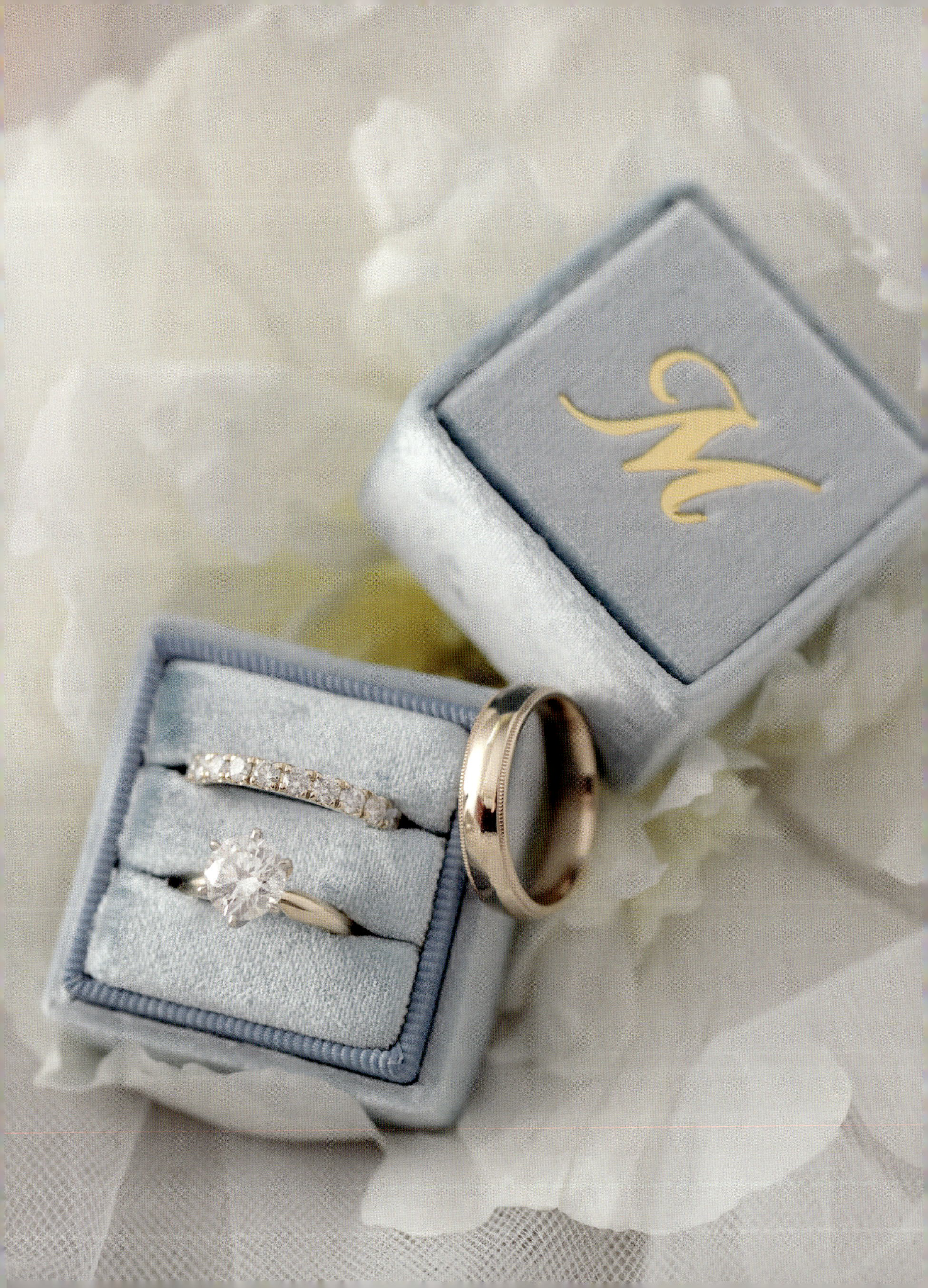

SCENARIO 18

Tiny Little Details

Creating a natural light look with the littlest of things.

GOAL IMAGE

One of my favorite parts of a wedding day is photographing the details, bathed in soft, beautiful light. However, very often I'm not photographing in a gloriously lit space, but in a tiny, dark room. This section will show you how to create better light in a flash (puns always intended).

I want my detail pictures to look like they were shot with natural light so they match the rest of the images that I take throughout the wedding day and fit my brand. To have a nice, soft look to your pictures, you need a big light source. I like to think of this technique as creating my own big, floor-to-ceiling window. The best part is that you really only need a speedlight to get it done.

GEAR NEEDED:

- Camera + Trigger
- Detail lens (I enjoy a 50mm or 100mm Macro)
- Off-camera flash
- Reflector *(optional)*

Step by Step

1. **Find your window:** By window, I mean wall. Find a white or lightly colored wall and plant yourself and the details you're shooting a couple feet away.

2. **Position your reflector:** If you're stuck in a black hole with nothing but dark walls, use a reflector. Lean it against a wall in place of a white wall.

3. **Position the light:** Place your speedlight on the floor or the speedlight stand and point it at your wall. Try to have it fairly close to you so the light spreads as largely as possible on the wall. Remember, the bigger the light source (in this case your light source is where your flash it hitting the wall), the softer your light will be.

4. **Set the camera exposure:** Set your camera for how you like to photograph details. For me, that's a fairly shallow depth of field and as low of an ISO as I can get. Because you're using a speedlight, you may want to raise your ISO a little bit so the flash doesn't need to pump out as much power. Raise your shutter speed to lower the ambient light in the room so you don't have overhead tungsten lights affecting the color and luminance of your image.

5. **Set the white balance:** Your flash will be hitting your subject, so set your white balance to flash or 5600 (depending on your flash).

6. **Set the flash:** I start with TTL here, and then flip to manual and go brighter or darker depending on what I'd like my images to look like. If you're shooting on manual, use a light meter or start at the mid power range and adjust from there.

OPTIONAL: Have a reflector opposite the wall that you're firing your flash into. This will fill in the shadows on the other side of the image and create an even softer look.

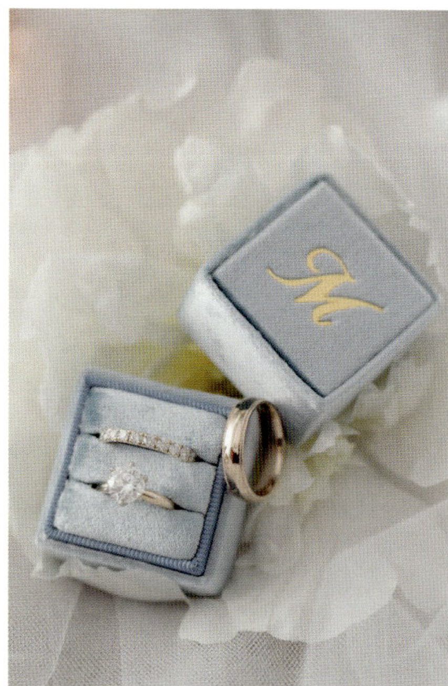

FIGURE 18.1

GOAL IMAGE. A PROFOTO A1 WITH DOME DIFFUSER BOUNCING OFF A WALL.
CANON 1DX MARK II, CANON 100MM 2.8 MACRO, ISO 500, APERTURE 4.5, SHUTTER 1/160

Shot by Shot

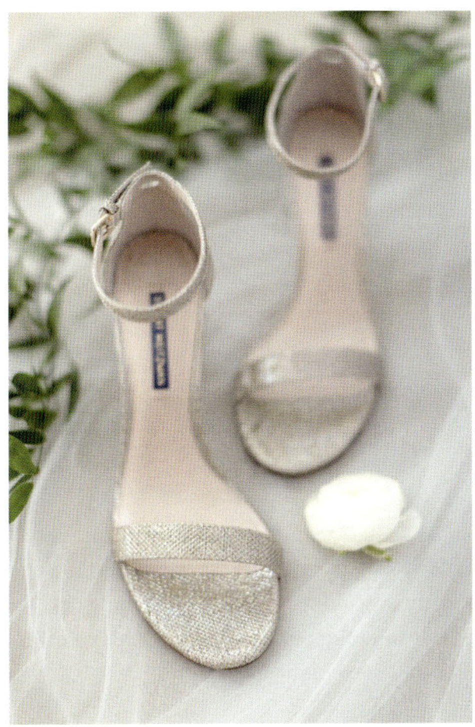

FIGURE 18.2
I USED A PROFOTO A1 WITH A DOME DIFFUSER
BOUNCING OFF A WALL.
CANON1DXII, CANON50MM 1.2, ISO 500,
APERTURE 1.8, SHUTTER 1/160

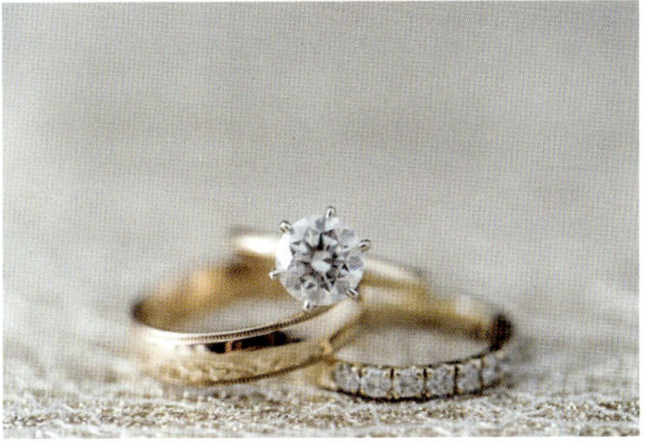

FIGURE 18.3
CANON 1DX II, CANON 100MM 2.8 MACRO, ISO 500,
APERTURE 3.5, SHUTTER 1/160.

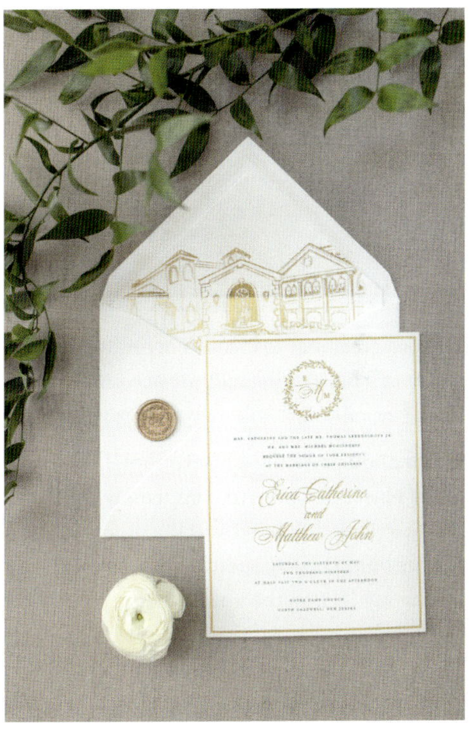

FIGURE 18.4
CANON 1DX II, CANON 50MM 1.2, ISO 500, APERTURE 2.2,
SHUTTER 1/160 TAKEN WITH A PROFOTO A1 SET TO 4.5
WITH A DOME DIFFUSER BOUNCING OFF A WALL.

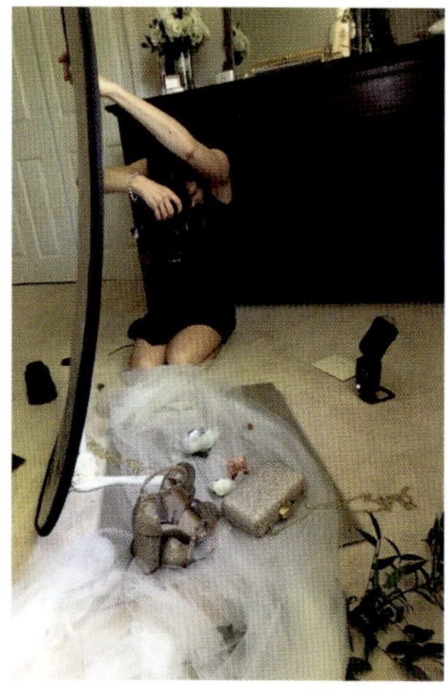
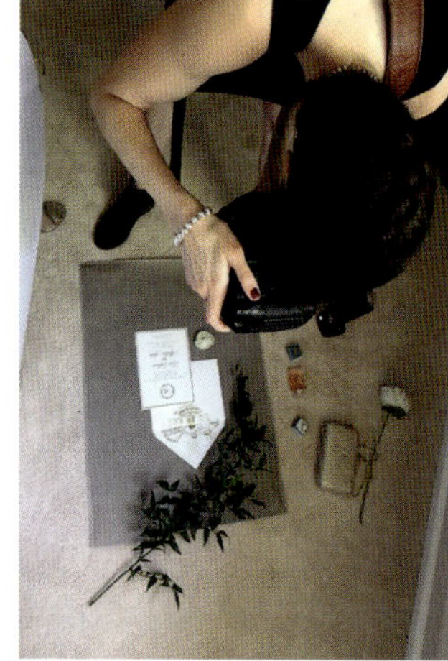
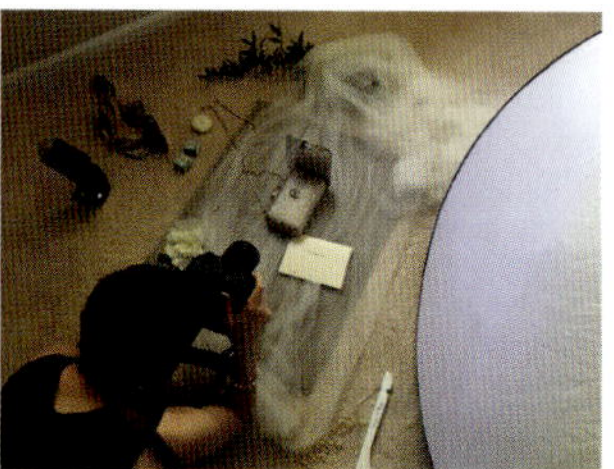

Potential Problems

You do not necessarily need to have a blacked out image to start with. If you want some of the natural light to affect your picture, then it's OK to have a bit of an exposure when you first set your camera. However, that could lead to weird colors mixing into your image depending on what the natural or ambient light in the room looks like. You might like it if it's a normal color, but if you're in some kind of magenta room, that color may seep into your pictures.

Practical Uses

This is a great tool to create a natural light look for your detail pictures. In addition, it's helpful if you're in a dark room and just need more light. Even with a large window to light the room, if it's cloudy or raining it still may not provide enough light for the look you want.

When photographing a macro shot, I may need to raise my aperture to f/6.3 or higher to get more of the object in focus. To compensate for that I'll usually need to raise my ISO. This causes the image to look different from the others in the series because of the added noise. Using flash here lets me bump up my aperture. I raise the flash power to compensate for the light loss instead of raising my ISO, so the images in the series all match in an album spread.

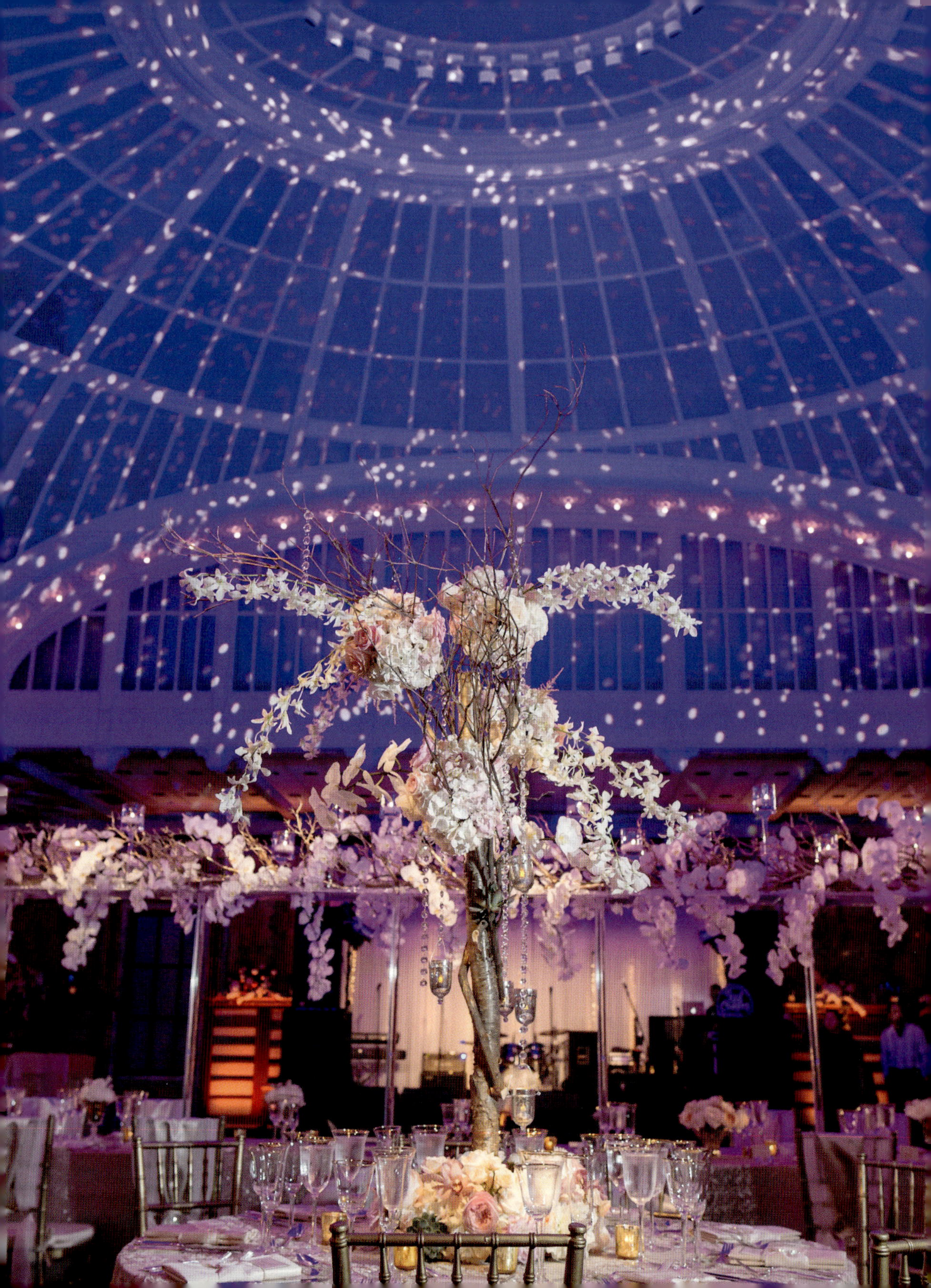

SCENARIO 19
Table Details

My go-to, easy-peasy wedding reception lighting setup that shows off every little detail.

GOAL IMAGE

I absolutely love my time at wedding receptions photographing all of the décor. My goal is to capture it as it looks, so sometimes that means using only natural light.

If you're photographing a daytime wedding, this lighting setup isn't appropriate or necessary. But if you're photographing a night wedding, this will show you how to capture every little detail and keep the ambiance of the room (**Figure 19.1**).

My goal at a wedding is to create imagery that represents what guests and clients see when they walk into a room. I used to color balance for an orange-glowing room, but then I realized I was taking all of the natural color out of the images. My clients would wonder why the images didn't show the warm candlelight feel they were going for, so I stopped color balancing my lights to match the ambient light.

GEAR NEEDED:

- Camera + Trigger
- 50mm or 85mm focal length lens
- 2 Off-camera flashes
- 2 Light stands
- 2 Grids
- Third off-camera flash *(optional)*
- Gel set *(optional)*

I used to just bounce flash the detail pictures. The problem with that is that you're not controlling the light, so it's bouncing and lighting both the table and backdrop, killing the ambient light. Bouncing the light doesn't show off the details quite as well as pointing it more directly at your subjects does.

My favorite method uses two lights on either side of the table. This allows for light and shadow to show off the texture and color of what I'm photographing. Occasionally, I'll let one of the lights flare into my shot, giving the image a glamorous feel.

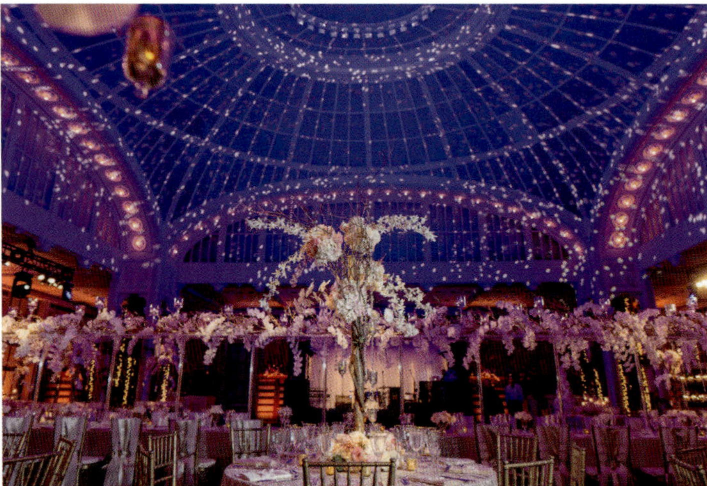

Step by Step

1. **Grid the lights:** It would be best to use two grids of the same size. However, I own 20-, 10-, and 5-degree grids. I have only one of each size, so I use the 20- and 10-degree grid one on each light. I then position the 10-degree gridded light a few feet farther away from my subject than the 20-degree gridded light. This prevents the spread of light so that both sides of my subject (the table) are lit evenly. This does potentially mean that the light that's farther away may need to have a brighter power setting.

2. **Position the lights:** Choose what you're photographing and place one light directly to the left of it and one light directly to the right of it. Raise the lights to just at or above the height of the centerpiece of the table.

3. **Set the camera exposure:** Create an exposure that shows off the level of ambient light (e.g., candlelight, uplighting) that you want to see in the image. I like using a shallow depth of field, somewhere around f/2.2–3.2, to get the look I'm going for.

4. **Set the white balance:** Because the flash is your main light source, set your white balance to the flash preset or 5600 Kelvin depending on the temperature of your light. If you want the entire image to have a slightly warmer look, you can raise your white balance to achieve this.

5. **Set the flash power:** Turn both lights on and take a shot using TTL. Flip to manual mode and adjust. You do not have to have both sides of the subject evenly lit. You could decide to have the right side a bit brighter than the left. That is completely up to you. If you don't have TLL available, start on the lowest manual setting your flash has and slowly move up until you have the desired brightness, or use a light meter. Do this one light at a time.

6. **Move lights to shoot table details:** When you've shot the whole table and centerpieces and want to move on to the details on the table like the plates, glasses, and silverware, you may need to lower the lights. This way they will light the table and décor more prominently.

OPTIONAL: Place one of the lights a little more behind the subject and pointed towards you to get a bit of flare in your image.

OPTIONAL: If you have a boring room without much light in the background, throw a third light with any color gel in the back. Point it towards a background wall to add some life to the shot.

Shot by Shot

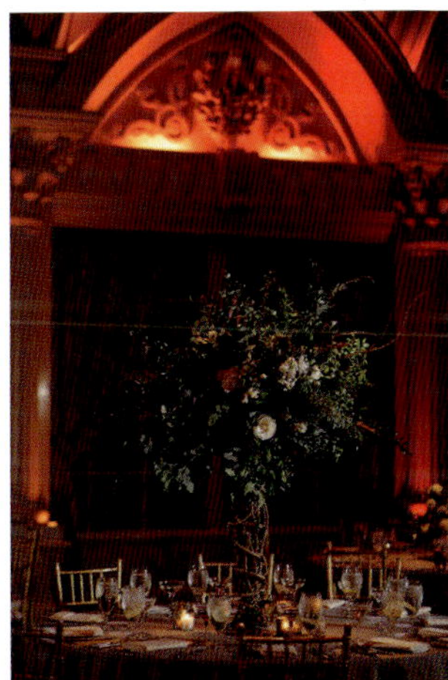

FIGURE 19.2
THIS FIRST LIGHTING SETUP IS ON THE RIGHT SIDE. I USED A PROFOTO B1 WITH A GRID.
CANON 1DXII, CANON 85MM 1.4, ISO 1250, APERTURE 2, SHUTTER 1/200

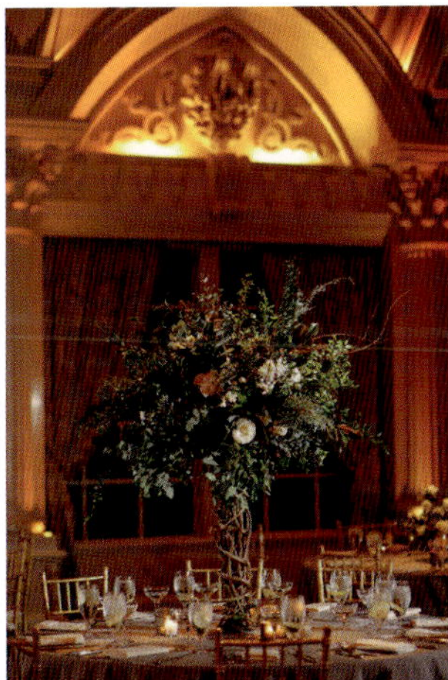

FIGURE 19.3
I ADDED A SECOND LIGHT ON THE LEFT. THE BACKGROUND UP-LIGHTING CHANGED BUT DIDN'T AFFECT IMAGE TOO MUCH. I USED TWO PROFOTO B1S WITH GRIDS.
CANON 1DXII, CANON 85MM 1.4, ISO 1250, APERTURE 2, SHUTTER 1/200

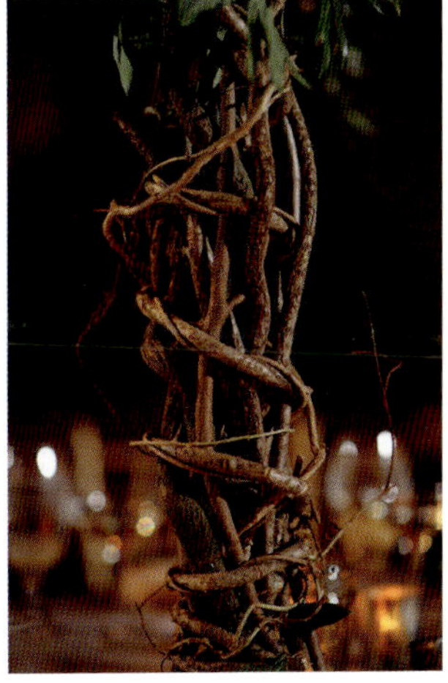

FIGURE 19.4
IT'S EASY TO MOVE AROUND FROM THERE TO CAPTURE SMALLER DETAILS. I USED TWO PROFOTO B1S WITH GRIDS.
CANON 1DXII, CANON 85MM 1.4, ISO 1250, APERTURE 2, SHUTTER 1/200

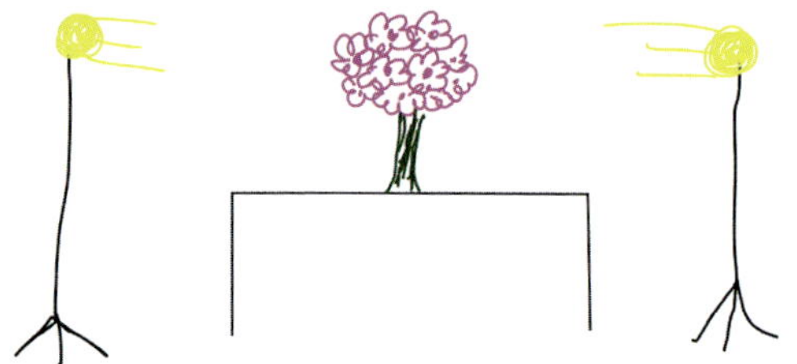

Potential Problems

The reason I place the lights above the table centerpiece is because the tablecloths at weddings are typically white or a light color, while the flowers are a mix of colors. Because of this, it can be very easy to overexpose the table itself, even when the centerpiece is exposed correctly.

Avoid this by raising the lights to specifically light the centerpiece when you're photographing the table as a whole. Then when you're ready to move onto the smaller details on the table you can lower the lights as you see fit.

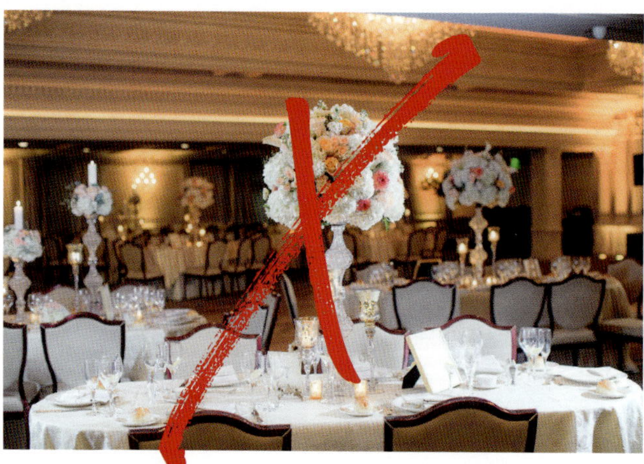

FIGURE 19.6

THE WHITES ON THIS TABLE ARE BLOWN OUT BECAUSE I DIDN'T USE A GRID FOR THE TWO PROFOTO B1S. THIS IS BAD.
CANON 1DX, CANON 50MM 1.2, ISO 1600, APERTURE 2.5, SHUTTER 1/125

I have certainly had my share of marathon wedding-reception-room shoots. If you're short on time just use one light. Set the light on manual and walk around (faster with an assistant, but you can keep moving around a light stand) from detail to detail, holding the light at the same distance from and angle to your subject each time.

We had about six and a half minutes to photograph the most glorious wedding reception of my career. It was a bummer to have to rush, but gosh darn it, we did it, and it was epic none-the-less.

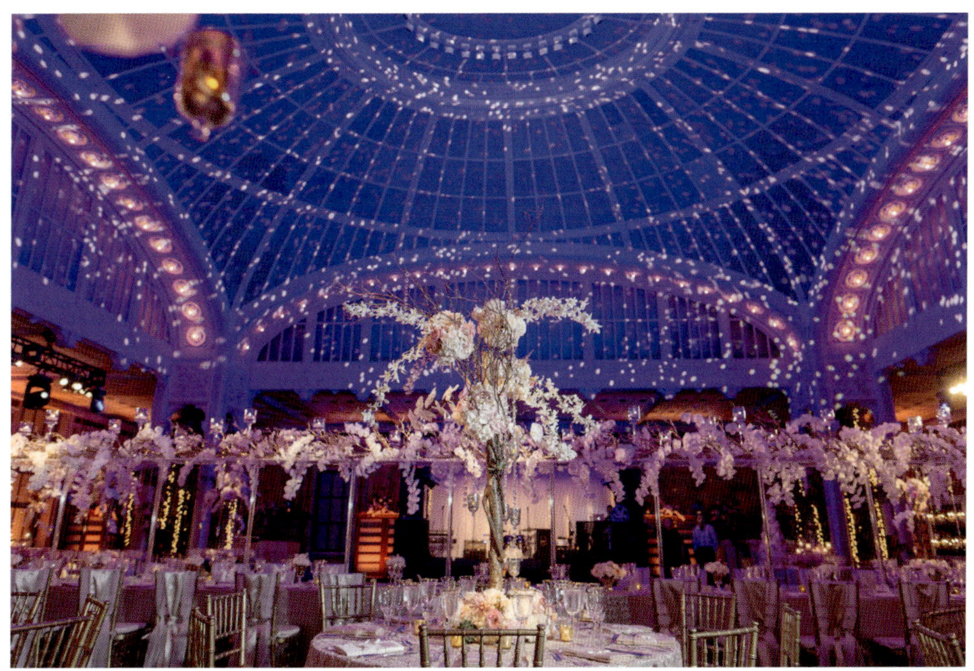

FIGURE 19.7

SHOT WITH ONE PROFOTO B2 ON CAMERA RIGHT.

CANON 1DX, CANON 24MM 1.4, ISO 1600, APERTURE 3.2, SHUTTER 1/125

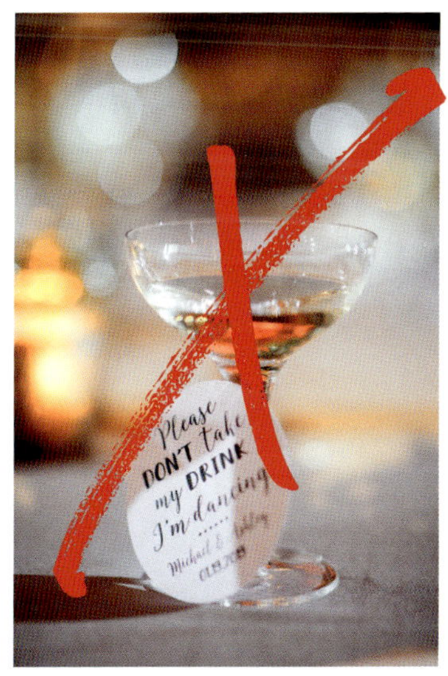

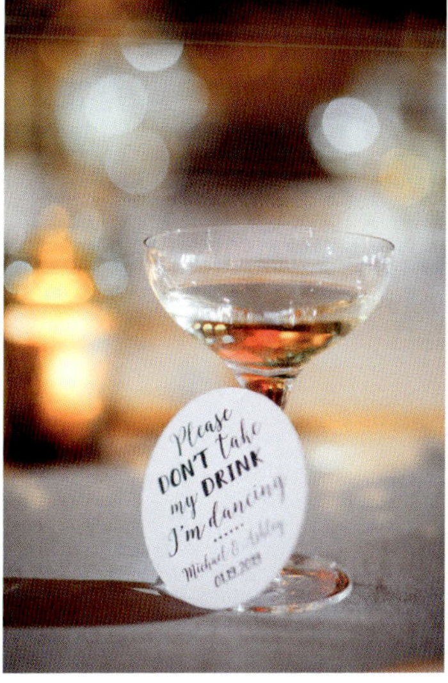

FIGURE 19.8

HERE THERE IS AN UNDESIRABLE SHADOW ON THE DRINK COASTER. I REMOVED THE ITEM
THROWING THE SHADOW AND USED ONE PROFOTO B1 WITH A GRID.

CANON 1DXII, CANON 85MM 1.4, ISO 1250, APERTURE 2, SHUTTER 1/200

Since you're likely inside trying to keep your ISO as low as possible to get a clean image, I imagine your shutter speed will be a bit on the lower side. Sometimes this can let in a little too much light. Try raising your shutter speed to darken the ambient light in the space. Alternatively, if you're taking a picture and you feel like it looks like you're shooting in a black cave, lower your shutter speed to make the background brighter.

Sometimes you'll need to move table details that are not in the shot so they don't throw a shadow on what you're photographing. You could also move the light, but I often find it's easier just to move whatever is throwing the shadow.

Practical Uses

With this method you can have a bit more creative fun shooting wedding reception details. You can use a nice long lens like an 85mm and shoot under, over, or through wedding décor in the foreground. It makes for a very pretty, intimate-looking photo that wouldn't be possible with a bounce flash. The bounced light off of the foreground makes it distracting instead of being an entry point into the photograph that draws the viewer's eye through to the detail you're photographing.

You can use this same method to photograph a wide shot of the entire room as well. Choose what tables you'd like to light (ahhhh, wouldn't it be nice if we had 26 lights to spot light every single one?). Alternatively, you can position one light at the right side of the room pointed at the left side of your frame, and the second light on the left side of the room pointed at the right side of your frame. With grids on the lights they won't entirely bathe the room in light, letting you keep the ambience of the room while you strategically light your subject. See more on this in Scenario 26, "Lighting a Dark Room."

Finally, if you are shooting a day wedding but your client wishes they had an intimate, dark reception; or you happen to only have time to shoot the details during the day when it is a night reception; you can use this method to make it look like the image was shot at night. Follow the same instructions, except set your initial exposure to be very dark (as though it was night) instead of setting it for the correct daylight exposure. Continue through the steps and consider the option of adding a third light with a gel on it.

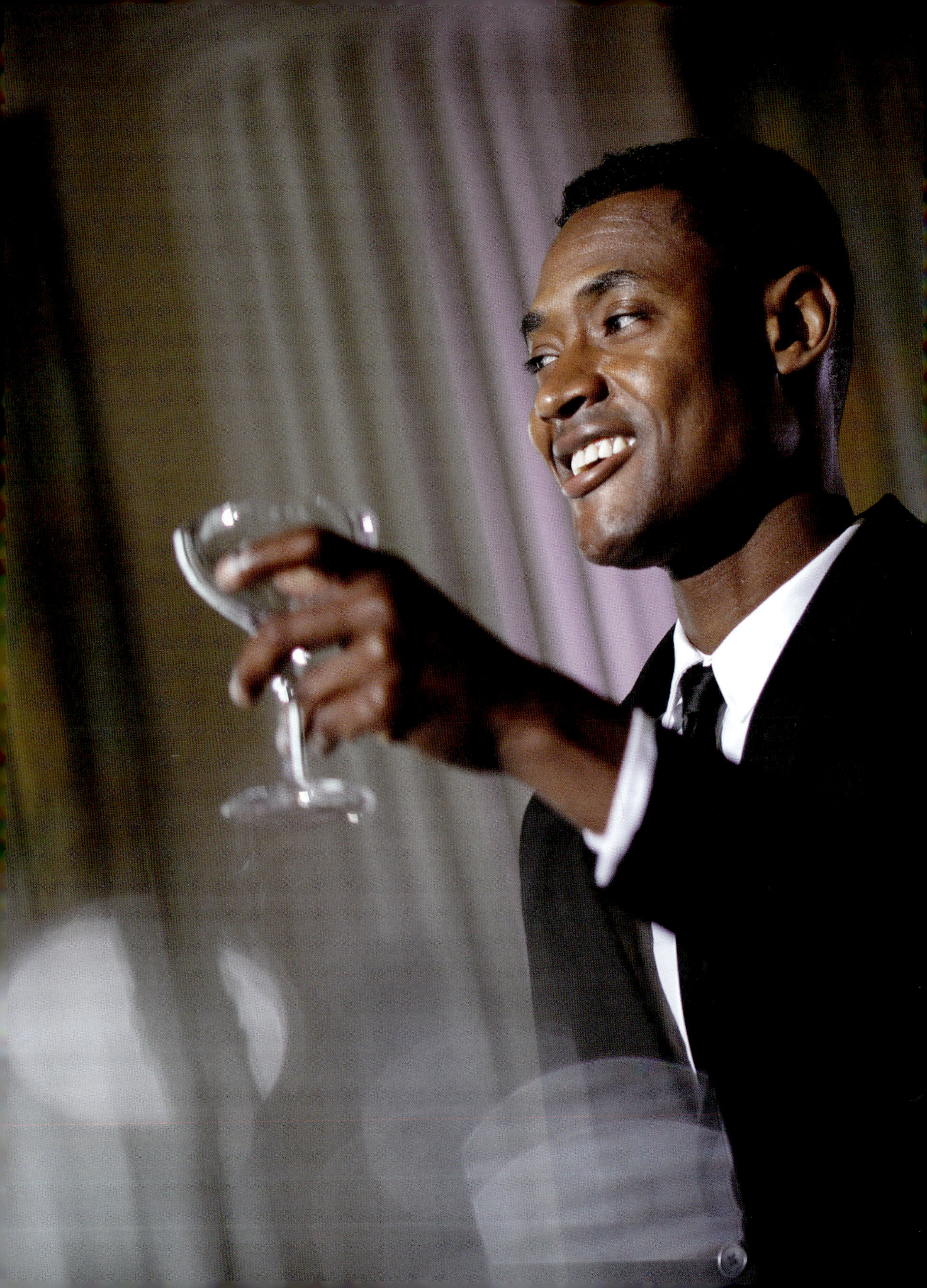

SCENARIO 20

Event Speeches

*Assuming they stand in one place, of course,
which never happens.*

GOAL IMAGE

Let me preface this section by saying that in order to re-create light like this during toasts, you have to either have a voice-activated light stand (a.k.a. an assistant) or hope that the speaker doesn't move around like they're a rock performer dancing around the stage. If you're working with a DJ or videographer, ask if they have a mic stand so that the speaker has to stay in one spot. They'll have a little bit of leeway, but it doesn't hurt instructing the speaker to stand and stay (**Figure 20.1**).

I titled this section "Event Speeches," but you could use this technique for lighting the entire event. This method creates a dramatic look that's full of contrast and depth. I love using this type of lighting, but depending on the event, timing, and space, it's not always my first priority and I divert to bounce flashing as needed.

I'm going to explain this as a two-light setup, but you can do this with just the front light to start and work on adding your second light once you feel comfortable. From there you can go on even further to three or four lights. I'll explain the idea, but personally I find it to be overkill for the events that I do and the way I shoot.

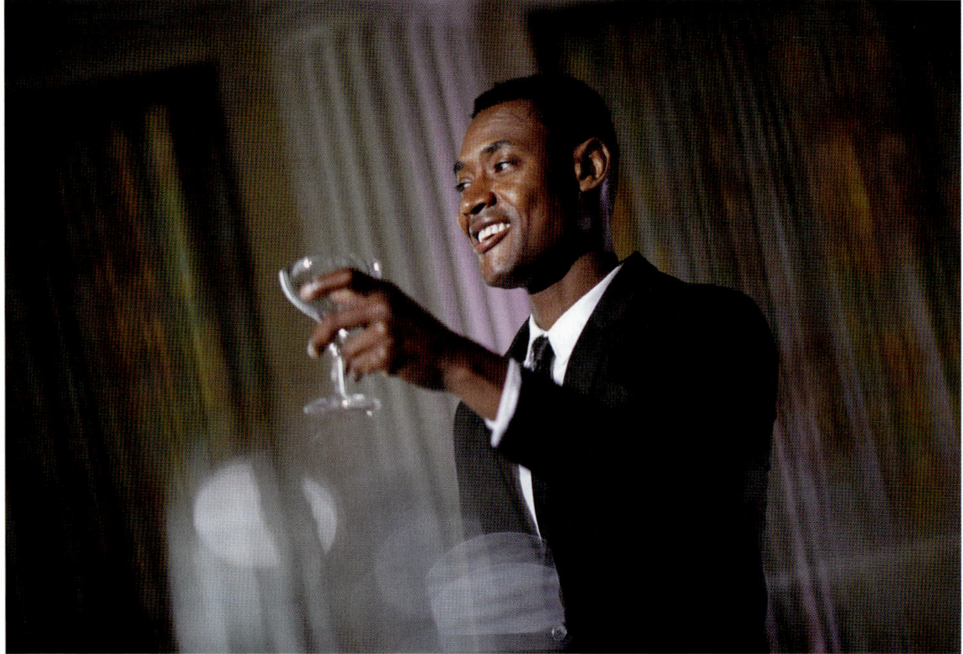

FIGURE 20.1
GOAL IMAGE. EDITED FOR CONTRAST IN LIGHTROOM.
CANON 1DXII, CANON 135MM 2.0, ISO 500, APERTURE 2, SHUTTER 1/250

Step by Step

1. **Grid the lights:** You'll be placing the lights father away from the speaker so that they're not obtrusive. You'll need to direct the light to hit only your speaker rather than flooding the whole space. If you flood the whole space, you may as well just bounce the flash.

   How large the space is and how far away your light is from your subject will determine what grid to use. Use a 5- or 10-degree grid to start. Turn on your modeling light and see where the light is falling. If it's too much like a spot light, use a 20- or 30-degree grid.

2. **Position the lights:** One light will be lighting the face of the speaker, and the other light will be rim lighting the back of their head.

   A. **Face light:** Position the light to point toward wherever the speaker is looking. This will ensure that even if you move around a bit, the front of their face will be illuminated. When you're on one side or the other of the subject, this light will create a nice shadow on the cheekbone and jaw.

B. **Rim light:** Place this light behind the speaker, pointed towards their head, slightly off to the right or left. You don't want it directly behind them because it won't look natural and will likely be in the crowd's view.

3. **Set the camera exposure:** Create an exposure as if you're photographing the room's natural light. I like a shallow depth of field, so I set my camera around f/2.2–3.2 to get the look I'm going for, especially when I'm using my longer 135mm lens. I'll likely be using around $\frac{1}{125}$ of a second so I don't have motion blur, and 1600–2500 ISO, depending on how dark the room is.

4. **Set the white balance:** Set your white balance to the flash preset or 5600 Kelvin depending on the temperature of your light.

5. **Set the flash power:** Turn both lights on and take a shot using TTL. Flip to manual and adjust. Both lights may not be on the same power setting, depending on how far away they are from the subject. If you don't have TLL available, start on the lowest manual setting your flash has and slowly move up until you have the desired brightness. Do this one light at a time. I don't find this particular setup practical for using a light meter because you don't have the time and it would be obtrusive to walk up to someone giving a toast to meter the light.

6. **Move around while shooting:** As you move around, the lighting pattern won't change on your subject, but the mood of the image will. I highly suggest moving around to see what the light looks like depending on where you're standing. It's a great way to learn about light and how it looks as you change your angle.

OPTIONAL: Throw a colored gel on the rim light to add a bit of fun color to the image.

Shot by Shot

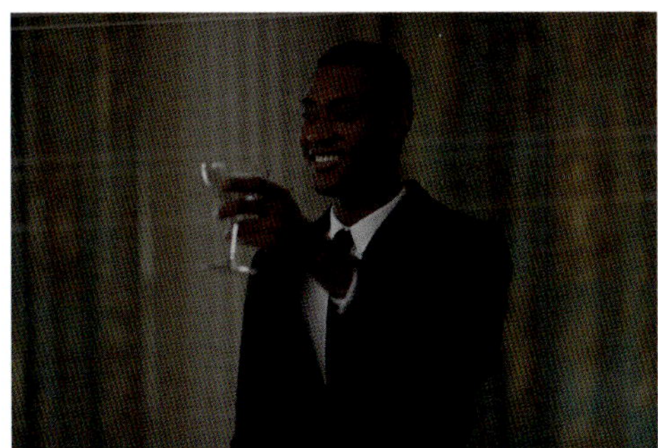

NATURAL LIGHT IMAGE, EXPOSING FOR THE BACK-GROUND.
CANON 1DX II, CANON 135MM 2.0, ISO 1000, APERTURE 2, SHUTTER 1/250

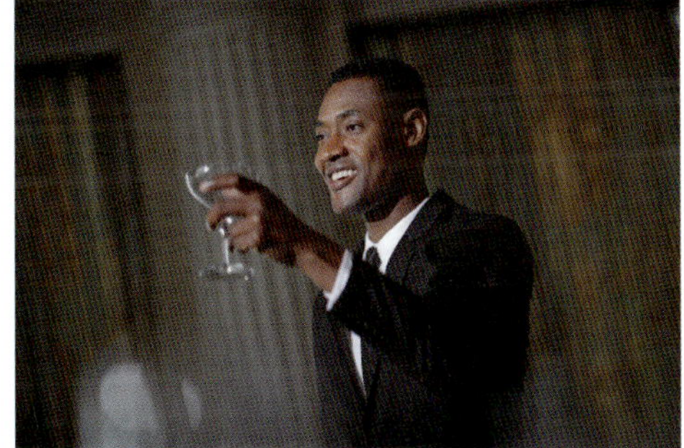

I ADDED FRONT LIGHT (A PROFOTO B1) AND DARKENED THE EXPOSURE FOR A NIGHTTIME EFFECT.
CANON 1DX II, CANON 135MM 2.0, ISO 500, APERTURE 2, SHUTTER 1/250

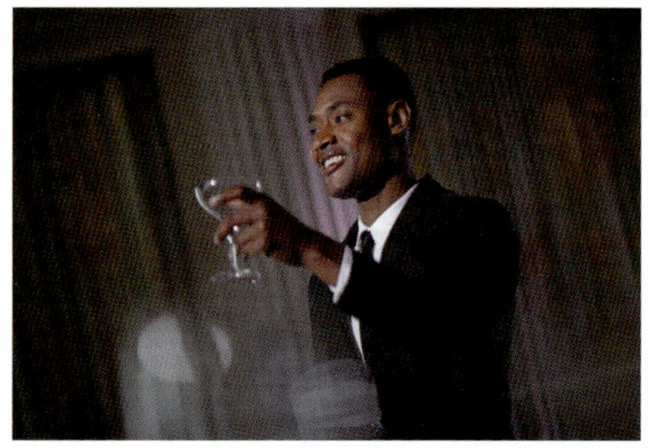

I ADDED RIM LIGHT (A PROFOTO B10 WITH PURPLE GEL).
CANON 1DX II, CANON 135MM 2.0, ISO 500, APERTURE 2,
SHUTTER 1/250

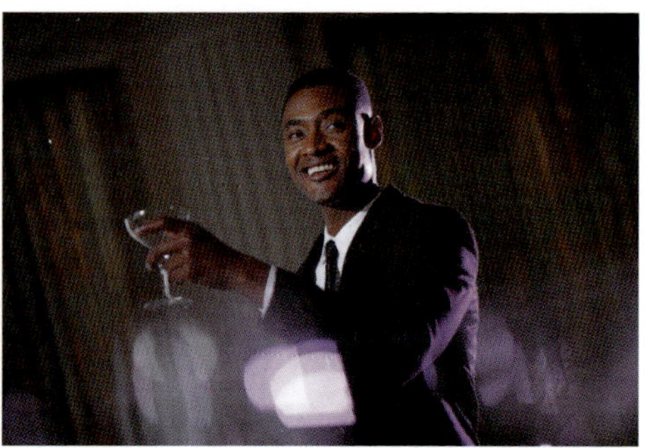

I RAISED THE POWER OF MY RIM LIGHT (THOUGH IT IS
OVEREXPOSED, IN MY OPINION).
CANON 1DX II, CANON 135MM 2.0, ISO 500, APERTURE 2,
SHUTTER 1/250

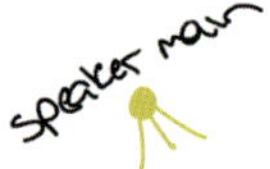

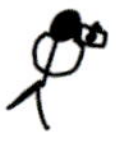

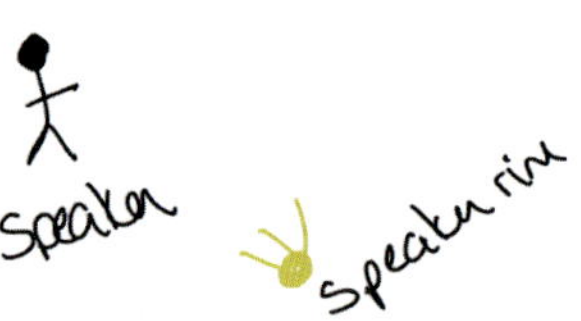

FIGURE 20.6

LIGHTING DIAGRAM.

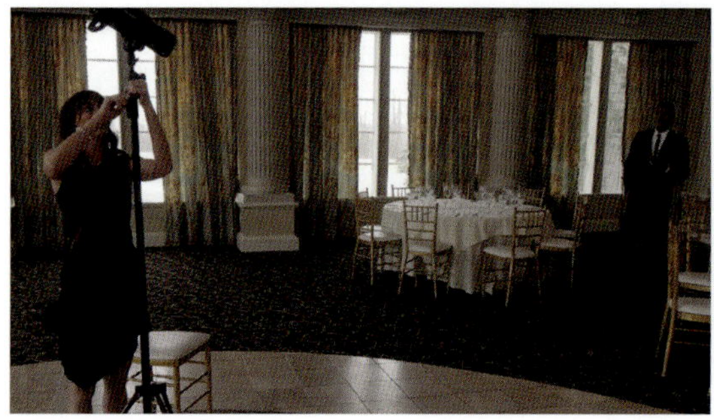

FIGURE 20.7

BEHIND-THE-SCENES VIDEO GRABS.

Potential Problems

Make sure that the backlight isn't hitting your subject on the side of their face. It can easily blow out the skin tones and usually isn't very flattering. Position the light so it's more behind the speaker in relation to where you're shooting versus on the same side as you.

Sometimes speech-givers ask the reception goers to stand for a toast. When that happens, they all stand and block your lights. I highly recommend 12-foot light stands so that you can securely put the lights up that high. Make sure your lights are at least 9 feet high (thought 12 feet is ideal) to overcome people standing and their hands being in the air.

I know I told you that it's great to use a mic stand and communicate with the person that's speaking that they shouldn't move too much, but some speakers are cooler than you and do whatever the %$*& they want. I once had a best man that decided to pace the entire reception room giving a speech like he was Eminem trying to bust a rhyme. Awful.

If this happens you have three choices in the moment: you can move your lights (repeatedly), pull the grids off your lights and flood the room, or (and this is what I recommend) use bounce flash. When I set this up, I use a trigger that's also a speedlight so that if the speaker goes rogue, all I have to do is turn on the flash that's already on my camera. If you don't use a system that has a speedlight trigger, keep a speedlight nearby just in case.

If you're shooting a wedding, you also need to photograph the wedding couple that the speaker is addressing. If that's the case, here are two lighting options:

#1: Position the speaker to face the couple. The speaker's rim light is the couple's face light. The speaker's face light is the couple's rim light (**Figure 20.8**).

#2: Position the speaker to be side-by-side with the couple. The speaker's face light is also the couple's face light. The speaker's rim light is also the couple's rim light. Spread the light across all three people by pointing it at the person that's farthest away from the light (**Figure 20.9**).

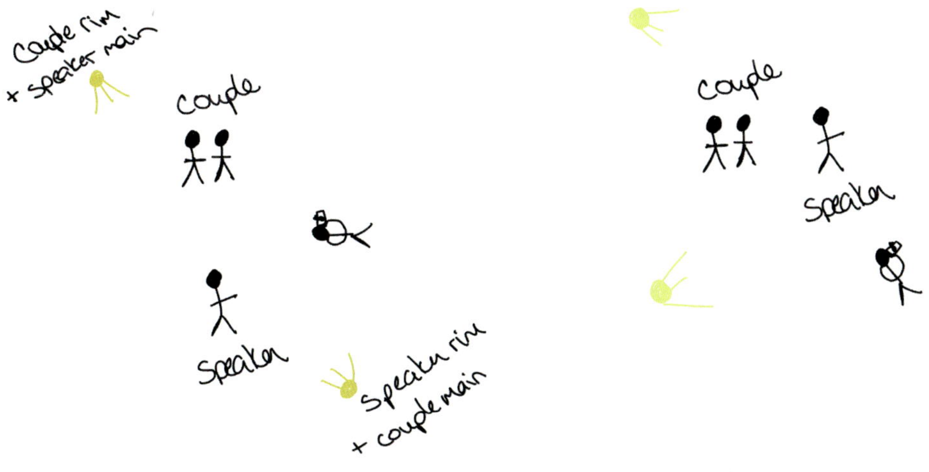

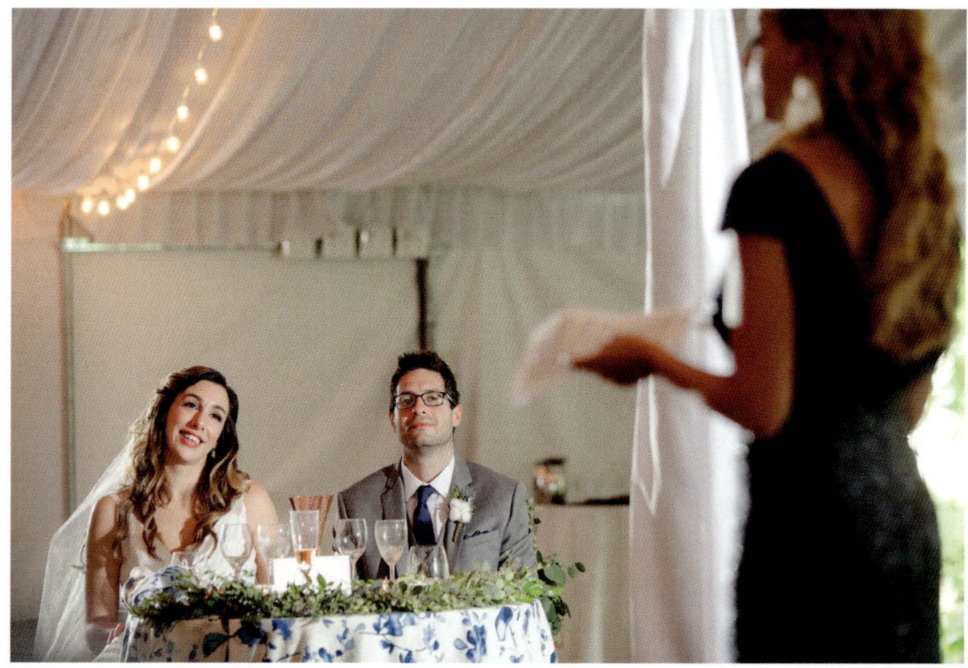

FIGURE 20.10

CANON 1DX, CANON 135MM 2.0, ISO 1600, APERTURE 2.8, SHUTTER 1/250

Practical Uses

In addition to creating dramatic images, this method of lighting is a must-use for events that are in halls without "bounceable" walls. If you're in a dark room with dark walls, use this lighting setup with the lights pointed towards the dance floor versus the speaker. You may want to put wider grids on your lights to cover more of the dance floor or add a third or fourth light, but that's up to you.

Other Techniques

This method of lighting can be used throughout an event or in any dark room in general. Consider using it for shots of dancing throughout the night and taking an overall room shot. You can add a third or fourth light to it if you want. For more on this in detail, take a look at Scenario 26, "Lighting a Dark Room," to use a similar setup in other ways.

To use this for shooting dancing throughout the night, take this technique but point the lights into the center of the dance floor. I recommend either putting the lights on opposite corners of the dance floor or putting both lights in the corner of the same side of the dance floor. If there's a

DJ booth or entertainment with lighting that moves over the crowd, place the two lights on the opposite side of the dance floor and use the extra lights as backlight. Depending on your shooting style, you may like one of these setups better than the other.

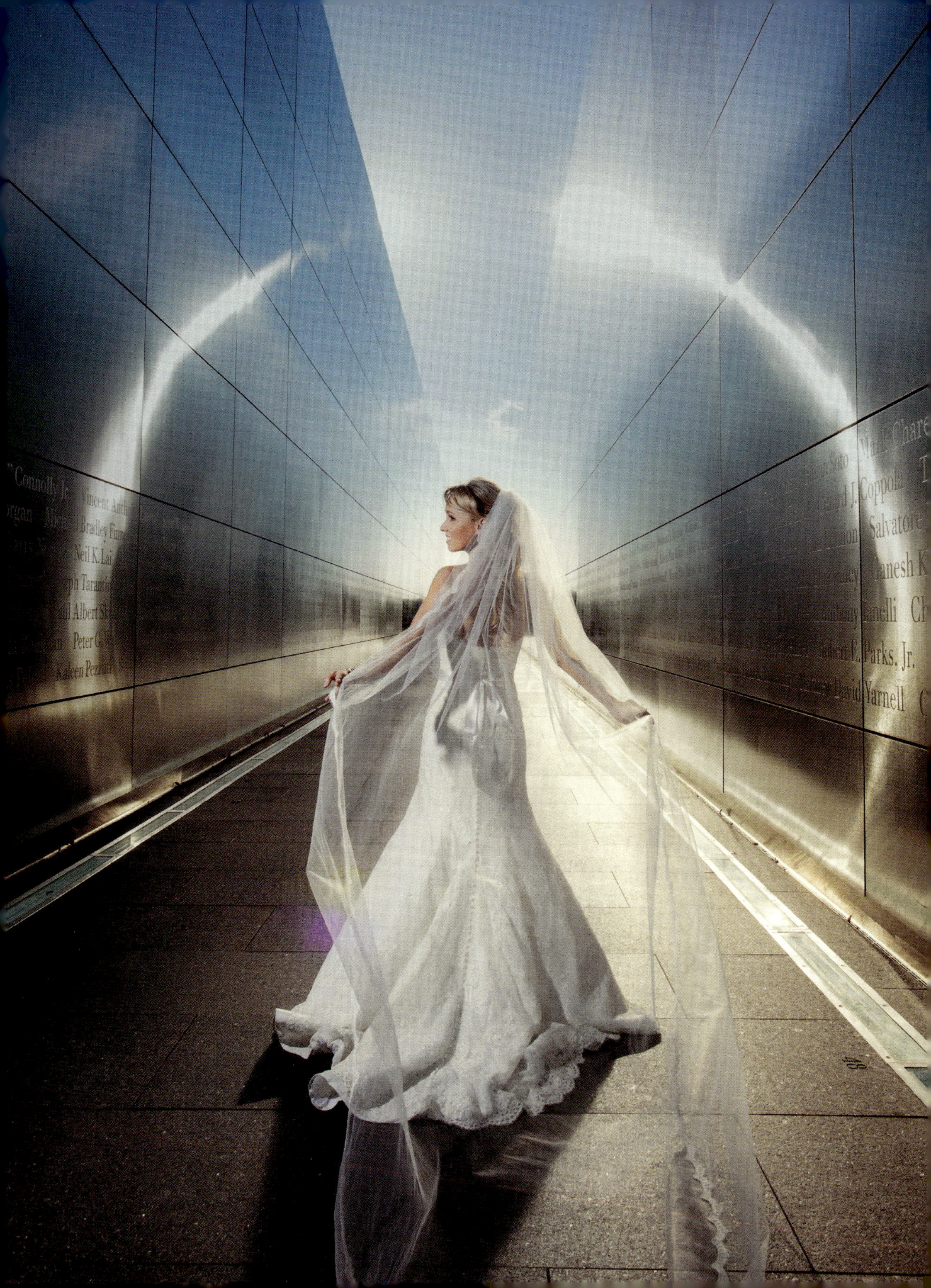

SCENARIO 21

In Harsh Sunlight

Solutions that don't leave you running for shade.

GOAL IMAGE

We've all been there. Not a cloud in the sky. You're literally and figuratively sweating, and there is nowhere to run for cover from harsh lighting. **Figure 21.1** is actually the very first time I used a strobe for a wedding. It was the Profoto B1, and I had no. Freaking. Clue. What I was doing. Naturally, quite a bit of Photoshop work has been done on this image (it was also 2014 and I didn't know the meaning of the word "subtle"). I also didn't know what I was doing and made up for it in post. However, the concept, which I executed by the skin of my teeth, is the same.

For this concept to work, you'll need to figure out which direction your subject needs to face to get the most shade on their face, even if it's a very little bit of shade. Ideally the light is hitting them in the back as much as possible. The sun ends up becoming your rim light, and you fill in your subject's face as much as possible with a flash.

This is a great example of why flash is more useful than continuous light, or why sometimes you need a strobe instead of a speedlight. The flash or strobe will emit a much more powerful burst of light, allowing you to overpower the sun in situations like this. You could not do this with a continuous light source—unless you've got crazy bright one attached to a generator.

Step by Step

1. **Position your light:** Because you're fighting the sun, and especially if you're using a light modifier, you'll need the light to be fairly close to your subject. Find a spot that's only a few feet away to get as much power from your light as possible.

2. **Set the camera exposure:** Get an exposure for the natural light *behind* your subject, taking into consideration both the background of the photo and any light that is hitting them. You don't want any highlights on shoulders created by the sun.

3. **Set the white balance:** Because the flash is affecting the light on your subject, set your white balance for flash or 5600K depending on the flash you're using.

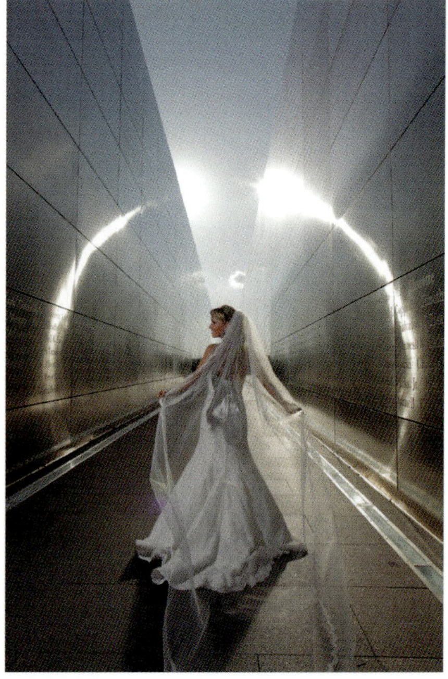

FIGURE 21.1

GOAL IMAGE. FLASH SET ON TTL +2; SATURATION BROUGHT UP AND BACKGROUND DARKENED IN LIGHTROOM AND PHOTOSHOP. SEE THE STRAIGHT-OUT-OF-CAMERA IMAGE IN FIGURE 21.4.
CANON 1D MARKIV, CANON 24MM 1.4, ISO 100, APER-TURE 14, SHUTTER 1/200

4. **Set the flash power:** I usually set my light using TTL in this scenario, and then adjust it from there. If you're using a manual flash, start in the middle-high power range or use a light meter and adjust up or down to your liking. Take a test shot and adjust your light to be more or less powerful. If you need more light but are at max power on your flash, move closer, add a grid to concentrate the light, or take off a layer of diffusion from your modifier.

5. **Balance the light:** If you're noticing hot spots on your subject's face or shoulders, you need to darken down your exposure and brighten your flash.

OPTIONAL: Put a gel on your flash and change your white balance or color tint to balance the skin tone, but change the color of the background. You can do some pretty fun things with this technique!

OPTIONAL: If you're having trouble with hot spots on your subject (as mentioned in step 5), use a translucent reflector to shade them from the harsh sun coming from behind.

Shot by Shot

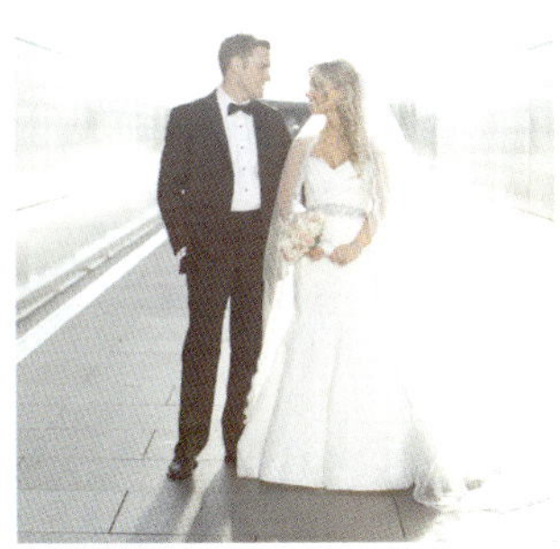

FIGURE 21.2

EXPOSING FOR THE SUBJECT'S FACE IN NATURAL LIGHT. NIGHTMARE! CANON 1D MARK IV, CANON 50MM 1.2, ISO 200, APERTURE 2.8, SHUTTER 1/1000

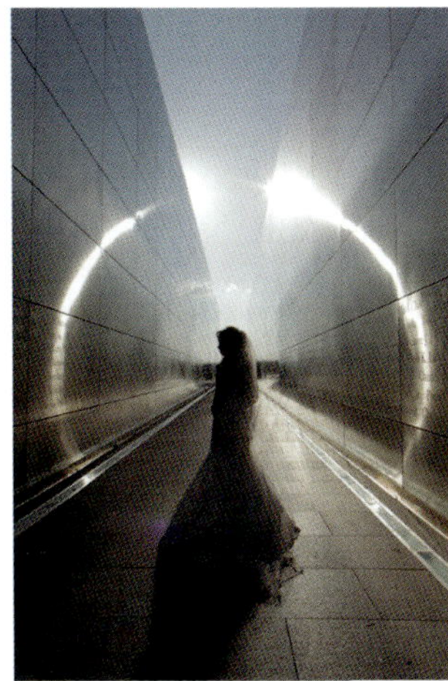

FIGURE 21.3

EXPOSING FOR THE BACKGROUND. THIS VERSION OF THE B1 DID NOT HAVE HIGH SPEED SYNC, SO I HAD TO KEEP IT BELOW SYNC SPEED. CANON 1D MARK IV, CANON 24MM 1.4, ISO 100, APERTURE 14, SHUTTER 1/200

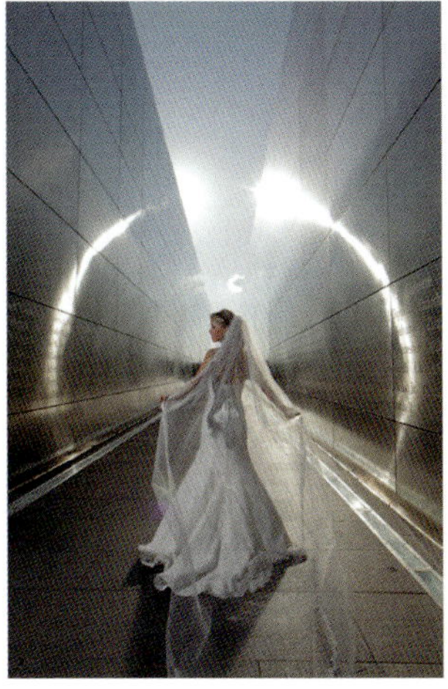

FIGURE 21.4

SHOT WITH A PROFOTO B1 ON CAMERA LEFT WITH NO MODIFIER. FLASH WAS SET TO TTL +2 (IT WAS DEFINITELY MAXED OUT AT 10). CANON 1D MARK IV, CANON 24MM 1.4, ISO 100, APERTURE 14, SHUTTER 1/200

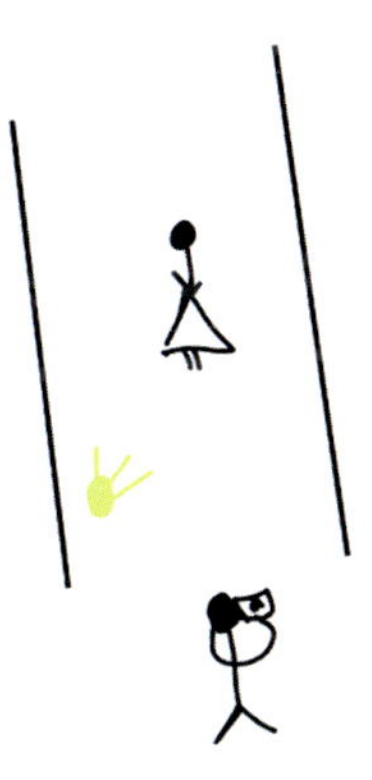

FIGURE 21.5

BOTH OF THESE SHOTS USE THE LIGHTING SETUP IN THIS DIAGRAM.

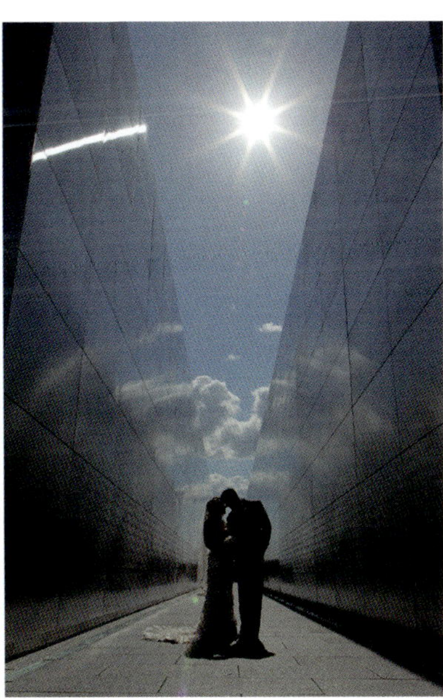

FIGURE 21.6

EXPOSING FOR THE BACK-GROUND. CANON 5D MARK II, CANON 24MM 1.2, ISO 100, APERTURE 14, SHUTTER 1/200

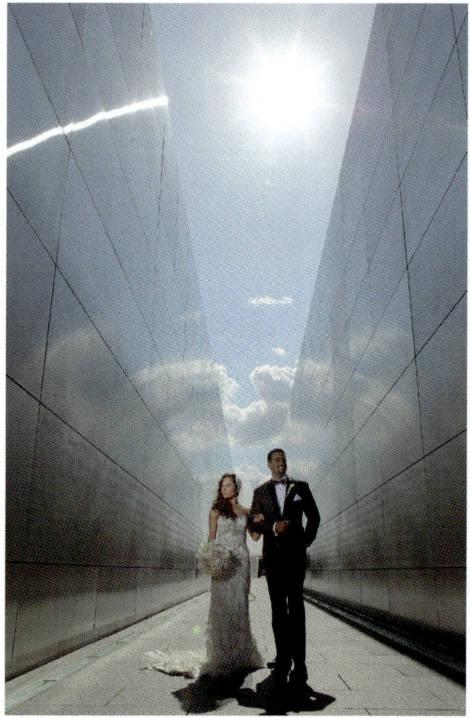

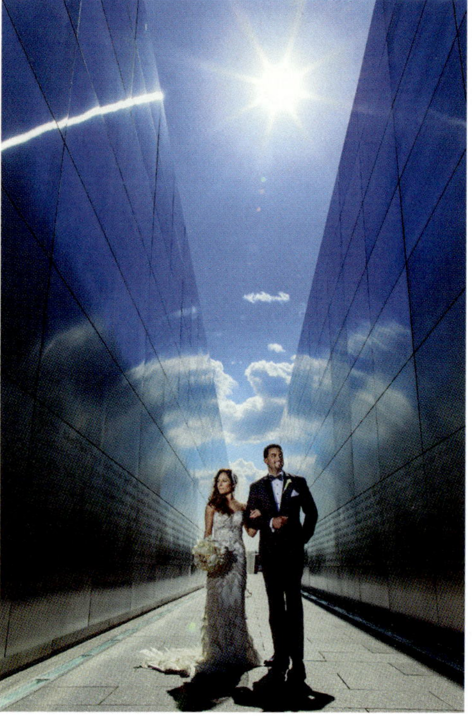

FIGURE 21.7
SHOT WITH A PROFOTO B1 ON CAMERA LEFT WITH NO MODIFIER.
CANON 5D MARK II, CANON 24MM 1.2, ISO 100, APERTURE 14, SHUTTER 1/200

FIGURE 21.8
THIS IMAGE WAS PHOTOSHOPPED TO DARKEN AND SATURATE THE BACKGROUND. IT WAS 2014, I HAD NO HIGH SPEED SYNC, NO ND FILTER, AND I WAS MAXED OUT ON LIGHT POWER. OH, AND THIS WAS ONLY THE SECOND TIME I USED THE LIGHT. SEE? IF I CAN DO IT, SO CAN YOU!

Potential Problems

This chapter focused on how to overcome harsh sunlight for individuals or couples. I didn't address how to do so for groups, but the concept is still the same. The problem with groups is that you'll need a lot more light and a large light spread in order to fight the sun. If you have a group of, for example, ten people, you may want to use umbrellas to spread the light more extensively. Place one light on either side of the group pointing towards the opposite end of the frame or group of people. See Scenario 6, "Group Shots with One Light," for more about balancing the light evenly across a group of people. In harsh sunlight, you'll likely need two lights, probably strobes, to light across the group to balance your flash with the sun.

You may encounter the problem of the background getting blown out. I solve this problem by searching for a darker background to shoot into, as well as using a longer lens so it compresses and makes the background a bit softer. A shallow depth of field helps with this as well. Be careful not to go too shallow if you're working with a group of people.

Other Techniques

Since my first example is a "flashy" looking image, I wanted to show you a more natural headshot as well. The key, like always, is making your light source larger. I used a Profoto B10 with an OCF beauty dish for this image.

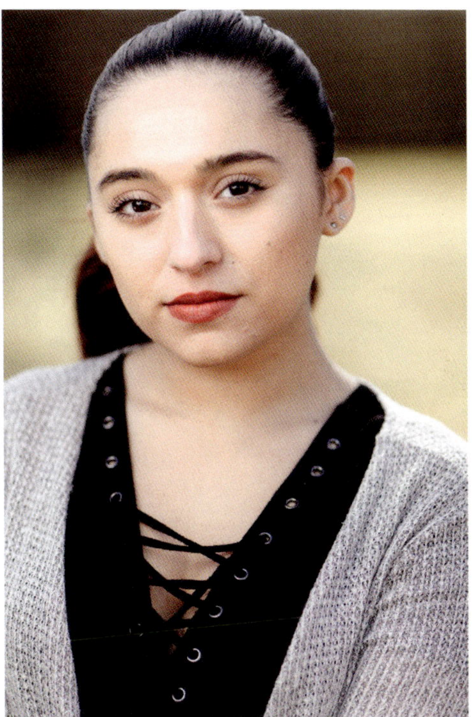

FIGURE 21.9
SHOT WITH A PROFOTO B10 WITH OCF BEAUTY DISH TO CAMERA LEFT.
CANON 1DX II, CANON 135MM 2.0, ISO 125, APERTURE 2, SHUTTER 1/640

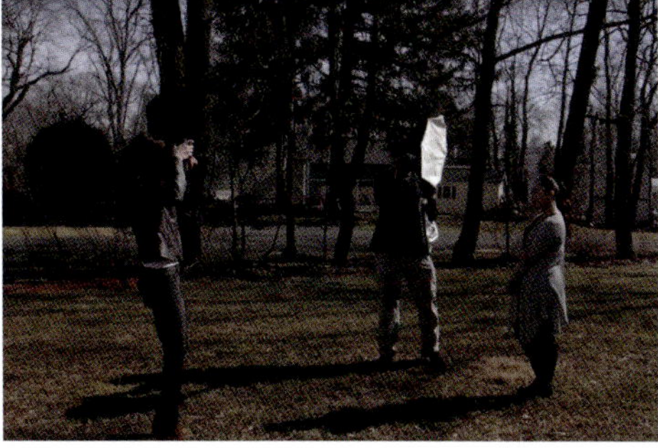

FIGURE 21.10
NOTE HOW SHE'S PLACED WITH THE SUN HITTING HER BACK, AND THE LIGHT IS NICE AND CLOSE, ILLUMINATING HER FACE.

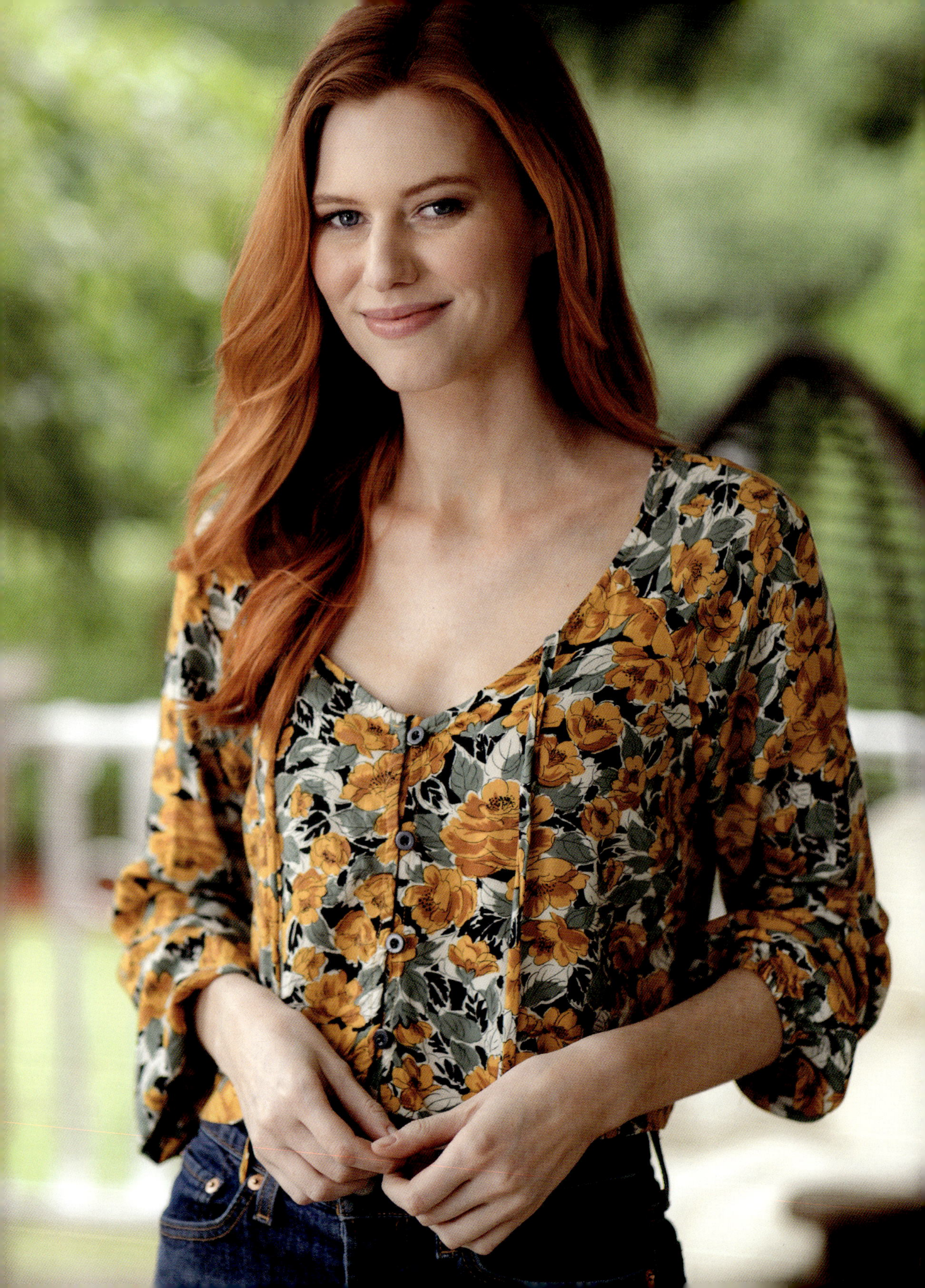

SCENARIO 22
Shooting with Reflectors

A few options for one of your favorite natural light tools.

GOAL IMAGE

I don't really have a goal image for this chapter, more like a goal outcome. Just because you're shooting with off-camera flash doesn't mean that you have to throw away some of the tools you've learned to use with natural light.

My reflector is one of my absolute favorite tools. It is a very inexpensive light modifier that's light-weight, easy and fast to set up, and can drastically change the look of your image. Using reflectors with off-camera flash can be equally, if not more, useful as using them with natural light.

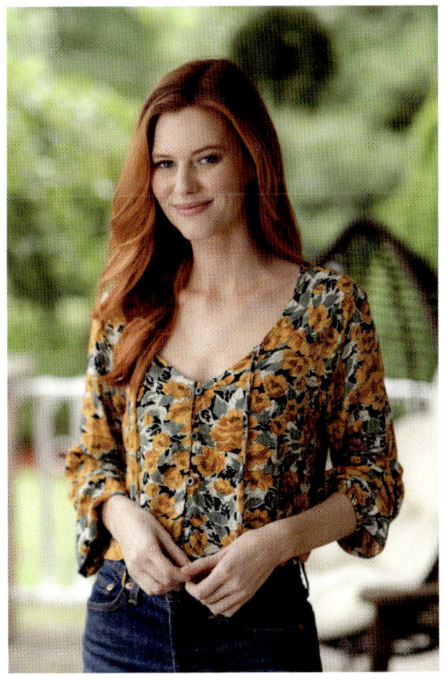

FIGURE 22.1

GOAL IMAGE. SHOT WITH A PROFOTO A1 BOUNCING OFF A WHITE 42″ REFLECTOR.
CANON 1DX II, CANON 85MM 1.4, ISO 125, APERTURE 2.2, SHUTTER 1/250

GEAR NEEDED:

- Camera + Trigger
- Lens of any focal length
- Off-camera flash
- 42" 5-in-1 reflector (recommend style and size)

ABOUT REFLECTORS

Whenever you use a reflector, go back to the pool hall or high school geometry class. The angle of incidence equals the angle of reflection. Or, the light will hit the reflector at one angle degree and bounce off at the opposite but equal angle degree.

Think about standing next to a wall with a tennis ball. If you throw the ball directly at the wall, it'll come directly back at you. If you throw the ball at an angle, it's going to bounce off the wall in the opposite direction it was thrown. It's just physics, my friend.

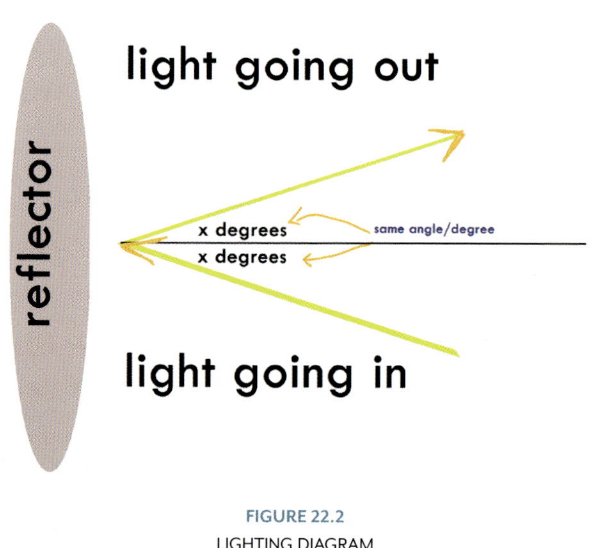

FIGURE 22.2
LIGHTING DIAGRAM

Sides of the Reflector

Reflectors like this have a number of sides. If you have the Glow 5-in-1 Reflector from Adorama.com that I do, you have all of these parts in one reflector, except the gold side (which I almost never use). It's important to know the differences between them all (which are sometimes very subtle) so that you're utilizing the best tool for your desired outcome.

White Side

This is the side I use the most. It reflects the same color light back onto my subject. It's great for filling in soft light in most cases, unless I'm intentionally letting the sun hit it directly.

Gold Side

The gold side will reflect a warmer light back at your subject, and it will also add to the specular highlights. It reflects a brighter light back than the white light will, but that's not the only difference. The white highlights will become whiter and create more of a contrast to the rest of the image. If you have a subject with oily skin, it will intensify the blown-out shiny areas of the skin. This is used often for beauty shots where you want to highlight the skin in a more glowing way.

Silver Side

This silver side behaves exactly as the gold, but instead of reflecting a warm tone back, it reflects a cooler tone more representative of the light it's reflecting. It adds to the specular highlights just like the gold side.

Mixed Silver and Gold

This silver and gold side is just a combination of the two. It reflects back a warm tone, but half as warm as a fully gold side would. It adds to the specular highlights and has a brighter reflection than the white side.

Black Side

I know what you're thinking: "Duh Vanessa, black doesn't reflect anything." Correct. Instead, it controls unwanted reflections. Say you have your subject standing on green grass. With natural light or off-camera flash you stand the chance of the light reflecting that green color back up at your subject. Yuck. Throw the black side of the reflector down in front of your subject (or wherever the green light is bouncing back from). You'll save yourself some time in Photoshop, and your subject won't resemble the Wicked Witch of the West.

Translucent Middle

This is my favorite side of my reflector, and it's not even a side. The middle of my reflector is a translucent white cloth. I can reflect very soft light off of it and shoot light through it. When I shoot light through it, it essentially becomes a nice big softbox.

Reflector Uses

Shoot through it: You'll need someone to hold the translucent middle of the reflector in front of the light while you shoot. Shoot through it to create a soft, diffused light. This is a great alternative to purchasing potentially expensive light modifiers, and will produce similar results.

Shoot into it to use it as a main light: Holding your reflector in front of the light to bounce it back at the subject.

Reflect light off of it: Maybe you want a two-light look, but you only have one off-camera flash. Place your light behind your subject like in Scenario 1, "Creating Gold Haze," and use your reflector (likely the silver side to provide enough light) to reflect that light back into your subject's face.

Control the light: Sometimes you get unwanted light from your OCF or ambient light hitting parts of your scene other than your subject. Use the black side of the reflector to block the light, change the shape of the light, or control where the light spreads. This is sometimes referred to as flagging the light.

Fill light: Place your reflector opposite your main off-camera flash and use it as a fill light to lighten the shadows in your image.

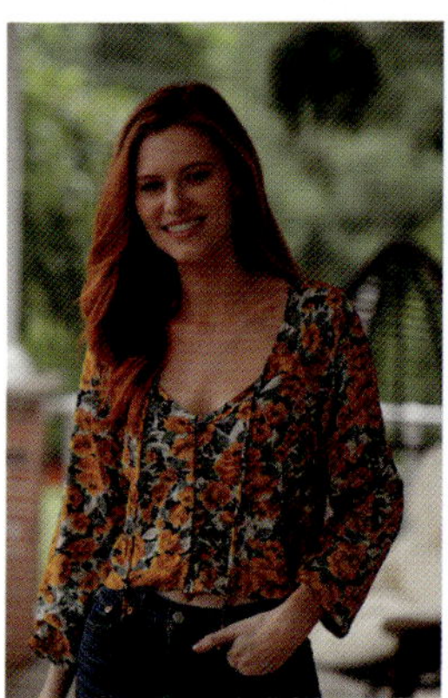

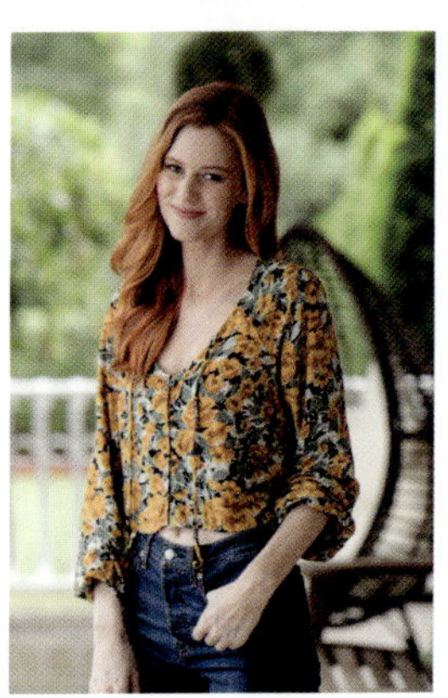

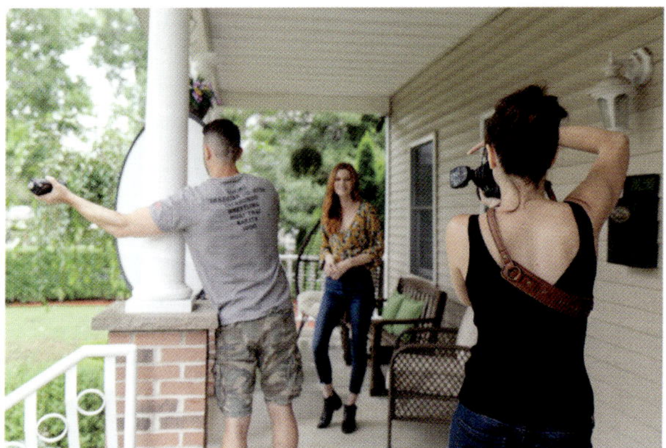

FIGURE 22.4
ON THE LEFT: SHOOTING THROUGH A REFLECTOR DIFFUSER. ON THE RIGHT: BEHIND THE SCENES.
CANON 1DXII, CANON 85MM 1.4, ISO 125, APERTURE 2.2, SHUTTER 1/250

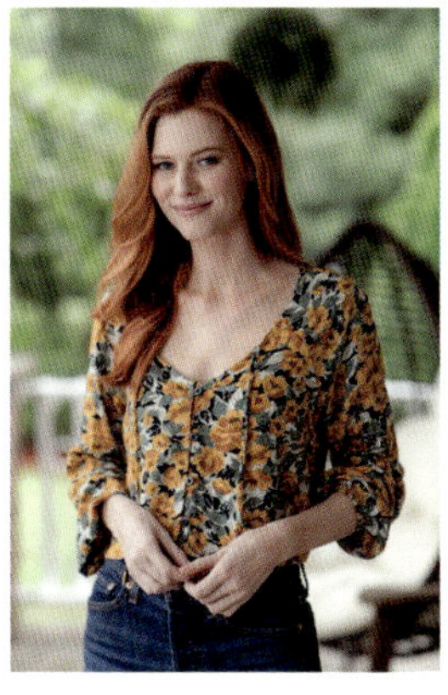
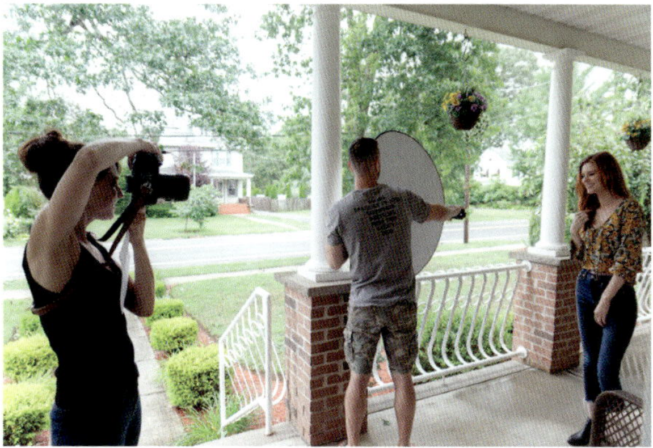

SHOOTING A PROFOTO A1 INTO A WHITE REFLECTOR.
CANON 1DXII, CANON 85MM 1.4, ISO 125, APERTURE 2.2, SHUTTER 1/250

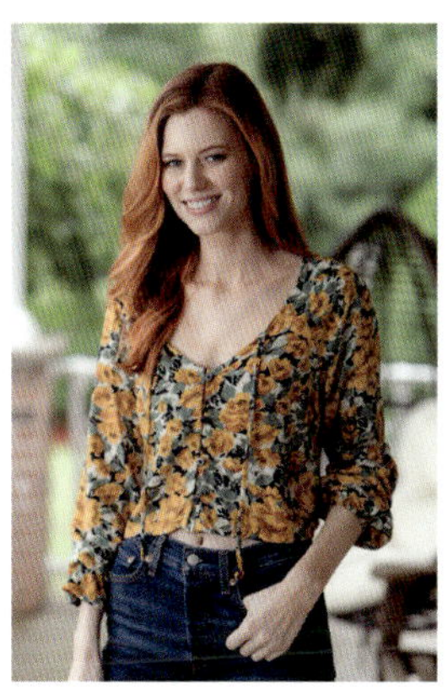
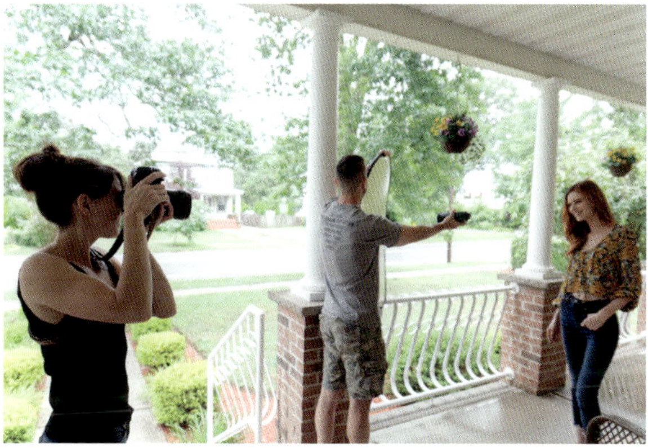

SHOOTING A PROFOTO A1 INTO A SILVER REFLECTOR.
CANON 1DXII, CANON 85MM 1.4, ISO 125, APERTURE 2.2, SHUTTER 1/250

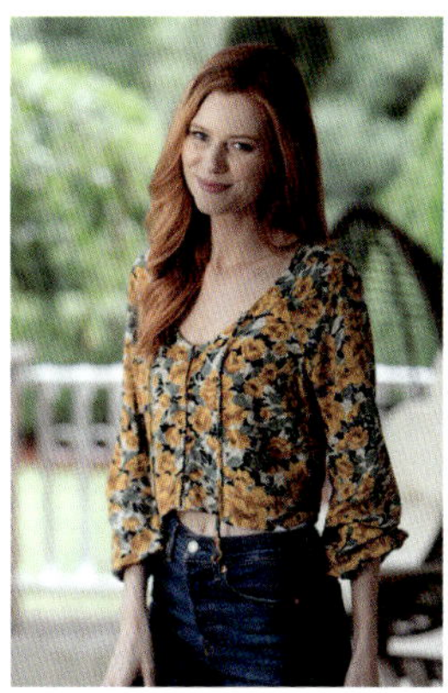

SHOOTING A PROFOTO A1 INTO A SILVER/GOLD REFLECTOR. I WHITE
BALANCED IN POST FOR THE SKIN TONE. NOTICE THAT THE BACK-
GROUND IS COOLER IN THIS PHOTO THAN THE ONE SHOT WITH THE
SILVER REFLECTOR.
CANON 1DXII, CANON 85MM 1.4, ISO 125, APERTURE 2.2, SHUTTER 1/250

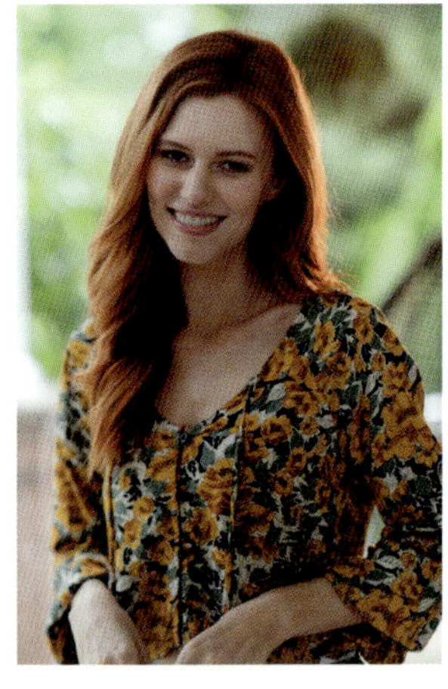

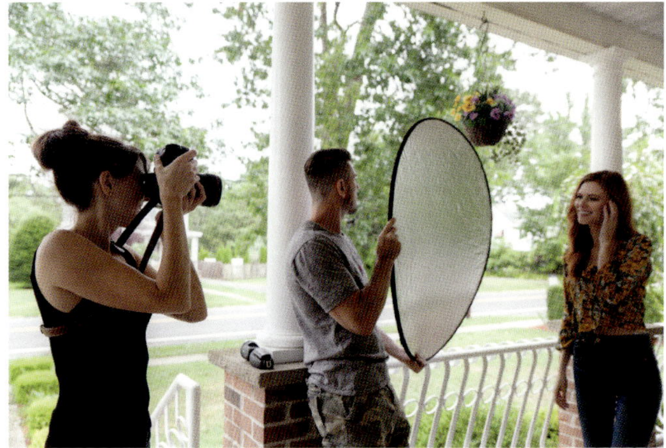

FIGURE 22.7

SHOT WITH A PROFOTO A1 WITH FULL CTO (ORANGE) GEL IN THE BACK, HITTING THE SILVER SIDE OF THE REFLECTOR TO LIGHT THE SUBJECT'S FACE.

CANON 1DXII, CANON 85MM 1.4, ISO 250, APERTURE 2.2, SHUTTER 1/160

FIGURE 22.8

THE PROFOTO A1 IS OFF CAMERA RIGHT BEHIND THE MODEL WITH A FULL CTO GEL.

CANON 1DXII, CANON 85MM 1.4, ISO 250, APERTURE 2.2, SHUTTER 1/160

FIGURE 22.9

THE BLACK SIDE OF THE REFLECTOR IS BLOCKING THE GREEN REFLECTION FROM THE BUSH.

CANON 1DXII, CANON 85MM 1.4, ISO 160, APERTURE 2.8, SHUTTER 1/250

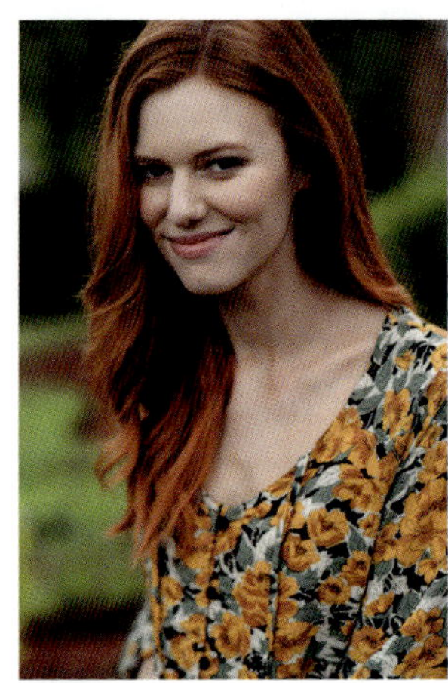

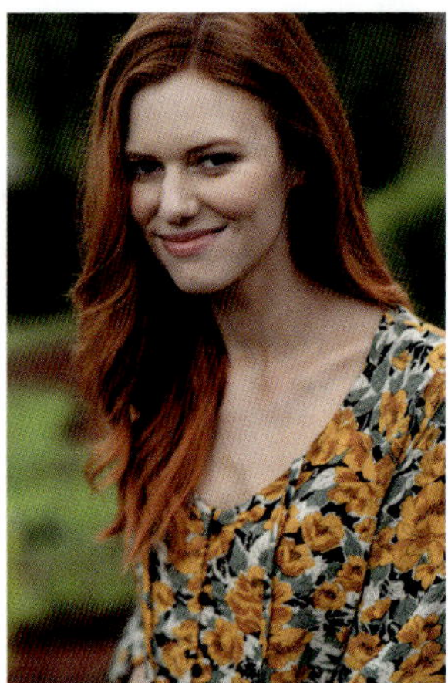

FIGURE 22.10

THIS SHOT IS NOT USING THE REFLECTOR TO BLOCK THE GREEN REFLECTION FROM THE BUSH. NOTICE THE SLIGHT GREEN HUE IN THE SHADOWS UNDERNEATH HER CHEEKS AND ON HER NECK.

CANON 1DXII, CANON 85MM 1.4, ISO 160, APERTURE 2.8, SHUTTER 1/250

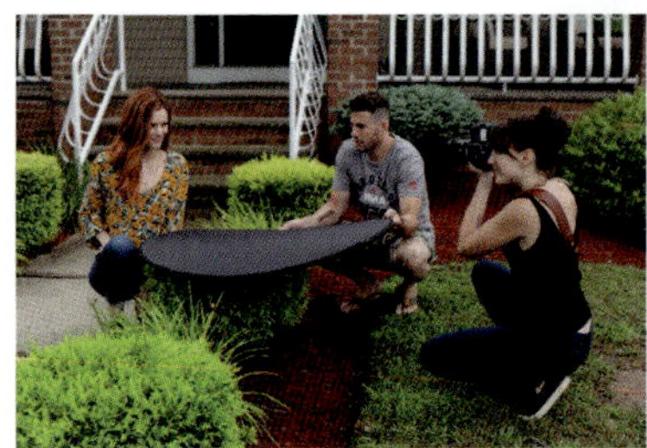

Practical Uses

You can use a reflector in pretty much any scenario—as a fill light, to control light, in place of a softbox, etc. The scenarios in which I specifically suggest using a reflector for particular effects are the following:

- Creating Gold Haze
- Epic Rain or Snow
- Super Soft Portrait Light
- Tiny Little Details
- Creating Golden Hour
- Making Indoors Look Like Outdoors
- Individual Portraits
- In Harsh Sunlight

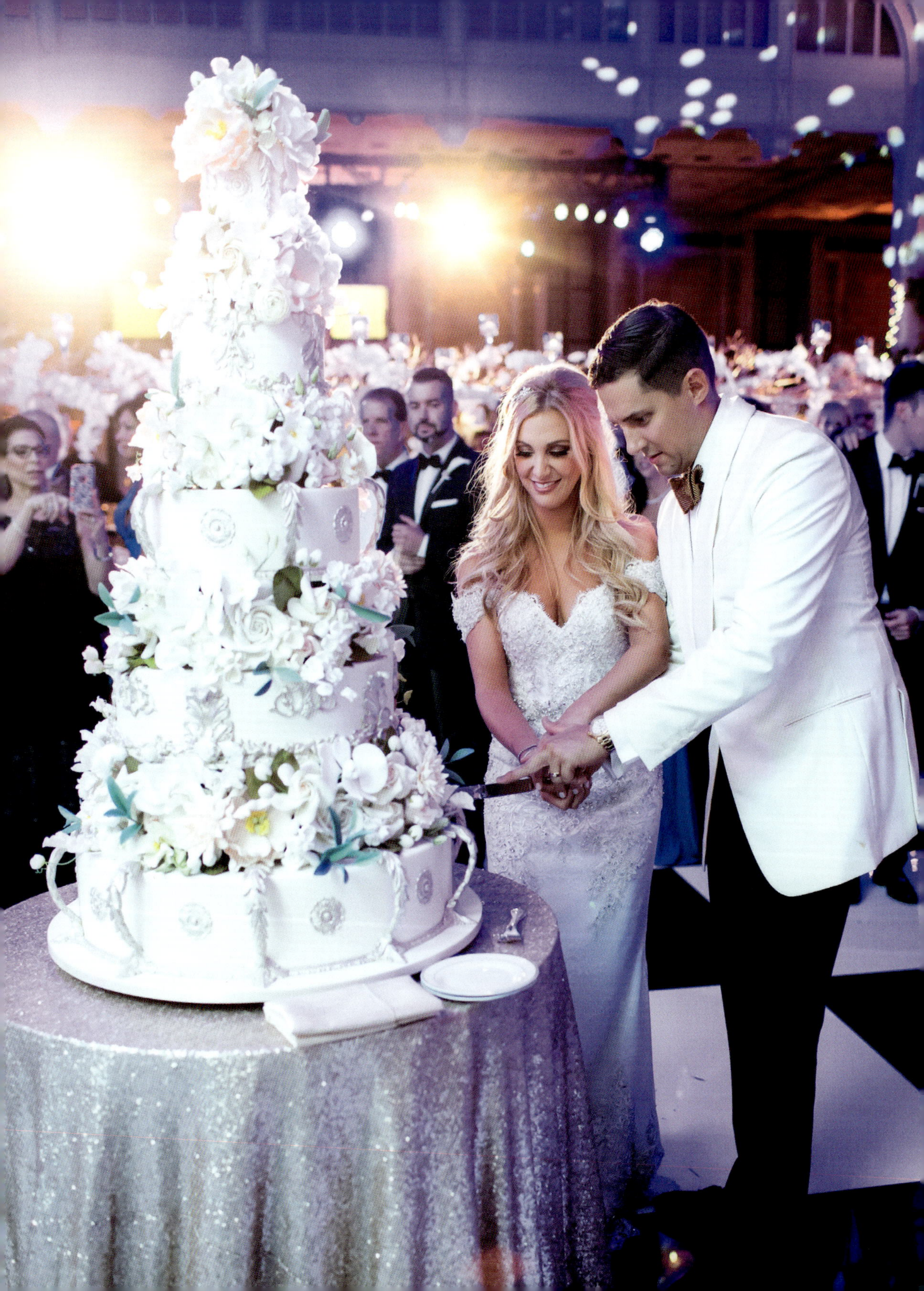

SCENARIO 23
Event Bounce Flash

My go-to method for lighting events.

GOAL IMAGE

I almost didn't write about my event (wedding) lighting system because truthfully, I shoot with my speedlight on camera at almost all costs. After all, this book is all about off-camera flash, right? Well, the concepts regarding flash are the same whether it's on or off the camera. It's simply the light direction that changes (**Figure 23.1**).

I use bounce flash at receptions if it's at all possible. I prefer this because I can move anywhere and take a photo. Some events are in separate rooms, and I can't have lights set up in every room. Sometimes I get dragged to another building to take a photo for the mother-of-the-bride. Keeping my flash on-camera allows me the freedom to move in a moment's notice and capture anything, anywhere.

That being said, I can't always shoot bounce flash. And sometimes, even when I can, I want to do something different or create a more dramatic image than bounce flash can produce. This scenario will walk you through bounce flash and adding flashes from there to embellish.

GEAR NEEDED:

- Camera + Trigger
- Lens of a focal length
- On-camera flash
- 1 or more off-camera flashes
- 1 or more light stands
- 1 or more grid

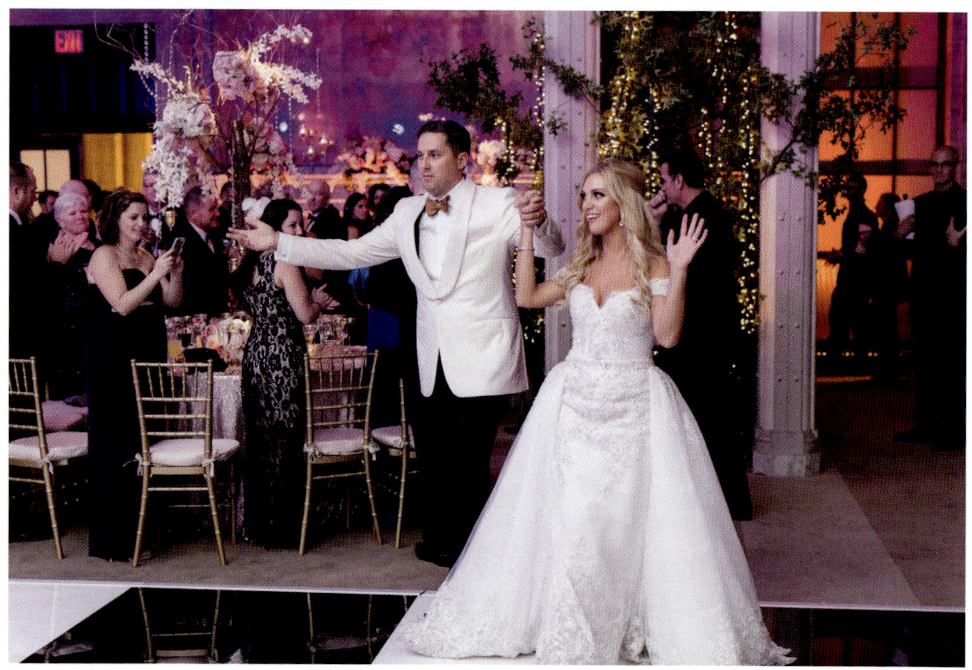

FIGURE 23.1
GOAL IMAGE.
CANON 1D X, CANON 50MM 1.2, ISO 2000, APERTURE 3.2, SHUTTER 1/160

Step by Step

1. **Evaluate the room:** For bounce flash to work, you need to have a white or lightly colored surface to bounce it off of. If it's a room with nothing but dark walls, bounce flash isn't going to work. It'll suck up a ton of power and reflect back whatever color the wall is. However, if you have just one lightly colored wall or ceiling, that's all you need.

2. **Learn to move your flash head:** Throughout the event, you will move your flash head around constantly. Your goal is to not only point it at a "bounceable" wall, but point it in the direction where your subject's nose is pointed. This will cause the light to bounce back and beautifully light their face instead of the back of their head.

3. **Set the camera exposure:** Since the point of this setup is to photograph as quickly and effectively as possible, you'll want to have an exposure that you don't need to futz with much. Depending on the ambient light in the space, I usually set my ISO around 1600 or 2000 (a bit higher if I want to save battery life), my shutter speed at $\frac{1}{160}$, and my aperture at f/2.5–3.2.

4. **Set the white balance:** The light you're working with will be a mix of flash and ambient light hitting your subject. You can set your WB to auto, and it may work better than dialing it in manually if you have (for instance) continually changing colored DJ lights. It depends on how

much ambient light you're letting in versus the flash overpowering it, but you'll likely be around 4600K. Start there, check your coloring, and adjust.

5. **Set your metering mode:** Because I'm going to advise that you use TTL to bounce your flash, set your metering mode to spot metering and your focus to single-point. This will make TTL work more accurately by reading the light where you're placing your focus (typically your subject's face) versus reading the entire room. It results in a much more accurate TTL reading.

6. **Set your flash power:** TTL is my best friend in this scenario. It's what TTL was practically invented for. If you choose to set your flash manually, just know that you'll have to continually adjust it based on how far away your subject is from the wall (your light source) and your camera.

Shot by Shot

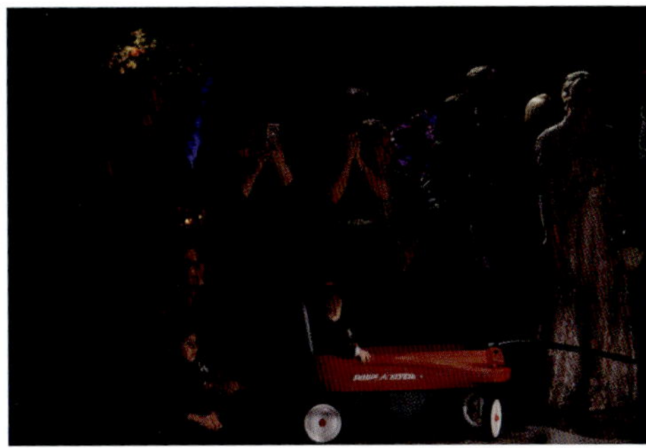

FIGURE 23.2
NATURAL LIGHT.
CANON 1D X II, CANON 135MM 2.0, ISO 2000,
APERTURE 2.5, SHUTTER 1/320

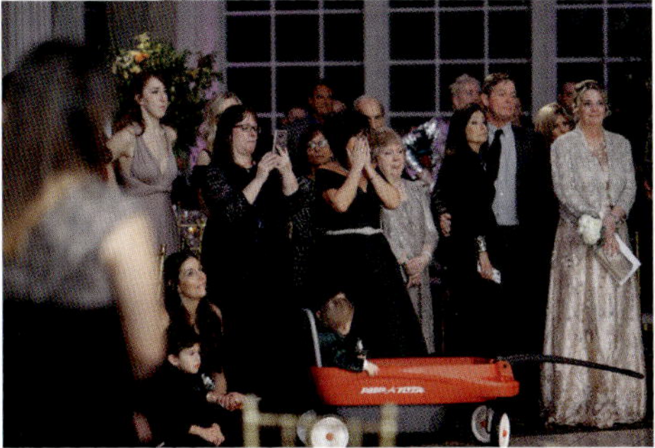

FIGURE 23.3
SHOT WITH BOUNCE FLASH.
CANON 1D X II, CANON 135MM 2.0, ISO 2000, APERTURE
2.5, SHUTTER 1/250 (STRAIGHT OUT OF THE CAMERA)

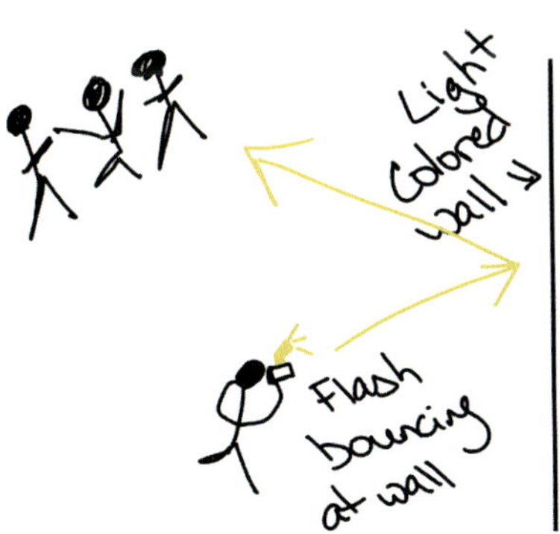

FIGURE 23.4
LIGHTING DIAGRAM.

OPTIONAL STEPS:

1. **Add a backlight:** This is one of the easiest ways to embellish your event shots. Personally, I don't use this if I have a videographer with a lighting setup or DJ lights that I can shoot into. If I have either of those present, I'll use those lights as my backlights to add more dimension to the shot. If I don't, here's what I do:

    A. **Set up the backlight:** Think of this as adding a light to your existing shot. I don't like using TTL for the backlight because, depending on your flash, it'll vary too much. Look at the light power from your last TTL on-camera bounce flash, add +1 power (if you can) and set your backlight to manual on that power setting. Adjust up or down from there depending on how you'd like the image to look.

    B. **Position the light:** My favorite way to use this at weddings is during the first dance. I have my assistant hold the light directly behind the couple and move it as I move. This will rim light them, and if you want to, let a little flare in by showing some of the flash in your shot. Be careful not to show your assistant, though. If you don't have an assistant, use a light stand. It will, however, limit your movement.

    C. **Experiment:** Once you've tried it during the first dance, try backlighting some crazy dance sets with a wide-angle lens. Let the light maybe overexpose everything a bit, and fire through the crowd like a spotlight behind them. Add a gel for a bit of colored fun.

2. **Add colored up lighting:** If you have a cave-like dark room without any lighting, you can add your own. Choose a colored gel and set up your light exactly like step 6. Instead of pointing the light at your couple, point it at the wall behind where you're shooting.

Shot by Shot

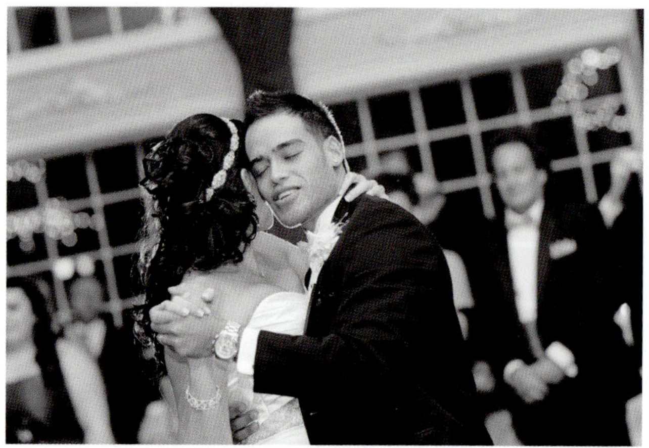

FIGURE 23.5

SHOT WITH A BOUNCE FLASH AND AN ASSISTANT HOLDING A SECOND FLASH BEHIND THE COUPLE.

CANON 1D MARK IV, CANON 85MM 1.2, ISO 1600, APERTURE 2.5, SHUTTER 1/80

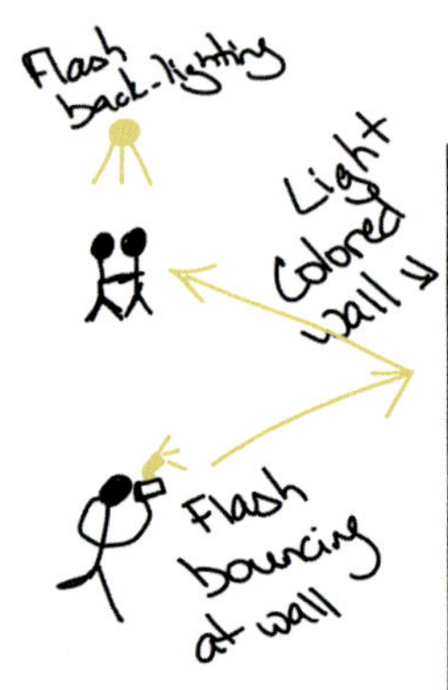

FIGURE 23.6

LIGHTING DIAGRAM.

Potential Problems

Whenever I train new shooters, reception lighting is almost always the trickiest for them to learn. Don't feel bad if you're not getting it right away. Don't freak out if the consistency isn't there. It takes time to see the light, notice potential issues before they happen, and adjust for them.

One of the biggest complaints I see event photographers have online is about the entertainment's club-like light show. This is super simple to work around. Just shoot into them. They become really cool backlights that liven up the image. If you're worried about shooting into the DJ booth, just shoot slightly to the right or left of it rather than straight into it. The lights won't hit your subject's faces, and you'll end up getting some pretty fun shots from it.

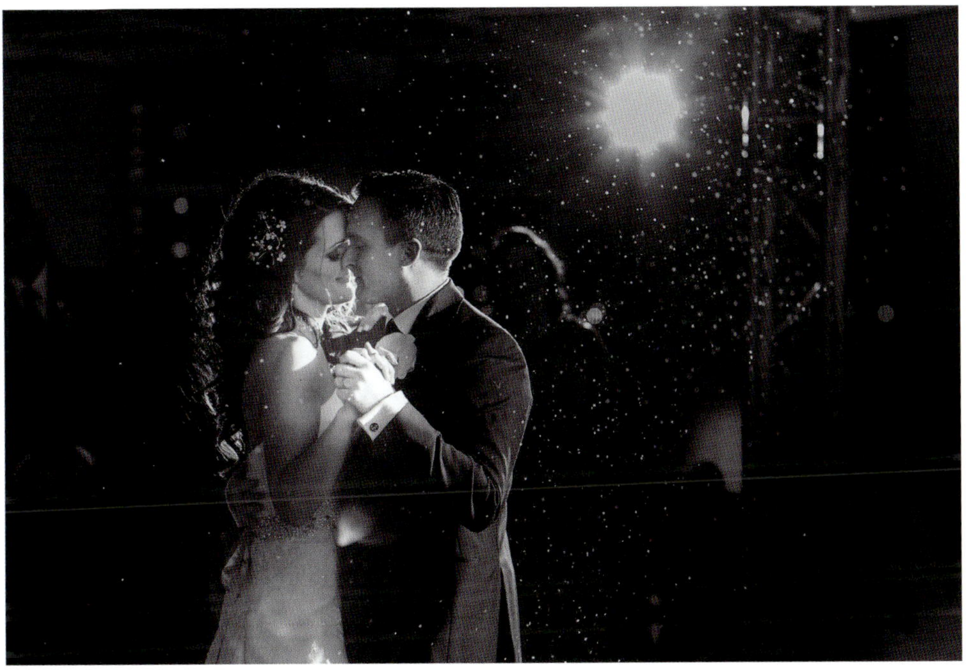

SHOT WITH BACKLIGHT FROM THE DJ AND BOUNCE FLASH.
CANON 1D MARK IV, CANON 85MM 1.2, ISO 1600, APERTURE 2.8, SHUTTER 1/200

I mostly ignore my metering setting because I shoot in manual 99.9% of the time. Recently, my friend Seth Miranda reminded me that when you use TTL on your flash, it's utilizing whatever metering method your camera is set to. Duh (insert face-palm here)! Set your camera to spot metering so that whatever face your focus point lands on is what the TTL will use to determine the correct power setting for your flash. You'll find a lot less fluctuation in the power coming out of your flash.

The flash not firing is a biggie when you're shooting events. No one wants to be the photographer that missed the big moment because the flash didn't fire. Most of the time this is due to the recycle time on your flash. It's definitely something to consider when purchasing a flash. If you own a speedlight that has a battery pack option, you'll find a world of a difference in your recycle time.

Most photographers are trained that a flash will freeze your subject. Yes and no. Yes, it freezes your subject, but if you have the natural ambient light of the room affecting your shot, that will also be a part of the exposure. The flash will freeze the subject, but the ambient light may end up giving your subject motion blur. If you're finding this to be a problem, raise your shutter speed until you don't see the motion blur any longer. You can create motion blur intentionally, however, and create some very cool ghosting effects if you want to experiment a little.

Make sure your foreground isn't too bright! Bounce flash can only get you so far and it's limiting if you want to shoot through different objects or people in the foreground. It'll likely overexpose them, and instead of your carefully placed foreground directing the viewer to the subject, it'll distract them from it. To eliminate the problem, you'll need to learn how to shape directional light. Check out Scenario 20, "Event Speeches," for specifics.

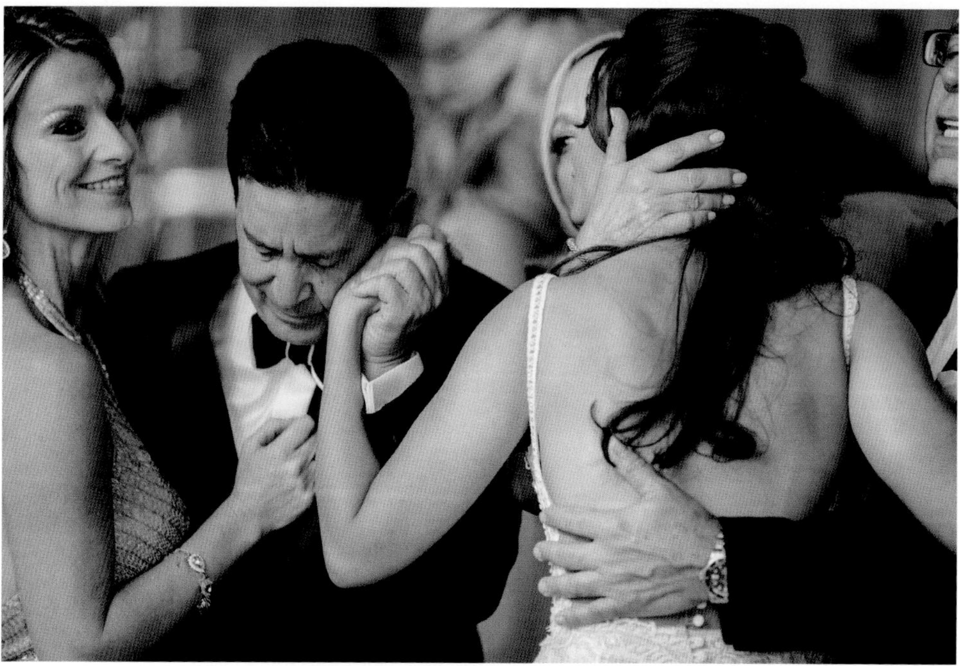

FIGURE 23.8
BOUNCE FLASH.
CANON 1D X II, CANON 135MM 2.0, ISO 4000, APERTURE 2, SHUTTER 1/160

Practical Uses

Learning to bounce your flash will likely become a staple in your photography skills. When you're shooting indoors, it's a quick soft, directional light that you can provide for any event; birthday parties, weddings, Bar and Bat Mitzahs—you name it. It's the lightest, fastest, and most portable flash that you'll ever use. Oh, and if you don't have a white wall to bounce light off of, you can use this technique by bouncing light off of a reflector. I even once bounced the light off of a white piece of paper at a rehearsal dinner once when I forgot my reflector, didn't bring an assistant or light stand, and needed to shoot some details in a floor-to-ceiling dark-wood barn room. Worked like a charm.

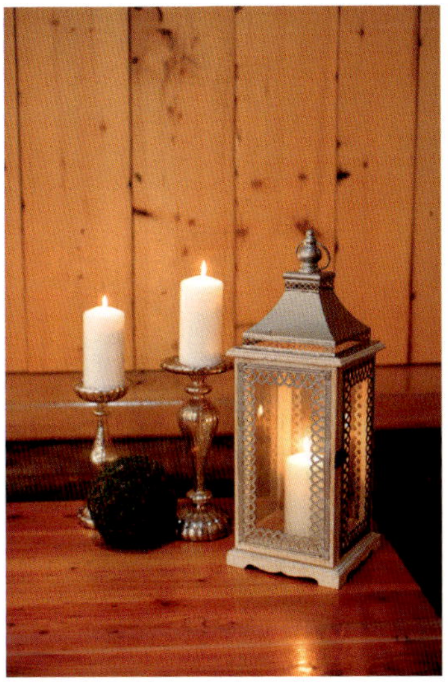

FIGURE 23.9
NATURAL LIGHT SHOT FOR EXPOSING THE BACKGROUND. – CANON 1DXII, CANON 85MM 1.4, ISO 125, APERTURE 2.2, SHUTTER 1/250

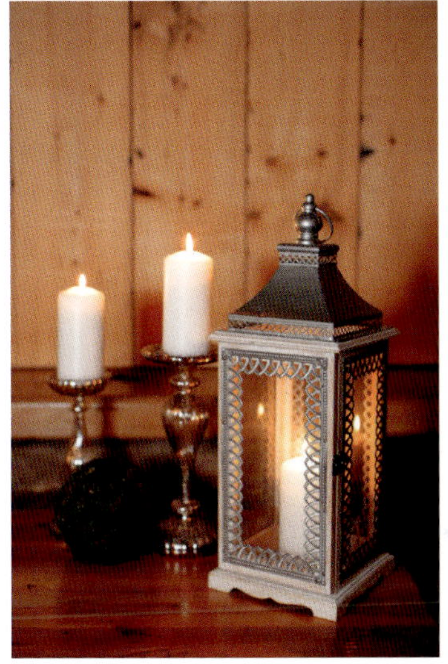

FIGURE 23.10
SHOOTING THROUGH A REFLECTOR DIFFUSER. CANON 1DXII, CANON 85MM 1.4, ISO 125, APERTURE 2.2, SHUTTER 1/250

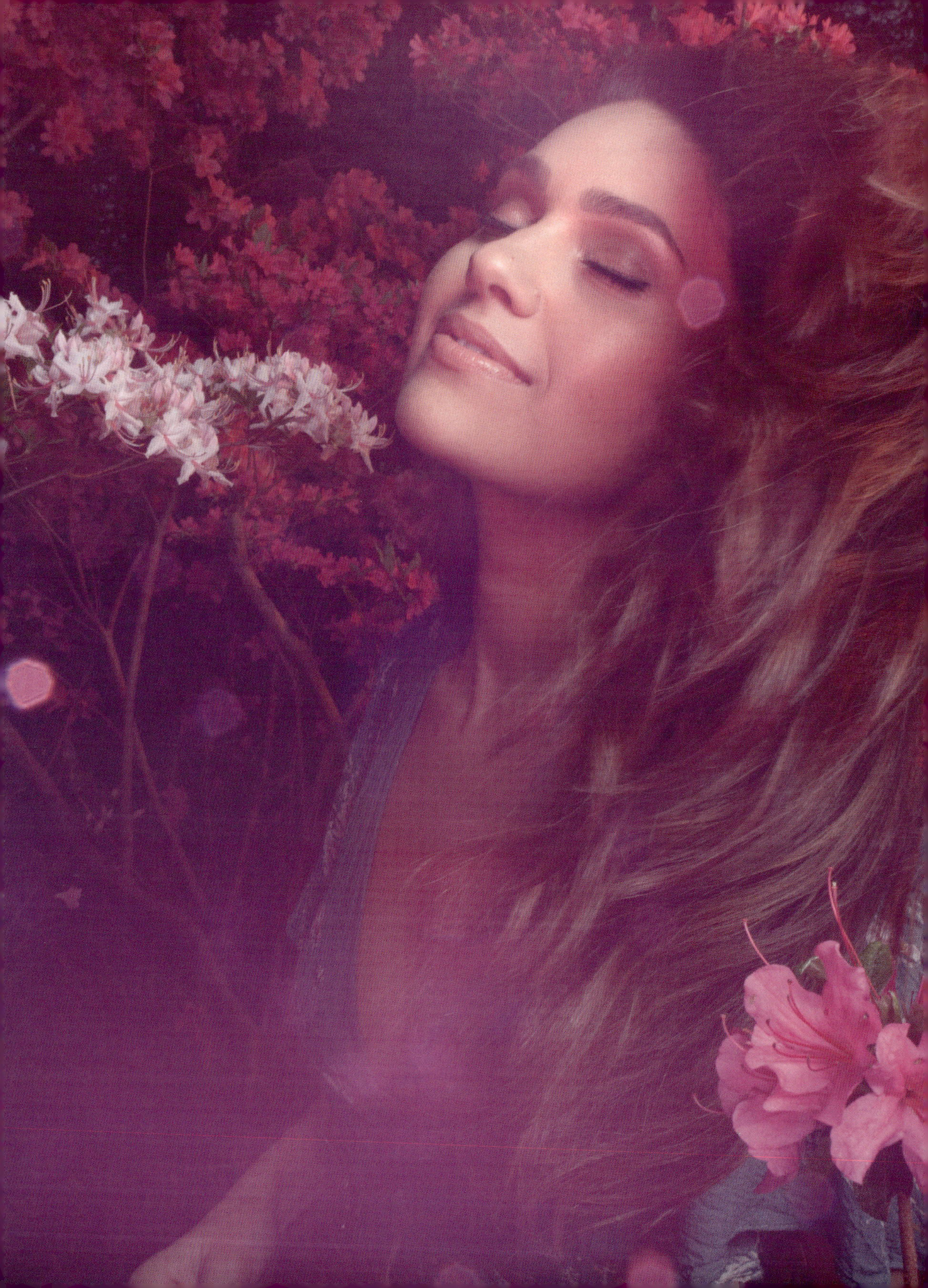

Using Gels for Fun Color Effects

Because why not color it pretty?

GOAL IMAGE

The possibilities are endless in using gels for color effects. You can use them to cast rim lights of different colors on a face. You can backlight a subject with a gel and silhouette them (similar to Scenario 16, "Creating a Silhouette," but pointing the gel toward the couple instead of toward the wall). For this scenario though, we're going crazy. I'm going to show you how to use a gel to fill light a subject while creating front bokeh (**Figure 24.1**). It's pretty darn fun.

GEAR NEEDED:

- Camera + Trigger
- Wide-angle lens
- 3 Off-camera flashes
- 2 or 3 Light stands
- Light-softening modifier
- Fun-colored gel
- Reflector *(optional)*

Before you read this section, I would take a look at Scenario 29, "Making Front Bokeh." I'll be applying those techniques in this chapter as well as techniques from Wow, this Indoor Light Sucks and Individual Portraits. This is a more advanced scenario, so make sure you're good on those simpler techniques first.

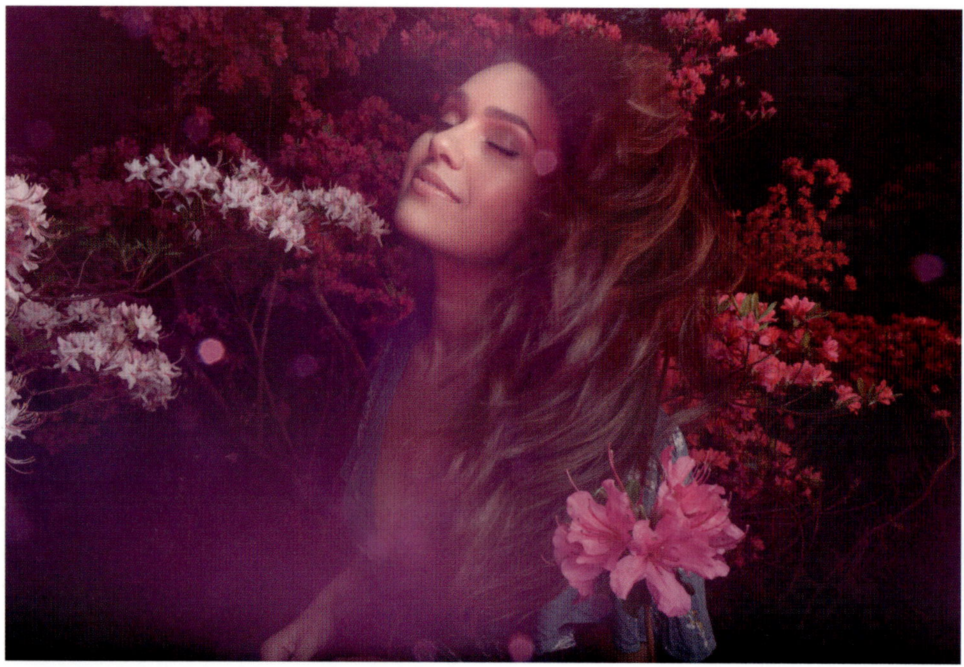

For this shot, we're going to *almost* black out the scene so that *mostly* just the off-camera flash is affecting the image. We'll light the subject with a main light on her face as well as a backlight behind her to light her hair and part of the background. Finally, we'll have another light, with a gel on it, to add a fun, mood-changing element.

You can choose any color of gel you like. The color you choose will dramatically change the mood of the shot so feel free to experiment with a few different ones. The colored gel will fill in the shadows of the image, as well as create front bokeh balls and a bit of haze in that color. You just might become addicted to this technique!

Step by Step

1. **Position the backlight:** For this example shot, I had two CTO gels on my backlight. You don't need this, but since we're playing with gels, why not? Try to get your light at least 20 feet away from your subject, slightly to the right or left, and behind trees or bushes that'll break up the light and make it look more natural. Don't point the light directly at their head! Aim to point it behind and past their head so that the light spreads softly across them and their surroundings.

2. **Position your front light:** This light will have the umbrella or large modifier on it. You'll want it as close to your subject as possible without being in the frame. I suggest placing it just to your right or left at about a 45-degree angle to your subject and about 8 feet high. Feather the light a bit in front of and across your subject so it lights them and their surroundings.

3. **Set the camera exposure:** Set your exposure to *almost* black out your surroundings. I prefer having a little detail in the shadows so I don't have to light all of my background and sky, but dark enough that my OCF is primary light in the shot.

4. **Set the white balance:** The flash that will hit the front of your subject won't have a gel on it so set your WB to the color temperature of the flash (usually ~5600K). If you're not into dialing in your white balance Kelvin manually, try using the sunny day preset. Take a test shot and check the coloring of your photo. Feel free to warm or cool it slightly depending on your taste.

5. **Set the back flash:** Turn on just your back flash and use TTL to get a power setting. Flip to manual keeping the same power setting and adjust it until you like how it looks. Turn this flash head off.

6. **Set the front flash:** Turn on just your front flash and use TTL to get a power setting. Flip it to manual keeping the same power setting and adjust brighter or darker for proper exposure on your subject's face. Alternatively, for both lights you could set your camera to manual, set the flash to mid power range, and adjust up or down to your liking. You can also use a light meter to measure and set both lights to be the same exposure on the front and back of your subject.

7. **Check both flashes:** Turn your back flash back on, still set with the power setting you got in step 5, and take a test shot with both flashes firing together. Adjust your flashes up or down until you get the look you're going for.

8. **Set the main gel flash:** This is where you can pick your pretty color. I went for purple in this example. You need a lot of light for this, so I set my light (assuming it's a smaller speedlight) to full power and adjust from there.

    If you're using a more powerful light, start at half power and move it up if you don't see the bokeh affect.

9. **Position the light:** This is the tricky part. I usually hold my light (a light one, like a speedlight or Profoto A1) in my left hand, super close to (if not touching) and pointing into my lens.

    If you have a heavier light, or if you just don't feel like holding your light, you can set it on a light stand right in front of where you're standing.

10. **Change your angle:** This is the very tricky part. Every little millimeter that you move your light changes the angle that it hits your lens, thus changing how it looks in your image. Move the light all around your lens. Shoot with it above, below, left, and right—everywhere—and see what it does to the bokeh pattern in your image. Your goal is to also let the light hit your subject to fill in the shadows and create a bit of colorful haze in the image.

11. **Make adjustments:** Once you see the light effect show up, play with it. Make is brighter or darker, and change your f-stop to change the size of the bokeh. Change your lens to see what effect the different focal lengths have on the bokeh. There are limitless possibilities.

OPTIONAL: Add a reflector to fill in some of the shadows with the main light color if you want less contrast.

Shot by Shot

FIGURE 24.2
NATURAL LIGHT.
CANON 5DS R, CANON 24MM 1.4, ISO 250, APERTURE 22, SHUTTER 1/250

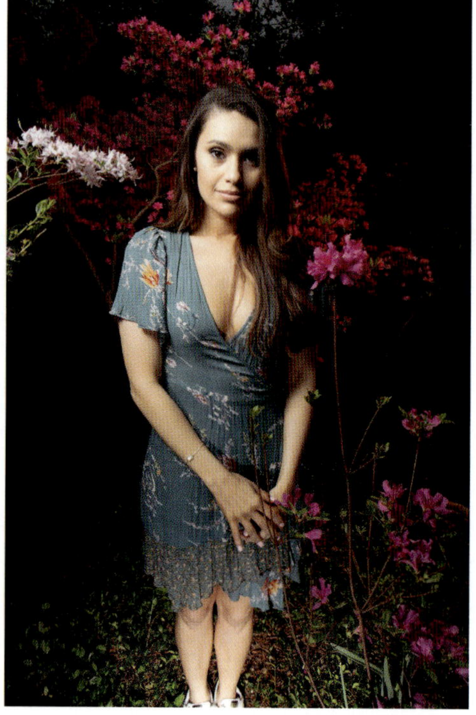

FIGURE 24.3
THE OCF ON THE SUBJECT IS METERING WITH TTL. ONE LIGHT WITH A MEDIUM-DEEP UMBRELLA IS ON CAMERA LEFT. ANOTHER LIGHT WITH A CTO GEL IS BEHIND THE SUBJECT TO GIVE HER HAIR SOME LIGHT. TTL WAS TOO BRIGHT SO I TURNED THE FLASH POWER DOWN IN THE NEXT SHOT. I LOWERED THE SHUTTER SPEED TO LET IN A LITTLE BIT OF NATURAL LIGHT. THIS WAS SHOT AT 10 A.M. OUTSIDE ON A CLOUDY DAY.
CANON 5DS R, CANON 24MM 1.4, ISO 250, APERTURE 22, SHUTTER 1/125

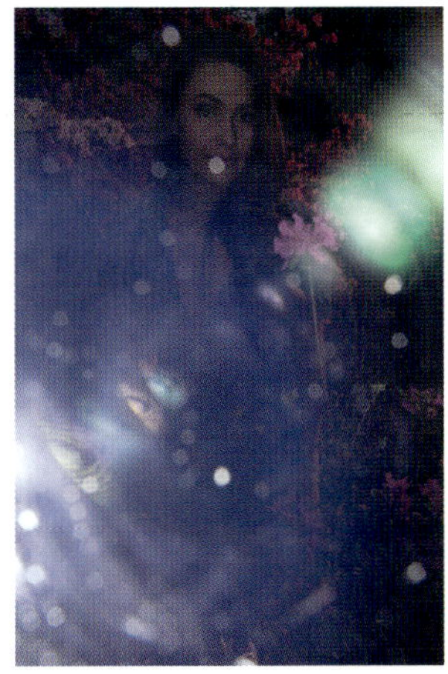

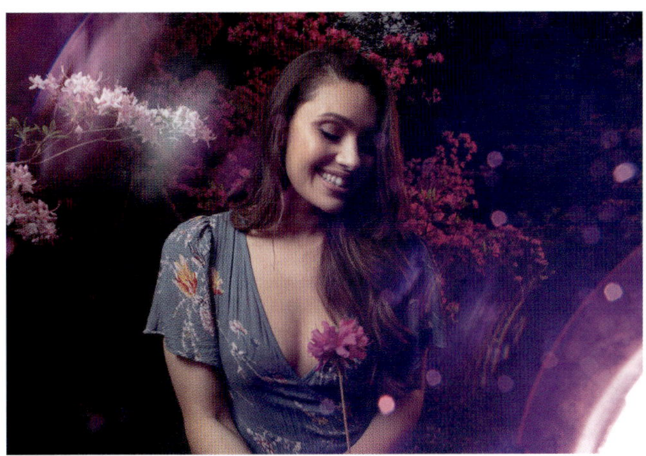

FIGURE 24.4

TESTING THE "BOKEH" FLASH BY TURNING IT ON TO FULL POWER. THE FLASH LIGHTING HER FACE WAS TURNED OFF.

CANON 5DS R, CANON 24MM 1.4, ISO 250, APERTURE 22, SHUTTER 1/125

FIGURE 24.5

I TURNED THE FRONT FLASH BACK ON AND ADDED A PURPLE GEL ON THE BOKEH FLASH.

CANON 5DS R, CANON 24MM 1.4, ISO 250, APERTURE 22, SHUTTER 1/125

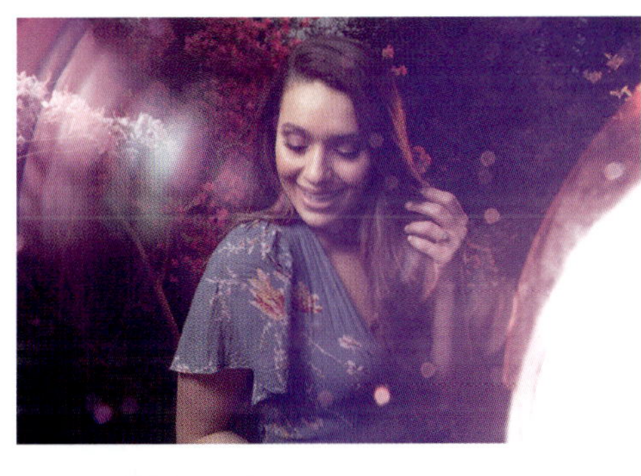

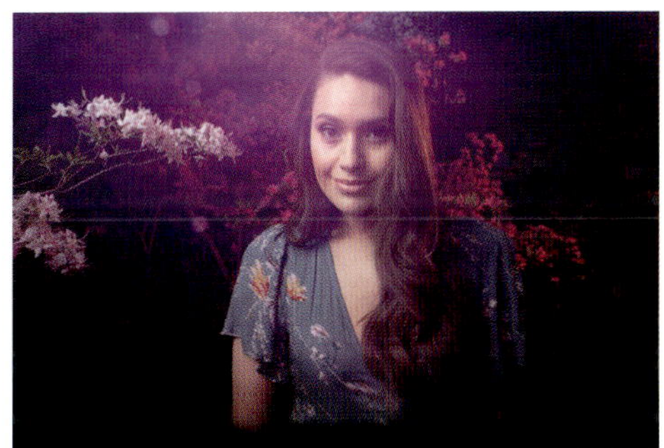

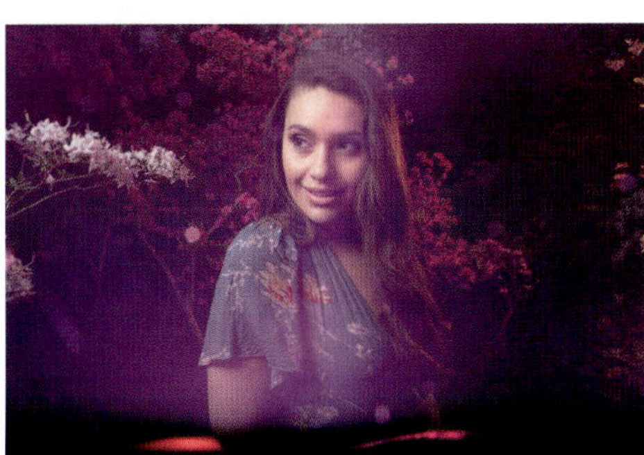

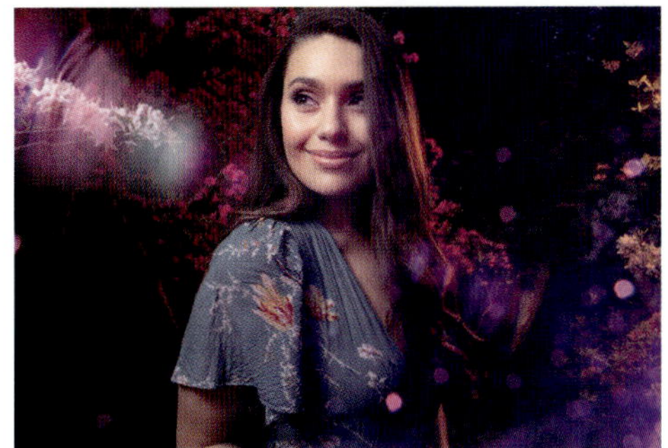

FIGURE 24.6

I MESSED AROUND WITH THE BOKEH LIGHT POSITION. I VARIED THE SHUTTER SPEED BECAUSE I LIKED SEEING A LITTLE BIT OF THE BLUE SKY IN THE UPPER-RIGHT CORNER OF THE IMAGE.

CANON 5DS R, CANON 24MM 1.4, ISO 250, APERTURE 22, SHUTTER 1/125 (OR 1/250)

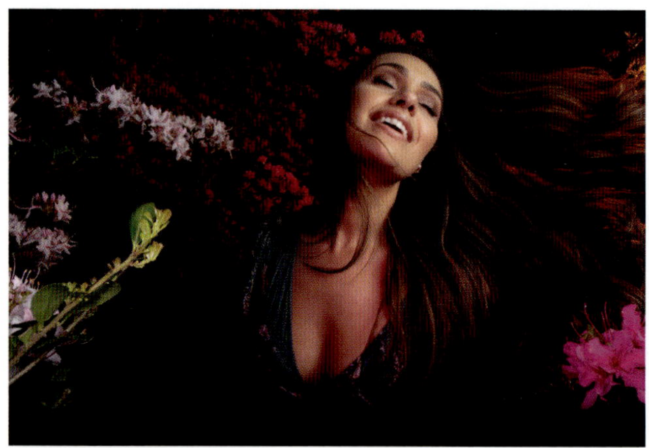

I DECIDED TO HAVE THE MODEL DO A HAIR FLIP SO I MOVED THE LIGHT BEHIND ME. THIS KEPT THE SHOT LIT FLATLY AND GAVE HER MORE ROOM TO MOVE. THE FRONT BOKEH DIDN'T WORK IN THIS SHOT BECAUSE THE LIGHT WAS POINTED TOO MUCH TOWARD THE MODEL. I STAYED AT A 1/250 SHUTTER SPEED HERE SO I MADE SURE TO FREEZE THE ACTION AS MUCH AS POSSIBLE; BUT THERE IS SOME MOVEMENT IN THE HAIR, WHICH I ACTUALLY LIKE.
CANON 5DS R, CANON 24MM 1.4, ISO 250, APERTURE 22, SHUTTER SPEED 1/250

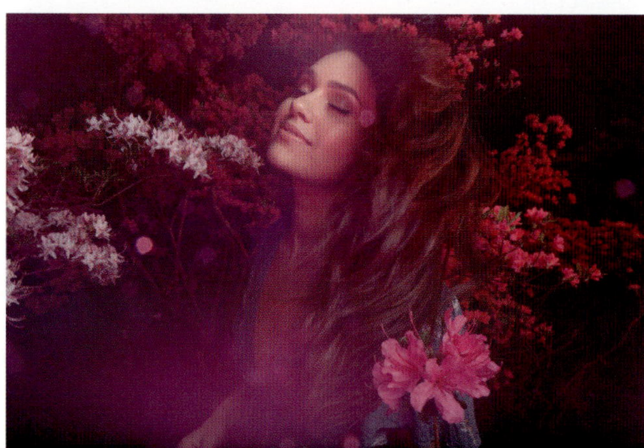

THIS BOKEH LIGHT WAS POSITIONED PERFECTLY TO GIVE FLARE IN THE LENS AND FILL THE SHADOWS ON THE MODEL WITH A PURPLE COLOR (YOU CAN SEE THE COLOR ON HER TEMPLE AND CHEEK BONE AND BELOW HER NECK). IT GAVE A NICE HAZE TO THE IMAGE.
CANON 5DS R, CANON 24MM 1.4, ISO 250, APERTURE 22, SHUTTER 1/250

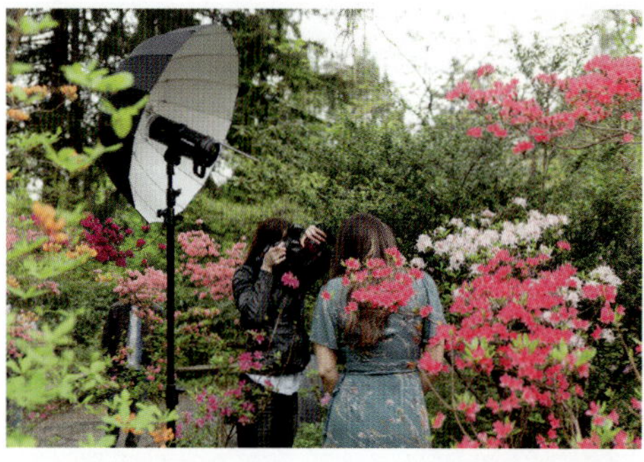

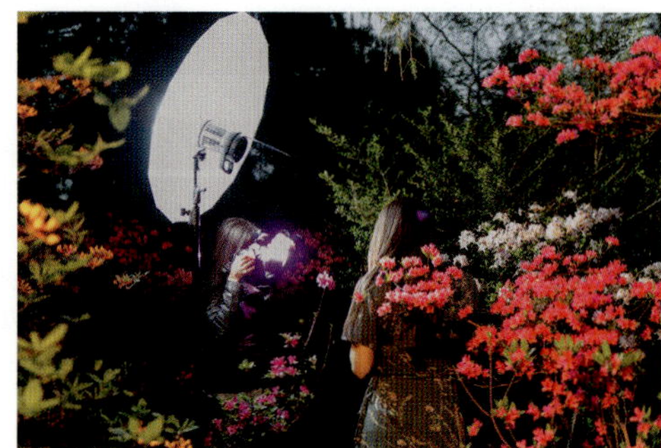

FIGURE 24.9

BEHIND THE SCENES: THIS IS ONE OF THE VERY FINAL IMAGES OF THE SHOOT. THROUGHOUT THE SHOOT I MOVED THE FLASH IN MY HAND AROUND MY LENS FROM THE TOP TO THE SIDES AND THE BOTTOM.

Potential Problems

This trick can be difficult depending on your lighting circumstances. Ultimately, the effect shows up best on the darker parts of the image, so try this in a darker lighting scenario first instead of in a scene with bright outdoor light. A wider-angle lens with a high f-stop, such as f/22, will create the most dramatic look in terms of front bokeh. Getting it at just the right angle to get bokeh *and* fill flash your subject is quite tricky!

Other Techniques

Adding movement to a shot is really fun. Because you've almost completely darkened the natural light, your flash will freeze any action. However, with the natural light still peeking into the shot, you can lower your shutter speed and have you or your subject move to get a little motion in the image. For my last (and favorite) shots from this shoot, I had the model flip her hair. Even at a shutter speed of ½₅₀ of a second, she moved fast enough to show a little motion in her hair while the flash froze her face perfectly sharp. It took a few tries, but it's a ton of fun!

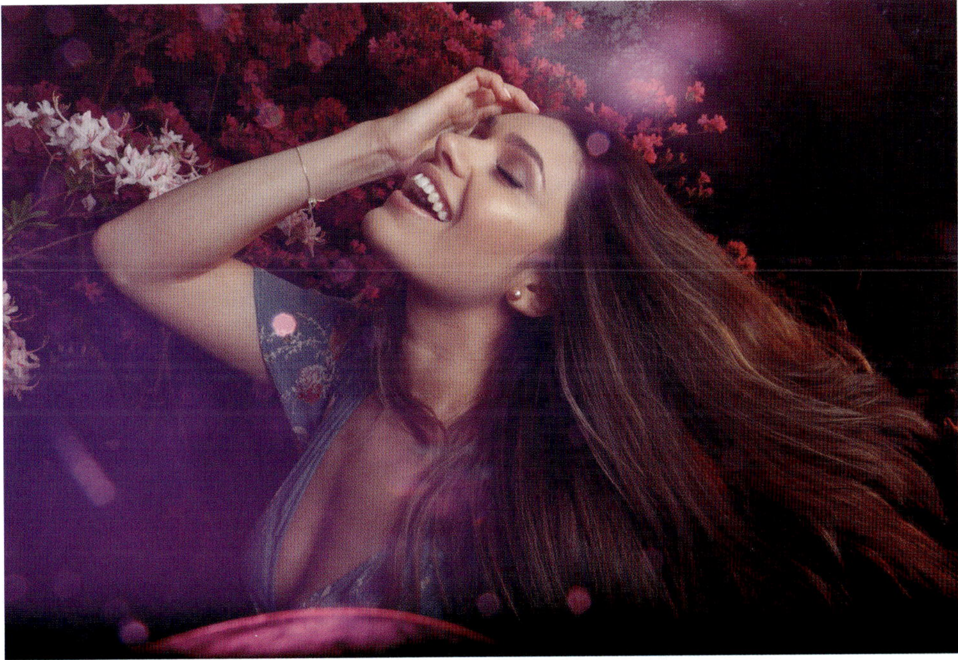

FIGURE 24.10

THE FINAL IMAGE (THOUGH I THINK I LIKE THE MOOD OF THE PREVIOUS IMAGE BETTER).
CANON 5DS R, CANON 24MM 1.4, ISO 250, APERTURE 22, SHUTTER 1/250

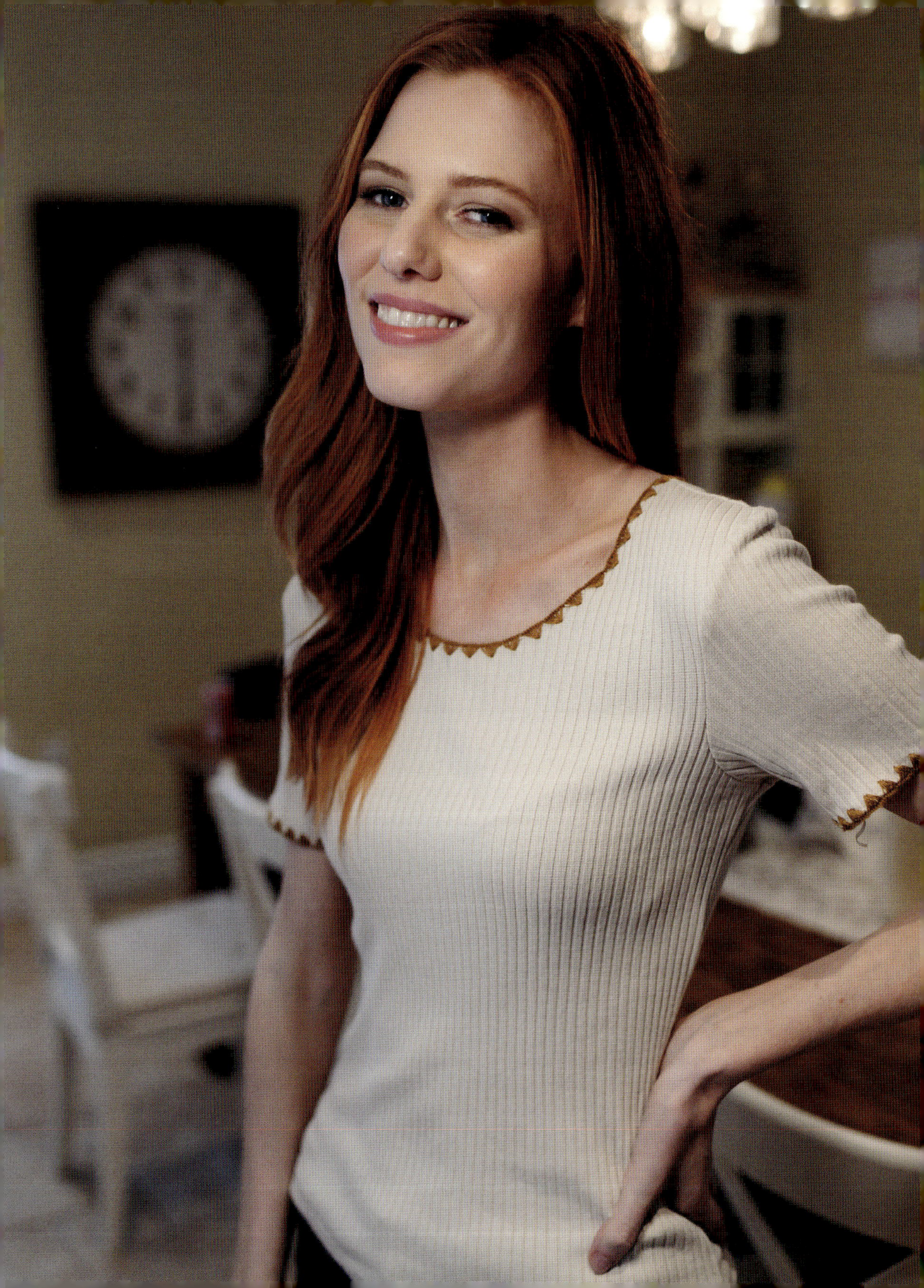

SCENARIO 25

Using Gels to Color Correct

Because sometimes the light is uuuuugly!

GOAL IMAGE

I will say that I very rarely practice this. I used to do it, but now, because I mostly shoot events in properly up-lit rooms, it's not as necessary. However, it's a technique that you definitely want to understand photographically and be able to use whenever you need to.

The most popular time to use this technique is when you're indoors using a flash (off-camera, on-camera, or bouncing) and the background looks a disgusting yellowy-orange. It happens in most normally lit rooms because the lights that are dimly illuminating the space are tungsten lamps, which provide an orange color.

To fix this, match your flash to whatever color is naturally occurring in the space. It's almost like you want to pull out one of those lightbulbs and use it as a flash so it's the same as all the other lights in the room.

To do this, gel the flash with the same color as tungsten (typically a half or full CTO gel), and then shift your white balance to adjust for the orange light so that it becomes white. Everything from flash to natural light will magically be beautifully balanced.

Step by Step

1. **Position your lights:** As I mentioned, this technique can be used at any point with on-camera, off-camera, or bouncing flash. You can put a gel on your strobe or speedlight and then position it based on the scenario you're in.

2. **Set the camera exposure:** Create an exposure as if you're just photographing the room's natural (ugly) light.

3. **Set the white balance:** Set your white balance to the tungsten preset or around 3200 Kelvin depending on how much of a gel you've put on your light (half or full CTO). The darker the orange, the lower your Kelvin setting needs to be.

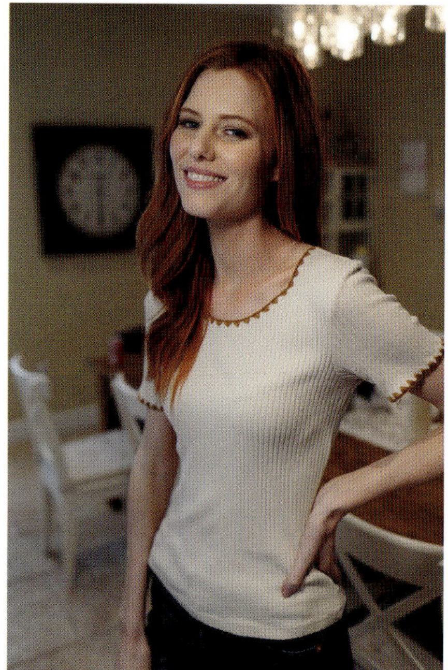

4. **Set the flash power:** Do this according to your lighting setup. You're essentially combining this with other lighting scenarios like in the sections on Event Speeches, Lighting a Dark Room, or Table Details—but adding a gel. You can use TTL, manual, or a light meter to set your flash power.

5. **Take a test shot:** Notice if the natural light looks too orange or too blue. If it looks too blue, take off some of the gel color (if you're using a full CTO, try half; if you're using a half, try a quarter) and warm up your white balance (raise the number). If the natural light looks too orange, blue down your white balance (lower the Kelvin number) and add more of the gel color.

Shot by Shot

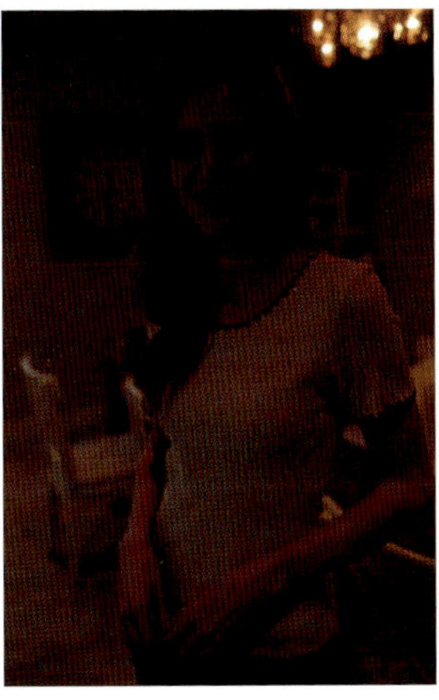

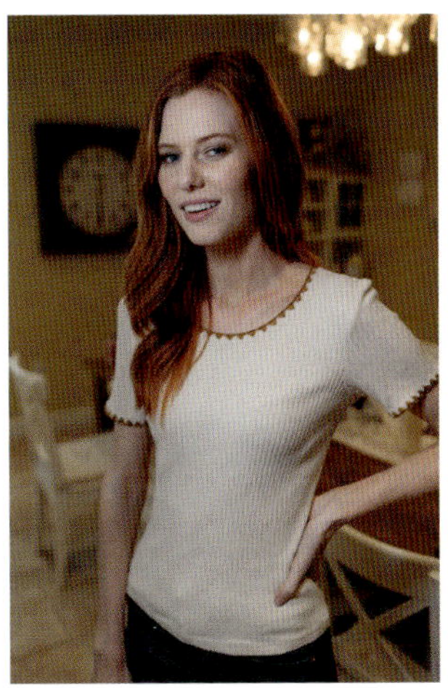

FIGURE 25.2

NATURAL LIGHT.
CANON 1DX II, CANON 35MM 1.4,
ISO 250, APERTURE 2.5, SHUTTER
1/250, WB 5100K

FIGURE 25.3

OCF WITHOUT A GEL.
CANON 1DX II, CANON 35MM 1.4,
ISO 250, APERTURE 2.5, SHUTTER
1/200, WB 5100K

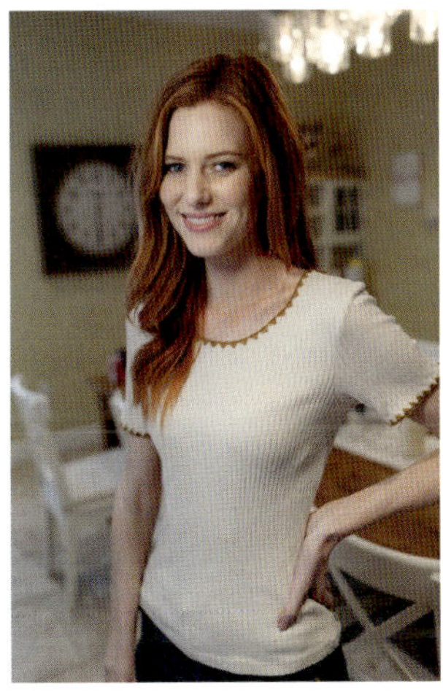

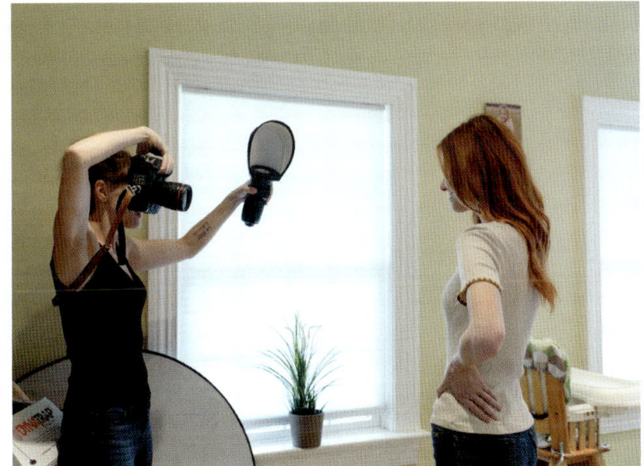

FIGURE 25.4

OCF WITH A GEL AND A LOWERED
WHITE BALANCE. NOTICE HOW
MUCH LESS ORANGE THE BACK-
GROUND IS.
CANON 1DX II, CANON 35MM 1.4,
ISO 250, APERTURE 2.5, SHUTTER
1/200, WB 3100K

FIGURE 25.5

BEHIND THE SCENES (NO GEL ADDED IN THIS SHOT).

Potential Problems

The most difficult part is getting the two light sources to balance. You might not be able to get it perfect, but it's OK to have a bit of warmth to your background. To me, that's how the light looks. Your clients may also want to capture the warmth of the environment, especially if it's lit by candles, so be sure to set expectations with them one way or the other.

Practical Uses

My example was with tungsten light, but this concept can be used with many natural/ambient light colors. The idea is to match your flash color to the color of whatever light is in the space. Maybe you're shooting in an environment with crazy pink up-lighting, and it's just too much. Gel your flash pink or magenta to change the color tone to be more green (and maybe your white balance bracket to be more green as well).

Whatever color the lights are that you want to desaturate, that's the color you put on your flash. Then, with your camera's color settings (white balance, color tone, and/or white balance shift), you take that color away from the whole photograph by adding the *opposite color* (opposite of blue is yellow, opposite of magenta is green, etc.). It takes a bit of practice to wrap your head around this idea, but once you do it adds another element of control and skill to your photography.

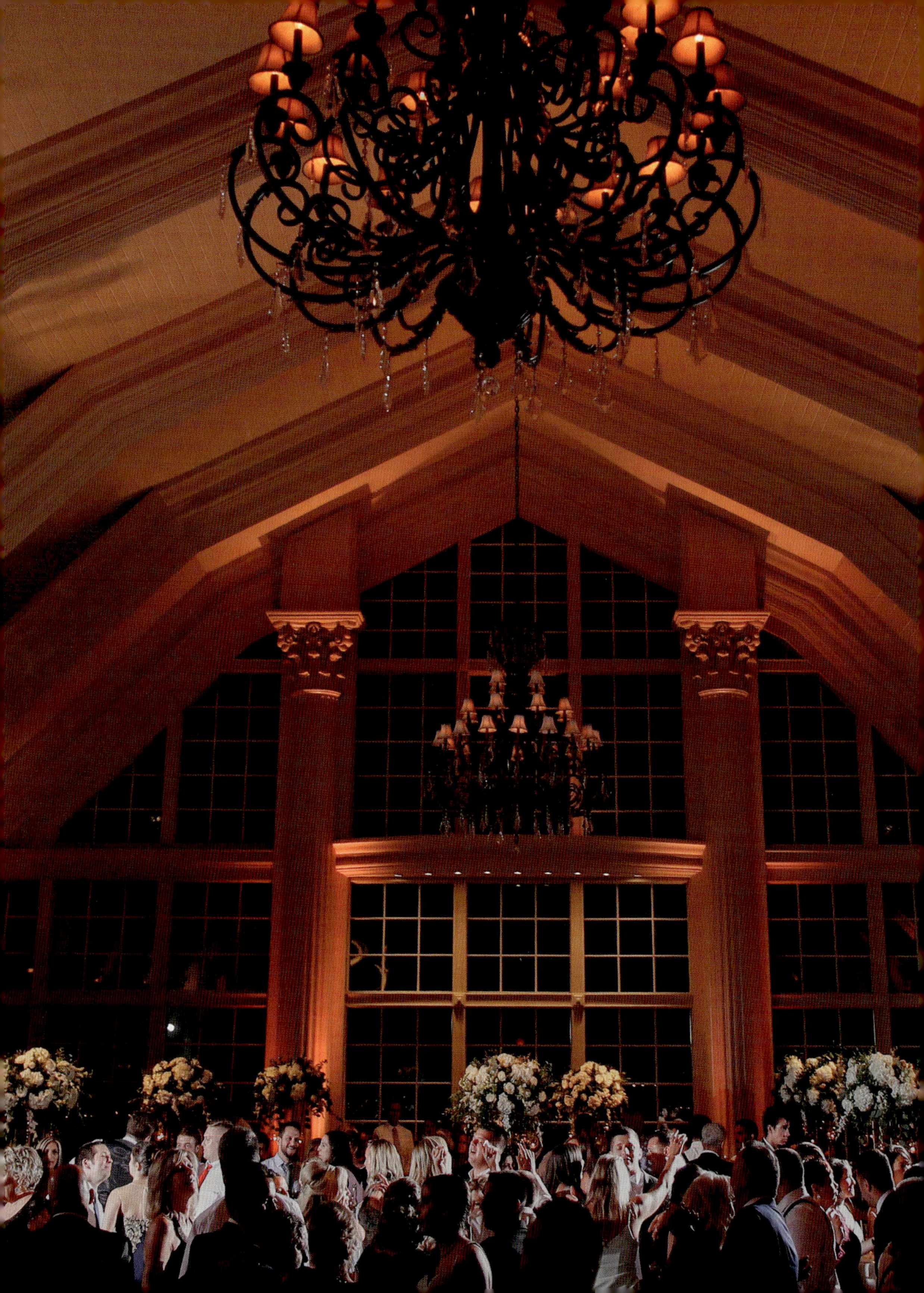

Lighting a Dark Room

Dynamic lighting for weddings, Bar/Bat Mitzvahs, and corporate events.

GOAL IMAGE

If you've already read Scenario 23, "Event Bounce Flash," then you know this is not my go-to lighting for wedding receptions. However, this kind of lighting is 100% more dynamic than what I typically do. Even though, for reasons I mentioned in that scenario, I prefer to bounce flash throughout the night, I do often set up a few shots using the following technique. It adds a lot of dimension to the images and definitely a level of quality.

GEAR NEEDED:

- Camera + Trigger
- Fast-focusing lens of any focal length
- 2 Off-camera flashes
- 2 9-12' Light stands
- 2 Grids
- Gel set *(optional)*

I choose to use this lighting setup for large overall room shots, but you can use it in a variety of places. With two lights in a dark room, you have two options. Either you have them on opposite corners or sides of the room or dance floor. Or you have them on the corners of the same side of the dance floor or room.

Where you decide to place the lights is up to you. However, where you place them and where you stand in relation to them will give you a different light pattern as you move around the room. You have to decide what kind of looks you'd like to have, and then choose which lighting setup is best for creating that.

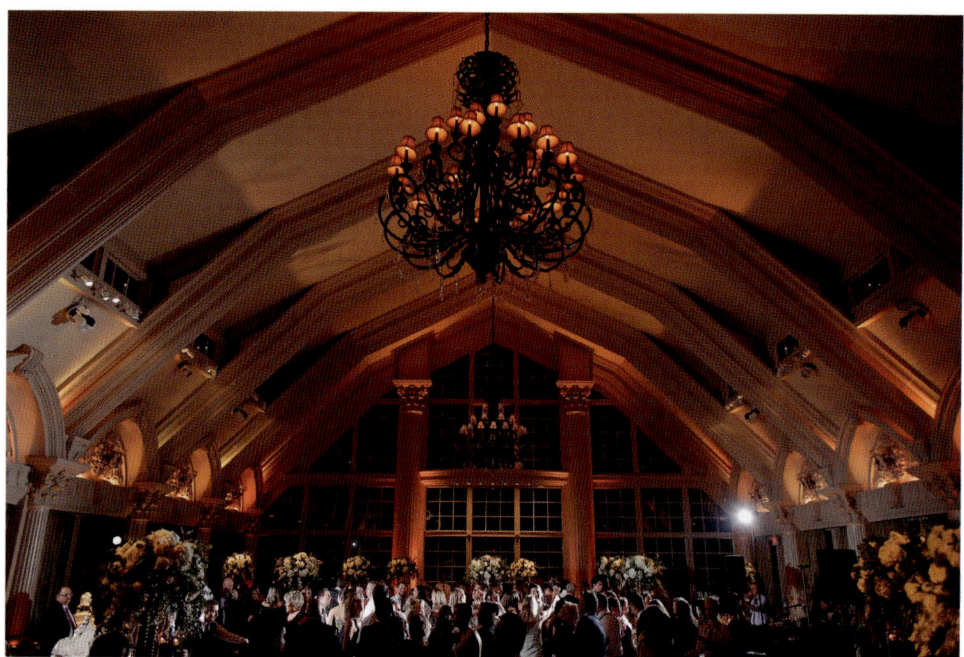

SHOT USING TWO PROFOTO B1S WITH GRIDS.
CANON 1DXII, CANON 24MM 1.4, ISO 1250, APERTURE 2.5, SHUTTER 1/125, WB 5600K

If you are doing this at an event with a ton of potentially drunk people flailing about thinking they're dancing, *please* weigh down your lights, affix them to sturdy light stands, and place them where they won't be easily tripped over. You also need to consider the aesthetics of how your lights look in the room. If you can set your lights in the corner or against the wall of the room, do it. It's the safest place for them to be, and usually they don't look as bad as they do when they are haphazardly placed on an open corner or side of the dance floor.

You must use grids! Without grids the light goes everywhere and kills the ambiance of the room.

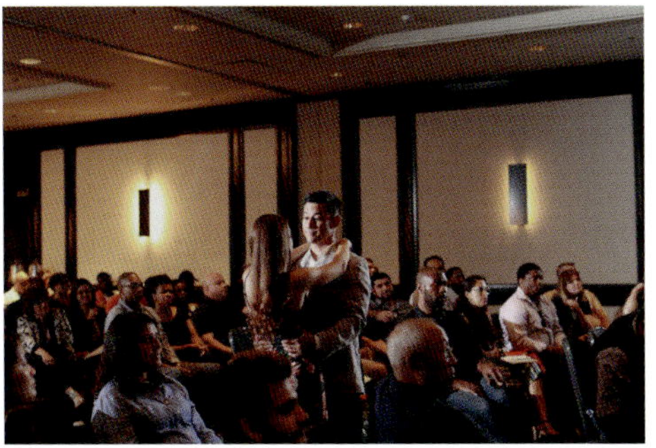

FIGURE 26.2
SHOT USING TWO PROFOTO B10S WITH GRIDS.
CANON 1DXII, CANON 50MM 1.2, ISO 2500, APERTURE 2.8,
SHUTTER 1/250, WB 5600K

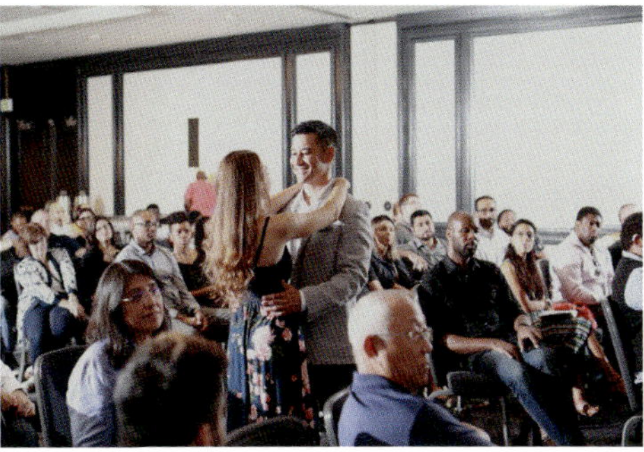

FIGURE 26.3
SHOT USING TWO PROFOTO B10S WITHOUT GRIDS.
CANON 1DXII, CANON 50MM 1.2, ISO 2500, APERTURE 2.8,
SHUTTER 1/250, WB 5600K

Option 1: Place your lights on opposite corners or sides of the dance floor or room. This option lets you put one light next to the DJ or band, which is usually a safe, unobtrusive spot; and the other light can go in the opposite corner. With this lighting setup, you'll have a light pattern that will, depending on where you're standing, be a rim light with a front flash, or lights hitting your subjects at 90 degrees on either side. There is, of course, everything in between those two as you walk from one side of the room to the other.

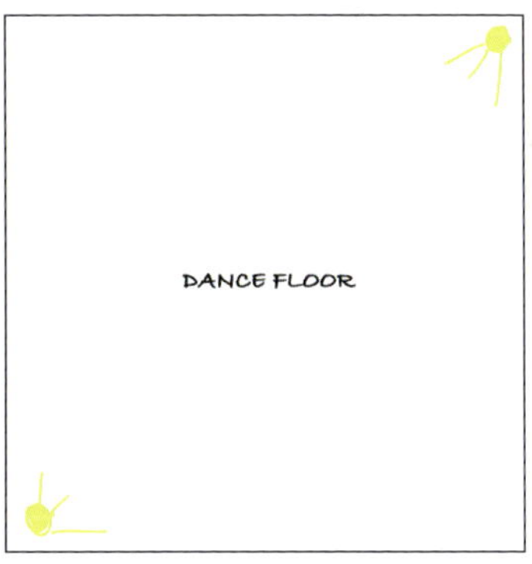

FIGURE 26.4
LIGHTS IN OPPOSITE CORNERS.

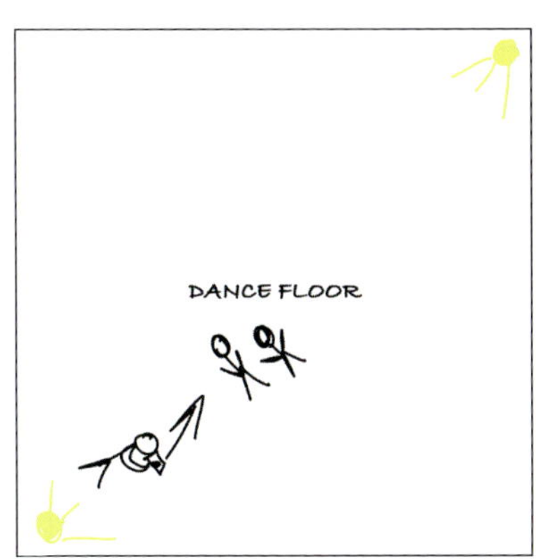

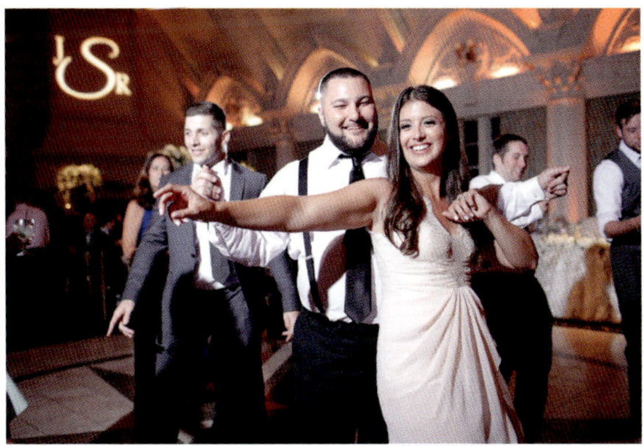

FIGURE 26.5
SHOT WITH TWO PROFOTO BIS WITH GRIDS: THE MAIN LIGHT AND THE RIM LIGHT.
CANON 1DXII, CANON 35MM 1.4, ISO 2500, APERTURE 2.5, SHUTTER 1/125, WB 5600K

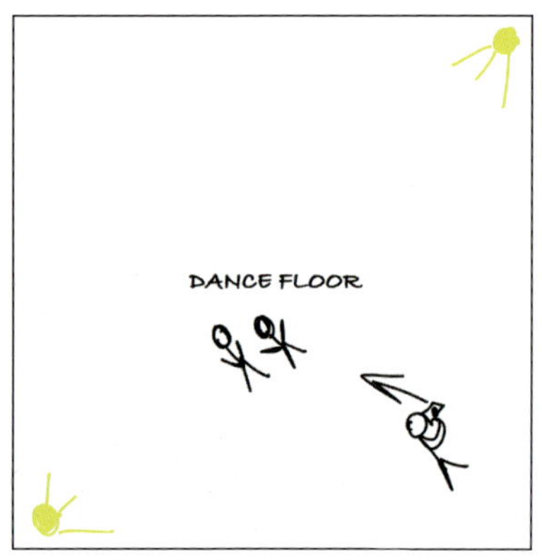

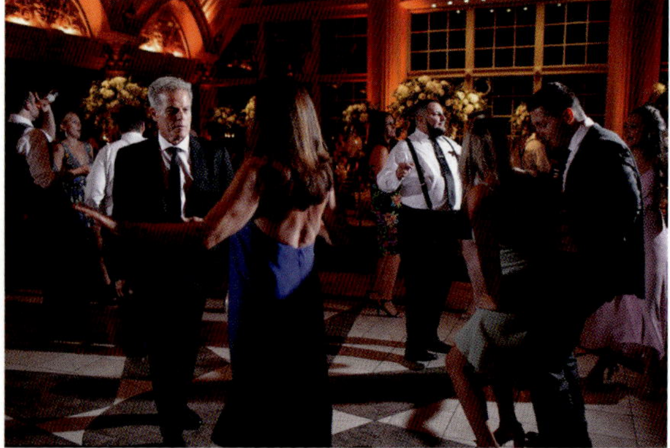

FIGURE 26.6

SHOT WITH TWO PROFOTO B1S WITH GRIDS IN SIDELIGHT POSITION.
CANON 1DXII, CANON 35MM 1.4, ISO 2500, APERTURE 2.5, SHUTTER 1/125, WB 5600K

Option 2: Place your lights on the corners of the dance floor or room on the same side. This option puts both lights on one side of a 180-degree axis. Basically, draw a line down the center of the room (in whatever direction) and both lights are on one side of it. This lighting setup will give you three different types of lighting patterns depending on where you stand (and naturally everything in between, as well). You'll have either a silhouette of your subjects with two lights on either side of the frame, a fairly flat look with two lights shooting from either side of you at your subject, or side lighting on the subject.

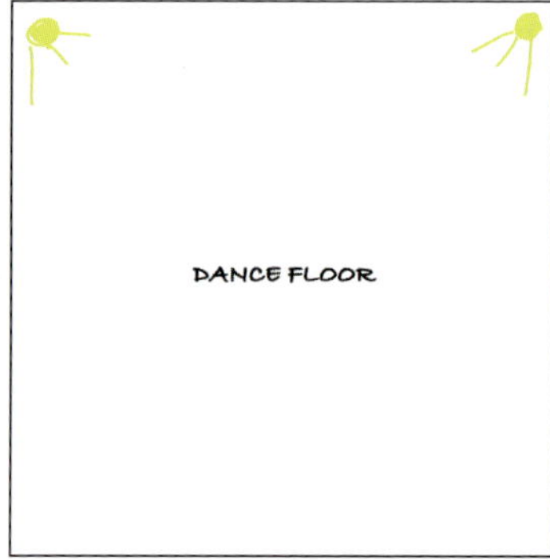

FIGURE 26.7

LIGHTS POSITIONED IN THE CORNERS ON
THE SAME SIDE OF THE DANCE FLOOR.

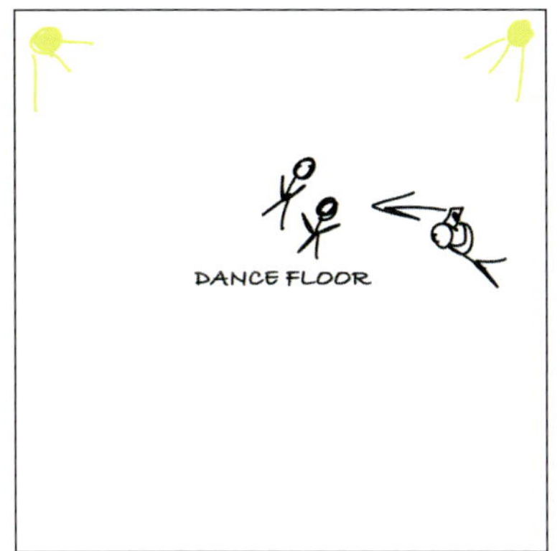

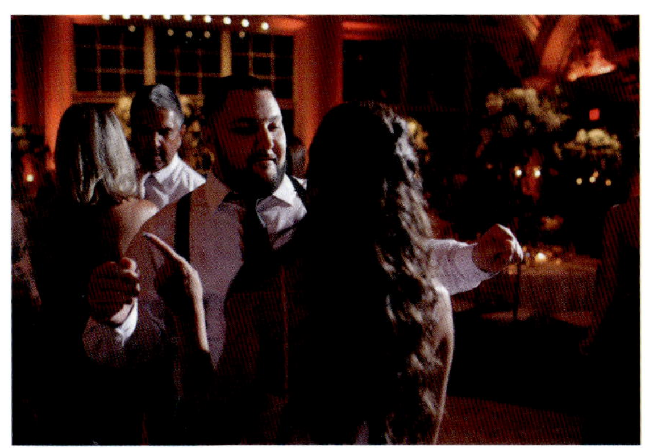

TWO PROFOTO B1S WITH GRIDS, BOTH ON ONE SIDE OF THE ROOM.
CANON 1DXII, CANON 35MM 1.4, ISO 2500, APERTURE 2.5, SHUTTER 1/125, WB 5600K

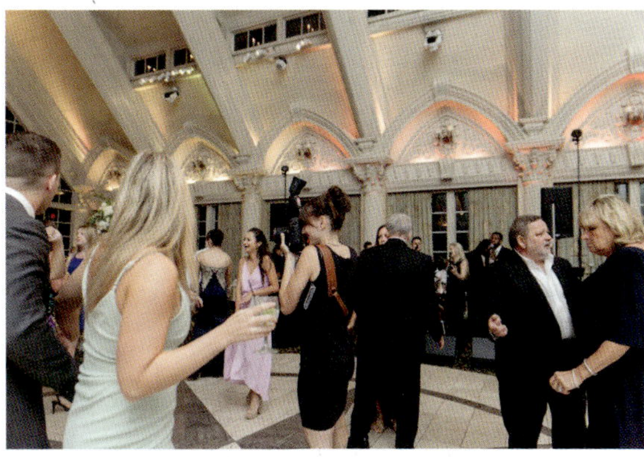

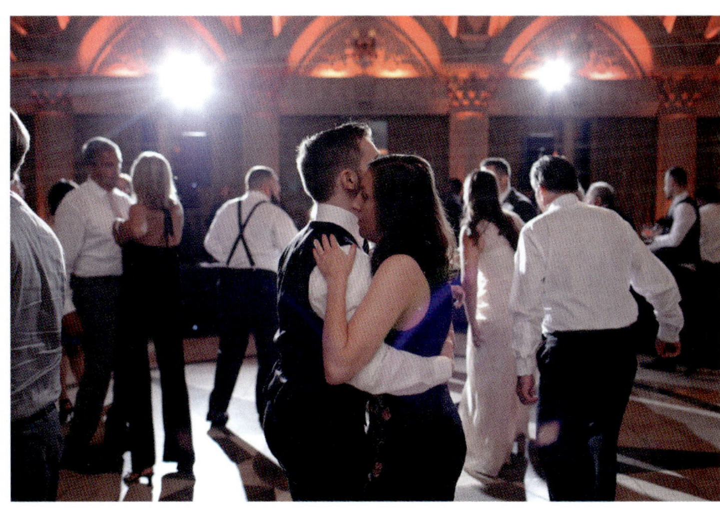

FIGURE 26.9

TWO PROFOTO B1S WITH GRIDS CREATING BACK-LIGHTING.
CANON 1DXII, CANON 35MM 1.4, ISO 2500, APERTURE 2.5, SHUTTER 1/125, WB 5600K

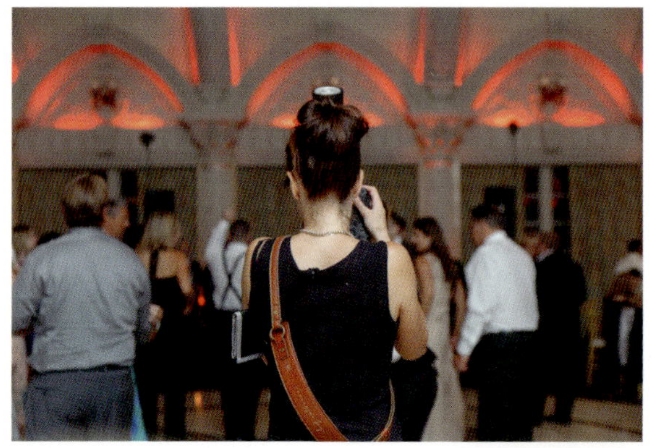

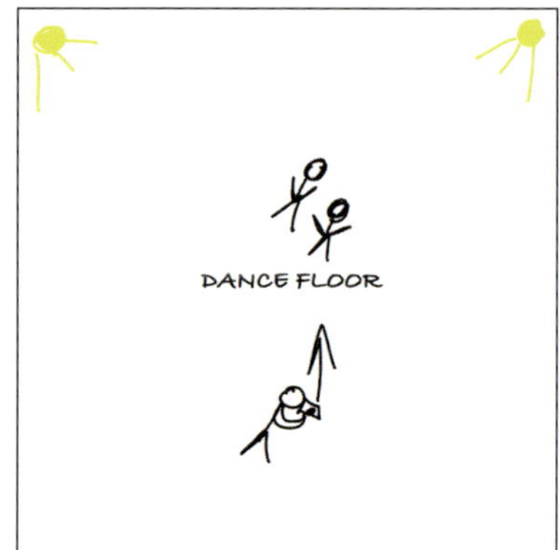

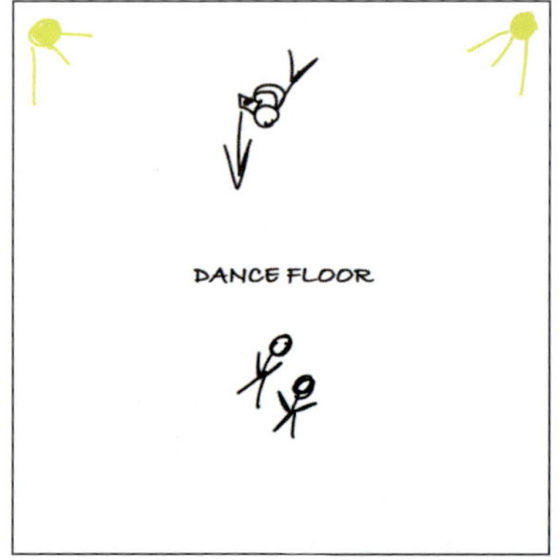

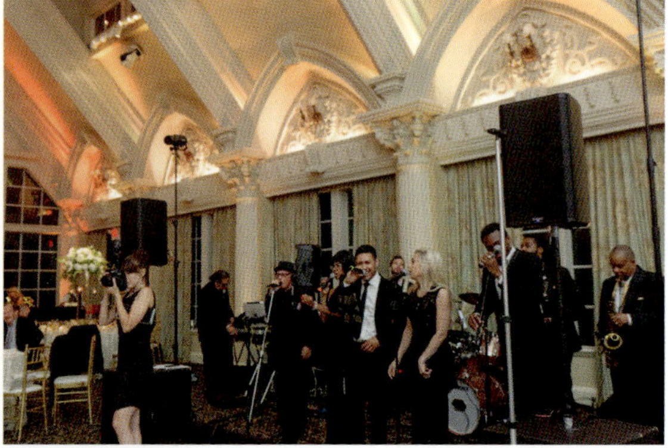

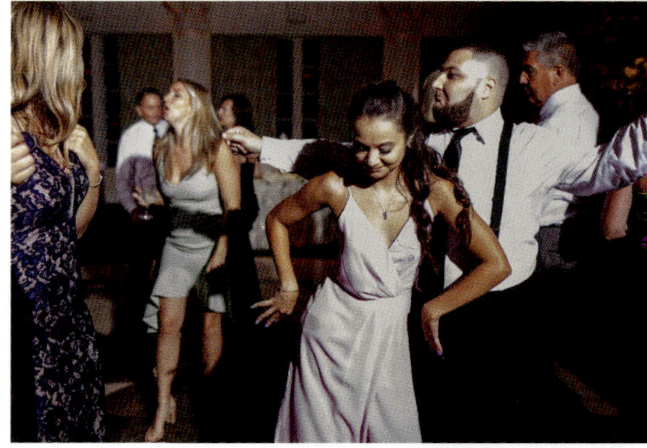

FIGURE 26.10

TWO PROFOTO B1S WITH GRIDS CREATING
FRONT LIGHTING.
CANON 1DXII, CANON 35MM 1.4, ISO 2500,
APERTURE 2.5, SHUTTER 1/125, WB 5600K

Both options require a similar setup, which we'll go through in a minute. The last thing I wanted to address in this are the room lights, or the lights from the DJ or band. I prefer to use those as backlights because they're natural rim lights and they create a fun, colorful background. Plus, I won't have to worry about crazy polka-dot patterns showing up on people's faces. Does this mean that my background is the entertainment? Yeah, it does. But just a slight shift to the side or playing with a shorter depth of field lets me still shoot into their lights without having the DJ booth or band in the image.

Step by Step

1. **Grid the lights:** You'll be placing the lights father away from the center of the action so they're not obtrusive and not a tripping hazard. You'll need to direct the light toward the dance floor rather than flooding the whole space. If you flood the whole space you may as well just bounce flash.

   How large the space is and how far away your light is will determine what grid to use. Use a 5- or 10-degree grid to start, turn on your modeling light, and see where the light is falling. If it's too spotted and you can't follow enough action around, use a 20- or 30- degree grid.

2. **Position the lights:** I recommend pointing both lights towards the center of the dance floor. A little variance is fine, and you may end up liking to shift them a little once you get a feel for these setups. Most importantly, the lights need to be at least 9 feet high (preferably 12 feet) to light over people standing with their hands up dancing. You don't need to tilt the lights down toward the ground on the center of the dance floor or room; they can still be straight, or slightly tilted down depending on the size of the grid you are using. A modeling light is very helpful here to see where the light is hitting as you're setting it up.

3. **Set the camera exposure:** Create an exposure as if you're photographing the room's natural light. I like a shallow depth of field so I set my camera around f/2.2–3.2 to get the look I'm going for. I'll likely be around $\frac{1}{160}$ of a second, so I don't have motion blur with all the crazy dancing, and 1600–2500 ISO depending on how dark the room is.

4. **Set the white balance:** Set your white balance to the flash preset or 5600 Kelvin depending on the temperature of your light.

5. **Set the flash power:** Turn both lights on and take a shot using TTL. Flip it to manual and adjust. Both lights may not be at the same power setting depending on how far away they are from the subject. If you don't have TLL available, start on the lowest manual setting your flash has and slowly move up until you have the desired brightness of the light, or use a light meter and measure from the center of the room. Do this one light at a time.

   A. You may find that keeping your lights set to TTL works best for you, and this setup keeps up with you as you move around the room.

   B. You may like adjusting your light power manually as you move around the room. Maybe you like a super powerful backlight. If that's the case, brighten whatever light is behind your subjects, and reverse it if you move and that backlight becomes your front light.

6. **Focus:** You'll need a fast-focusing lens for this technique. Because you'll be shooting in a dark room, you'll really want a lens that's great at focusing quickly and in low light. However, some of the newer mirrorless cameras have insane face-detection autofocus that works really well, even in low light. I recently tried the Canon EOS with the newest firmware upgrade (August 2019), and it blew my mind. It focused perfectly in the dark when even I couldn't see any faces.

7. **Move around while shooting:** As you move around, the lighting pattern will change on your subjects, and the mood of the image will alter. I highly suggest moving around to see what the light does depending on where you're standing. It's a great way to learn about light and how it looks as you change your angle. Feel free to let in some light flare for fun!

OPTIONAL: Throw a colored gel on one of the lights to add a bit of fun to the image. You might not want that colored light to be the main light hitting your subject's face though!

Shot by Shot

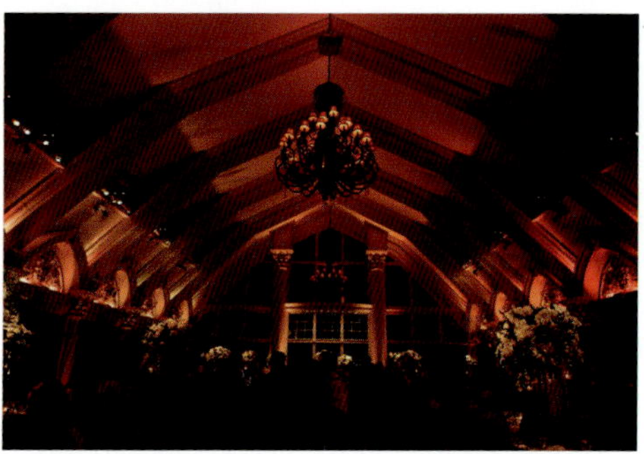

FIGURE 26.11
NATURAL LIGHT.
CANON 1DXII, CANON 24MM 1.4, ISO 2000, APERTURE 2.5,
SHUTTER 1/125, WB 5600K

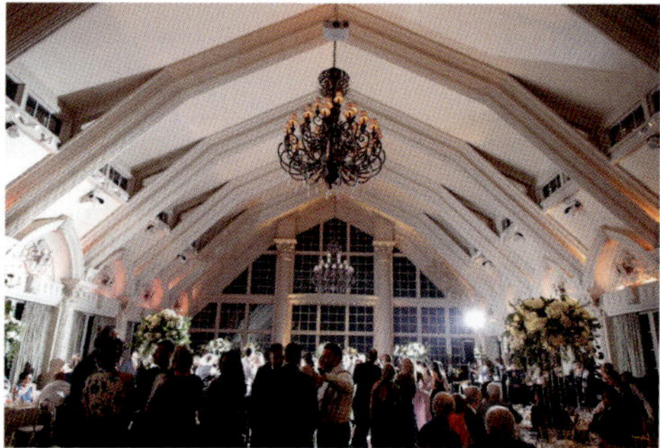

FIGURE 26.12
SHOT WITH TWO PROFOTO B1S WITH GRIDS, OCF ON TTL
CANON 1DXII, CANON 24MM 1.4, ISO 2000, APERTURE 2.5,
SHUTTER 1/125, WB 5600K

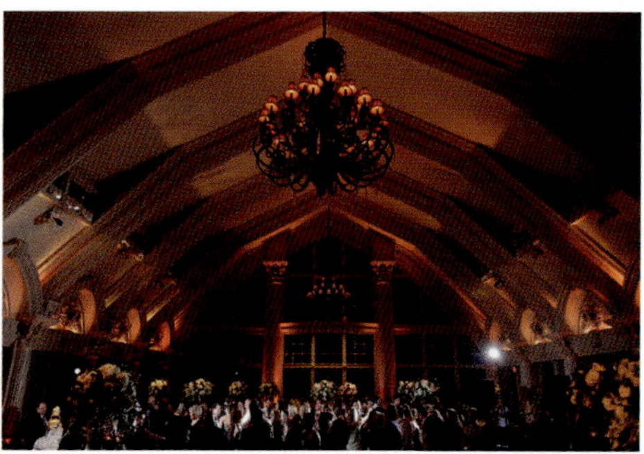

FIGURE 26.13
I SWITCHED TO MANUAL AND LOWERED MY LIGHT
POWER AND ISO TO BETTER THE QUALITY OF THE IMAGE
SINCE I HAD ENOUGH LIGHT POWER USING TWO PRO-
FOTO B1S WITH GRIDS.
CANON 1DXII, CANON 24MM 1.4, ISO 1250, APERTURE 2.5,
SHUTTER 1/125, WB 5600K

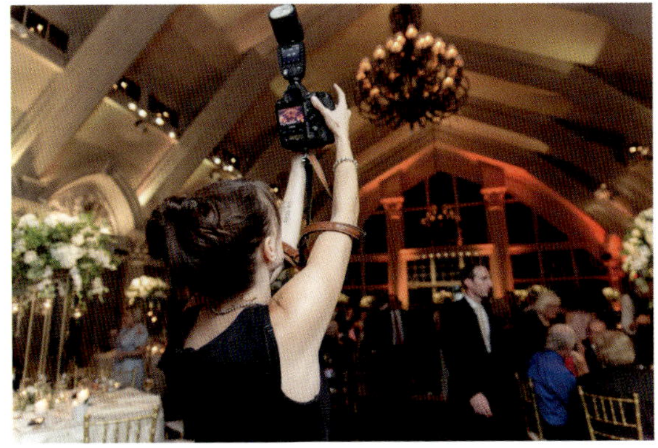

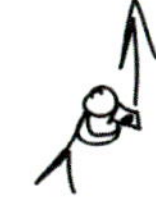

FIGURE 26.14

LIGHTING DIAGRAM AND BEHIND THE SCENES; THE PROFOTO A1 WAS
NOT FIRING, JUST TRIGGERING THE OTHER TWO LIGHTS.

Potential Problems

Make sure the backlight isn't hitting your subject on the side of the face. It can easily blow out
the skin tone and usually isn't very flattering. Be conscious of where you're standing and where
the lights are set. For this reason, a lot of people choose to have an assistant with them, walking
around holding up a light on a light stand or monopod in relation to the shooter, throughout
the night.

Sometimes speech-givers ask the reception to stand for a toast. When that happens they all stand
up and block your lights. I highly recommend using a 12-foot light stand so you can securely put
up lights high enough to be over the crowd. Make sure your lights are at least 9 feet high to
anticipate sudden standing so it won't affect your shot.

Just because the room is big, it doesn't mean you have to put your lights all the way in the corners
of the room (although I do find that's the safest location for them, liability-wise). Bring your
lights to the edge of the dance floor instead of the edge of the room.

If there are a lot of harsh shadows, try using an on-camera flash with a bounce card that will
trigger your lights and act as a fill flash. You'll lessen the shadows and find it easier to shoot in
more locations around your lighting setup.

NATURAL LIGHT.
CANON 1DXII, CANON 35MM 1.4, ISO 1600, APERTURE 2.5,
SHUTTER 1/160, WB 5600K

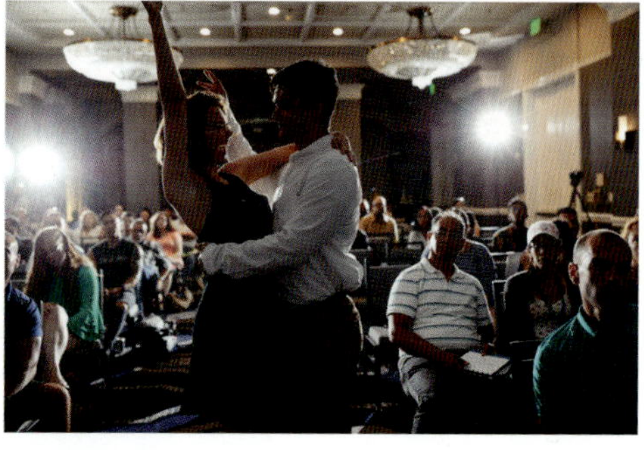

SHOT WITH TWO CANON 600EXII SPEEDLIGHTS WITH
MAGMOD GRIDS.
CANON 1DXII, CANON 35MM 1.4, ISO 1600, APERTURE 2.5,
SHUTTER 1/160, WB 5600K

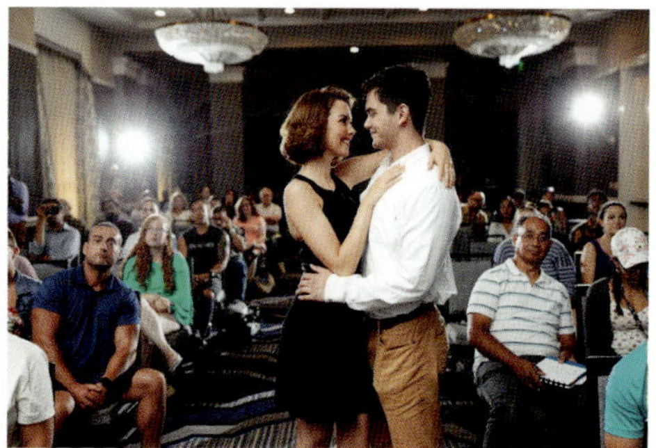

SHOT WITH AN ON-CAMERA CANON 600EXII ADDED FOR
BOUNCE FLASH AND TWO CANON 600EXII SPEEDLIGHTS
WITH MAGMOD GRIDS.
CANON 1DXII, CANON 35MM 1.4, ISO 1600, APERTURE 2.5,
SHUTTER 1/160, WB 5600K

Practical Uses

This setup is fun for shooting dancing or any type of special event (first dance, parent dances, cake cutting, bouquet/garter toss) that happens in the center of the room. I also enjoy using it to take a full-room shot that emphasizes the size and liveliness of the party.

Get an overall shot of the reception hall. Throwing one light to one side of the room or adding a second light to the opposite side of the shot works for me. I use an ultra-wide lens and get a shot of the entire room (hopefully from a higher angle). Try doing this with a really slow shutter speed of around 1/10 of a second (and maybe a tripod) to capture the movement of the dancing while keeping the other elements of the photo crisp.

You have the option to add more lights to give you the freedom of moving around and shooting from different places while maintaining a consistent look to your images. Add these lights one by one to the corners of the dance floor or room. If you're quick, you can turn on and off the lights from your trigger as you move around the dance floor to keep the same light pattern image to image no matter where you're standing. You can also choose to fire all of them at the same time and not worry about it at all.

One of the perks of this technique is being able to use the foreground because it won't be lit. This will help lead the viewer's eye toward what your subject. It creates a beautifully dramatic image for speeches, dances, or anything else going on at an event.

The key to lighting like this is understanding that your shooting location will determine what the light looks like in the image. It's fun to be able to photograph a flat-lit photo, then a sidelight, a rim light, and then create a silhouette shot without changing anything on your camera or lighting. However, it can also be limiting if there is movement happening outside of your lit area. If possible, use a system that triggers your off-camera flashes with a flash on your camera. This way if you have to move outside your lit area, you can easily bounce flash with the flash that's already on your camera. Oh, and turn off the other lights when you do so they're not flashing like crazy for nothing! #beenthere

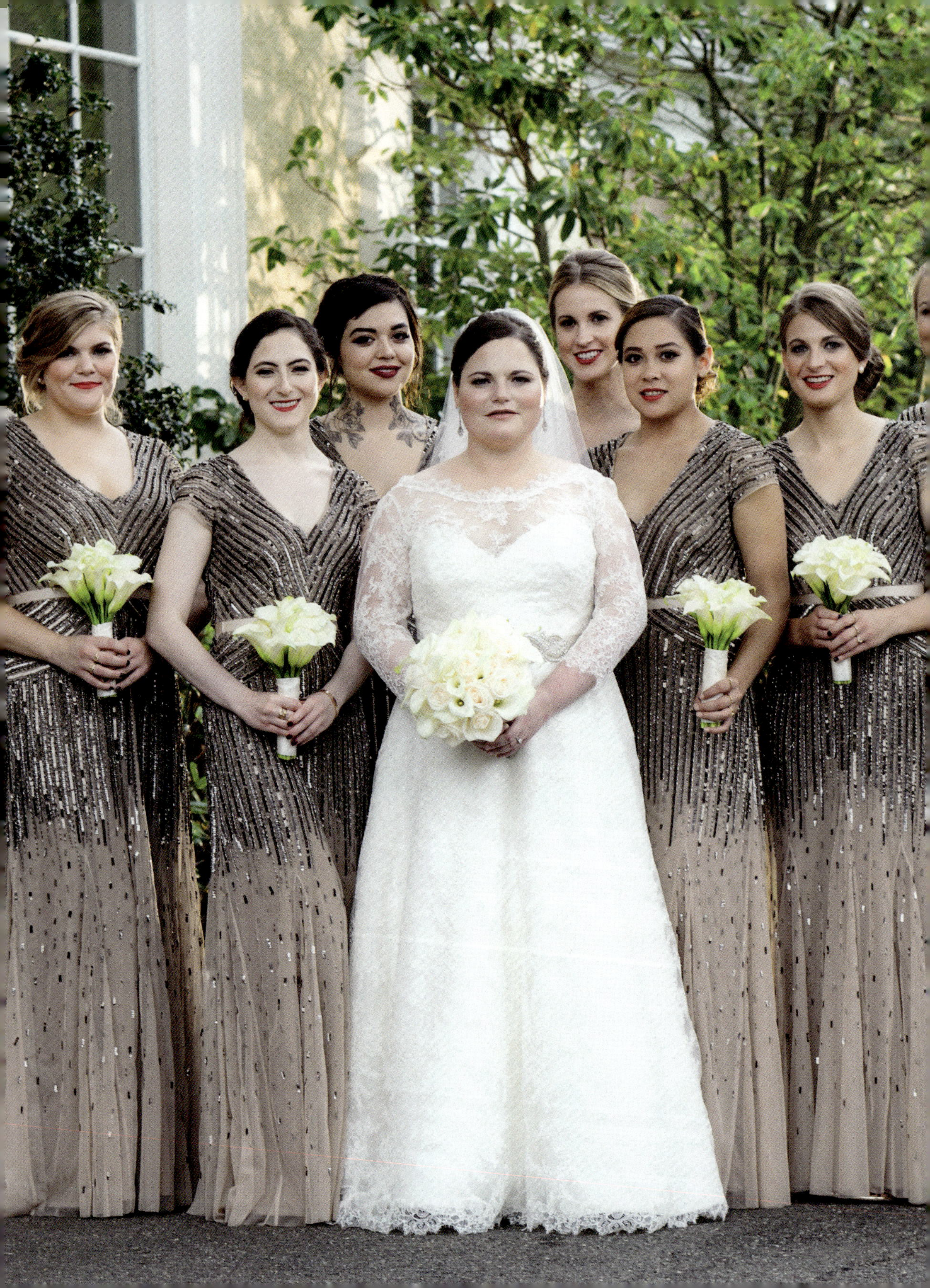

SCENARIO 27

Making a Rainy Day Sunny

How to "bring the sun" to any shoot.

GOAL IMAGE

I work in weddings in the Northeast, and it rains like hell all the time. I envy people in California who get 300+ days of sunshine. For me, it feels like we get 300+ of rain (or at least clouds). It's super depressing. I have a vitamin D lamp for the winter. I call it my happy lamp.

OK, back to photography. The point is that the threat of rain is very real on any given wedding day. My couples dread their bright and vibrant wedding day being turned into doom and gloom. I tell them not to worry because "I bring the sun." I love having the confidence to know I can give them beautifully bright and sunny-looking images no matter what the weather.

GEAR NEEDED:

- Camera + Trigger
- Medium to long focal length lens (50mm or higher recommended)
- Off-camera flash
- 2 Full CTO (color temperature orange) gels
- Light stand
- 2 Umbrellas *(optional, but probably a good idea)*
- Second off-camera flash and light stand *(optional)*

The key to this shot is being able to find a place outside with an overhang. *Warning:* You will likely get wet. You want to place your subject(s) just at the edge of the overhang so that the natural light is hitting their faces, without them getting wet. This means you need to be out in the rain. So grab an umbrella for yourself, and another one for your light, which will also be out in the rain.

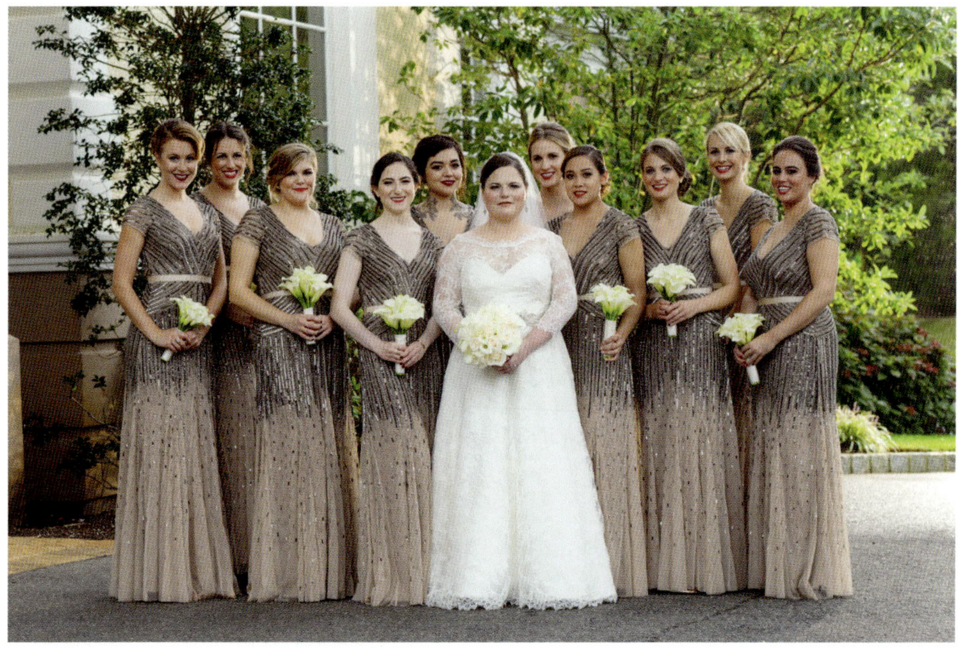

SHOT WITH A PROFOTO B1 BEHIND THEM ON CAMERA RIGHT WITH A CTO GEL.
CANON 1DX, CANON 85MM 1.2, ISO 320, APERTURE 5.6, SHUTTER 1/160

Step by Step

1. **Position your subjects:** Place your subjects just at the edge of the overhang so that the natural light is hitting their faces (without them getting wet!). Ideally the background behind your subjects is a bright and has foliage and depth.

2. **Position the "sun" backlight:** This is the light that will have the two CTO gels on it. Try to place it at least 20 feet away from your subject and behind trees or bushes that'll break up the light and make it look more natural. Don't point it directly at your subjects, but place it in a way that allows the light to pass across their backs.

3. **Set the camera exposure:** Get an exposure for the natural light on your subjects' faces. Ideally the exposure will also create a bright background that's as evenly exposed as their faces. If that's not the case, consider moving your position to a spot where you can have a background that has the same amount of light on it as the light hitting your subjects' faces.

4. **Set the white balance:** Auto white balance would work in this case because the light hitting the faces is natural. Alternatively, dial in your Kelvin temperature according to the natural light hitting your subjects' faces.

5. **Set the back flash:** Turn on just your back flash and use TTL to get a power setting. Flip to manual, keeping the same power setting, and adjust until you like how powerful the "sun" looks. You can also use a light meter or start on mid-high manual power and adjust to taste.

6. **Make adjustments:** Once you have a solid image, feel free to change your exposure, white balance, or flash settings. Be sure to only change one thing at a time so you don't get too far away from what was working originally and you can't get back. Your goal is to balance the natural light with your flash so that it looks like the sun is lighting the background and hitting the back of your subjects.

OPTIONAL: Use another off-camera flash with a soft modifier to light your subjects' faces if you don't like the existing light pattern or you need more light.

Shot by Shot

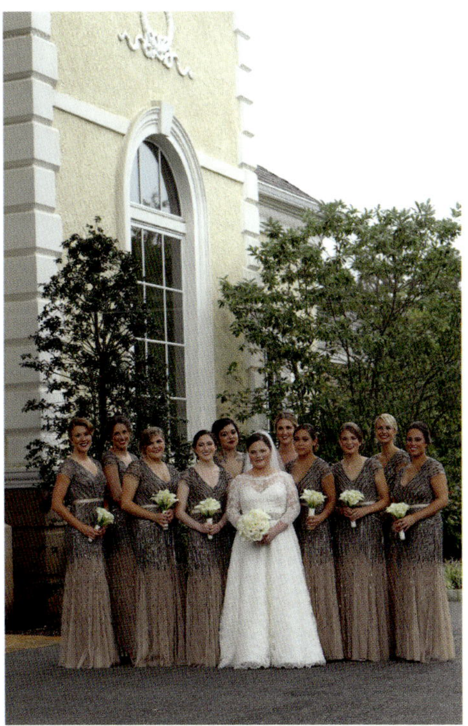

FIGURE 27.2
NATURAL LIGHT.
CANON 1DX, CANON 85MM 1.2, ISO 320, APERTURE 5.6,
SHUTTER 1/160

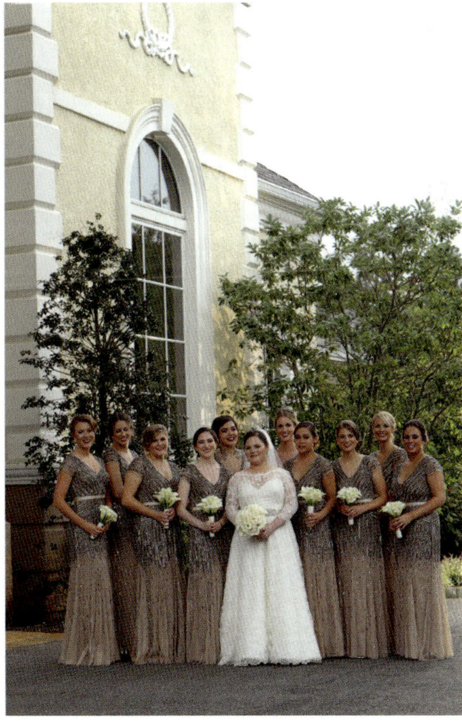

FIGURE 27.3
SHOT WITH A PROFOTO B1 AND CTO GEL BACKFLASH.
CANON 1DX, CANON 85MM 1.2, ISO 320, APERTURE 5.6,
SHUTTER 1/160

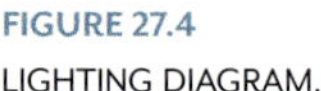

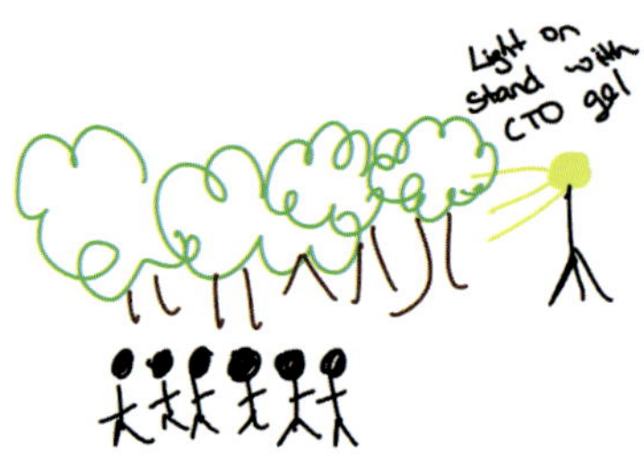

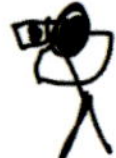

Potential Problems

The most difficult part of this scenario in my opinion is finding the perfect spot. You need to have some kind of greenery (or something) in the background for the flash to hit so it looks like it's the sun hitting the background. In addition, you want to have the light hitting your subjects' faces match the light that's hitting your background. On a naturally sunny day, the light is usually fairly even on your subjects and the background, so you need to find a way to mimic that.

Move your subjects closer or farther away from the edge of the overhang until the light on their faces matches the light on the background. If there's not enough light on their faces and they can't move forward without starting to get wet, consider using a second flash with a soft modifier to add a bit more light to their faces.

Practical Uses

Depending on how large of an overhang you can find, it can be used for individuals, couples, and large groups. The best part is that once you have your light set, you can move people all around and switch from groups to individuals in a heartbeat. The light is spread around so far behind them that a little movement throughout the session shouldn't affect your photo too much.

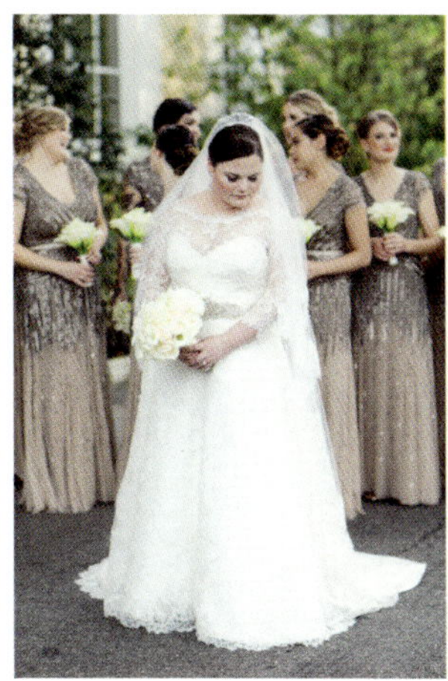
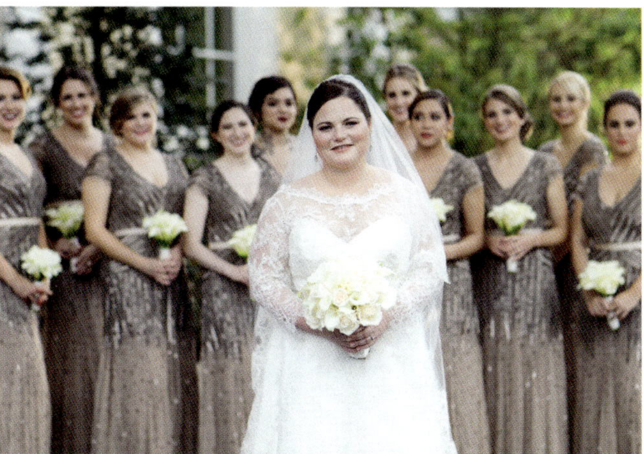
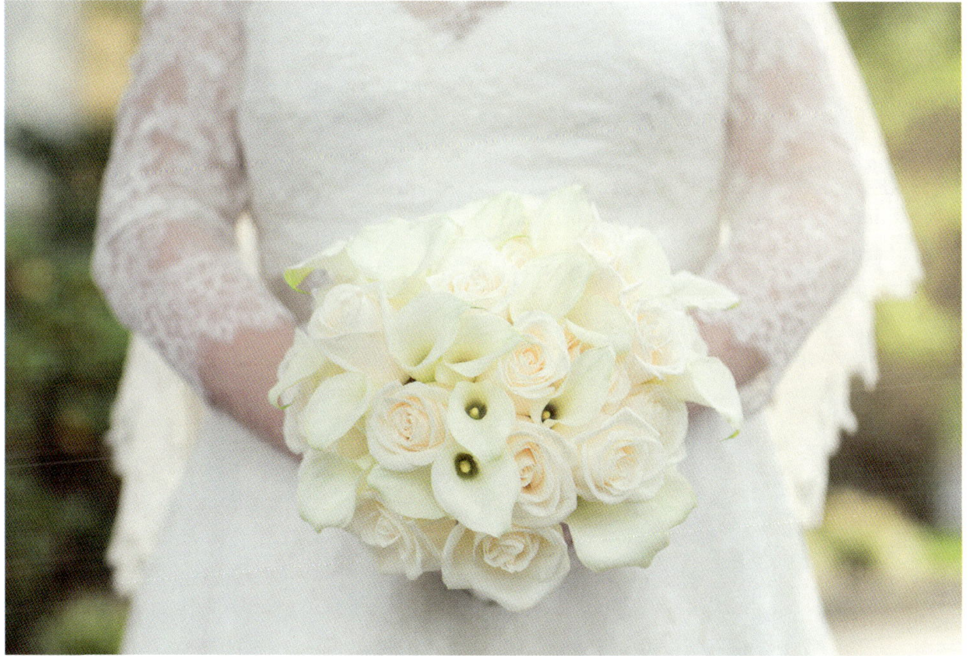

THIS METHOD IS A SET-IT-AND-FORGET-IT SYSTEM, SO AFTER YOU'VE DIALED IT IN, IT'S EASY TO WALK AROUND AND GET DIFFERENT SHOTS THAT YOU NEED WITHOUT CHANGING YOUR SETTINGS.

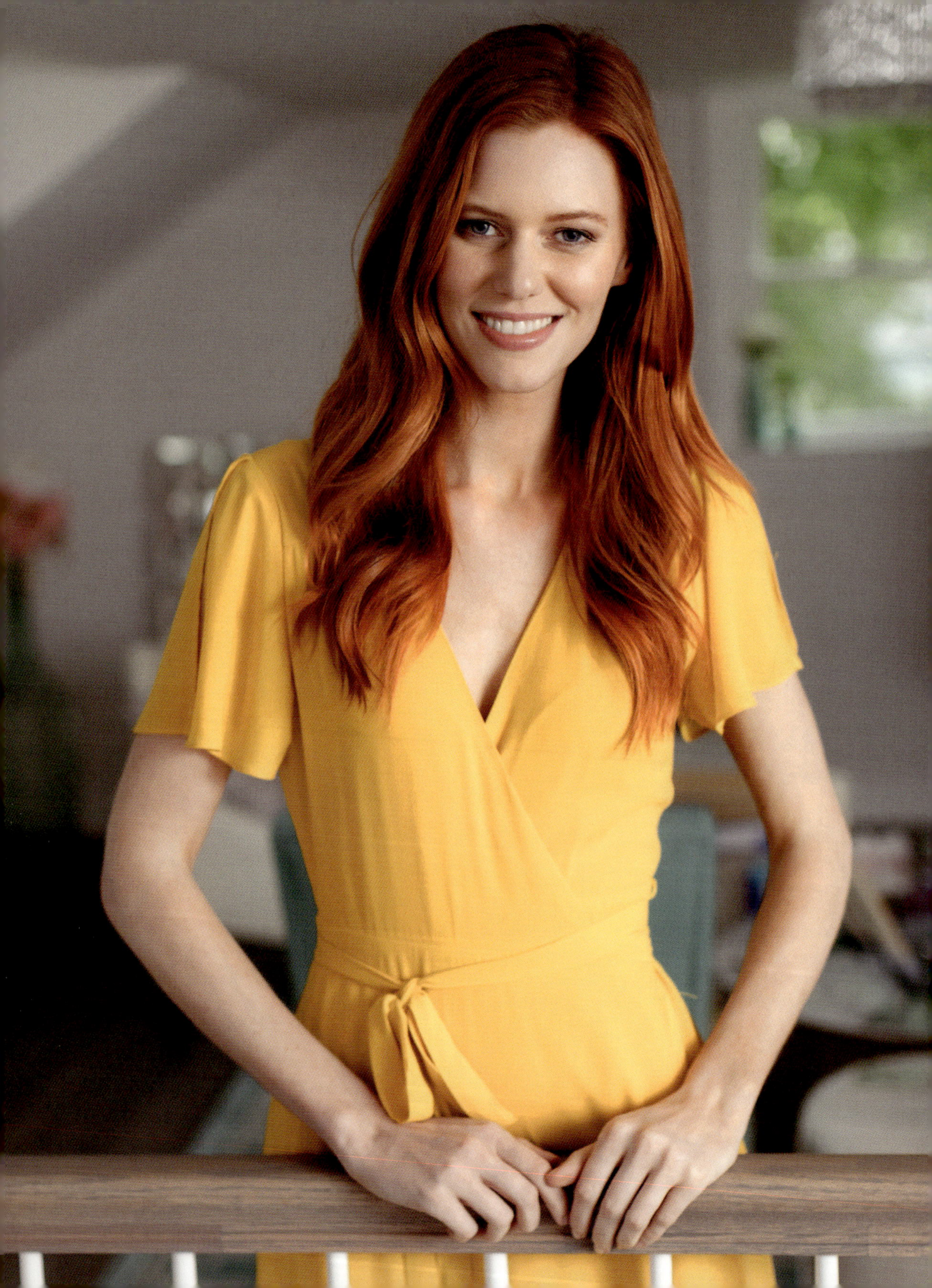

SCENARIO 28

Lighting to Look Like Window Light

For soft, even light that looks like it's natural—but it's not!

GOAL IMAGE

As much as I love shooting in places with floor to ceiling windows, it doesn't always happen. Even if I have windows to use, it doesn't necessarily mean that the light quality will be what I want it to be. This setup is an easy way to make it look like there's beautiful natural window light, even if there really isn't.

There are two ways to create this light. This scenario covers scenarios with white or light-colored walls to bounce light off of. If you don't have one, you'll have to make do by using the largest light modifier that you can get your hands on.

<table>
<tr><td>GEAR NEEDED:</td></tr>
<tr><td>

- Camera + Trigger
- Lens of any focal length
- Off-camera flash
- Light stand *(optional)*
- Reflector *(optional)*

</td></tr>
</table>

Think about rooms with large windows. The light comes in from the window side and pours into the room. That light then bounces off every surface around the room and back at your subject.

With that in mind, you'll want to position your light so that it double bounces off the walls. You need to have your subject in between two white or light-colored walls. Position the light towards one of the walls, and set it to output enough power that the light will reach the other wall and bounces all around (**Figure 28.2**).

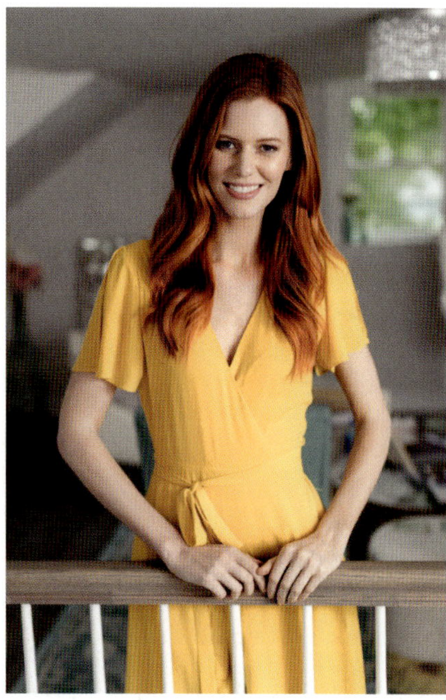

FIGURE 28.1

GOAL IMAGE: THE LIGHT DOUBLE BOUNCING. CANON 1DX II, CANON 50MM 1.2, ISO 800, APERTURE 2.5, SHUTTER 1/200

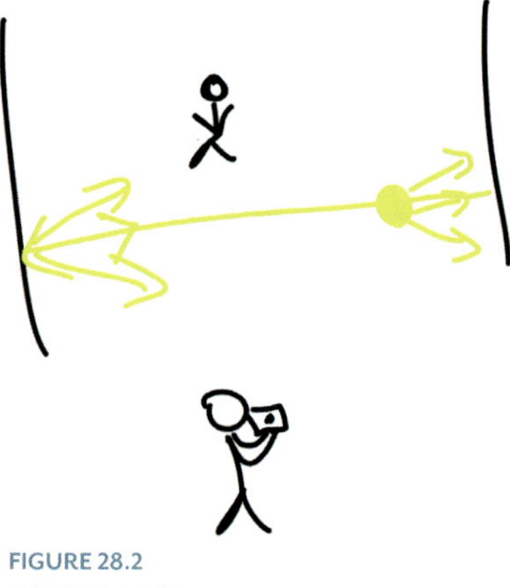

FIGURE 28.2
LIGHTING DIAGRAM.

Step by Step

1. **Position the subject:** Place your subject with a white wall to their right and left. If there are windows in the room, positioning your shot so they are behind you could be ideal because they can add some fill light. However, you could also place the window behind your subject.

2. **Position the light:** Place the light on whichever side has the largest wall with the least amount of interference (furniture, pictures on the wall, etc.). The light should be far enough away from your subject that it won't be in frame, but far enough away from the wall that it lights up the entire wall. Point the light at the wall and, but slightly toward you so that the light bounces back, hitting your subject at about a 45-degree angle.

   Make sure that the light also bounces off the opposite wall. Test fire your light and look at the opposite wall to see where it is hitting. Adjust your positioning if it's not hitting enough of either wall.

3. **Set the camera exposure:** Set your camera exposure as if you're taking a picture of the background. I do not try and eliminate the natural light in this scene because I want to use both light sources—unless the lights aren't so attractive (like overhead tungsten lights). In that case I turn them off, either by actually turning them off or darkening my exposure so that

light doesn't affect the image as much. Try to set your shutter speed to around $\frac{1}{160}$ of a second so you have room to raise or lower your shutter speed to darken or lighten the natural light in the room without affecting your flash.

4. **Set the white balance:** Because the flash is your main source of light, set your white balance to flash or 5600 Kelvin depending on the original color temperature of your light. If you're bouncing the light off of a wall that is colored, you'll need to adjust your Kelvin temperature to compensate for that.

5. **Set the flash power:** Set your flash power to TTL and take a test shot. Flip it to manual, holding that power setting, and adjust if necessary. If you're using a manual flash, start in the medium-high power range or use a light meter. Then adjust up or down to your liking. Take a test shot and adjust your light to be more or less powerful according to your taste.

OPTIONAL: Use a reflector close to your subject to bounce the light back on your subject in a more specific direction. This may be a better choice if you don't have two light-colored walls, or if the walls are too far away for the double bounce to be effective.

Shot by Shot

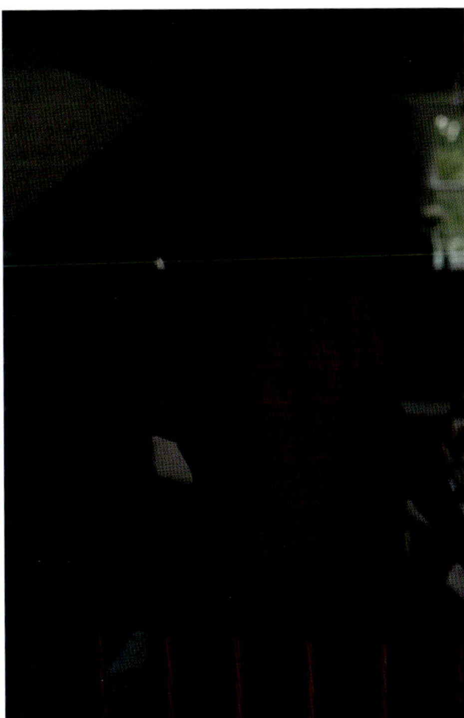

FIGURE 28.3

NATURAL LIGHT INDOORS.
CANON 1DX II, CANON 50MM 1.2, ISO 800, APERTURE 2.5, SHUTTER 1/200

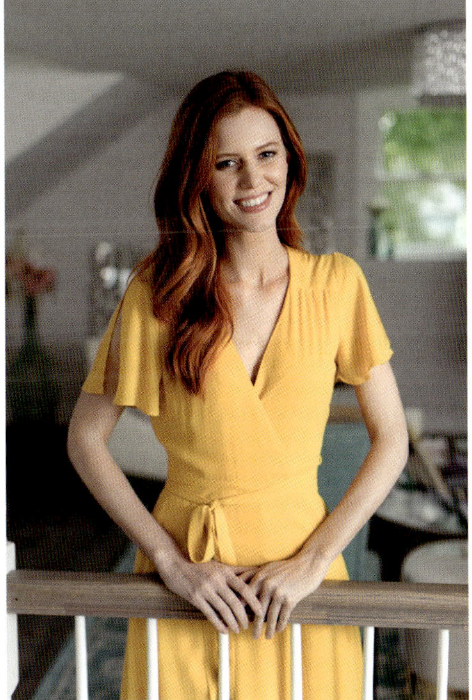

FIGURE 28.4

OCF ADDED.
CANON 1DX II, CANON 50MM 1.2, ISO 800, APERTURE 2.5, SHUTTER 1/200

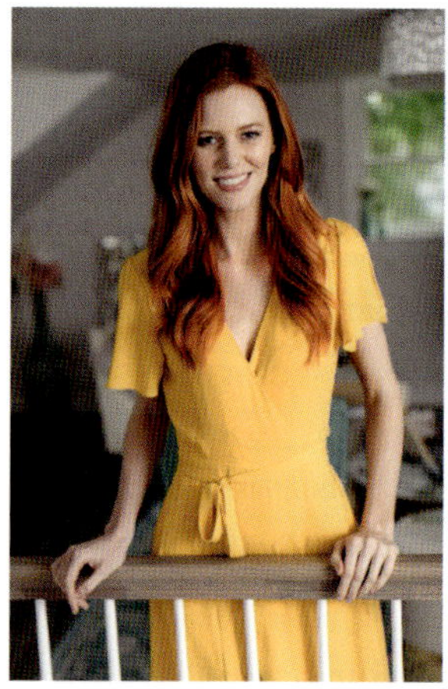

FIGURE 28.5
REFLECTOR ADDED.
CANON 1DX II, CANON 50MM 1.2,
ISO 800, APERTURE 2.5, SHUTTER
1/200

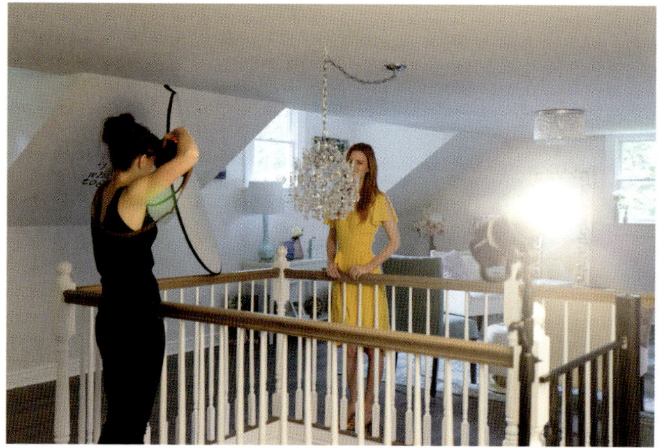

FIGURE 28.5
BEHIND THE SCENES.

Potential Problems

Especially when you place the subject against the window and you need to light their face in a flattering manner, you may not having enough flash power to overcome the ambient light. This may be a problem if you only have a speedlight in a large room. To double bounce, you'll need a good amount of light, especially if your walls are fairly far apart.

Even if you have white or light-colored walls, the ambient light source in the room may give off an ugly color, like Tungsten bulbs. You might need to use some of that light for your shot, but to make it look more natural, you need to balance the color of the lights to your flash. Read Scenario 25, "Using Gels to Color Correct," for more information.

Practical Uses

This technique is great for a room without windows or a room with windows on a cloudy day that doesn't have enough natural light for your shot.

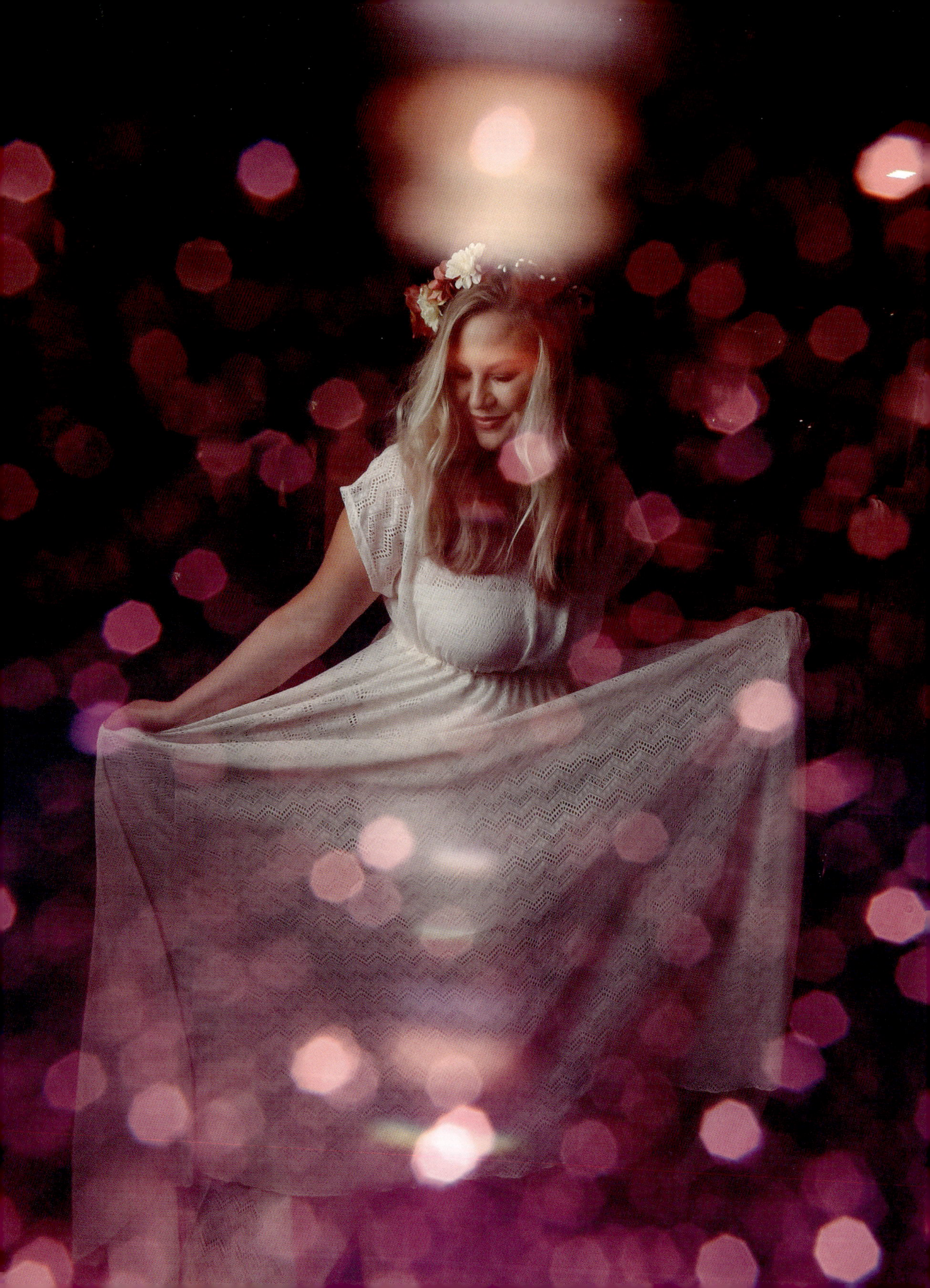

SCENARIO 29

Making Front Bokeh

Or as I like to say, "Go flash yourself."

GOAL IMAGE

This is one of the coolest stinking tricks I've ever done. It can change any image. I can't take full credit for this one—my friend Seth Miranda (IG: @LastXWitness) came up with it and showed me how to do it. I expanded on it from there.

To wrap your head around this technique and how it works, you have to know a bit about lenses and how they work. When light hits your lens, it's not just hitting one piece of glass. It's passing through multiple pieces of glass and making its way to your sensor. When your images have lens flare in them, it's the light hitting those pieces of glass and bouncing around in there. Some lenses have ASC (Air Sphere Coating) to enhance the anti-reflective properties, so those lenses may be trickier to use successfully for this trick.

GEAR NEEDED:

- Camera + Trigger
- Wide focal length lens (50mm or wider recommended)
- Off-camera flash
- Light stand *(optional)*
- Colored gels *(optional)*
- Second off-camera flash *(optional)*

The wider your lens is, the smaller your bokeh balls will be. The longer the focal length of your lens is, the bigger your bokeh balls will be. Sometimes they'll just be haze versus bokeh balls. It's all about how the lens processes light as it passes through your camera.

Step by Step

1. **Position your subject:** Because the bokeh balls are essentially light circles, finding a darker background will help them show up more prominently. A lighter background will hide a lot of the light effect that you're trying to create.

2. **Set your camera exposure:** You have two options here. You can set your camera to create a dark or black exposure and light your subject with another light; or, you can set your camera to take a properly exposed natural-light photograph. The first option will make your bokeh balls show up more.

3. **Set your white balance:** Your white balance can be set to auto for this or manually dialed in to whatever your natural-light exposure calls for.

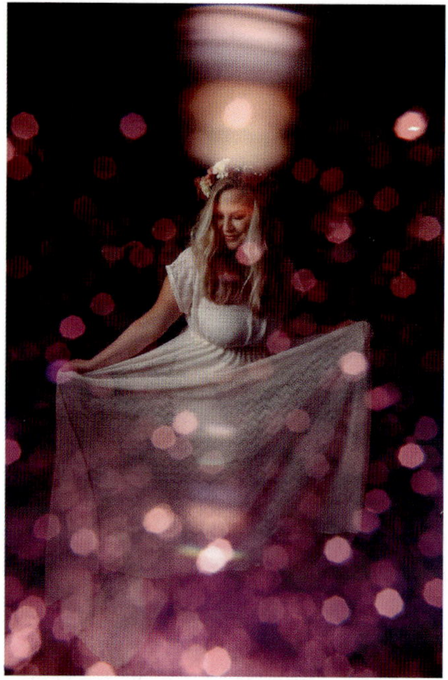

FIGURE 29.1

GOAL IMAGE. I USED A STROBE ON CAMERA LEFT WITH A LARGE UMBRELLA. YOU'LL SEE BEHIND-THE-SCENES SHOTS AND OTHER VARIATIONS LATER IN THE SECTION.

CANON 1DX MARK II, CANON 24MM 1.4, ISO 1250, APERTURE 16, SHUTTER 1/250

4. **Set your bokeh flash:** You need a lot of light for this, so set your light (assuming it's a smaller speedlight) to full power and adjust from there.

    If you're using a more powerful light, start at half power and move it up if you don't see the bokeh effect showing up.

5. **Position your light:** This is the tricky part. I usually hold my light (a light one like a speedlight or Profoto A1) in my left hand, super close (if not touching) my lens, and pointing into my lens.

    If you have a heavier light, or if you just don't feel like holding your light, you can set it on a light stand right in front of you.

6. **Change your angle:** This is the tricky part. Every little millimeter that you move your light will change the angle that it hits your lens. This will change how it looks in your image. Move the light all around your lens. Shoot with it above, below, left, and right—everywhere. See what it does to the bokeh pattern.

7. **Make adjustments:** Once you see the light effect show up, you can play with it to change the effect. You can use more or less power to make the effect brighter or darker, and you can change your f-stop to change the size of the balls. Change your lens to see the difference it has on the effect. Have fun with this! There are limitless possibilities.

OPTIONAL: Throw any color gel you'd like on the flash to change the color of the bokeh balls. Experiment with different colors!

OPTIONAL: Black out your exposure and light your subject with a second off-camera flash. This will make your bokeh show up even more. It will also prevent the bokeh from showing up on the subject's face because that light can be set to be brighter than your bokeh light. This is the technique I use in the example below.

Shot by Shot

FIGURE 29.2
TAKE AN ALL-BLACK EXPOSURE FIRST.

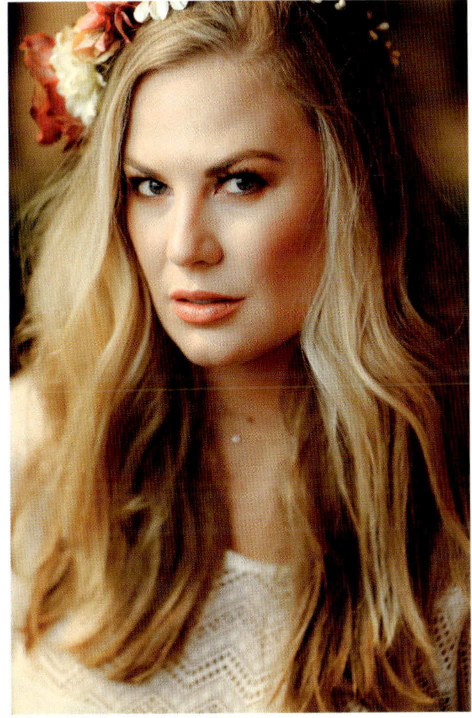

FIGURE 29.3
FOR THIS IMAGE, I TURNED ON THE FRONT CANON 600EXII SPEEDLITE TO TTL AND USED A 3' OCTA. CANON 1 DX II, CANON 135MM 2.0, ISO 400, APERTURE 2, SHUTTER SPEED 1/250

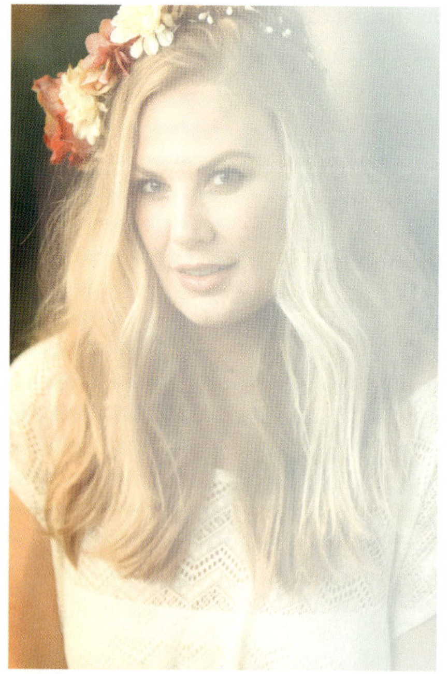

FIGURE 29.4

I ADDED FRONT "BOKEH" LIGHT, A CANON 600EXII SPEEDLITE.

CANON 1 DX II, CANON 135MM 2.0, ISO 400, APERTURE 2, SHUTTER SPEED 1/250

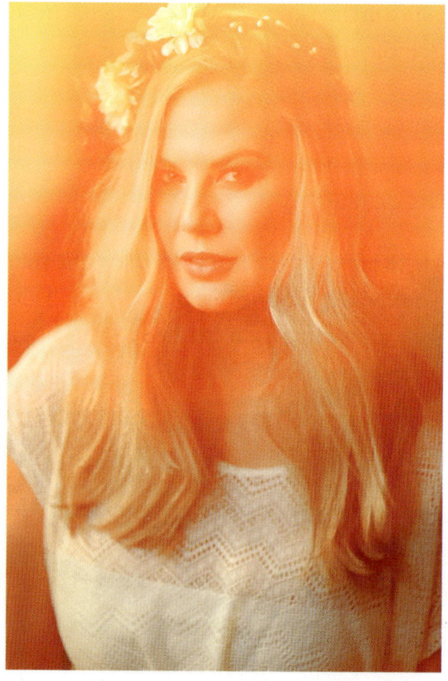

FIGURE 29.5

I ADDED A CTO GEL TO THE FRONT BOKEH LIGHT, A CANON 600EXII SPEEDLITE.

CANON 1 DX II, CANON 135MM 2.0, ISO 400, APERTURE 2, SHUTTER SPEED 1/250

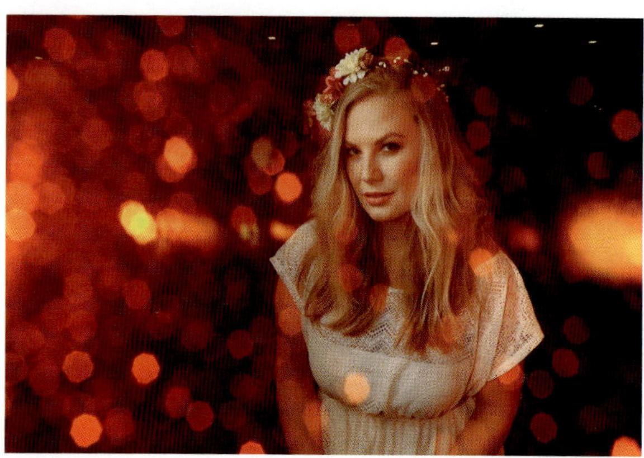

FIGURE 29.6

USING A LONGER LENS WITH A LOWER APERTURE TURNS THE LIGHT INTO A HAZE RATHER THAN SMALLER BOKEH BALLS. I CHANGED THE LENS TO THE CANON 24MM 1.4, THE APERTURE TO 16, AND THE ISO TO 1250, SO THAT THE SMALLER BOKEH BALLS WOULD SHOW UP. CANON 600EXII SPEEDLITE.

CANON 1 DX II, CANON 24MM 1.4, ISO 1250, APERTURE 16, SHUTTER SPEED 1/250

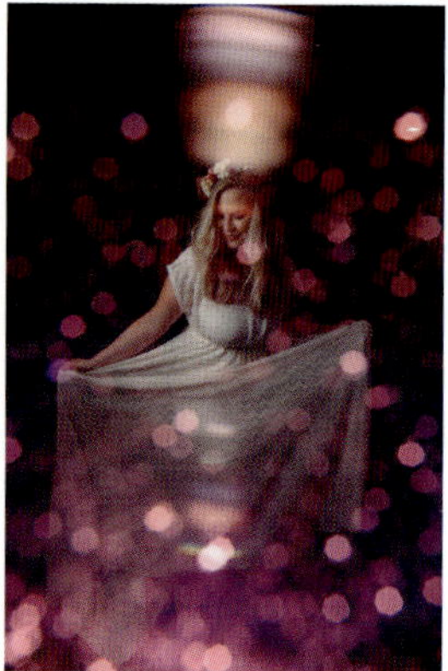

FIGURE 29.7

I USED A PURPLE GEL ON THE CANON 600EXII SPEEDLITE FOR THIS IMAGE.

CANON 1 DX II, CANON 24MM 1.4, ISO 1250, APERTURE 16, SHUTTER SPEED 1/250

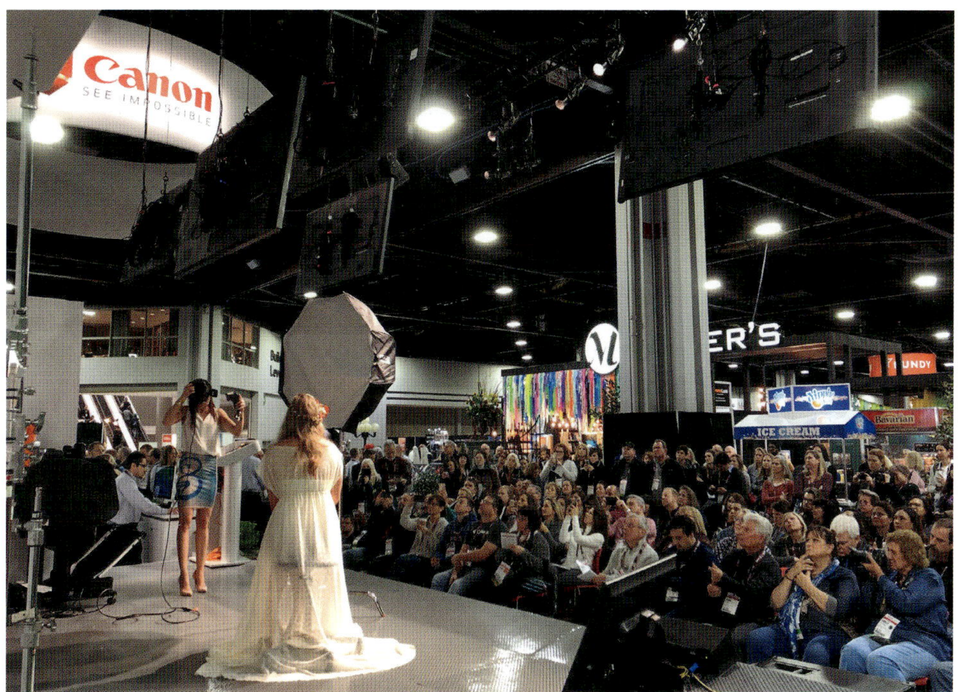

FIGURE 29.8
BEHIND THE SCENES AT IMAGING USA ON THE CANON STAGE.

Potential Problems

This trick can be difficult depending on your lighting circumstances. Ultimately, the effect shows up best on the darker parts of the image, so try this in a lower-light scenario first. A wider-angle lens with a high f-stop (such as f/22) will create the most dramatic look.

You can do this outside on an overcast day. It just takes a lot of flash power, and you won't necessarily see the bokeh quite as prominently because the light isn't contrasting against anything dark behind it.

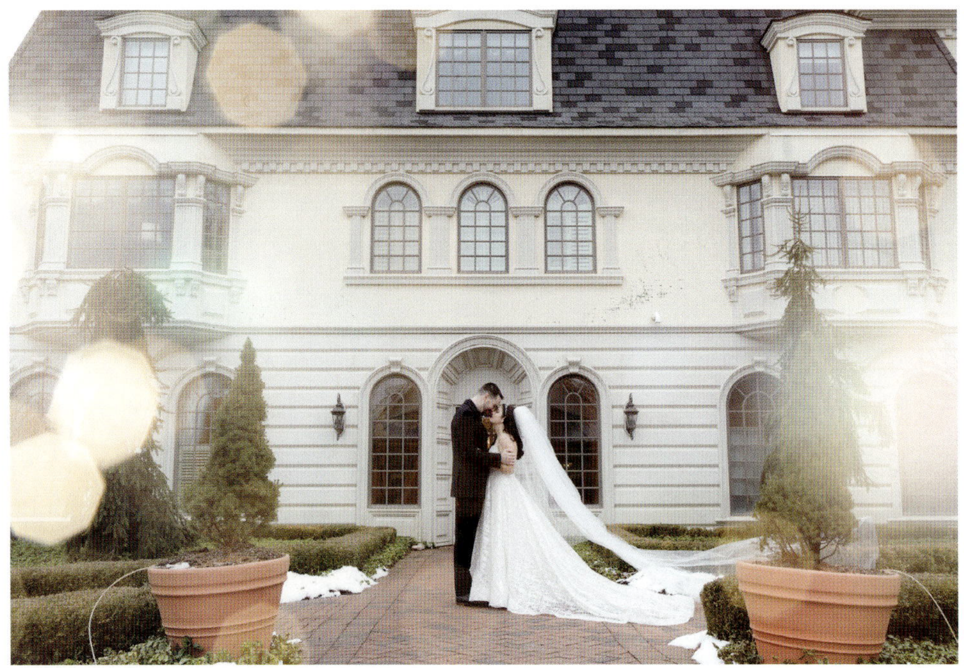

Practical Uses

This is a handy tool to use when you want to create a crazy look or elevate a photograph. Be careful not to overdo it. It's a neat technique, but it can be easily overdone and most clients won't want a full album of photos like this.

It really is a ton of fun to try this out, so get out there and go flash yourself! Oh, and hashtag it #goflashyourself so I can see it.

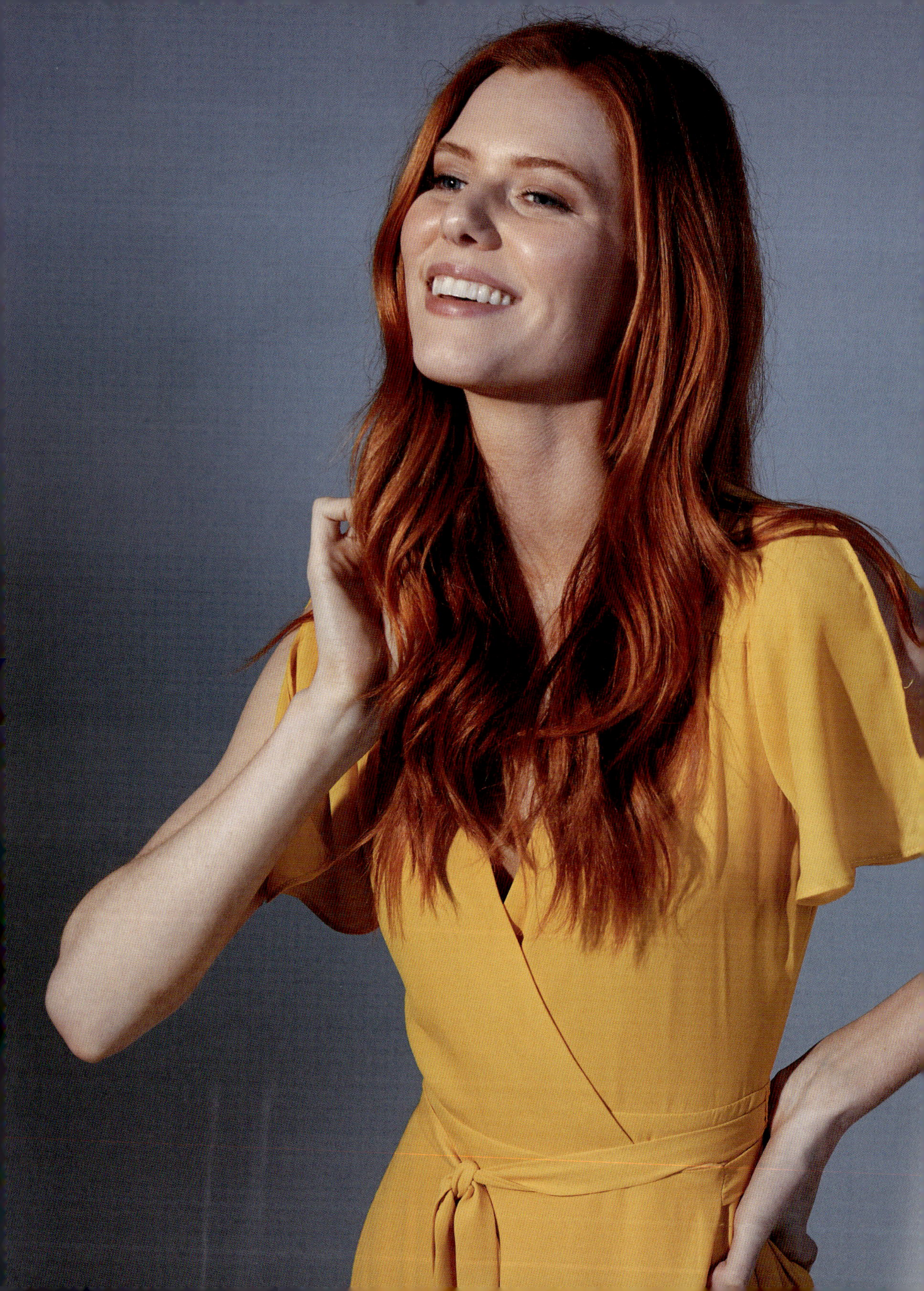

SCENARIO 30
Filling in Shadows

Because lights can do it too—not just reflectors.

WHAT IS FILL LIGHT?

I believe fill light is one of the most misunderstood concepts in photography. Understanding how to use it in a shot seems simple, but most photographers don't realize exactly what's happening photographically. Let's get you up to speed using some pretty colors.

For the best video explanation of fill light, watch this Instagram TV video: *www.instagram.com/tv/BkR9nJpDMkd.* In written form, here's what we're looking at.

GEAR NEEDED:

- Camera + Trigger
- Lens of any focal length
- 2 Off-camera flashes
- 2 Light stands
- Colored gel *(optional)*

The light that fills in the shadow area (the light hitting where the main light is absent) is called the fill light. It's filling in where the main light is not. The fill light doesn't just lessen the shadow; you can also fill shadows in with colored light.

The fill light, even if it's colored, doesn't affect the parts of the photo that the main light is lighting (unless you want it to). The fill light should have a much lower flash power output than the main light, assuming you don't want it to affect the parts of the photograph that are lit by the main light.

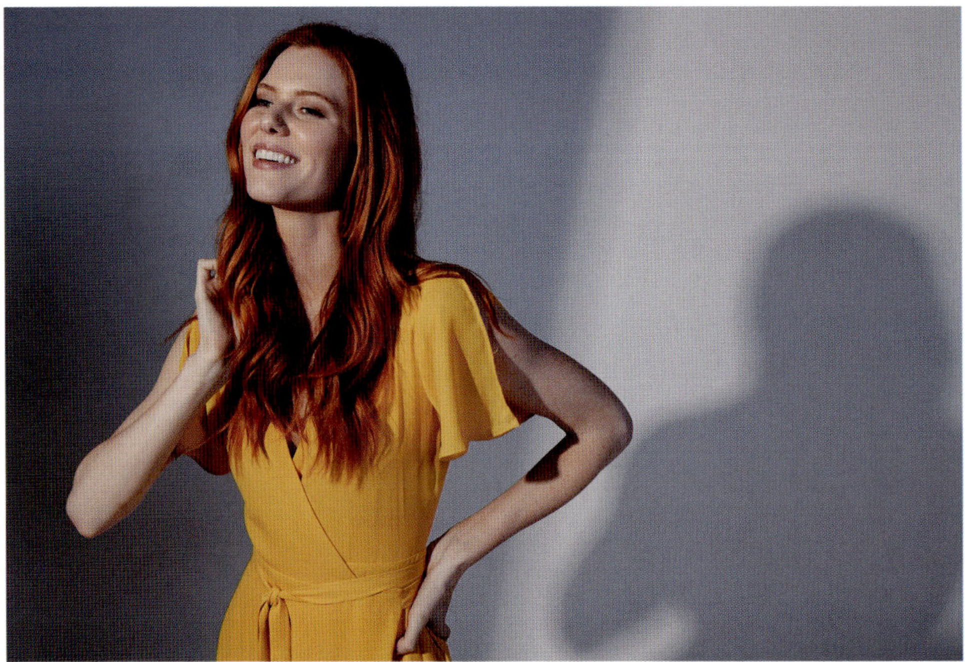

GOAL IMAGE. EDITED IN CAPTURE ONE. THE STRAIGHT-OUT-OF-CAMERA IMAGE IS BELOW.
CANON 1DXII, CANON 35MM 1.4, ISO 100, APERTURE 9, SHUTTER 1/250, WB 5600K

Yes, you can use a "fill light" to affect the main light and cast different shadows. However, it's not really a fill light, because it's taking over another light instead of just filling in shadows. For our purposes, let's start with a basic fill light that fills in shadows. I find this to be the best way to learn how fill light works. From there, you can experiment away and break all the rules.

Step by Step

1. **Position your subjects:** For our purposes, we want to see prominent shadows. Place your subjects close to a wall where a shadow can be thrown from the main light. Or, plan to position them to have shadows thrown on their faces.

2. **Position the lights:**

   A. **Main light:** We want shadows in the picture and a hard-light look, so I'm placing the light to the right or left of my subject, and a bit far away to create a smaller light source that will throw a shadow on the wall. Use your modeling light to see exactly where your shadow is falling.

   B. **Fill light:** Your goal in positioning the fill light is to let the light hit the shadows in your photo. Because we're not setting it to overpower the main light, it doesn't make too much of a difference where you position it in relation to the main light, but I like positioning my fill light fairly close to the camera. In fact, you could even use a speedlight on-camera directly flashing at your subjects to provide perfectly adequate fill light.

3. **Set the camera exposure:** I'm in the studio for this shot, so I set my exposure so the frame goes completely black. I don't want any natural light affecting my shot. To complement the hard-light look, I also set my f-stop fairly high.

4. **Set the white balance:** Because the flash is your main source of light, set your WB to daylight, flash, or 5600K depending on the color temperature of your flash.

5. **Set the flash power:** This is a scenario in which a light meter would help tremendously, but in case you don't have one available, here are two ways of determining your flash power:

   A. **Without a light meter:**

      I. Turn the main light on to TTL. Take a shot, flip to manual, and adjust the light to be brighter or darker as necessary. If you don't have TTL, start in the mid-high power range and adjust from there.

      II. Note what power your main light is set to.

      III. Turn the main light off.

      IV. Turn on the fill light, and set it manually to half the power (or less) of the main light.

      V. Turn both lights on. Take a shot and adjust for more or less fill light.

   B. **With a light meter:**

      I. Turn the main light on to the mid-high power range. Take a light meter reading on your subjects' faces. Adjust the light until the output matches the f-stop you have chosen to use.

      II. Note what power your main light is set to.

      III. Turn the main light off.

      IV. Turn on the fill light and set it manually to half the power (or less) of the main light.

      V. Take a light meter reading where the shadow will fall on the wall or your subjects. Adjust the light until the output is 2–3 stops lower than what your main light is set to.

      VI. Turn both lights on. Take a shot and adjust for more or less fill light.

6. **Adjust your fill light:** Your fill light should not change the exposure that the main light is giving you. If it is, and you see the colored light or a shadow being throw onto the main-light side of your subject, then lower your fill-light flash power or raise your main-light flash power (and change your f-stop).

OPTIONAL: Add a colored gel to your fill light to create fun shadows.

Shot by Shot

FIGURE 30.2

NATURAL LIGHT SHOT THAT MOSTLY
DARKENS THE AMBIENT LIGHT IN THE
PICTURE.
CANON 1DXII, CANON 35MM 1.4,
ISO 100, APERTURE 9, SHUTTER 1/250,
WB 5600K

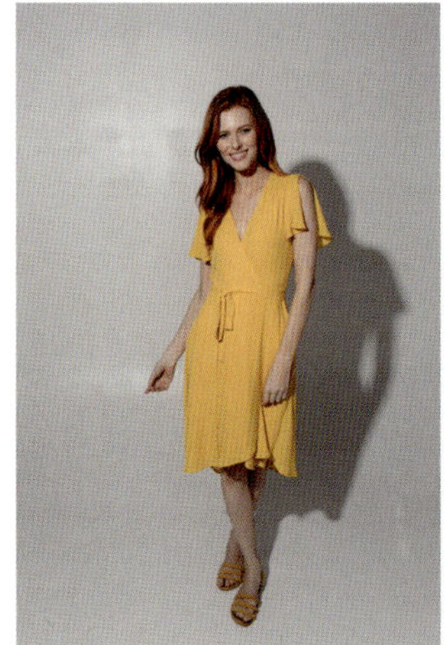

FIGURE 30.3

SHOT WITH A MAIN LIGHT, A PRO-
FOTO D1 BAREBULB, TO CREATE A
HARSH SHADOW.
CANON 1DXII, CANON 35MM 1.4,
ISO 100, APERTURE 9, SHUTTER 1/250,
WB 5600K

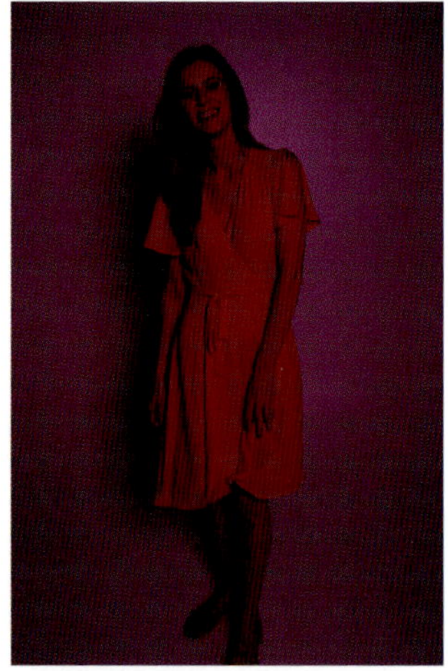

FIGURE 30.4

SHOT WITH A FILL LIGHT, A PROFOTO
D1 WITH AN UMBRELLA AND
MAGENTA GEL.
CANON 1DXII, CANON 35MM 1.4,
ISO 100, APERTURE 9, SHUTTER 1/250,
WB 5600K

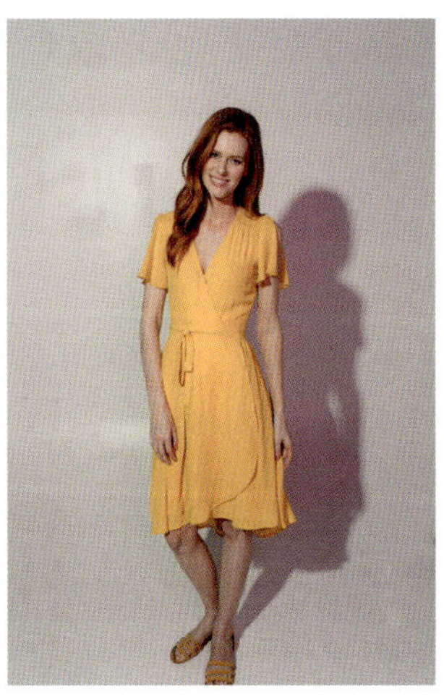

FIGURE 30.5

SHOT WITH BOTH LIGHTS. NOTICE
HOW ALL OF THE SHADOWS ARE
TINTED MAGENTA, INCLUDING THE
SHADOWS ON HER FACE.
CANON 1DXII, CANON 35MM 1.4,
ISO 100, APERTURE 9, SHUTTER 1/250,
WB 5600K

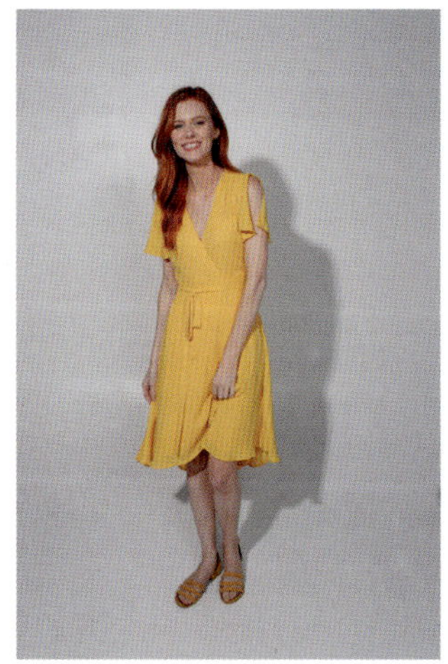

FIGURE 30.6

SHOT WITH BOTH LIGHTS, WITHOUT
A MAGENTA GEL.
CANON 1DXII, CANON 35MM 1.4,
ISO 100, APERTURE 9, SHUTTER
1/250, WB 5600K

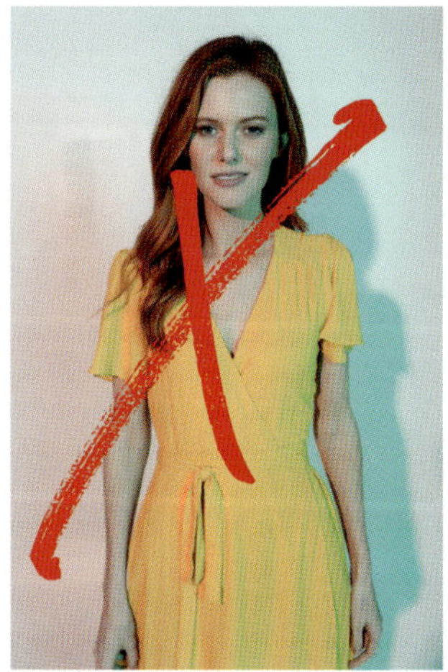

FIGURE 30.7

THIS SHOT HAS TOO MUCH FILL LIGHT!
NOTICE SHE HAS TWO NOSE SHADOWS
UNDER AND ON THE SIDES OF HER NOSE.
I COLORED BOTH LIGHTS (THE TEAL MAIN
LIGHT AND THE MAGENTA FILL LIGHT) TO
EXAGGERATE THE EFFECT.
CANON 1DXII, CANON 35MM 1.4, ISO 100,
APERTURE 5, SHUTTER 1/250, WB 5600K

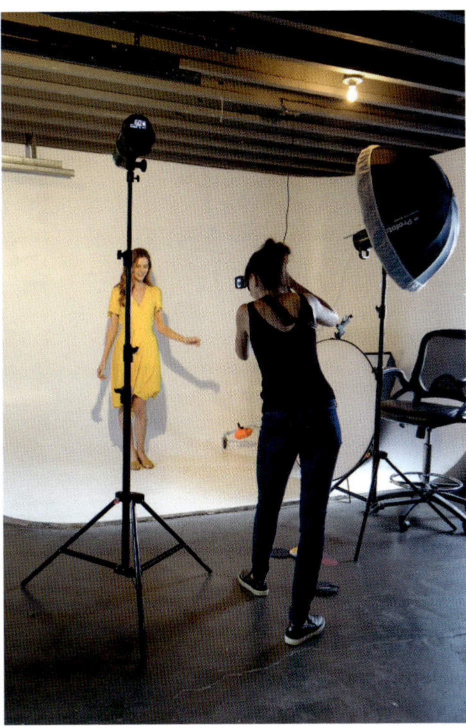

Potential Problems

If the fill light is overpowering the main light in an undesirable manner, consider doing one of the following:

- Feather the fill light so it's not directly hitting the shadows.

- Add a diffuser in front of the fill light so it decreases the light output hitting your shadows.

- Move the light farther away.

- Raise the main light's power. Raise your f-stop or lower your ISO to compensate until there's a big enough light ratio between the main and fill light so that the fill light isn't overpowering the main light.

Practical Uses

Fill light has infinite uses in photography. Practice these techniques a few times until you master them and can control them. Then have a bit of fun!

Give this a try for reducing the contrast in a photograph and for filling in shadows when the main light is the sun. You can also add fun-colored shadow effects to your photos. Also try making it look like a daylight shot by filling in shadows with blue light by using a big diffuser, as in **Figure 30.10**.

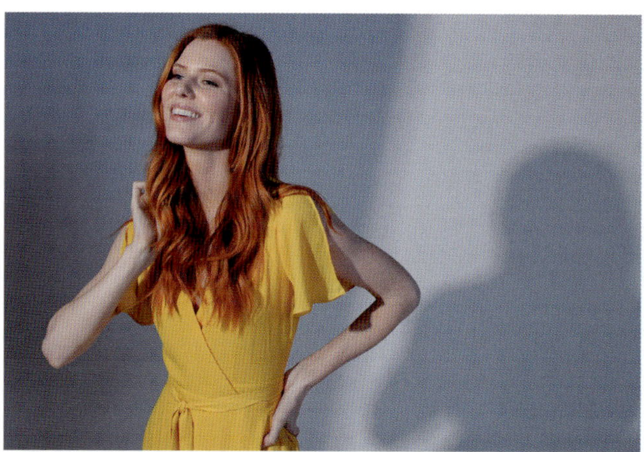

FIGURE 30.9
ADDED FILL LIGHT WITH FULL CTB (BLUE) GEL. THE SHADOW WAS CAUSED BY A 2X3 SOFTBOX, WHICH WAS NOT ON.
CANON 1DXII, CANON 50MM 1.2, ISO 100, APERTURE 5.6, SHUTTER 1/250, WB 5600K

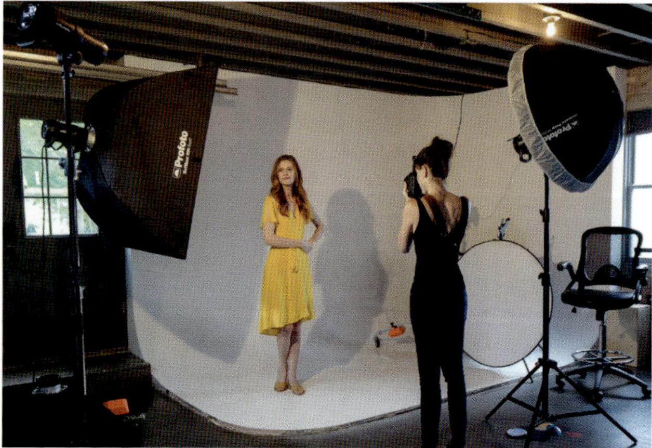

FIGURE 30.10
BEHIND-THE-SCENES SHOT.

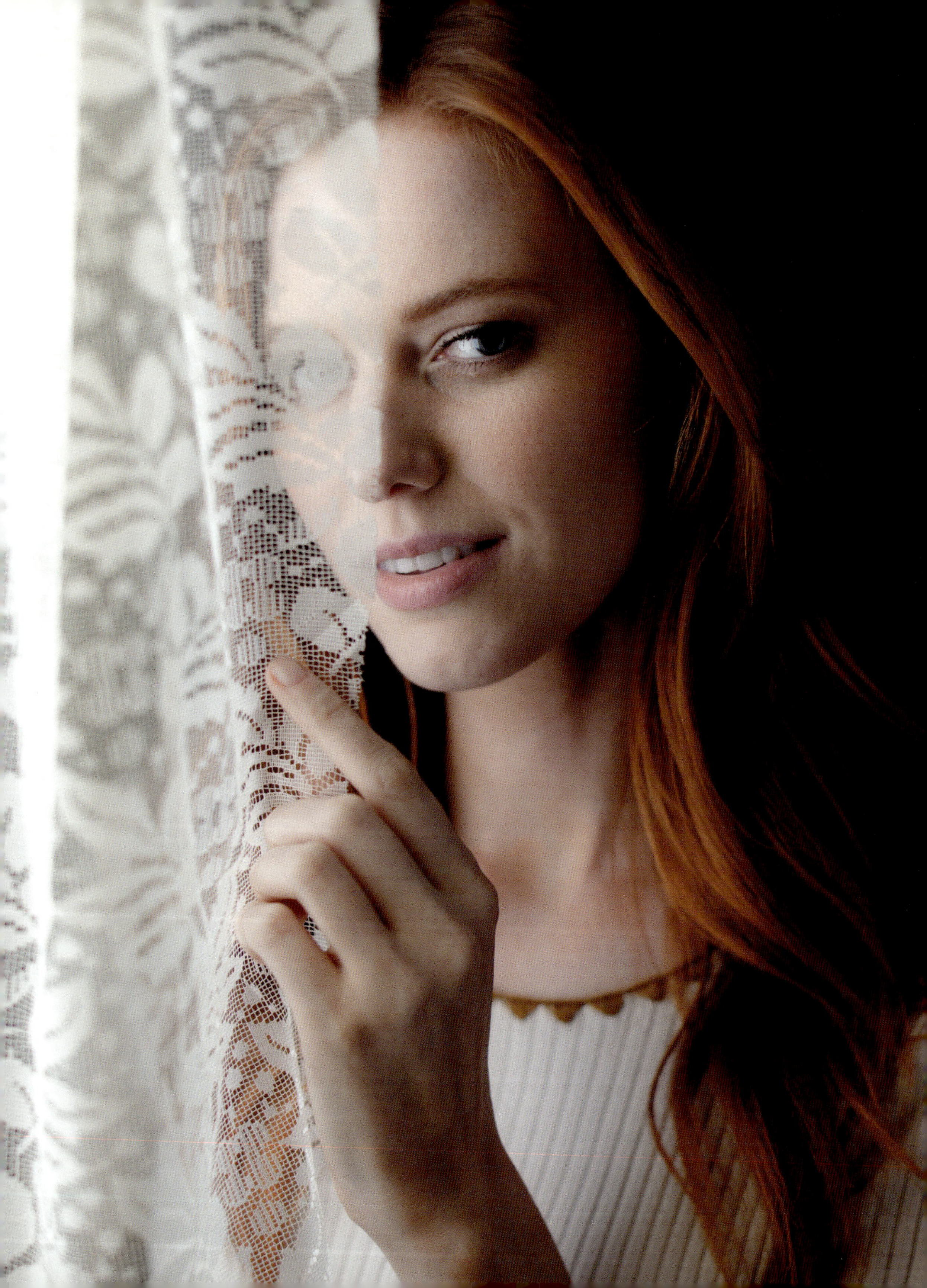

SCENARIO 31

Wow, This Indoor Light Sucks

"And there are pink walls..."

GOAL IMAGE

Have you ever walked into a shoot, or the morning preparations for a wedding, and been smacked in the face with the ugliest peachy-pink walls you've ever encountered? Yeah. Me too. You can't use natural light, because ew. You can't bounce flash because you'll be bouncing the color of grandma's peach cobbler back at them. Double ew. What to you do?

Think of this process as remodeling the room with light. You hate everything that's there, so you're going to erase it and add your own. The trick to coming out of this lighting nightmare alive is combining several techniques we've talked about in this book: faking window light and using gels to color correct (**Figure 31.1**).

You have to first evaluate your room and decide what course you want to take to correct the colors. Typically, there are windows in a room. If there are no windows, it is by definition a closet and not a room. Believe me, I have photographed my fair share of bridal prep sessions in what is, by definition, a closet. Here's the thought process you need to go through when entering places where light has gone to die:

- Do you have a gel that matches the color of the walls?

    A. If Yes: Refer to Scenario 25, "Using Gels to Color Correct."

- Is there a window?

    B. If Yes: Refer to Scenario 15, "Light Like It's Coming Through a Window."

- Is there at least one white wall?

    C. If Yes: Refer to Scenario 28, "Lighting to Look Like Window Light."

- Did you answer no to all, or there's a window but you can't get outside of it? That's what this troubleshooting section is about.

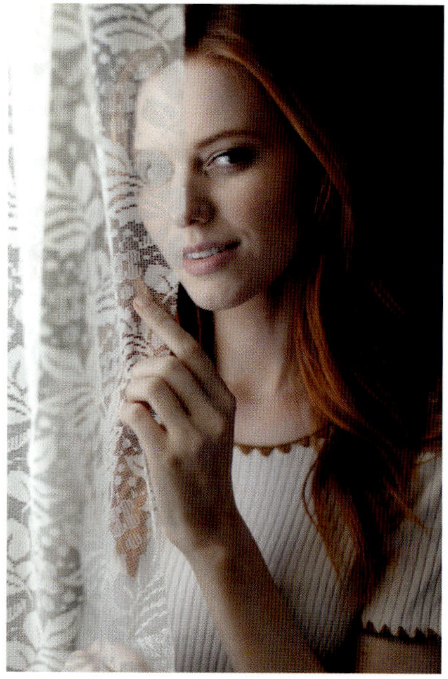

FIGURE 31.1
GOAL IMAGE.
CANON 1DXII, CANON 50MM 1.2, ISO 100,
APERTURE 2.5, SHUTTER 1/250

Step by Step: With a Window

1. **Light position option 1:** Position the light against the window, and "fake" the window light by using a big modifier and maybe even putting some of the curtains a little in front of it. You'll have to step back a little bit and frame the shot so that you don't see the very silly-looking light setup. I only had a 2x3 softbox in this scenario, but had I used a larger modifier, I could've backed up a bit and had more room.

    I highly recommend a Savage MultiFlex Light Stand. For situations like this, you can position the light on a stand completely against the wall.

    The problem with this setup, depending on your settings, is that your fill light will end up being the color of whatever ugly color the walls are. If this is a problem, either use light position 2 or have a reflector on the other side of your subject to block the fill light. Replace it with your own white light from the white side of the reflector.

2. **Light position option 2:** Place the light directly opposite the window so that any fill light will be bouncing back from the window or the (hopefully white) shades.

Step by Step: Without a Window:

1. **Position the light:** Place the light in a spot so it aims at a clean background. Treat the light like a window when you position your subjects.

2. **Position the reflector:** Have a reflector on the other side of your subjects to block the ugly-colored fill light, and replace it with your own white light from the white side of the reflector.

Step by Step: After Positioning the Light

1. **Set the camera exposure:** Set your camera so that the frame is completely black. You hate the natural light in the room, so turn it off by creating an exposure that's one or two stops underexposed for any light in the room.

2. **Set the white balance:** Because the flash is your main source of light, set your white balance to flash or 5600 Kelvin, depending on the original color temperature of your light.

3. **Set the flash power:** Set your flash power to TTL and take a test shot. Flip it to manual, holding that power setting, and adjust if necessary. If you're using a manual flash, start in the medium-high power range, or use a light meter and adjust up or down to your liking. Take a test shot and adjust your light to be more or less powerful according to your taste.

Shot by Shot: With a Window

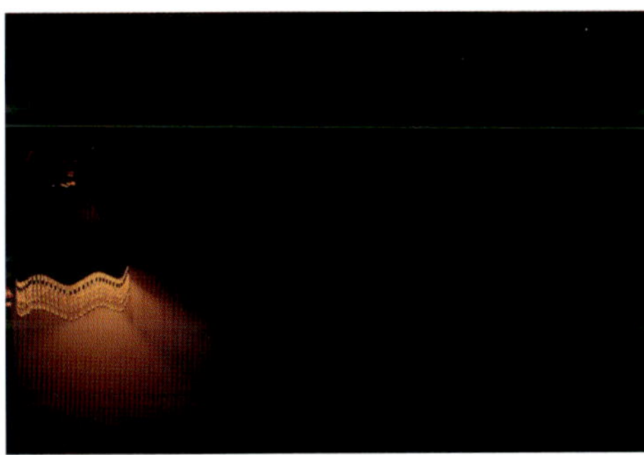

FIGURE 31.2
NATURAL LIGHT INDOOR SHOT.
CANON 1DXII, CANON 35MM 1.4, ISO 400, APERTURE 2.2, SHUTTER 1/250

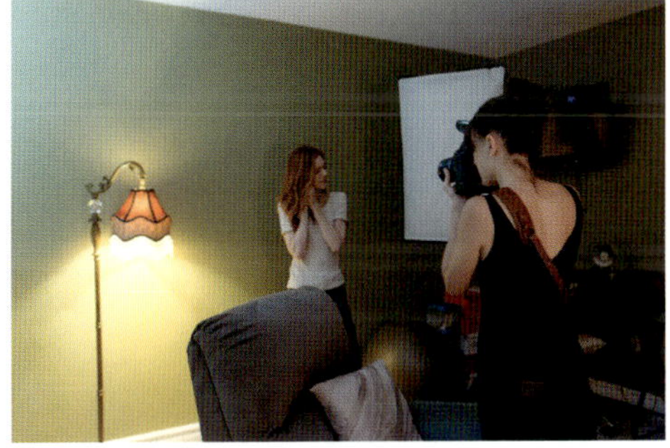

FIGURE 31.3
LIGHT POSITION 1, BEHIND THE SCENES (POINTING THE FLASH TOWARD A WINDOW).
CANON 1DXII, CANON 35MM 1.4, ISO 400, APERTURE 2.2, SHUTTER 1/250

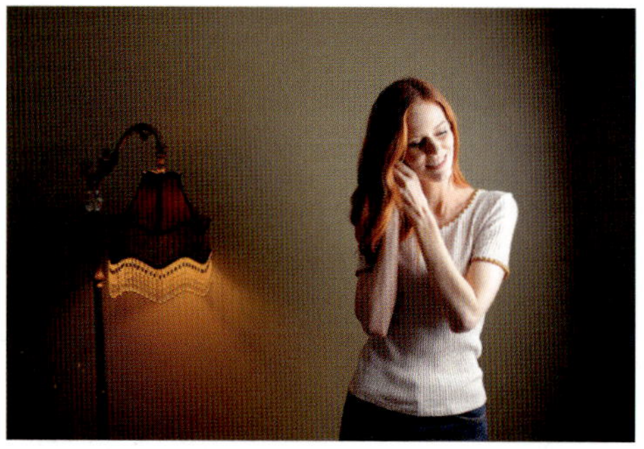

I ADDED A PROFOTO B1 WITH A 2X3 SOFTBOX ON TTL, BUT THE LIGHT WAS TOO BRIGHT AND WAS HITTING THE WALL TOO MUCH.
CANON 1DXII, CANON 35MM 1.4, ISO 400, APERTURE 2.2, SHUTTER 1/250

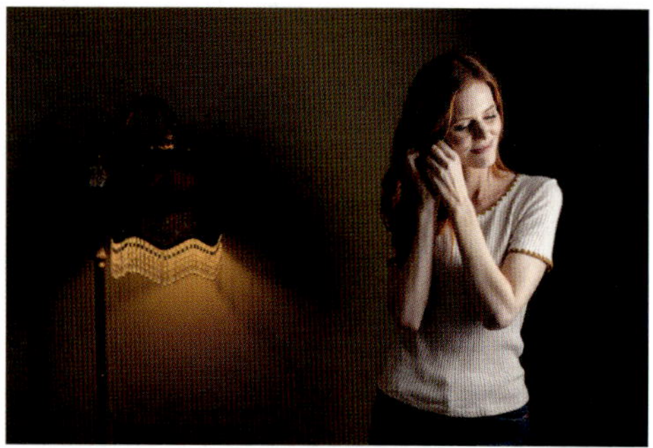

SWITCH THE LIGHT TO MANUAL, LOWER THE POWER, AND TILT IT AWAY FROM THE WALL.
CANON 1DXII, CANON 35MM 1.4, ISO 400, APERTURE 2.2, SHUTTER 1/250

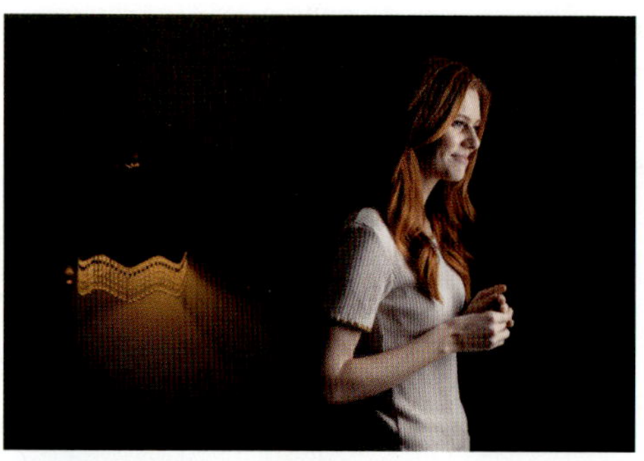

TILT THE LIGHT FARTHER AWAY FROM THE WALL AND LOWER THE ISO IF THE WHOLE SCENE IS TOO BRIGHT.
CANON 1DXII, CANON 35MM 1.4, ISO 200, APERTURE 2.2, SHUTTER 1/250

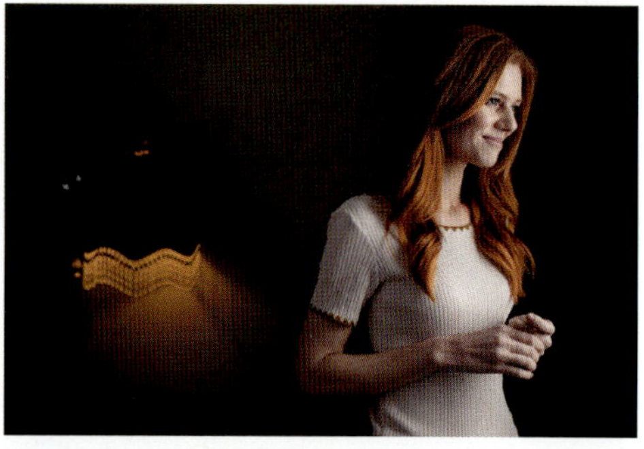

I ADDED A 42-INCH WHITE REFLECTOR ON THE LEFT SIDE OF THE SETUP.
CANON 1DXII, CANON 35MM 1.4, ISO 200, APERTURE 2.2, SHUTTER 1/250

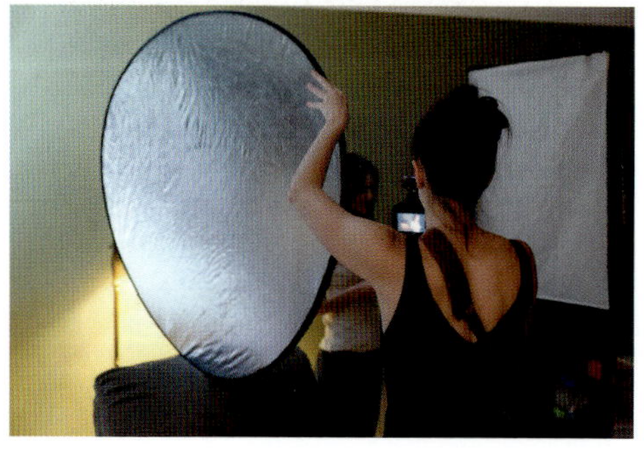

FIGURE 31.8

BEHIND THE SCENES SHOT WITH A REFLECTOR.

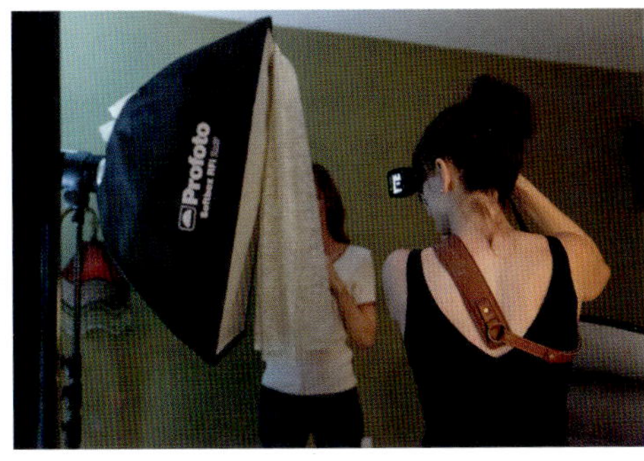

FIGURE 31.9

LIGHT POSITION 2, BEHIND THE SCENES. FAKING WINDOW LIGHT HERE BY PLACING LIGHT IN FRONT OF A WINDOW AND USING CURTAINS. IN MY CASE I DIDN'T HAVE CURTAINS, SO I USED A PIECE OF LACE.

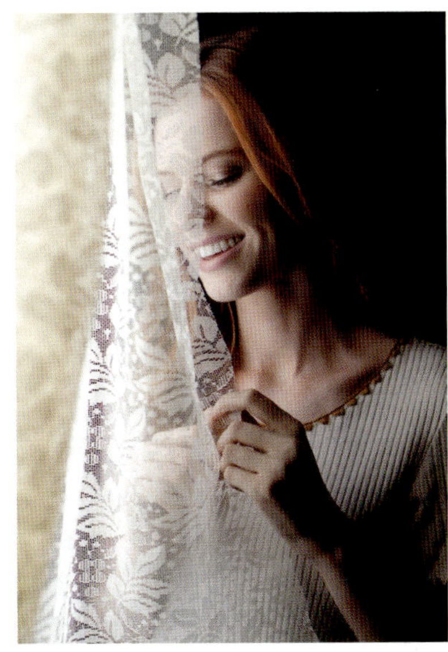

FIGURE 31.10

THIS IMAGE USES A PROFOTO B1 ON TTL WITH A 2X3 SOFTBOX AND LACE.
CANON 1DXII, CANON 50MM 1.2, ISO 100, APERTURE 2.5, SHUTTER 1/250

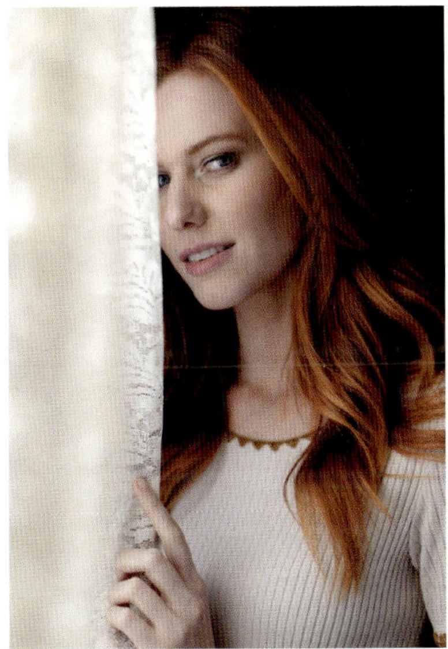

FIGURE 31.11

I ADDED A 42″ WHITE REFLECTOR ON THE RIGHT SIDE OF THE SETUP FOR THIS IMAGE TO BRING IN SOME LIGHT ON HER HAIR.
CANON 1DX II, CANON 50MM 1.2, ISO 100, APERTURE 2.5, SHUTTER 1/250

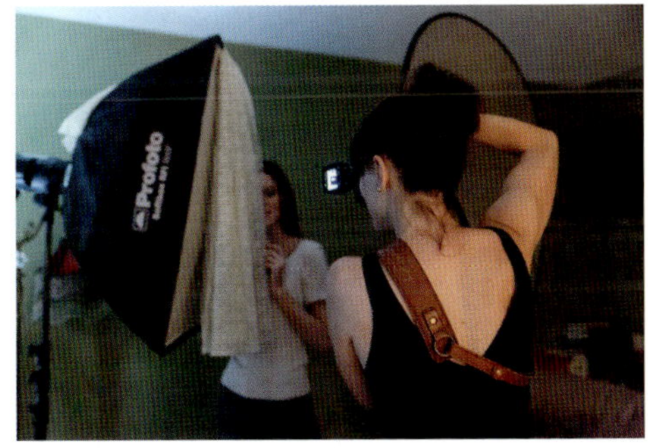

FIGURE 31.12

LIGHT POSITION 2 (FAKING A WINDOW) WITH A REFLECTOR, BEHIND THE SCENES.

Shot by Shot: Without a Window

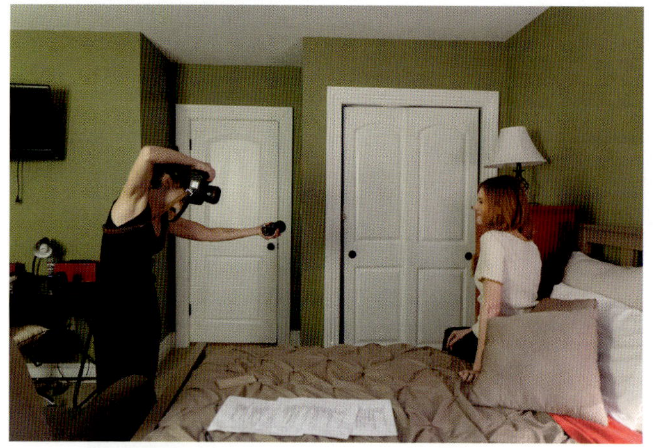

FIGURE 31.13

LIGHT POSITION 1 (BEHIND THE SCENES). HERE I AM BOUNCING A PROFOTO A1 OFF CLOSET DOORS. YOU COULD ALSO BOUNCE IT OFF OF A REFLECTOR.

FIGURE 31.14

NATURAL LIGHT INDOOR SHOT. CANON 1DXII, CANON 50MM 1.2, ISO 250, APERTURE 2.5, SHUTTER 1/250

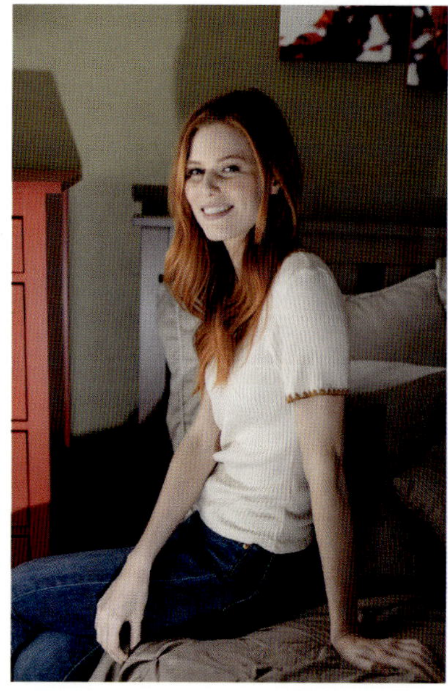

FIGURE 31.15

I ADDED A PROFOTO A1 ON TTL, BUT THE LIGHT WAS POINTED TOO LOW, AND CAUSED CIRCLES UNDER THE SUBJECT'S EYES.
CANON 1DXII, CANON 50MM 1.2, ISO 250, APERTURE 2.5, SHUTTER 1/250

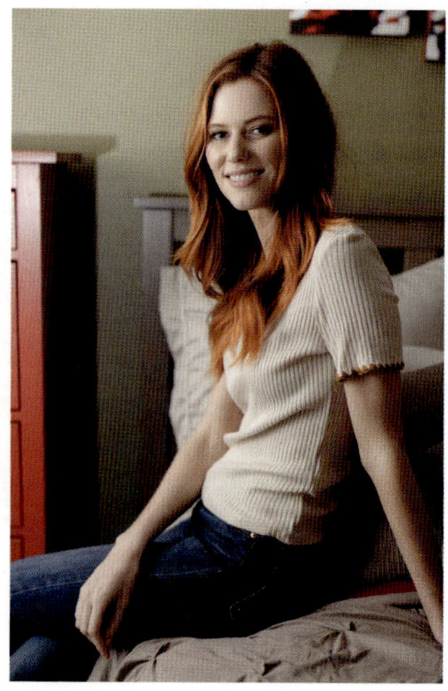

FIGURE 31.16

I SWITCHED THE LIGHT TO MANUAL AND LOWERED THE POWER, BUT THE LIGHT WAS HITTING TOO MUCH OF THE WALL AND WAS STILL A LITTLE TOO BRIGHT.
CANON 1DXII, CANON 50MM 1.2, ISO 250, APERTURE 2.5, SHUTTER 1/250

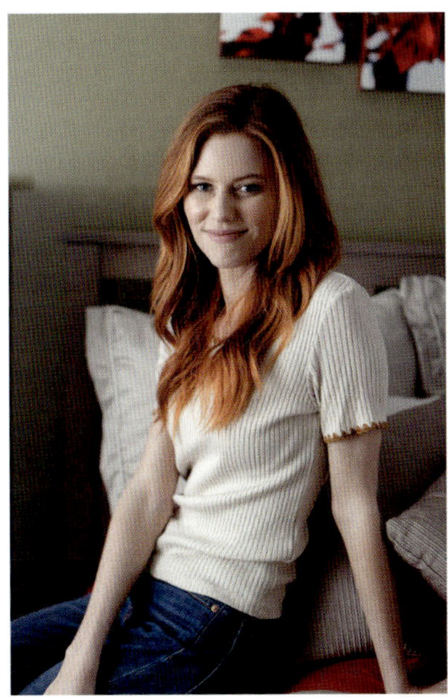

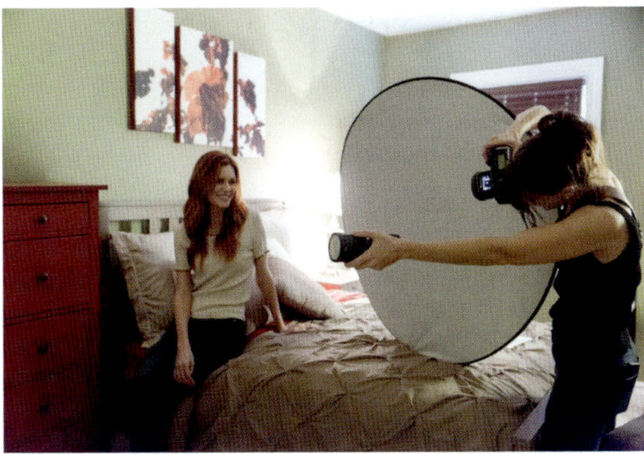

Potential Problems

If the shot looks unnatural, make sure that you're using the largest light modifier possible and keeping the light as close to your subject as possible. This will produce the softest quality of light possible.

If the background goes black, consider using a fill light with a large modifier to bring up the shadows and light the room. Refer to Scenario 30, "Filling in Shadows," to see how to do this.

Practical Uses

This technique is great for a room without windows, one with an undesirable color, or a room with windows that don't provide enough natural light.

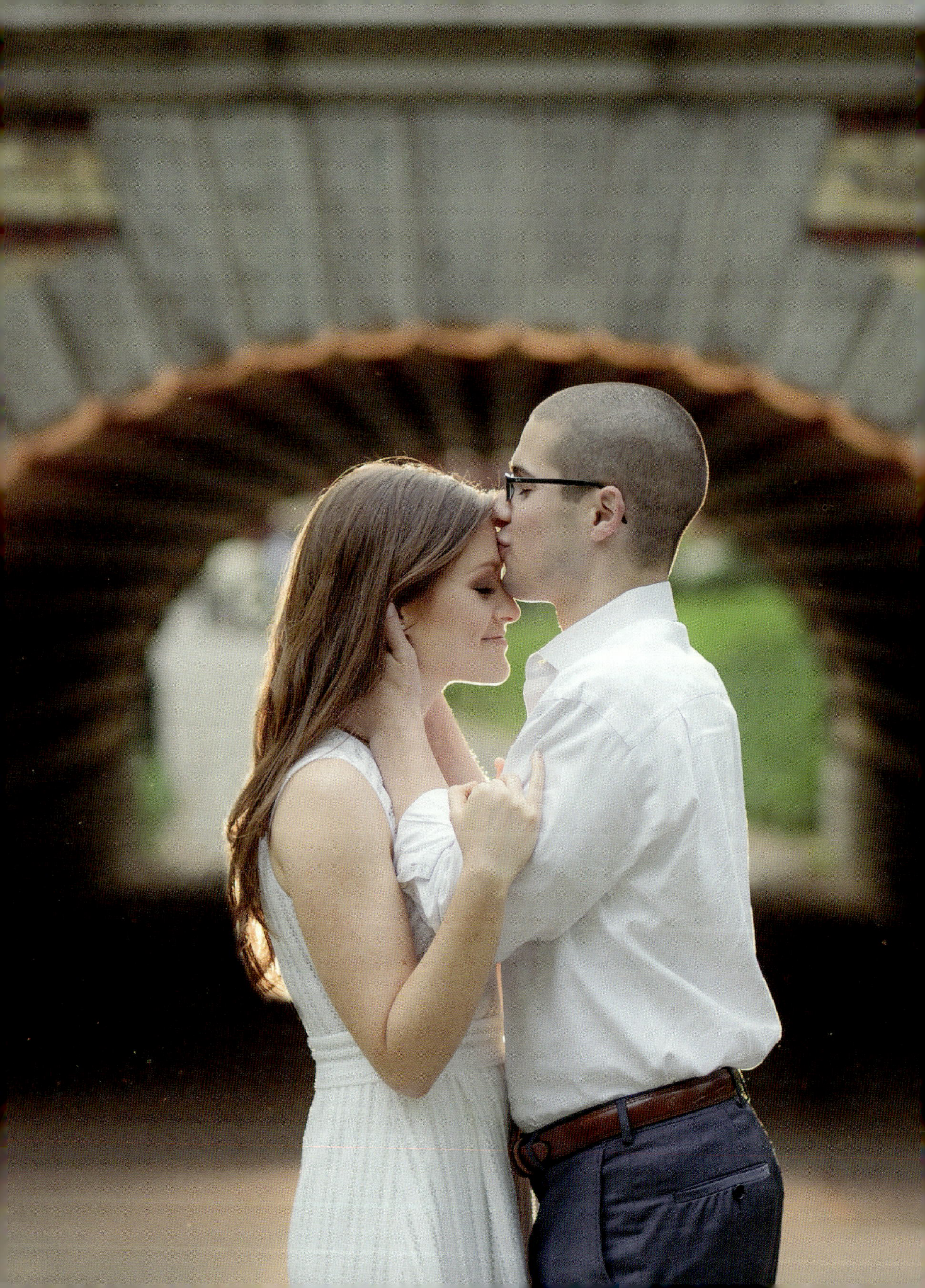

SCENARIO 32

Rim Lighting

Rim lights are great for giving your photo that little extra umph.

GOAL IMAGE

Rim lighting your subjects is a great way to separate them from the background. Often I notice my subject's hair or outfit blending right in, and the viewer can't tell where they end and the background begins. Rim lighting solves that problem and can make your photo stand out in a way that enhances the natural light in the scene (**Figure 32.1**).

Try this out on any given shoot. It works fairly universally no matter what lens you're using or scene you have. The biggest pain with this technique is hiding your light and light stand/assistant behind your subjects so you don't have to do any post-production work removing legs (real or metal).

For this example, I'm rim lighting the entire subject. You could vary this if you only wanted rim light on one side of your subject. As long as the light is coming from behind and outlining your subject, you're using the light correctly.

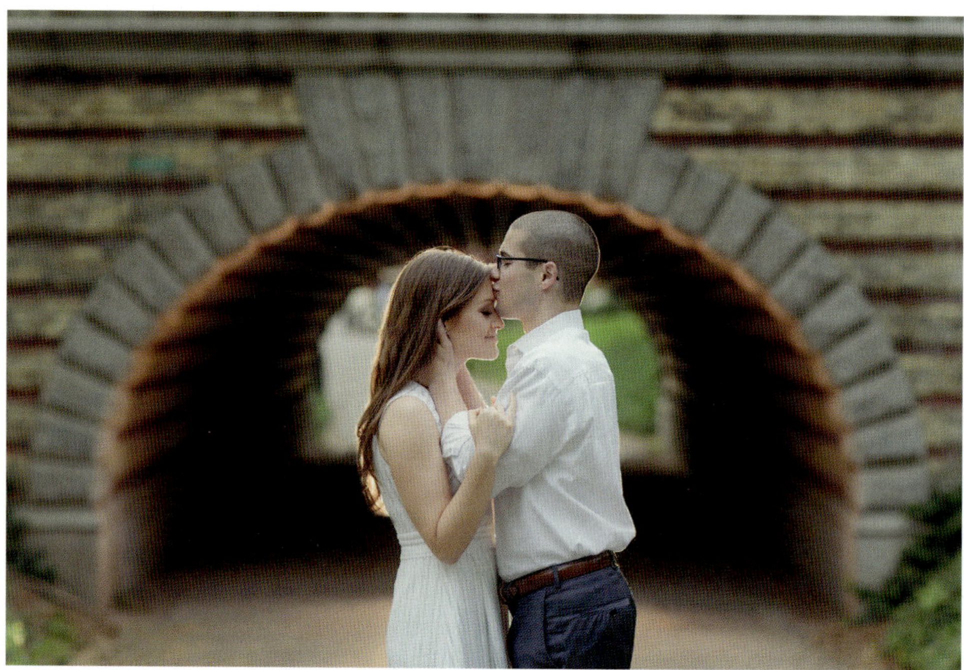

FIGURE 32.1

GOAL IMAGE.

CANON 1DX, CANON 85MM 1.2, ISO 200, APERTURE 2.2, SHUTTER 1/200

Step by Step

1. **Position the light:** Try to place your light at least 10 feet away from your subject. The goal is to have it close enough that you don't have to blast your flash power, but far enough away that you have a nice even spread of light around your subject.

2. **Set the camera exposure:** Get an exposure for the natural light on your subject as if you weren't going to be using an off-camera flash. Since the light won't be hitting the front of your subject, you want to make sure that the image is exposed properly from the front.

3. **Set the white balance:** Because the ring-light flash won't affect the light on your subject, set your white balance for the light hitting your subject. Auto WB is an option with this setup.

4. **Set the flash:** I usually set my light using TTL in this scenario and then adjust from there. If you're using a manual flash, start in the middle-high power range, or use a light meter and adjust up or down to your liking. Take a test shot and adjust the power of your light. The trick is to see the light around your subject but not have it completely blown out.

5. **Change your angle:** If you notice that the rim light isn't surrounding your subject evenly, you can move your camera angle or move the light. I find it's easier to move yourself, but if you don't want to change the composition you have, then move the light instead.

OPTIONAL: Put a gel on your flash to change the color of the rim light. If I'm shooting outdoors, I typically use a warm color like a full CTO gel so it fits nicely into the scene. If you're going for something more fun or vibrant, feel free to experiment with different colors.

Shot by Shot

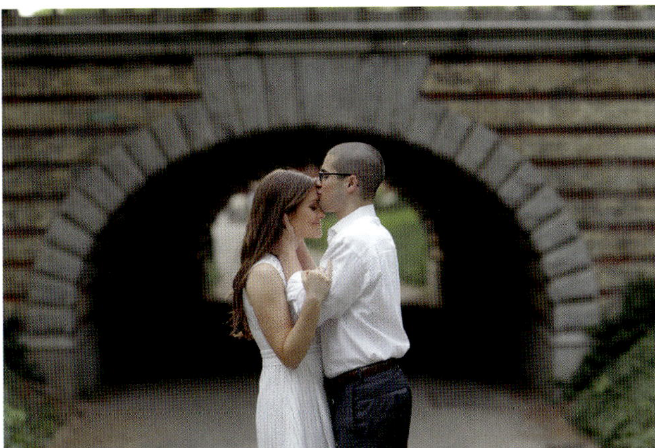

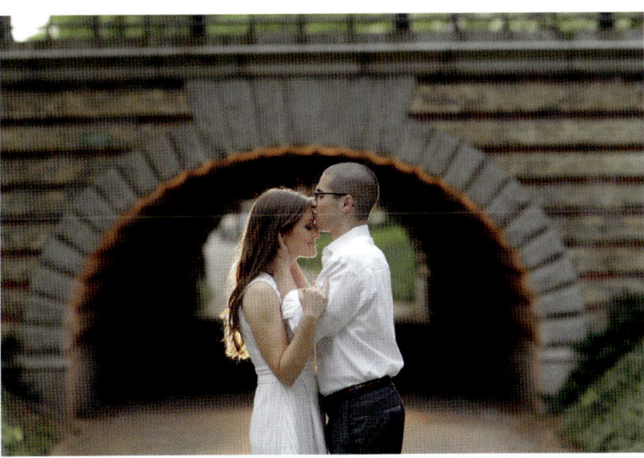

FIGURE 32.3
I USED A CANON 580EXII SPEEDLIGHT WITH A CTO GEL IN THIS IMAGE.
CANON 1DX, CANON 85MM 1.2, ISO 200, APERTURE 2.2, SHUTTER 1/200

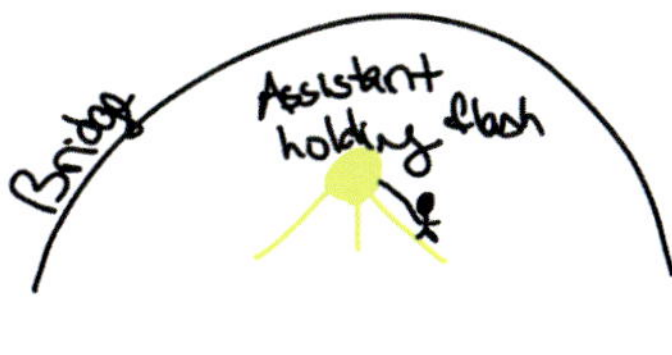

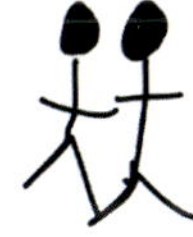

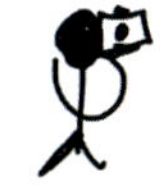

FIGURE 32.4
LIGHTING DIAGRAM.

Potential Problems

Be careful not to blow out the edges of the rim light. It's easy to pump a lot of power through your flash and take it too far. If your subject has frizzy hair, the backlight will extenuate it.

Additionally, if you're using TTL, get your power setting and then switch to manual. Sometimes when you're shooting directly into a flash, it confuses the TTL settings and sets the power too low. It's much easier to manage by setting your flash to manual and controlling it yourself.

Finally, while this isn't necessarily a problem per se, you may find your flash showing up in the photo. If you catch a little of the light, you can turn it into a starburst by setting your aperture high. Or, to make it seem hazier, set your aperture low.

Practical Uses

If you find yourself shooting into a dark background and your subject has dark clothing or dark hair, this is going to be your best friend. Without separation from the background, your subject may end up looking larger than they are and lacking in definition.

Personally, I love using this flash to enhance a typical natural light scene. Adding the rim light brings life to the image in a way that the natural light can't do.

Give this a try for individual and couples portraits. It adds a wow-factor to an otherwise regular natural light photo, and it's also great for separating your subject from the background.

PART 3

Features, Troubleshooting, and FAQs

CHAPTER 6

WTF Are You Talking About?

That's "What the Flash," dear. WTF were you thinking it was?

IT'S A WHOLE NEW LANGUAGE

That's how I think about learning lighting. When you learned the basics of photography, everything was Latin to you then. It's the same when you start learning about flash. It all seems like a bunch of mumbo jumbo. This chapter is all about clarifying the terms that go along with learning flash. I personally do not think you need to know all of the things I'm going to outline in this chapter in order to start using flash. I think studying flash terms without studying flash function is useless; much in the same way I think learning a language is useless if you're not learning the culture that goes with it. They go hand-in-hand and both symbiotically help you understand the other. There's no reason for you to not start playing with flash just because you don't fully understand what sync speed is, yet.

I'll explain the following terms as simply and quickly as possible. Many of these terms have far more depth than these descriptions, but the goal of this list is for you to get a basic understanding so you can apply it to shooting and understand WTF others are talking about in flash conversations or educational settings.

Flash Duration

Flash duration is how long your strobe or flash is "on" (bursting light). Essentially, when your light flashes, it's emitting light for a very fast period of time. That length of time is called flash duration. Flash duration is different for each flash or strobe. It is *very* fast. Usually it is faster than your shutter speed can typically go, so if you want a flash that can really freeze motion, you want a very fast flash duration.

The Profoto B10 plus has settings up to $\frac{1}{50,000}$ of a second t.05 flash duration, while the Profoto A1X has up to $\frac{1}{20,000}$ of a second.

What's t.05? In a nutshell, t.05 indicates that the flash duration was measured when the light was at 50% of its maximum brightness for the burst. These are all crazy micro-measurements we're talking about here. Flash duration changes along with flash power. Flash duration is faster at a lower power setting than it is at a higher power setting. This is because the flash never changes the amount of light it bursts, only how long the flash bursts.

Sync Speed

Sync speed is the highest shutter speed in which your camera can "keep up" with how fast the flash fires. Your shutter and flash have to sync to fire along with each other. Sync speeds are different depending on the camera you're using, but are generally around $\frac{1}{200}$ of a second for cameras with focal plane shutters.

If you're set at a shutter speed that is faster than your camera's sync speed, your camera will either automatically jump your shutter speed to the camera's sync speed (likely resulting in an overexposed photograph), or produce a picture that's half blacked out. To combat this, you need to have a flash with High Speed Sync (HSS), or choose your camera settings for a shutter speed that will sync with the flash.

High Speed Sync (HSS)

High Speed Sync (HSS) is a combo feature of your camera and flash that allows you to shoot at shutter speeds faster than your camera's native sync speed. To make this work, your camera adjusts the way that it opens the shutter (the rear curtain starts to close before the front curtain is completely open). Your flash doesn't just burst out one flash (even though it looks like it to the naked eye); instead, in HSS, there are a series of flashes in a row that properly expose the entire image.

HSS is useful in situations where you want your aperture more open at a lower f-stop, but you need a higher shutter speed to create a proper exposure. HSS does drain more battery power from the flash, and the flash output is not as strong. An alternative to using HSS would be to use a neutral density filter.

Neutral Density Filter (ND Filter)

A neutral density filter (ND filter) is a translucent filter that goes on the front of your lens (or sensor, as I've seen in a recent invention called the Clip Filter Series by STCoptics.com) to darken the image by obstructing the light in the scene from hitting the camera's sensor. It's helpful when you'd like a certain exposure, but the natural-light scenario is too bright for the settings you'd like to use. Using an ND filter results in being able to lower your settings overall, and is especially useful when using flash because you can lower your shutter speed to avoid draining your battery power using HSS, and get a more powerful light out of your flash.

Battery Power

Every flash has a different battery life. Your battery life is directly related to how hard your flash is working. The higher the power setting of the flash, the more battery it will drain. FYI: HSS drains more battery power at its lowest flash power setting than the flash does in normal sync mode at it's highest flash power setting.

Flash Power

Flash power is the brightness of the light that comes out of your flash. Flash power is measured in fractions. Flashes have power settings of full power (1/1), half power (1/2), quarter power (1/4), one-eighth power (1/8), one-sixteeth power (1/16), etc. Profoto measures this in numbers 1–10. 10 is full power, 9 is half power, 8 is quarter power, etc.

The flash power is actually measured in stops, just like your camera. Going from half power to quarter power is one stop lower. So, if you lower your flash by one stop, you need to lower your camera by one stop. By the way, that's not one "click" of your aperture or shutter, that's one *real* stop.

Real/Full Stops

I had to put this in here because it makes a difference when we're talking about changing light stops on your flash in tandem with your camera stops. I've seen a lot of photographers think 3.2 is an f-stop. It's actually not, technically. It's a setting in between the real or full f-stop setting on your camera (most cameras allow you to fine-tune your settings by changing them by a half or third of a stop).

If you lower your light by one full stop, you need to change your camera settings by one full stop, not just one "click" to a half stop. By the way, the same goes for shutter speed and ISO values. You can set them to half or third stops. Here's a (partial) list of full f-stops, shutter speeds, and ISO values. You'll notice they have a mathematical pattern that'll help you memorize them. This will help you when adjusting your flash manually.

- **Full f-stops:** f/1.4, f/2.0, f/2.8, f/4.0, f/5.6, f/8.0, f/11, f/16, f/22, etc.

- **Full shutter speeds:** 1, ½, ¼, ⅛, ¹⁄₁₅, ¹⁄₃₀, ¹⁄₁₂₅, ¹⁄₂₅₀, ¹⁄₅₀₀, ¹⁄₁₀₀₀, ½₀₀₀, etc.

- **Full ISO values:** 100, 200, 400, 800, 1600, 3200, 6400, 12,500, etc.

TTL versus Manual

Essentially auto for your flash, *TTL* measures the amount of light the flash will emit by reading it as it comes through your lens. TTL emits a burst of light before the actual real flash to measure the light, and then sets the flash power to a setting it thinks is appropriate.

Manual is you deciding on and dialing in your flash power yourself. Some people are diehard manual flashers. I'm a TTL-Manual-combo person. I like TTL getting the initial flash power output setting first, and then I take control from there, adjusting as I see fit.

Flash Zoom

Speedlights typically have a flash zoom function. The light can move closer to the end of the flash head, resulting in a wider light spread; or it can move back, further away from the end of the flash head, resulting in a more direct spread of light.

Light Spread

Light spread is the degree value in which the light is spreading out from your flash head. A really directed light with a grid on it could have a 10-degree spread of light. A flash with no modifier on it would have something closer to a 180-degree spread. This is a degree value measured from the light source. From there it spreads out according to inverse square law.

Inverse Square Law

The *inverse square law* is the mathematical formula that explains how light spreads and trails off from the light source. It describes the relationship between the distance of the light source and the brightness of the light. Of course, this is a super simplified version of inverse square law. I want to explain it as simply as possible to put the idea in your head, but not too much to be confusing in practice. You can build from there.

The inverse square law tells us that the intensity of the light decreases in a measureable and predictable way the farther from the light source it gets. Every time you double the distance between the light and your subject, you actually lessen the intensity of the light to ¼ the intensity. If I move my light from one foot away from my subject to two feet away from my subject, my light will be ¼ as intense. Logically you might have thought it would be half as intense—there's a lot of math involved. Instead of unraveling that, let's look at it as it applies to you in real life.

The most practical application of the inverse square law that I see in my day-to-day shooting is when I light a group of people with one light. If I place a light close to one side of the group, that side will be super bright, while the other side of the group will be super dark. However, if you move that light further away from the group, even if it's still on that one side, the light will even out across the entire photograph. Why? Because the difference of how intense the light is from one side to the other is significantly less dramatic the farther away the light source is from the subject, making the light fall off less drastic from bright to dark. See Scenario 6, "Group Shots with One Light," for more on how to make this work for you.

Light Fall Off

Light fall off refers to the difference of the intensity of the light on the side of the subject closest to the light versus the side farthest away from the light. Because the inverse square law tells us that the light is drastically more intense the closer we are to it, the more rapid the fall off will be in that situation. If your subject is super close to your light source, there will be a big difference between the bright side and the shadow side. Practically, this means that if you want a very contrasty image, get your subject closer to the light. If you want a less contrasty image with more even light, move your subject farther away from the light.

Soft Light versus Hard Light

I just finished telling you that the further away the light is from your subject, the less of a difference between the light side and shadow side there will be. So you're thinking, "Why don't you just say the farther away the light is, the softer the light will be?"

Because it's not true. Soft and hard light refer to the way that the light wraps around the subject and the gradation transition between the light side and the shadow side. The bigger the light source is, in relation to your subject, the softer the light will be, and you'll see a more gradual progression of light into shadow. The smaller the light source is, in relation to your subject, the harder the light will be and you'll see a more harsh line distinguishing between the light and shadow side the photo.

Note that I said "in relation to your subject." You might have a 2'x3' softbox on your light, but if it's far enough away from the subject, the light source is still small in relation to your subject and will become a hard light source. My example from earlier in the book is my favorite. The sun is a hard light source because it is so far away from us that it registers as a a small light source. However, if we convinced NASA to fly us next to the sun, it would be a big light source in relation to us, and it would create a beautiful, soft line from light to shadow across our completely burned-up faces.

To sum up, soft light is like how Anikan Skywalker made his way to the dark side slowly and painfully over three, horrible movies that we hope will be redone at some point. Hard light is like how he came back to the light in an instant when he saw his son Luke in pain at the hand of the Emperor. Sorry. I couldn't help myself there.

Light Ratios

Light ratios are how we measure the difference between the intensity of two light sources, or between the light side and shadow side of the subject. This is directly related to f-stops. A 1:1 light ratio means that both lights are illuminating your subject evenly; or, the same intensity of light is hitting both the light and shadow side of your subject (though in this case, that means no shadow).

A 2:1 ratio means that one light is twice as bright as the other and has a difference of one full stop. A 4:1 ratio means a two-stop difference between the light side and shadow side of the subject; an 8:1 ratio is a three-stop difference; and so on. Our cameras can utilize half and full stops, and you can have half-stop ratios as well. A 3:1 light ratio is about a 1 ½-stop difference; 6:1 is about a 2 ½-stop difference.

Why know this when you can just eyeball it on the back of your camera? This was a bit more necessary when lighting a photograph that you were shooting on film and you couldn't see your results immediately to alter them like you can with a digital camera. However, this concept is important to understand, even if you shoot digital only, if you want to advance in your photography and light knowledge. It's good to know how to measure light ratios, likely with a light meter, to quickly get the lighting for the image you want or to see how much leeway you have with your settings.

Gels

We talk about gels a lot in this book, so I'm only going to address a few overall points here. Not all gels are created equal. There are different quality gels, and a million different color gels, and you might like some over others. Shooting through a gel will decrease the amount of light output hitting your subject. The higher the flash power output, the less saturated the color from the gel will be.

"Term Overload!"

This was a lot, I know. This is another reason why this is a handbook, meant for you to reference as you go along. I don't expect you to read all of this and understand it the first time around. In fact, all there is to know about all of these terms isn't even included here. Use this as a guide, look back on it as much as you need, and further your education beyond this book when you're ready.

CHAPTER 7

But Light Doesn't Do That

Learning to weed out the b.s.

WHY DO I SUCK?

I remember looking at photos on Instagram and thinking how much I sucked at photography. Sound familiar? I'm sure I'm not alone here. I would scroll through my feed looking at shots perfectly lit with off-camera flashes and wonder why there wasn't any light spill at all. Or, why the subjects' faces had the most perfect light graduation with absolutely no flaws.

It wasn't until a friend of mine was listening to me lament about it that I found out just how much I had been deceived. Hanging out after Adorama's yearly Inspire event, I mentioned how I just couldn't get light to look the way I've seen it on certain photographers feeds. Seth Miranda turned toward me and said, "Wait, you think these photos are real?!" I squirmed.

"Um, yeah, aren't they?"

He proceeded to show me then, and over the next few months, all that was faked in Photoshop. More importantly, he taught me how I could start seeing it for myself in any given photo. In fact, I can credit this entire chapter to Seth because without his photography intervention, I don't think I would know any of this.

I knew Photoshop, but I didn't know it as well as I thought I did and didn't realize just how doctored so many of the photos I was admiring were. They weren't just retouched. They were reconstructed. Composited. Re-texturized and fabricated. And not just the blemishes, the light quality and direction as well.

Since then, I've learned to look at photos differently. I take what I know about photography and see if the photo is following the basic rules of light. If it's not, then I don't need to get all bent out of shape about how great it is—I concentrate on photography, not Photoshop. To each their own, of course, but since this book is about photography, I'll show you a few things to look for when you're ready to eat your feelings thumbing through social media imagery.

MAGICALLY SHAPED LIGHT

I see a lot of wedding photos. Consistently, I would look at pictures that were obviously lit with off-camera flash. The image would have just the face and dress lit, but there was absolutely no spill of light onto the ground. In my mind I thought that I just didn't know how to control my light enough to create that look.

I was wrong. Why? Because light travels in straight lines. It does not travel in wedding-dress shaped lines. So if a dress is illuminated but the dark ground right next to it is not, it is very likely that it was adjusted in post. Now, yes you can control your light and prevent it from overexposing the ground, but without cutting out a light modifier in the exact shape of a bride's dress train, you're going to get some spill.

INSPECT THE EYEBALLS

This is more of a reverse engineering lighting technique rather than a "catch the Photoshop" cue. If you zoom into a photo you can take a look at the reflections in the eyes of the subject(s) and see quite a bit about the light. Light reflections in the eyes are called catch lights. Assuming it's a sharp photo, you can see where the light is coming from, the shape of the light modifier that was used, and how many lights were hitting the subject's eyes. If the eyes aren't lit, then you won't be able to see anything because there aren't any reflections of the light. If you can, it's a wonderful way to learn how the photograph was lit.

ORANGE-PEEL SKIN

You know those beauty shots where the model has this surreal, perfectly glowing skin without any pores, but with the texture of a perfectly ripe orange peel? Fake, fake, fake, *fake*, and **fake**! Unless you've been living in a bubble, your skin is going to have some kind of texture that doesn't resemble a fruit.

In this case, it's likely an editing technique using frequency separation. Not only does it make the skin look flawless, but it smoothens out the lighting as well. Mind you, this isn't a useless Photoshop trick. A lot of clients want this type of work. I just want you to be able to look at photographs and know the difference. This is important for everyone, not just photographers: Don't believe everything you see in photos, especially if it looks perfect.

I highly suggest doing a quick YouTube search and teaching yourself how to retouch using frequency separation. I learned how to do it to my photos from Mark Wallace's video on AdoramaTV. Try applying the technique to a photo of yours just to see how it works, and you'll learn to recognize it in other photographs that much easier.

LIGHT RATIO INCONSISTENCY

This is an itty-bitty detail that'll help you see a bit of dodging and burning in a photograph. Take note of the ratio between light and shadow in the shot. Look at how much or how little contrast there is between the two. If you notice that parts of the photograph that have less of a difference between the light and dark areas as compared to other parts of the image that are the same distance from the light source, then there has likely been some doctoring there. I notice this most when people are wearing white. You'll see a fairly contrasting light ratio on their faces, but then not so much of a difference on their white clothing. The highlights have likely been painted in to prevent blowing out the clothing in the shot. There is nothing necessarily wrong with that, but it's good to be able to notice what's constructed and what's not.

PHOTOGRAPHER OR PHOTOSHOPPER?

This is not meant to be a facetious ending to this chapter. It's meant to make you think. I want you to think about where you want to spend your time. Do you want to be behind a camera, or behind a computer? There is no right or wrong answer.

You might start out as a photographer and discover that you love working the back-end magic more than the behind the shutter magic. That's OK. However, if your goal is to make money as a photographer, taking pictures, the quickest way to fail at that goal is to spend too much time holding a mouse. Why? Because editing takes time, and the more time you spend on a job, the less money you're making per hour for that job. One of the ways to maximize how much you make per hour is to do your "Photoshopping" in-camera. OK, there I am being facetious, but you get what I mean. Getting it as close to right as you can in-camera, and minimizing your post-production time or dollars is a sure-fire way to make money as a photographer versus as a Photoshopper. Decide what's right for you and stick to it.

CHAPTER 8

FAQs About OCF

I'm sure there are a ton more,
but here are the most common questions I get.

Why are my batteries dying so fast?

You're likely using the flash at full power. Try lowering your f-stop or raising your ISO so that the flash doesn't need to work so hard to light the image.

Why does the light look so harsh?

The light may look harsh for a variety of reasons. It could be too bright in comparison to the ambient light, in which case you can lower your light power or brighten your background. It could be a hard light source creating hard-lined shadows, which you can fix by creating a bigger light source in relation to your subject. It could also be because the color of the light doesn't match the ambient light, and you need to gel your flash to color correct. Feathering the light also helps smooth out the look of the flash.

What is ambient light?

Ambient light is the light that's in the space where you're shooting that is not the flash. It could be synonymous with natural light, except that ambient light also refers to lights that are on in a room.

How can I get photos taken with a speedlight to look better?

Because they are small, speedlights generally create a harsh look in images. Use a modifier to transform a speedlight into a larger light source. There are a lot of modifiers available for speedlights such as softboxes, umbrellas, and even something as simple as a white piece of paper that you bounce the light into. Use them.

Why isn't my light firing?

Because you stink at this. *No!!!* I'm just messing around, mostly because that's what I used to think when my light didn't fire. The truth is, a light may fail to fire for a variety of reasons. I once shot on a day so hot and humid that one of the pieces physically got so hot it *melted down* in front of the sensor. Unreal!

If your flash isn't firing, you next step is to locate where the problem is. Here's what you do, in this order:

1. **Test fire the flash itself:** If it doesn't fire, you know there's something wrong with the actual flash. If it does fire, move on.

2. **Test fire the flash from the transmitter:** If it doesn't fire, you know there's something wrong with the transmitter or its ability to communicate with the flash. If it does fire, move on.

3. **Take a picture:** If it doesn't fire, there's likely something wrong with the connection between your camera and the transmitter. Take the transmitter off your hot shoe and put it back on, making sure that it's secure.

Common Reasons Your Flash Isn't Firing:

- Something is broken.

- A general flash misfire (sometimes technology glitches).

- The flash is too far away from the transmitter.

- The transmitter isn't secured on the hot shoe.

- The flash hasn't fully recycled and isn't ready to fire.

- The transmitting function isn't turned on correctly (e.g., the flashes are not set correctly as masters or slaves, the air transmitting isn't set up properly, etc.).

- The signal from the transmitter is being blocked by something. This typically only happens with transmitters that are line-of-sight, which means there can't be anything blocking the view from the transmitter to the flash.

Why isn't TTL working?

TTL is auto mode for your flash. However, that doesn't mean it has any idea what you're actually photographing. Any auto exposure feature on your camera or flash is essentially trying to bring everything to 18% gray, which is considered middle exposure. Not too dark, not too light. It'll try to make both a white wedding dress and a black shirt gray. TTL is great, but you have to know what is does and how to work with it.

Get TTL to work better by using spot metering and a single-point focus. This tells your camera exactly where the light that you want to expose for is in your image. The focus point will be the sample spot the TTL is reading, so, for me, the TTL is usually dead on because I focus right on my subject's face. Previously, I was using evaluative metering and my TTL was all over the place, which was very frustrating. Thanks to a suggestion from Seth, I switched my metering mode. I'd never even thought about this because I shoot in manual camera exposure mode, get my exposure via live view, and typically don't pay too much attention to the metering mode.

Why does the flash power or color keep changing?

There are two reasons this could be happening. It could be that you have your flash set to TTL. Use TTL and then flip to manual. Keep the same power setting if you want to use it throughout a set of pictures.

It could also be the inconsistency of your flash. One of the big features of flashes and strobes is how consistent they are from one shot to the next. However, due to the nature of flash, even when your light is set to manual and at the same power, the flash can have small variations resulting in a shift in intensity output and color. Sometimes the color shifts from shot to shot. Other times, as the flash heats up, there is a gradual change in color. Both are no bueno. A characteristic of a very good flash or strobe, and consequently usually a more expensive one, is how consistent the light is. It may not make a difference if you're just shooting here and there, but it certainly makes a difference if you're shooting thousands of pictures throughout a job. It's no fun adjusting those colors later in post-production!

Why is my picture half black?

You're taking a picture that's higher than your camera's sync speed. You can either lower your shutter speed to your camera's sync speed (different for every camera, but usually somewhere around ½₀₀ of a second). Or, you can use High Speed Sync (more information on this in Chapter 6, "WTF Are You Talking About?").

Why is my light spilling everywhere?

You need light modifiers to control your light. If it's spilling around in places you don't want it to go, putting a grid on the light will help it travel in tighter, straighter lines. Don't be afraid to feather the light up so it doesn't hit the ground. I know it'll seem like you're pointing your light at the sky, but the bottom of the light will still hit your subjects while avoiding the ground below them.

Why are there ugly shadows?

Shadows are a result of how you've positioned your light. The smaller the angle between you, your light, and your subject, the less shadow you'll have. Shadows help us shape a subject, but you need to know how to do that in a flattering way. I highly recommend getting a mannequin head practicing with a flashlight or a strobe with a modeling light to get a sense of what light does to a person's face at certain angles.

Additionally, don't forget that you can use fill light, in any circumstance, to lessen your shadows. See Scenario 10, "Filling in Shadows," for more about how fill light works and how to get the look you're going for.

Do I need expensive lighting gear?

No, you don't. All of the 32 scenarios I present in this book can be achieved with flashes or strobes of any price. Get what you can afford and start learning. Expensive lighting gear will be part of your future if you want it to be, and better equipment with newer technology gives you more convenience, customer service, power, and consistency. I will say that I believe in investing in lights and lenses more than camera bodies. They last longer than camera bodies, and I prefer only buying them (and crying over the price) once. My Profotos are definitely worth every single penny I spent on them.

What light modifiers should I buy first?

This depends on what you'll be using them for. If I were buying light modifiers for the first time, I'd want a set of grids, gels, and at least one soft modifier, like an umbrella. They're an inexpensive option and can be used for group and individual portraits.

Why doesn't shutter speed affect my flash power?

Shutter speed will change the ambient light in your photo, but it won't affect the flash power. You may notice a change in exposure, but that's due to more of the ambient light hitting your subject, not because the shutter speed is affecting the flash power.

This happens because the flash duration is much shorter than your shutter speed. As my friend Seth Miranda likes to say, "When you're using flash, you essentially have two shutter speeds: the camera's shutter speed and the flash's." Each one creates a burst of light in your exposure. The shutter of your camera is open longer than the flash is firing, so making your shutter speed faster or slower won't make a difference for the flash itself.

Do I have to be 1 or 2 stops below ambient light when using flash?

No. I honestly don't know where this idea came from. Maybe because when you flash in an outdoor environment the light bounces all over and brightens the entire image. If you're looking for a more dramatic image, then yes, lower the exposure of your natural/ambient light in the background. If you don't want to have a dramatic difference between your flash and the natural light I your scene, then keep it as is.

Do I have to know all of this to shoot flash?

No. Stinking. Way. There's no test you need to pass to start shooting with flash. Try it. Suck at it. Do it again. Get better. Shoot again. Fail some more. As Martin Luther King Jr. said, "If you can't fly, then run. If you can't run, then walk. If you can't walk, then crawl, but whatever you do, you have to keep moving forward."

Index

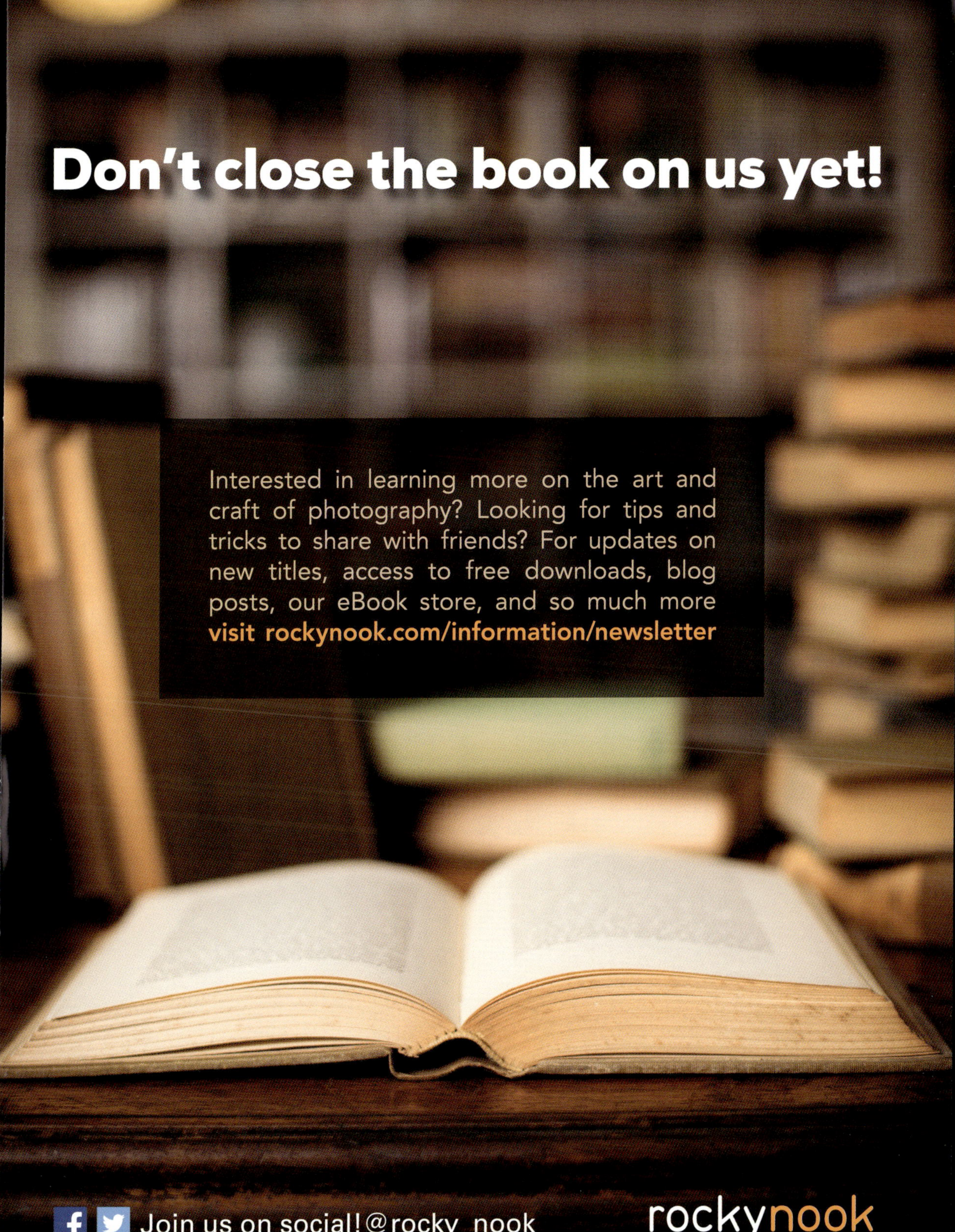